The Lewis and Clark Expedition

was launched by President Jefferson, who had long desired to open to trade and frontier expansion the unexplored territory stretching from the upper reaches of the Missouri River across the Rockies to the Pacific Coast.

The Journals are the colorful daily record of that epic trek, in which a select band of some 28 men, led by Captains Meriwether Lewis and William Clark, and a Shoshone squaw and her indestructible infant son (born on the expedition) traversed a territory that has since become ten states.

Here are the dangers and wonders they encountered in the wilderness; accounts of awesome natural phenomena never before described by civilized man; and detailed records of the life and customs of Indian tribes, friendly and hostile.

JOHN BAKELESS, editor of this edition, was born and raised among the Indians of the Carlisle Indian School in Pennsylvania. He is a *cum laude* graduate of Williams College and holds M.A. and Ph.D. degrees from Harvard. Dr. Bakeless is the author of *Daniel Boone: Master of the Wilderness* and *Lewis and Clark: Partners in Discovery*.

MENTOR Books of Related Interest

(0451)

☐ **THE OXFORD HISTORY OF THE AMERICAN PEOPLE, Volume I: Prehistory to 1789 by Samuel Eliot Morison.** From the Pulitzer Prize-winning historian, the first of this magnificent three volume set covers the period of American history from the earliest Indian civilizations to the beginnings of George Washington's first administration. (621921—$3.95)

☐ **THE OXFORD HISTORY OF THE AMERICAN PEOPLE, Volume II: 1789 to 1877 by Samuel Eliot Morison.** The second volume opens with the election of George Washington as first President of the United States and extends through the troubled era of Reconstruction following the War Between the States. (624084—$4.95)

☐ **THE OXFORD HISTORY OF THE AMERICAN PEOPLE, Volume III: 1869 to the Death of John F. Kennedy 1963 by Samuel Eliot Morison.** This volume opens with America united after the carnage of the Civil War, through the Industrial Revolution, World Wars I and II, and closes with the death of the president who symbolized both the greatness of America and its continuing dilemmas. (622553—$4.50)

☐ **URBAN LEGACY: The Story of America's Cities by Diana Klebanow, Franklin L. Jonas and Ira M. Leonard.** A vivid history of American cities from colonial times to the '70s that traces the progressive urbanization and suburbanization of American society and the impact of urbanism upon American life, including unemployment, the flight to the suburbs, bankruptcy and crime. Illustrations, maps, bibliography, political cartoons included. (615867—$2.95)

THE JOURNALS OF
LEWIS AND CLARK

*A New Selection
with an Introduction by*
John Bakeless

A MENTOR BOOK

NEW AMERICAN LIBRARY

NEW YORK AND SCARBOROUGH, ONTARIO

MENTOR TRADEMARK REG. U.S. PAT. OFF. AND FOREIGN COUNTRIES
REGISTERED TRADEMARK—MARCA REGISTRADA
HECHO EN WINNIPEG, CANADA

SIGNET, SIGNET CLASSIC, MENTOR, PLUME, MERIDIAN AND NAL
BOOKS are published *in the United States* by
New American Library,
1633 Broadway, New York, New York 10019,
in Canada by The New American Library of Canada Limited,
81 Mack Avenue, Scarborough, Ontario M1L 1M8

11   12   13   14   15   16   17   18

PRINTED IN CANADA

Introduction

The Lewis and Clark Expedition of 1804–1806 was the fruition of a dream that had haunted Thomas Jefferson all his life. Widely interested in music, science, and literature, as well as in political life, that remarkable man had always been especially curious about the vast expanse of North America, stretching from the Mississippi across the Rockies to the Pacific. In spite of French, Spanish, and American settlements on the Mississippi and Spanish settlements in California, most of this area was totally unknown to white men, though a few bold traders were venturing part of the way up the Missouri and overland from Canada.

A large part of Jefferson's motive was purely disinterested scientific curiosity. His perpetually active and inquisitive mind had long been intensely interested in the Indian tribes, plants, animals, fossils, aboriginal languages, and geography of the great mysterious area which, in that day, might well have been described as "darkest North America."

Partly, too, Jefferson was motivated by patriotic and political considerations. He realized more clearly than most Americans of his day the immense prospects these new and unknown lands offered for national expansion in trade, territory, and population. From them would come the wealth and power that would make secure forever the democratic ideals of the struggling young republic.

The American Revolution was not yet ended when, in 1783, Jefferson made his first tentative effort to send an exploring expedition to the Pacific coast. He wrote General George Rogers Clark, elder brother of Lieutenant William Clark, who was later to be a leader of the Lewis and Clark expedition, inquiring whether the general himself was willing to lead such an exploring party. General Clark declined.

Later, Jefferson made two other attempts. In 1786, he started John Ledyard, an adventurous Connecticut Yankee, across Russia and Siberia, in an effort to work his way eastward. Ledyard at first attempted to sail from London to Nootka Sound (which was to be his North American starting point); but British customs officers seized the ship. He then managed to pass through Russia and most of Siberia, reached Yakutsk, and then rashly returned to Irkutsk—where Catherine the Great's police arrested him and expelled him from the imperial dominions. Undaunted, Ledyard proposed still a third attempt, this time from Kentucky westward; but he died before he could attempt it.

In 1792, Jefferson tried again. He was a leading spirit in the American Philosophical Society's plan to send a French botanist, André Michaux, across the continent. Along with Jefferson, Washington and Hamilton also contributed to the expenses. Michaux was undoubtedly an eminent man of science. Unfortunately, as was soon discovered, he was also a French secret agent; and his proposed expedition ended abruptly. Meriwether Lewis, a neighbor of Jefferson's in Albemarle County, Virginia, tried to join this expedition, but his application was refused because Jefferson thought the eighteen-year-old militiaman too young.

Nine years later, when Jefferson became President, he knew it would at last be possible to mount the long-planned expedition. One of his first acts was to ask Meriwether Lewis, now a captain in the Regular Army, to take leave from his military duties and come to the White House as secretary to the President. Since Lewis—whose spelling was almost hopeless—was very nearly the one man in North America least qualified to be secretary to the President (or anybody else), it is plain that Mr. Jefferson was already thinking of him as leader of the expedition.

For such a role Lewis was uniquely qualified. Strong, vigorous, and country-bred, he had a keen interest in plants, animals, and nature in general. From his mother, an active amateur physician, he had learned enough about simple country remedies to look after the health of his command, without a medical officer, especially after a little hasty instruction from the celebrated American physician, Dr. Benjamin Rush, of Philadelphia. Lewis had already been on staff and troop duty in the wildest part of the northwestern frontier of that day—experience that well prepared him for the wild lands of the new northwestern frontier and the still wilder tribes with whom he would have to deal there.

As Mr. Jefferson wrote to a friend: "We cannot in the U. S. find a person who to courage, prudence, habits and health adapted to the woods, and some familiarity with the Indian character, joins a perfect knowledge of botany, natural history, mineralogy, and astronomy, all of which would be desirable."

No such universal genius being available, the President decided he would have to let Captain Lewis command his expedition. He had "the true qualifications"—that is, courage, character, health, and acquaintance with Indians. As for the captain's strictly scientific attainments, he had made "a great mass of accurate observation" of animals, plants, and minerals, as many Virginia gentlemen of that day loved to do. This was not, said President Jefferson regretfully, "under their scientific forms, but so as that he will readily seize whatever is new in the country he passes through," an expectation that the assiduous scientific collecting of the Lewis and Clark Expedition amply fulfilled.

Not long after Lewis reached Washington, it was definitely settled that he would lead the expedition; and he was soon being given some rather hasty scientific training, by way of preparation. He was also taught navigation (inadequately, as it turned out), in the hope that he would be able to report the latitude and longitude of river junctions and other important geographical points in the unmapped country where the explorers would have no other means of indicating exact locations. In the first months of 1803, Lewis was already buying scientific equipment, medicines, portable soup, and other field supplies.

Not least of Lewis's qualifications was what he himself called his passion for "rambling." As a boy in Virginia, he had always loved long and vigorous "rambles" in the woods and fields, a taste which, at times, he had to control because of his determination to progress in his studies. Later, even when the expedition was in parts of North America so wild that it traveled for months without seeing other human beings, Lewis often left the boats in order to travel ashore on foot for long periods, either alone or with only a few companions.

Lewis was, in other words, a rather solitary individual, devoted to his family and a few friends, a man with a gift for leadership, who could maintain discipline and get loyal and willing service from his men in the wilderness, but not a man who got along well with ordinary people under ordinary conditions. In the popular jargon of our day, Meriwether Lewis was an "introvert." He was also a rather moody individual.

When the President authorized Lewis to select another officer for the expedition, his first choice was a man with all his own abilities but of a somewhat different psychological make-up, his old friend and former commanding officer, Lieutenant William Clark, who had resigned from the Regular Army some years before. Second choice was Captain Moses Hook, of Lewis's own regiment, the First U. S. Infantry. The Secretary of War had already authorized Captain Hook to place himself under Lewis's command, if Lewis so requested.

Though both Lewis and Clark came from Albemarle County families, they had had little, if any, acquaintance in boyhood, since Clark's father had moved to Caroline County before his son William was born. Their friendship seems to have begun when Ensign Lewis served in Lieutenant Clark's "chosen rifle" company in the Old Northwest, sometimes called "the Ohio Country," not long after General Anthony Wayne's victory at Fallen Timbers, in which Lieutenant Clark had participated.

Not until plans for the expedition were already well advanced did Lewis, on June 19, 1803, write a letter outlining his proposed route up the Missouri and down the Columbia and inviting Clark to join him. Receiving the letter on July 16, Clark at once consulted his brother, General George Rogers Clark. The general urged acceptance, as "a fine field was open for the display of genius." On July 24, Clark wrote Lewis: "My friend, I join you with heart and hand."

Clark was ideally suited to share command of the expedition with Lewis. Both had the same general background and the same somewhat limited education, common in their class at that time, that local Virginia schoolmasters could provide in small private schools. Both were Regular Army officers, accustomed to danger and accustomed to command. Both were familiar with outdoor life in wild country. Both had a strong interest in adventure, exploration, and natural history. Both were natural leaders of men—and both were known to Thomas Jefferson.

Clark also had a talent that would be much needed on the expedition. He was a competent topographer, able to make surveys and draw the original maps of the expedition's route, which are now among the treasures of the Coe Collection in the Yale University Library. Most of these were the first maps ever made of the country through which the "Corps of Discovery" passed.

Unlike Lewis, however, Clark was neither moody nor solitary. He was a hearty, genial, socially inclined individual —an extrovert. Given their common interests, long acquaintance, hearty friendship, and similar enthusiasms, they complemented each other in an almost ideal way.

It is a remarkable fact that there is no record of the slightest quarrel between the two, not even under the terrible strain and hardship of wilderness travel, which makes ordinary men's tempers snap like fiddlestrings. Their only known differences relate, first, to the palatability of dogmeat, which Lewis rather liked and Clark detested, and, second, to the necessity of salt, which Lewis craved and Clark thought a matter of "mere indifference." It is more than a matter of form when they refer—as both men do—to each other as "my friend, Captain Lewis," or "my friend, Captain Clark." Even as an old man—so testifies a young niece living in his household—Clark could never refer to Lewis's death without tears in his eyes.

Lewis's choice of Clark as his companion naturally had the full approval of President Jefferson. It is obvious that Jefferson meant Meriwether Lewis to command the expedition and William Clark to be second in command. But this would have been extremely embarrassing to both Lewis and Clark. Before resigning from the Regular Army, Clark had been Lewis's superior officer. So, when inviting Clark to join him, Lewis had promised him equal rank. To make this possible, President Jefferson had wished to make Clark a captain of engineers, since he would be the expedition's chief topographer. When War Department red tape prevented that, Clark was recommissioned as a second lieutenant (a demotion of one grade) in the artillery, though his entire military career had been in the infantry. Clark felt about this demotion of one grade, he drily remarked afterward, "as might be expected." Lewis was indignant but hesitated to make an issue of the matter.

The two officers quietly solved the problem in an unorthodox but effective way. The enlisted personnel of the expedition were not allowed to know that a disparity of rank existed. Each officer was referred to as "captain" and so referred to himself. All command decisions were taken jointly, except when the two officers happened to be separated and commanding detachments of their own. On a few occasions, when they had to sign "Indian commissions"—papers given to prominent and friendly chiefs, certifying their loyalty to the United States and bespeaking the friendship of other white men—Lewis signed with his proper military rank, as "Captain, 1st Infantry," and Clark as Captain in a "Corps of Discovery" or Captain in an "Expedition for N. W. Discovery." Just what would have happened if this strictly *ad hoc* arrangement had come to the attention of the War Department, it is difficult to say; but commissions issued to Indians on the wild prairies rarely got back to Washington. Later, when Congress proposed to reward Lewis with a land grant larger than that offered Clark, Lewis insisted that their grants be equal—and this time had his way.

Lewis and Clark had orders to ascend the Missouri River (the upper reaches of which were unknown) to its source, cross the "Highlands"—that is, the Rockies—and follow "the best water-communication which offered itself from thence to the Pacific Ocean." This was expected to be (and was) the Columbia River, which was also largely unknown to white men, except for a relatively short distance above its mouth.

The commanders hoped (one can hardly say they expected) to come home aboard one of the trading vessels that visited the Pacific Coast, though, as these ships usually returned by way of China, it would have been a long voyage. If disappointed in this, they were fully prepared to repeat their overland journey, as, in the end, they had to do. Not until some time after their return did they learn that the brig *Lydia*, of Boston, had been in the Columbia estuary while they were encamped ashore.

Each officer had orders to keep an individual daily record. Enlisted personnel were encouraged to keep journals of their own, and a few did so, producing documents that are today of great value when used together with the more ambitious journals of the two captains. The total disappearance of Robert Frazier's journal (after published copies had actually been advertised for sale) and the complete bowdlerizing of Patrick Gass's (through the revision of a well-meaning clergyman who had no appreciation of its frankness and earthy vigor) are regrettable losses.

The expedition was to establish friendly relations with the Indians, impress them with the power of their new "White Father" in Washington, take vocabularies of all native languages on blank printed word lists, specially prepared for the purpose, make maps and general geographical notes, preserve seeds and other horticultural material suitable for cultivation, and collect scientific material, particularly botanical, zoological, and anthropological specimens. The President also hoped they would find a trade route across unknown western North America—as, indeed, they did—and that they would open the way for a prosperous Indian trade. But, though the Missouri and Columbia rivers remained important routes, the traders and explorers who followed Lewis and Clark soon found better routes across the Rockies; and the flood of emigrants followed many different trails. The Indian trade and the fur trade developed as President Jefferson had hoped.

As soon as Clark had dashed off his letter to Lewis, accepting his invitation to join the expedition, he began—as Lewis had requested—recruiting "some good hunters, stout healthy unmarried young men, accustomed to the woods, and capable of bearing bodily fatigue to a pretty considerable extent." From the beginning, both officers were careful to sift all applicants, rejecting many that seemed mere curiosity-seekers or starry-eyed adventurers not likely to endure the grinding fatigue and constant danger of wilderness travel.

Since news of the Louisiana Purchase had not been received when Lewis wrote Clark and since the treaty could not, in any event, be ratified until autumn, Lewis urged his friend to spread the idea "that the direction of this expedition is up the Mississippi to its source, and thence to the Lake of the Woods." This was to avoid alarming the Spaniards, through whose western territories the expedition was to travel (though technically, of course, these lands had already been ceded back to France).

Clark had to reply that the true destination had been gossiped about in Louisville for weeks. Fortunately, the United States was able to take formal possession of Louisiana before the expedition got under way the following spring, so that there was no longer any danger that it would be intercepted by suspicious Spanish officials. This might have been a serious matter, for Zebulon Pike's expedition, which was sent out soon after Lewis and Clark, did stray into Mexican territory and ended its exploration in a Spanish jail.

The success of the Lewis and Clark Expedition was due to the remarkable qualities of leadership possessed by these two officers. They traversed North America from St. Louis to the Pacific Coast and returned, taking a woman and a newborn baby with them. They traversed a territory that has since become ten states, opening the way for the tide of settlement that came pouring after them. Though the cost of the expedition was considerably more than the $2,500 originally appropriated, the whole cost was trivial in comparison with the immense results.

All this they accomplished with only one Indian fight and with the loss of only one man—from disease. And if the "bilious colic" from which Sergeant Charles Floyd died was really appendicitis, no medical skill of that period could possibly have saved him. Perhaps, in view of the stir about race relations in our own era, it may be well to point out that Lewis and Clark led, without friction of any kind, a group of three races, their own white men, the Negro slave, York, and the Indian girl Sacagawea, not to mention her half-breed baby.

From the moment when the expedition left Fort Mandan, in North Dakota, in the spring of 1805, until the boats turned toward the shore at St. Louis in the autumn of 1806, discipline was absolutely perfect, in spite of danger, discomfort, alarmingly limited and often unpalatable rations, occasional starvation, cold, wet, exhaustion, and the isolation of a small group seeing far too much of one another over a long period, usually a dangerous cause of friction. All the factors that undermine morale were present most of the time—and morale remained high.

This was partly due to the leaders' original skillful choice of men, partly to their wisdom in carefully testing the men during the first leg of the journey from St. Louis to Fort Mandan, testing them further during the winter of 1804–1805 at the Fort, and then quietly shipping two potential trouble-makers back to the United States in the spring of 1805, before the expedition went on to the most dangerous and difficult part of the journey.

The only dubious individual taken along from the Mandan country was the ne'er-do-well squaw man, Toussaint Charbonneau. In this case the leaders had no choice. Charbonneau had to be taken along, because the expedition needed his Shoshone wife, Sacagawea, whose knowledge of her tribe's obscure language was all that enabled the white men to buy the horses that were absolutely indispensable in crossing the Rockies. Sacagawea's baby was, of course, a burden, but the baby had to be taken along if his mother's services as a Shoshone translator were to be secured.

Strict observance of security principles, especially continued guard and constant reconnaissance, enabled the expedition to escape surprises of the kind that led to so many massacres of white men by the Indians. The one Indian fight that did occur—Lewis's combat with Blackfeet and perhaps Indians of another tribe, in Montana in 1806—resulted from the carelessness of a sentry, who let his rifle lie where an Indian could seize it.

During the journey up the Missouri, there was constant reconnaissance by patrols ashore. Sentries in the boats were continually on watch. Camp sites and adjoining terrain were carefully reconnoitered each night.

A few Indians occasionally spent the night at Fort Mandan, the expedition's winter quarters on the Missouri; but at Fort Clatsop, the Pacific Coast winter quarters, all Indians were required to leave at sundown, though exceptions were made in special cases, as when a group of Indians were caught barefoot in a sudden snow squall.

Both Lewis and Clark understood Indians and rather liked them, but neither had any illusions about the redskins' capacity for treachery. They had the gates of Fort Clatsop closed nightly and kept a small guard constantly alert, because "we well know that the treachery of the aborigines of America and the too great confidence of our countrymen in their sincerity and friendship has caused the destruction of many hundreds of us." It was because of their constant vigilance that the captains were able to take their command safely to the coast and back, in spite of various plots by several tribes, who were tempted by the arms and equipment of the expedition—immense wealth in the eyes of western redskins.

The various tribes through whose territories the explorers passed, and with whom they counciled, differed widely— the prosperous and not very warlike Mandans and Minnetarees, who were used to white men and interested in the fur trade; the haughty and belligerent Sioux, who could not quite believe that a new nation, even more powerful than themselves, was coming on the scene; the half-starved Shoshones, partly shut off by lack of adequate firearms from the wealth of the buffalo plains; the Nez Percés, who at first were inclined to be hostile but then became friends of the white man and remained friendly for a long time after the exploration; the Blackfeet, who really did fight; and the Pacific Coast tribes, who had been dealing with white men for years.

Lewis and Clark dealt with all these in a friendly way but without any sign of weakness that might have precipitated trouble. When some surly Sioux actually began to string their bows in preparation for combat, they at once discovered that Lewis, the officer afloat in the boats, was fully prepared to open fire with the dreaded swivel gun if they showed violence to Clark, the officer commanding the shore party.

Except on the Coast and in the lower reaches of the Missouri, most of the Indians with whom the captains dealt had no conception of the growing power of the United States of America and, except on the Pacific Coast and the lower Missouri, little knowledge of white men. All, however, had a keen appreciation of the white man's manufactures, especially his firearms, and were eager to have traders come to sell them.

Otherwise, the tribes of the wild interior had gained little respect for the white race in such isolated contacts as had taken place. The squaw men who settled among them for life were misfits of white society—men like René Jussome, whom one acquaintance called an "old sneaking cheat," or the worthless Toussaint Charbonneau, whose redeeming virtues seem to have been only that he was an excellent cook and had an admirable wife. The white visitors to the Mandan villages, said a Canadian trader, were "a set of worthless scoundrels who are generally accustomed to visit those parts."

The leading traders representing the Hudson's Bay Company and the North-West Fur Company were men of higher type, though many of their junior assistants may have been on a level not much higher than the squaw men. The Hudson's Bay Company had originally been chartered in 1670, as one of the early British joint-stock companies, its purpose being trade with the Indians, with furs and skins as the most important commodity. It had almost sovereign power in the Hudson's Bay Territory until the Canadian government took over control of the area in 1869; and its traders had, for more than a century, been gradually penetrating every corner of the American wilderness where furs could be had. The company had possessed a monopoly of the trade until 1783–1784, when Montreal merchants organized the North-West Fur Company, which remained a bitter rival until the two companies were amalgamated in 1821.

Though the leading traders were of a much higher type than the squaw men, they had little sympathy with tribal life, no appreciation of aboriginal culture, and often a good deal of contempt for the Indians with whom they dealt. The two Americans, on the other hand, took a relatively enlightened attitude toward the tribes. An important part of their mission was to detach Indian sympathies from Spanish and British colonial administration, to arouse interest in the United States government, to prepare the way for future trade (a matter of even more importance to the Indians than it was to the whites), and to learn as much as possible about aboriginal life, customs, social attitudes, and languages. A large part of their mission was to prepare the way for friendly trade with the tribes—an endeavor that was always difficult and that became more so as white settlers began to encroach on ancient hunting grounds.

Clark, on the whole, took a more sympathetic attitude toward the Indians than Lewis. This is well illustrated in the two men's attitudes toward Sacagawea. Clark nicknamed her "Janey" and seems to have found her amusing and a little touching. For years after the expedition returned he did everything in his power to provide for the heroic squaw, her husband, and their child. To Lewis she seems to have been just "the Indian woman," another squaw who happened to speak a language the expedition needed. Both officers, however, labored mightily to cure her when she fell sick and to cure the baby when even that indestructible infant fell ill; but it is likely that most of the treatment was Clark's.

Lewis seems to have taken no interest in native life after the expedition returned. Clark became Superintendent of Indian Affairs at St. Louis and was, for the rest of his life, the one white man most influential among the western tribes—the "Red Head Chief." The private anthropological museum that he gradually built up was, for its time, the best in the country.

The numbers of the Lewis and Clark Expedition varied at different periods. Jefferson had at first hoped that one man might be able to cross the continent alone. When Ledyard failed, that scheme was given up. Then there was an idea that a small force of about a dozen men might make the crossing. There were, in the actual expedition, from first to last about forty-five persons, including enlisted men, *engagés*—that is, professional rivermen—Clark's slave York, Sacagawea, her husband and their baby, and the two officers. On various occasions Indians came aboard the boats and traveled for some time with the expedition.

However, a small force of only twenty-nine set off from the Mandan village in the spring of 1805 for the final journey to the coast. There had been one desertion. Two soldiers were sent back because they had proved unsatisfactory on the trip from St. Louis, and all the *engagés* returned with them, as had been originally arranged. Charbonneau, Sacagawea, and the baby joined the party at the Mandan village.

The party was large enough to defend itself and, in view of its armament (including the swivel gun, a small cannon that could be mounted anywhere on the gunwale of a boat or the wall of a stockade), looked formidable enough to discourage warriors contemplating an attack. At the same time, the expedition was small enough to be readily manageable and to live on what the hunters could kill in ordinary game country. Except in the Rockies and occasionally along the Columbia, the explorers rarely went hungry, though they were far from enthusiastic over the dogmeat, horsemeat, very thin elk, pounded salmon, and roots on which they sometimes had to live. Once they ate mushrooms, a food almost totally unknown in the early American diet—luckily, they picked a nonpoisonous species.

The fresh salmon of the Columbia River were a useful addition to the diet, but the same fish, preserved by the Indian process of pounding, was not popular with white men. One priest, a few years after Lewis and Clark, politely assured his native hosts that it was "good," but admitted afterward that he meant a "good mortification."

Where game was plentiful, the party lived royally off the country, eating four deer, or an entire buffalo, or a deer and an elk on an average day. The leaders had been careful to include skilled hunters among their men and to ensure an abundant supply of ammunition. The loose gunpowder was carried in sealed lead containers to keep it perfectly dry; as each container was emptied, it was melted down into bullets. Ammunition never failed; but, if it had failed, the expedition could still have killed enough game to sustain life by using its specially constructed air gun. As matters turned out, the air gun was never needed; but it proved so useful as a curiosity to impress the Indians that a few practice shots to demonstrate its powers became standard procedure in entertaining each tribe.

There were really only two logistic errors. One was the failure to realize in time the insatiable eagerness of the Oregon and Washington Indians for blue beads—regarded as especially desirable "chief beads"—and their relative indifference to beads of other colors. After they reached the coast, the Corps of Discovery ran out of these unexpectedly valuable articles and, in the end, had to beg Sacagawea to give up her own blue beads—which, to a Shoshone squaw's taste, were no more valuable than any other beads.

A second error involved Captain Lewis's portable boat, the *Experiment*, which he had designed himself. He proposed to put his boat together above the falls of the Missouri, thus saving a portage. The collapsible framework did not add much to the party's baggage, and the idea seemed excellent until Lewis tried to launch it.

Accustomed to eastern forests and the bark canoes of the eastern tribes, he assumed that there would be plenty of suitable bark. Only after reaching the falls did he discover that there were no suitable trees. Efforts to use hides failed miserably. They worked well enough on the little "bull boats" of the Mandan Indians; but when Lewis's men tried to stitch the leather to cover so large a craft as the *Experiment*, the hides shrank, crevices opened, and the boat sank at her moorings.

The story of the arduous journey is best told in the words of Lewis and Clark. Both officers were under orders to keep journals. So long as they were traveling together, their records are largely duplicate accounts of the same incidents; and at times one is obviously copying the other. Hence a complete reprinting is hardly necessary.

Since space is limited, I have ignored casual preliminary travel on the Ohio and Mississippi by a few members of the expedition and have started the narrative when the boats shoved off from Wood River and began to ascend the Missouri. That is where the real story begins.

The Journals end a few days after the boats swing into shore at Fort Bellefontaine, three miles up the Missouri from its junction with the Mississippi. Next day, Lewis took the Mandan chief, Sheheke, who had returned with the explorers to visit the Great White Father in Washington, to the fort's quartermaster stores and outfitted him with white men's clothing. When that was done, the Corps of Discovery went on to St. Louis and landed, firing their rifles "as a salute to the town." The great adventure had ended in triumphant success, September 23, 1806. The last entry, September 26, reads only: "A fine morning. We commenced writing." But there was, of course, much more to the Lewis and Clark story.

That story was not told in full until Biddle and an assistant eventually managed to publish their much edited and altered version of the Journals. The leaders did not submit a formal report, though their numerous unofficial letters served nearly the same purpose. Important among these are two long letters, one from Lewis to an unidentified friend, which the Canadian explorer, David Thompson, copied into a notebook; and another long letter from Clark to his brother, General George Rogers Clark.

Though many of the botanical specimens collected on the first part of the journey had been damaged while stored in the cache at Great Falls, much material of scientific interest was brought safely back to civilization. Collections made between St. Louis and the Mandan country in 1804 had, of course, been sent back with the returning *engagés* and soldiers in 1805.

A special packet of seeds new to science went to Monticello for Jefferson. Others went to some Philadelphia botanists, one of whom had seven new species "up and in a growing state" by April, 1807. A German botanist (Pursh), visiting the United States about this time, met Lewis, who allowed him to sketch some of his dried specimens. Of the 150 specimens he examined, the German could identify only twelve as already known. Though later botanical study has reduced the number of unknown specimens the necessity of erecting two new genera, one called Lewisia and the other Clarkia, shows how much of the collected material was new to science—not merely new species, but new genera.

The zoological and anthropological material has largely disappeared, though some of it remains. Some was burned in a fire at the University of Virginia. Other materials probably vanished when Clark's "Indian Museum" in St. Louis, to which he had devoted much attention in his later years as Indian Superintendent, was broken up after his death. Some material is at Harvard. The Indian vocabularies collected by the expedition have largely, if not entirely, disappeared, though they may eventually turn up in some missing legal or governmental file.

Clark's manuscript maps were voluminous. He continued to improve them during his years as Indian Superintendent at St. Louis, and so it is not always possible to determine how much of the topography was done on the expedition and how much from information that reached him later. Though long replaced by more scientific surveys by topographers who could move freely about the country, without fear of Indians or wild beasts, Clark provided the first basic survey.

Lewis and Clark's success in carrying out their orders is remarkable. In spite of all difficulties, they traversed and surveyed the unknown (or almost unknown) upper reaches of the Columbia and Missouri rivers, crossed the Rockies, and discovered a trade route to the Pacific Coast. That it was not a very good trade route is hardly their fault, since they were not free to investigate others; and that far better routes and better passes through the Rockies were later to be discovered by other travelers was only to be expected. Lewis and Clark also brought back a great deal of new scientific material and reported many observations of animals and plants. They probably brought back rather more than most modern expeditions, though this was partly because there were so many more new species to be discovered then than there are now.

So far as was humanly possible, the expedition paved the way for friendly relations with the Indians. The Blackfeet and Sioux remained hostile or at least suspicious; but many of the other tribes awaited the coming of white traders in an entirely friendly spirit, which was eventually destroyed by the unwise Indian policies of later days and the greed of white traders, miners, and settlers.

In October, the two captains set out for the East, taking Sheheke with them, and reached the Clark home at Louisville on November 5. Clark tarried here, while Lewis and Sheheke went on to Albemarle County and then to Washington, where, on January 10, 1807, President Jefferson gave them a White House reception.

There was great difficulty in getting the chief back home. The military escort detailed for his protection through hostile country was driven off in September, 1807. Not until the autumn of 1809 was Sheheke back in his native village—where nobody believed his tales of the wonders he had seen among the white men.

Congress granted each officer 1,600 acres of land and

each enlisted man 320 acres. All received double pay. Lewis became Governor of Louisiana Territory, Clark, brigadier-general commanding the Louisiana Militia. Clark married his Judy (Julia Hancock) in 1808 and took her to St. Louis. Lewis tepidly imagined himself in love several times—but remained a bachelor.

The moody, solitary Lewis, accustomed to military command and the wilderness, proved himself quite unfitted for political life and served a brief, unhappy term as governor. Finally becoming embroiled with government accountants in Washington, he started east to settle matters by personal interviews, taking his papers with him. He died by violence at Grinder's Stand, a frontier farm on the Natchez Trace, at Hohenwald, Tennessee, in the autumn of 1809. The evidence is about equally balanced between murder and suicide—so far as there is any evidence from that lonely spot that can be trusted. Clark, on first receiving the news, inclined to fear his friend was a suicide; in later life, he stoutly denied such a possibility.

Clark, appointed governor of Missouri Territory in 1813, was far more successful. When Missouri was granted statehood, he even submitted a half-hearted candidacy for election as governor; but, as he declined to do any political campaigning, he was defeated. Until his death, September 1, 1838, he remained Superintendent of Indian Affairs—widely known, immensely venerated, greatly loved, and just a little feared among the western tribes.

John Bakeless

Elbowroom Farm,
Great Hill,
Seymour, Connecticut

A Note on the Text

The text here used is based on the edition compiled by Reuben G. Thwaites from the original manuscripts in the American Philosophical Society, Philadelphia (New York: Dodd, Mead and Company, 1904, 8 volumes). Because of the great length of the Thwaites edition, it has been necessary to omit much detail here; and since the cutting has been extensive, it seems best to note the fact once and for all instead of disfiguring page after page with ellipses.

Both Lewis and Clark spelled and punctuated after the wild fashion of their time. Hence, for the modern reader, it has seemed desirable to respell and repunctuate where needed. Both officers wrote clear and vigorous English prose, but occasionally there were lapses, and so I have made both the present of a little grammar, without further comment. The names of various people, places, and Indian tribes were misspelled—often several different ways—throughout the journals. As far as possible, all these have been corrected and made consistent in accordance with modern style.

The use of brackets and parentheses in the text is explained in a footnote on page 25.

The much rewritten, overedited, refined, and bowdlerized text of Nicholas Biddle, who prepared most of the first edition of the journals, has not been used at all. Lewis was dead before Biddle had finished his share of the text. Clark sent a man to assist Biddle and tried to keep in touch with the editing, but as he and Biddle were usually hundreds of miles apart, his efforts were not very successful. The real flavor of the Lewis and Clark Expedition's high adventure is in the original journals, the text used here.

J. B.

CONTENTS

Chapter *I*

THE CORPS OF DISCOVERY
SHOVES OFF

River Dubois opposite the mouth
of the Missouri River,
May the 13th, 1804

[Clark]

I dispatched an express this morning to Captain Lewis at St. Louis. All our provisions, goods, and equipage on board of a boat of 22 oars [party],[1] a large pirogue of 71 oars [in which 8 French], a second pirogue of 6 oars [soldiers], complete with sails, &c. Men completed with powder cartridges and 100 balls each, all in health and readiness to set out. Boats and everything complete, with the necessary stores of provisions and such articles of merchandise as we thought ourselves authorized to procure—though not as much as I think necessary for the multitude of Indians through which we must pass on our road across the continent.

May 14th, 1804

Rained the fore part of the day. I determined to go as far as St. Charles, a French village seven leagues up the Missouri, and wait at that place until Captain Lewis could finish the business which he was obliged to attend to at St. Louis, and join me by land from that place (24 miles). I calculated that if any alterations in the loading of the vessels or other

[1] Those words and phrases which are enclosed in brackets do not appear in the original journals. They represent additions or corrections made by a number of people between 1806 and the present; the first of these was Clark himself, who went over the journals before their first publication. Explanatory or corrective inserts by the present editor are italicized; all others are in roman type. Words and phrases in parentheses were in parentheses in the journals as originally written.

changes were necessary, they might be made at St. Charles.[2]

I set out at 4 o'clock, P.M., in the presence of many of the neighboring inhabitants and proceeded under a gentle breeze up the Missouri to the upper point of the first island, 4 miles, and camped on the island.

May 15th

[Lewis]

It rained during the greater part of last night and continued until 7 o'clock A.M., after which the party proceeded. The barge ran foul there several times on logs, and in one instance it was with much difficulty they could get her off. Happily no injury was sustained, though the barge was several minutes in imminent danger. This was caused by her being too heavily laden in the stern. Persons accustomed to the navigation of the Missouri, and the Mississippi also, below the mouth of this river, uniformly take the precaution to load their vessels heaviest in the bow when they ascend the stream, in order to avoid the danger incident to running foul of the concealed timber, which lies in great quantities in the beds of these rivers.

St. Charles, May 16th, 1804

[Orderly Book]

Note: The commanding officer is fully assured that every man of his detachment will have a true respect for his own dignity and not make it necessary for him to leave St. Charles for a more retired situation.

May the 17th, 1804

[Clark]

A fair day. Compelled to punish for misconduct. Several Kickapoo Indians visit me today. George Drouilliard arrived.

[2] Intentionally or not, Clark wisely made what is sometimes called a "Hudson's Bay start." Hudson's Bay men are credited with a system of starting late and making the first camp not far from their starting point. The first night's camp reveals anything that has been forgotten and it is not hard to go back for it. Lewis had been in St. Louis on business—and also to say farewell to some "fair friends." Clark's affections were already centered on Julia Hancock, the Virginia girl whom he married immediately on his return.

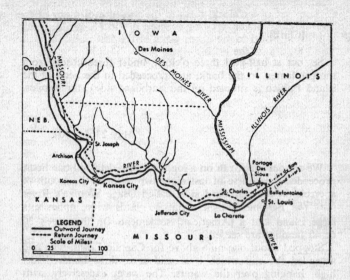

Orders, St. Charles, the 17th of May, 1804
[Orderly Book]

A sergeant and four men of the party destined for the
Missouri Expedition will convene at 11 o'clock today on the
quarterdeck of the boat and form themselves into a court-
martial, to hear and determine (in behalf of the captain),
the evidences adduced against William Warner & Hugh Hall,
for being absent last night without leave, contrary to orders;
and John Collins, first for being absent without leave; second,
for behaving in an unbecoming manner at the ball last night;
third, for speaking in a language last night after his return
tending to bring into disrespect the orders of the commanding
officer.[3]

[3] This court-martial was the beginning of Lewis and Clark's
careful testing out of their men on the first part of their journey.
It is interesting to see these two Regular Army officers introducing
enlisted men to sit on a court martial, about 150 years before
the U. S. Army itself did the same thing officially.

In this case, all three defendants were found guilty and sentenced to be whipped, the first two with 25 lashes, Collins with
50. Whipping remained a military punishment for many years.

The "orderly book" was a record kept in each command of all
written orders, whether issued or received.

May 21st, 1804

[Clark]

Set out at half-past three o'clock, under three cheers from
the gentlemen on the bank, and proceeded to the head of the
island (which is situated on the starboard side), three miles.

May 23rd, 1804

We set out early, ran on a log, and were detained one hour,
proceeded the course of last night two miles to the mouth of
a creek on the starboard side, called Osage Woman's River
[*i.e., the Femme Osage*], about 30 yards wide, opposite a
large island and a [American] settlement. On this creek 30
or 40 families are settled.

Stopped about one mile above for Captain Lewis, who had
ascended the cliff which is at said cave, three hundred feet
high, hanging over the waters. The water excessively swift
today. We encamped below a small island in the middle of
the river. Sent out two hunters. One killed a deer.

This evening we examined the arms and ammunition.
Found those men's arms in the pirogue in bad order. A fair
evening. Captain Lewis near falling from the pinnacles of
rocks, 300 feet. He caught at 20 feet.

May 25th, 1804

Camped at the mouth of a creek called Rivière la Charrette, above a small French village of seven houses and as
many families settled at this place to be convenient to hunt
and trade with the Indians. Here we met M. [*Régis*]
Loisel,[4] immediately down from the Cedar Island, in the
country of the Sioux, 400 leagues up. He gave us a good deal
of information.

---

[4] Régis Loisel was a well-known trader. He was not by any
means the sincere friend he posed as being. A few days after
this meeting he was giving the Spaniards a full report on Lewis
and Clark.

12th of June, 1804

At 1 o'clock we brought to, two chaussies [*cargo boats*], one loaded with furs and peltries, the other with buffalo grease and tallow. We purchased 300 pounds of grease; and, finding that old Mr. [*Pierre*] Dorion [5] was of the party, we questioned him until it was too late to go further.

Concluding to take old Mr. Dorion back as far as the Sioux nation, with a view to get some of their chiefs to visit the President of the United States—this man being a very confidential friend of those people, he having resided with the nation twenty-odd years.

June 17th, 1804

George Drouilliard,[6] our hunter, and one man came in with two deer and a bear, also a young horse they had found in the prairie. This horse had been in the prairie a long time and is fat. I suppose he has been left by some war party against the Osages. The party is much afflicted with boils, and several have the dysentery.

June 29th, 1804

[Orderly Book]

Ordered.—A court-martial will sit this day at 11 o'clock, to consist of five members, for the trial of John Collins and Hugh Hall, confined on charges exhibited against them by Sergeant Floyd, agreeable to the Articles of War. . . . John Collins charged with getting drunk on his post this morning out of whiskey put under his charge as sentinel, and for

[5] Pierre Dorion was a veteran of the western frontier. In 1780 he had been in correspondence with Clark's elder brother, George Rogers Clark.

[6] George Drouilliard's signature shows he spelled his name that way, though no one in the expedition ever learned how to spell it or even to pronounce it. In the MS. Journals he is usually "Drewyer." He was a young French-Canadian, a dead shot, a skilled frontiersman, well acquainted with Indian ways and the sign language, so that he could communicate with all western tribes, whether he knew their widely differing spoken languages or not. He was killed by the Blackfeet in 1810.

suffering Hugh Hall to draw whiskey out of the said barrel intended for the party.

To this charge the prisoner pleaded "not guilty."

The court, after mature deliberation on the evidence adduced, &c., are of opinion the prisoner is guilty of the charge exhibited against him, and do therefore sentence him to receive one hundred lashes on his bare back.

Hugh Hall was brought before the court charged with taking whiskey out of a keg this morning, which whiskey was stored on the bank (and under the charge of the guard), contrary to all order, rule, or regulation.

To this charge the prisoner pleaded guilty.

The court find the prisoner guilty and sentence him to receive fifty lashes on his bare back.

July 4th, 1804

Ushered in the day by a discharge of one shot from our bow piece, proceeded on, passed the mouth of a bayou leading from a large lake on the S.S.,[7] which has the appearance of being once the bend of the river, and reaches parallel for several miles. We came to on the L.S. to refresh ourselves. Joseph Fields got bitten by a snake, and was quickly doctored with bark by Captain Lewis.

We passed a creek twelve yards wide, on the L.S., coming out of an extensive prairie reaching within two hundred yards of the river. As this creek has no name, and this being the Fourth of July, the day of the Independence of the United States, we called it "Fourth of July 1804 Creek." We dined on corn. Captain Lewis walked on shore above this creek and discovered a high mound from the top of which he had an extensive view. Three paths came together at the mound. We saw great numbers of goslings today which were nearly grown. The lake is clear and contains great quantities of fish and geese and goslings. This induced me to call it Gosling Lake. A small creek and several springs run into the lake on the east side from the hills. The land on that side is very good.

[7] The abbreviation "S.S." stands for "starboard," or the right-hand side when one is facing forward on a ship. "L.S." means "larboard," or left-hand side. Probably because of the confusing similarity of sound in these two words, "larboard" has now generally been replaced by "port."

July the 7th, 1804

Set out early. Passed some swift water which obliged us to draw up by ropes. A sand bar at the point, opposite a beautiful prairie on the S. side, called St. Michael. Those prairies on the river have very much the appearance of farms from the river, divided by narrow strips of woodland, which woodland is situated on the runs leading to the river. Passed a bluff of yellow clay above the prairie. Saw a large rat on the bank. Killed a wolf. One man very sick—struck with the sun. Captain Lewis bled him and gave niter, which has revived him much.

July the 8th, 1804

Set out early. Passed a small creek and two small islands on the S.S. Five men sick today with violent headache, &c. We made some arrangements as to provisions and messes. Came to for dinner at the lower point of a very large island situated near the S.S. After a delay of two hours we passed a narrow channel 45 to 80 yards wide five miles to the mouth of Nodaway River.

Detachment Orders.
Nodaway Island, July 8th, 1804

[Orderly Book: Lewis]

In order to ensure a prudent and regular use of all provisions issued to the crew of the bateaux in future, as also to provide for the equal distribution of the same among the individuals of the several messes, the commanding officers do appoint the following persons to *receive, cook, and take charge of* the provisions which may from time to time be issued to their respective messes, viz., John B. Thompson to Sergeant Floyd's mess, William Warner to Sergeant Ordway's mess, and John Collins to Sergeant Pryor's mess.

These *Superintendents of Provision* are held immediately responsible to the commanding officers for a judicious consumption of the provision which they receive; they are to cook the same for their several messes in due time, and in such manner as is most wholesome and best calculated to afford the greatest proportion of nutriment; in their mode of cooking they are to exercise their own judgment. They shall also point out what part, and what proportion of the mess provisions are to be consumed at each stated meal, i.e., morning, noon, and night. Nor is any man at any time to take or consume any part of the mess provisions without the privity, knowledge, and consent of the superintendent. The superintendent is also held responsible for all the cooking utensils of his mess. In consideration of the duties imposed by this order on Thompson, Warner, and Collins, they will in future be exempt from guard duty, though they will still be held on the roster for that duty, and their regular tour shall be performed by someone of their respective messes; they are exempted also from pitching the tents of the mess, collecting firewood, and forks, poles, &c. for cooking and drying such fresh meat as may be furnished them; those duties are to be also performed by the other members of the mess.

M. Lewis
Wm. Clark

July 9th, 1804

[Clark]

One man sent back to the river we passed last night to blaze a tree with a view to notify the party on shore of our passing. Set out and passed the head of the island which was situated opposite to our camp last night—a sand bar at the head. Opposite this island a creek or bayou comes in from a large pond on the starboard side. As our flanking party saw great numbers of pike in this pond, I have laid it down with that name annexed. At 8 o'clock the wind shifted from the N.E. to the S.W. and it commenced raining. At six miles, passed the mouth of the creek on the L.S. called Montain's Creek. About two miles above are some cabins where our bowman and several Frenchmen camped two years ago. Passed an island on the S.S. in a bend of the river opposite some cliffs on the L.S. The wind shifted to the N.W. opposite this island, and on the L. side Wolf River comes in. This river is about 60 yards wide and heads with the waters of the Kansas, and is navigable for pirogues "some distance up." Camped at a point on the L.S. opposite the head of the island. Our party was encamped on the opposite side. Their not answering our signals caused us to suspect the persons camped opposite to us were a war party of Sioux. We fired the bow piece to alarm the party on shore, all prepared to oppose if attacked.

July 10th, 1804

Set out early this morning and crossed the river with a view to see who the party was that camped on the other side. We soon discovered them to be our men. Proceeded on past a prairie on the L.S. at 4 miles. Passed a creek L.S. called Pape's Creek after a man who killed himself at its mouth. This creek is 15 yards wide. Dined on an island called Solomon's Island. Delayed three hours on this island to recruit the men. Opposite on the L.S. is a beautiful bottom plain of about 2,000 acres covered with wild rye and potatoes (ground apple—*pomme de terre*), intermixed with the grass.

July 11th, 1804

Set out early. Passed a willow island in a bend on the S.S. Back of this island a creek comes in, called by the Indians Tarkio. I went on shore above this creek and walked up parallel with the river about half a mile distant. The bottom I found low and subject to overflow. Still further out, the undergrowth and vines were so thick that I could not get through with ease. After walking about three or four miles, I observed a fresh horse track; where he had been feeding I turned my course to the river and pursued the track, and found him on a sand beach. This horse probably had been left by some party of Ottawas, hunters who wintered or hunted in this quarter last fall or winter. I joined the party on a large sand island immediately opposite the mouth of Nemaha River, at which place they had camped. This island is sand, about half of it covered with small willows of two different kinds, one narrow and the other a broad leaf. Several hunters sent out today on both sides of the river. Seven deer killed today—Drouilliard killed six of them. Made some lunar observations this evening.

July 12th, 1804

Concluded to delay here today with a view of taking equal altitudes and making observations as well as refreshing our men, who are much fatigued. After an early breakfast I, with five men in a pirogue, ascended the river Nemaha about three miles to the mouth of a small creek on the lower side. Here I got out of the pirogue. After going to several small mounds in a level plain, I ascended a hill on the lower side. On this hill, several artificial mounds were raised; from the top of the highest of those mounds I had an extensive view of the surrounding plains, which afforded one of the most pleasing prospects I ever beheld: under me a beautiful river of clear water about 80 yards wide, meandering through a level and extensive meadow, as far as I could see—the prospect much enlivened by the few trees and shrubs which border the bank of the river, and the creeks and runs falling into it. The bottom land is covered with grass about 4½ feet high, and appears as level as a smooth surface. The second bottom [the upper land] is also covered with grass and rich weeds and flowers, interspersed with copses of the Osage plum, on the rising lands. Small groves of trees are seen, with numbers of grapes and a wild cherry resembling the common wild cherry, only larger, and growing on a small bush on the tops of those hills in every direction. I observed artificial mounds (or as I may more justly term graves) which to me is a strong evidence of this country being once thickly settled. (The Indians of the Missouris still keep up the custom of burying their dead on high ground.) After a ramble of about two miles, I returned to the pirogue and descended down the river. Gathered some grapes, nearly ripe. On a sandstone bluff about ¼ of a mile from its mouth on the lower side, I observed some Indian marks. Went to the rock which jutted over the water and marked my name [8] and the day of the month and year. Tried a man for sleeping on his post, and inspected the arms, ammunition, &c., of the party. Found all complete. Took some lunar observations. Three deer killed today.

[8] The universal passion for marking one's name in conspicuous places—one can't say public places, for there was nothing public about the Far West as yet—is very old. Greek mercenary soldiers in Egypt did it in ancient times, each using the characteristic alphabet of the city from which he came. The early American pioneers shared this taste, though without doing the harm their descendants do in marring ancient monuments. Daniel Boone habitually carved his name on trees. So did other pioneers, as innumerable entries in the Draper mss. in the State Historical Society of Wisconsin show. The signature that William Clark carved on Pompey's Tower (now called Pompey's Pillar) in Montana, while he was on his way home in 1806, is still visible. Pioneers on the Oregon Trail and other transcontinental trails also left abundant marks.

Latitude 39° 55′ 56″ N.

Camp New Island, July 12th, 1804

[Orderly Book: Lewis]

A court-martial consisting of the two commanding officers will convene this day at one o'clock, P.M., for the trial of such prisoners as may be brought before them. One of the court will act as judge advocate.

M. Lewis
Wm. Clark

[Clark]

The commanding officers, Captains M. Lewis and W. Clark, constituted themselves a court-martial for the trial of such prisoners as are guilty of capital crimes, and under the rules and articles of war punishable by death.

Alexander Willard was brought forward, charged with "lying down and sleeping on his post while a sentinel, on the night of the 11th instant." (By John Ordway, sergeant of the guard.)

To this charge the prisoner pleads guilty of lying down, and not guilty of going to sleep.

The court, after duly considering the evidence adduced, are of opinion that the prisoner Alexander Willard is guilty of every part of the charge exhibited against him. It being a breach of the rules and articles of war (as well as tending to the probable destruction of the party) do sentence him to receive one hundred lashes on his bare back, at four different times in equal proportion; and order that the punishment commence this evening at sunset, and continue to be inflicted, by the guard, every evening until completed.[9]

Wm. Clark
M. Lewis

July 13, 1804

[Clark]

Set out at sunrise, and proceeded on under a gentle breeze.

---

[9] Sleeping on guard may be punished by death, in any army. In view of the seriousness of the charge against Willard, the court-martial consisted of officers only.

At two miles, passed the mouth of a small river on the S.S. called by the Indians Tarkio. A channel running out of the river three miles above (which is now filled up with sand) runs into this creek, and formed an island, called St. Josephs. Several sand bars parallel to each other above. In the first bend to the left is situated a beautiful and extensive plain, covered with grass resembling timothy, except the seed which resembles flaxseed. This plain also abounds in grapes of different kinds, some nearly ripe. I killed two goslings nearly grown. Several others killed and caught on shore, also one old goose with pinfeathers. She could not fly. At about 12 miles, passed an island situated in a bend on the S.S.—above this island is a large sand bar covered with willows. The wind from the south. Camped on a large sand bar making out from the L side, opposite a high, handsome prairie, the hills about 4 or 5 miles on starboard side.

July 14th, 1804

Some hard showers of rain this morning prevented our setting out until seven o'clock. At half-past seven, the atmosphere became suddenly darkened by a black and dismal-looking cloud. At the time we were in a situation not to be bettered, near the upper point of the sand island, on which we lay, and [on] the opposite shore, the bank was falling in and lined with snags as far as we could see down. In this situation the storm, which passed over an open plain from the N.E., struck the oar boat on the starboard quarter, and would have thrown her up on the sand island dashed to pieces in an instant, had not the party leaped out on the leeward side, and kept her off with the assistance of the anchor and cable, until the storm was over. The waves washed over her windward side and she must have filled with water if the lockers, which are covered with tarpaulins, had not thrown off the water and prevented any quantity getting into the bilge of the boat. In this situation we continued about 40 minutes, when the storm suddenly ceased and the river became instantaneously as smooth as glass.

The two pirogues, during this storm, were in a similar situation with the boat about half a mile above. The wind shifted to the S.E., and we sailed up past a small island situated on the S.S., and dined, and continued two hours, men examined their arms. About a mile above this island we passed a small trading fort on the S.S., where Mr. Bennet of St. Louis traded with the Otos and Pawnees two years. I went on shore to shoot some elk on a sand bar to the L.S. I fired at one but did not get him. Several men unwell with boils, felons, &c. The river falls a little.

July 15th

A heavy fog this morning prevented our setting out before seven o'clock. At nine I took two men and walked on the L.S. I crossed three beautiful streams of running water heading into the prairies. On those streams the land very fine, covered with pea vine and rich weed. The high prairies are also good land, covered with grass, entirely void of timber, except what grows on the water. I proceeded on through those prairies several miles to the mouth of a large creek on the L.S. called Little Nemaha. This is a small river.

Chapter II

FROM THE PLATTE TO
THE VERMILION
July 23—August 24, 1804

Camp White Catfish,
nine [10] miles above the Platte River,
the 23rd of July, 1804

[Clark]

A fair morning. Set a party to look for timber for oars; two parties to hunt. At eleven o'clock sent off George Drouilliard and Peter Cruzat with some tobacco to invite the Otos if at their town, and Pawnees if they saw them, to come and talk with us at our camp, &c., &c. (At this season, the Indians on this river are in the prairies hunting the buffalo, but some signs of hunters near this place and the plains being on fire near their towns induce a belief that they—this nation— have returned to get some green corn or roasting ears.[1]) Raised a staff, sunned and dried our provisions, &c. I commence copying a map of the river below to send to the President, United States. Five deer killed today. One man with a tumor [2] on his breast. Prepared our camp. The men

---

[1] Corn was, of course, the usual staple of almost all Indian tribes. Oddly enough, there is no really good evidence that Indians ever ate corn on the cob. However, ears roasting whole were often found by white raiders on Indian villages, and it is natural to suppose that, in the era before the white man, squaws preferred serving the whole ear to trying to slice off the green kernels with a flint knife.

[2] The "tumor" was, of course, not malignant, but only a boil or a carbuncle. As these may be caused by extreme fatigue, it is easy to understand their frequency and severity in the early stages of the journey. Later, as the men grew harder, one hears very little about them.

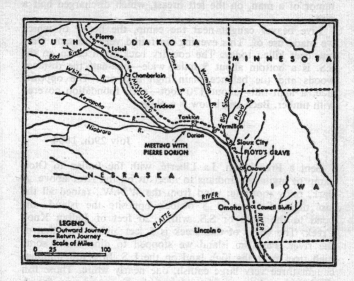

put their arms in order. Wind hard this afternoon from the N.W.

White Catfish Camp 10 miles above Platte,
24th of July, 1804

A fair day. The wind blows hard from the south. The breezes, which are very frequent in this part of the Missouri, are cool and refreshing. Several hunters out today, but, as game of all kinds is scarce, only two deer were brought in. I am much engaged drawing off a map. Captain Lewis also much engaged in preparing papers to send back by a pirogue, which we intended to send back from the River Platte. Observations at this place makes the latitude 41° 3′ 19″ North.

This evening Goodrich caught a white catfish, its eyes small and tail much like that of a dolphin.

Catfish, which is White Camp,
26th of July, 1804

The wind blustering and hard from the south all day, which blew the clouds of sand in such a manner that I could not complete my plan in the tent. The boat rolled in such a manner that I could do nothing in that, and was compelled to go to the woods and combat the mosquitoes. I opened the tumor of a man, on the left breast, which discharged half a pint.

Five beaver caught near the camp, the flesh [3] of which we made use of. This evening we found very pleasant. Only one deer killed today. The country back from camp on the S.S. is a bottom about 5 miles wide—one-half the distance woods and the balance plain high and dry. The opposite side, a high hill—about 170 foot—rock foundation covered with timber. Back and below is a plain.

July 29th, 1804

Sent a Frenchman, La Liberté, with the Indian to Otos' camp to invite the Indians to meet us on the river above. A dark, rainy morning; wind from the W.N.W., rained all the last night. Set out at 5 o'clock opposite the island—the bend to the right or S.S. within 20 feet of Indian Knob Creek. The water of this creek is 5 feet higher than that of the river. Past the island we stopped to dine under some high trees near the high land on the L.S. In a few minutes, caught three very large catfish, one nearly white. Those fish are in great plenty on the sides of the river and very fat. A quart of oil came out of the surplus fat of one of those fish.

July 30th, 1804

Set out this morning early. Proceeded on to a clear open prairie on the L.S. on a rise of about 70 feet higher than the bottom, which is also a prairie (both forming bluffs to the river) of high grass and plum bush, grapes, &c., and situated above high water. In a small grove of timber at the foot of the rising ground, between those two prairies, and below the bluffs of the high prairie, we came to and formed a camp, intending to wait the return of the Frenchman and Indians. The white horse which we found near the Kansas River died last night.

Posted out our guard, and sent out four men. Captain Lewis and I went up the bank and walked a short distance in

[3] Beaver was not an emergency diet. The tail was an especial frontier delicacy and was, in fact, a favorite dish with Captain Lewis. A seventeenth-century English traveler noted: "The Tail boiled, proved exceeding good meat, being all Fat, and as sweet as Marrow."

the high prairie. This prairie is covered with grass ten or twelve inches in height; soil of good quality; and at the distance of about a mile further back, the country rises about 80 or 90 feet higher, and is one continued plain as far as can be seen. From the bluff on the second rise immediately above our camp, the most beautiful prospect of the river, up and down, and the country opposite, presented itself, which I ever beheld.

July 31st

A fair day. Three hunters out. Took meridian altitude, made the latitude 41° 18′ 1 5/10″N. R. and Jo. Fields returned to camp; they killed three deer. The horses strayed off last night. Drouilliard killed a buck, one inch of fat on the ribs. R. and Jo. Fields returned without any meat, having been in pursuit of the horses. The Indians not yet arrived. Caught a young beaver alive which is already quite tame.[4] Caught a buffalo fish. The evening very cool, the mosquitoes are yet troublesome.

August the 1st, 1804

A fair morning. Dispatched two men after the horses lost yesterday. One man back to the place from which the messenger was sent for the Otos, to see if any Indians were, or had been, there since our departure. He returned and informed that no person had been there since we left it. The prairie which is situated below our camp is above the high-water level and rich, covered with grass from 5 to 8 feet high, interspersed with copses of hazel, plums, currants, like those of the U. S.

August 2nd, 1804

A very pleasant breeze from the S.E. The two men, Drouilliard and Colter, returned with the horses loaded with elk.

---

[4] The tame beaver was not so remarkable as it sounds. In the early days of Boston, Mass., one tame beaver frolicked unharmed through the streets. Daniel Boone rather liked to tame young otters, though even he failed to tame wolf puppies. Soldiers in the early American forests were likely to accumulate pets. Burgoyne's troops, at the surrender, were accompanied by animals they had tamed in remarkable numbers.

Those horses they found about 12 miles in a southerly direction from camp.

The country through which they passed is similar to what we see from camp. One beaver and a foot [of a beaver caught in a trap] caught this morning.

At sunset, Mr. Fairfong [5] [Oto interpreter resident with them] and a party of the Oto and Missouri Nations came to camp. Among those Indians, six were chiefs (not the principal chiefs). Captain Lewis and myself met those Indians and informed them we were glad to see them, and would speak to them tomorrow. Sent them some roasted meat, pork, flour and meal. In return, they sent us watermelons. Every man on his guard and ready for anything.

August 3rd, 1804

Made up a small present for those people in proportion to their consequence; also a package with a medal to accompany a speech for the grand chief. After breakfast, we collected those Indians under an awning of our mainsail. In presence of our party, paraded, and delivered a long speech to them, expressive of our journey, the wishes of our government, some advice to them, and directions how they were to conduct themselves. The principal chief for the nation being absent, we sent him the speech,[6] flag, medal, and some clothes. After hearing what they had to say, delivered a medal of second grade to one for the Otos and one for the Missouris, and presented four medals of a third grade to the inferior chiefs—two for each tribe. Those two parts of nations, Otos and Missouris, now residing together are about 250 men, the Otos composing ⅔ and the Missouris ⅓ part.

Those chiefs all delivered a speech, acknowledging their approbation to the speech and promising to pursue the advice and directions given them, that they were happy to

---

[5] Mr. Fairfong (or Faufon) was one of those not unusual white men who rather enjoyed the wild, free life of the prairies and happily settled down to it, more or less permanently cutting themselves off from white civilization.

[6] An Indian "speech" was not necessarily delivered orally. Any diplomatic communication was sometimes so described. The famous "speech" of Tahgahjute (Logan), which Thomas Jefferson thought a masterpiece of oratory, was simply written out for Logan by a trader and sent to Governor Dunsmore, of Virginia. In this case, the "speech" seems to have been written out, in the hope that sooner or later the recipient would find a literate white man who could read it to him.

find that they had fathers which might be depended on, &c.

We gave them a canister of powder and a bottle of whiskey, and delivered a few presents to the whole, after giving a breech cloth, some paint, gartering, and a medal to those we made chiefs. After Captain Lewis's shooting the air gun a few shots (which astonished those natives), we set out, and proceeded on five miles, on a direct line past a point on the S.S. and around a large sand bar on the L.S., and camped on the upper point. The mosquitoes excessively troublesome this evening. Great appearance of wind and rain to the N.W. We prepare to receive it. The man Liberté whom we sent for the Otos has not come up. He left the Otos' town one day before the Indians. This man has either tired his horse, or lost himself in the plains. Some Indians are to hunt for him.

5th of August, 1804

Set out early. Great appearance of wind and rain. I have observed that thunder and lightning is not as common in this country as it is in the Atlantic states. Snakes are not plenty; one was killed today, large, and resembling the rattlesnake, only something lighter. I walked on shore this evening, S.S. In pursuing some turkeys, I struck the river twelve miles below within 370 yards. The high water passes through this peninsula, and agreeable to the customary changes of the river, I should conclude that in two years the main current of the river will pass through. In every bend the banks are falling in from the current being thrown against those bends by the sand points which enlarge, and the soil, I believe, from unquestionable appearances of the entire bottom, from one hill to the other, being the mud or ooze of the river at some former period, mixed with sand and clay, easily melts and slips into the river, and the mud mixes with the water, and the sand is washed down and lodges on the points. Great quantities of grapes on the banks. I observe three different kinds, at this time ripe; one of the number is large and has the flavor of the purple grape. Camped on the S.S. The mosquitoes very troublesome. The man who went back after his knife has not yet come up. We have some reasons to believe he has deserted.

7th August, 1804

Last night at 8 o'clock a storm from the N.W. which

lasted ¾ of an hour. Set out late this morning. Wind from the north. At one o'clock, dispatched George Drouilliard, R. Fields, William Bratton, and William Labiche back after the deserter, Reed, with order if he did not give up peaceably to put him to death; to go to the Otos' village and inquire for La Liberté, and bring him to the Maha village, also with a speech on the occasion to the Otos and Missouris, and directing a few of their chiefs to come to the Mahas, and we would make a peace between them and the Mahas and Sioux; a string of wampum and a carrot of tobacco. Proceeded on and camped on the S.S.

8th August, 1804

Set out this morning at the usual time. At two miles, passed a bend to L.S. choked up with snags. Our boat ran on two, in turning to pass through. We got through with safety.

Captain Lewis took median altitude of the sun, made it 56° 9′ 00″, latitude 41° 42′ 34″. And I took one man and went on shore. The man killed an elk. I fired four times at one and did not kill him; my ball being small, I think, was the reason. The mosquitoes so bad in the prairies that with the assistance of a bush I could not keep them out of my eyes. The boat turned several times today on sand bars. In my absence, the boat passed an island two miles above the Little Sioux River. On the upper point of this island, some hundreds of pelicans were collected. They left three fish on the sand which were very fine. Captain Lewis killed one and took his dimensions. I joined the boat and we camped on the S.S. Worthy of remark that snakes are not plenty in this part of the Missouri.

11th August, 1804

About daylight this morning a hard wind from the N.W., with some rain. Proceeded on around the right of the island.

A hard wind accompanied with rain from the S.E. After the rain was over, Captain Lewis, myself, and ten men ascended the hill on the L.S. (under which there were some fine springs) to the top of a high point where the Maha king Blackbird was buried four years ago. [Died of smallpox.] A mound of earth about 12 feet diameter at the base and 6 feet high is raised over him turfed, and a pole 8 feet high in the center. On this pole we fixed a white flag, bound with red, blue, and white. This hill about 300 feet above the water forming a bluff, between that and the water, of various heights from 40 to 150 feet—yellow soft sandstone. From the top of this knoll, the river may be seen meandering for 60 or 70 miles.

14th August, 1804

A fine morning. Wind from the S.E. The men sent to the Maha town last evening have not returned. We conclude to send a spy[7] to know the cause of their delay. At about 12 o'clock, the party returned and informed us that they could not find the Indians, nor any fresh sign. Those people have not returned from their buffalo hunt. Those people, having no houses, no corn, or anything more than the graves of their ancestors to attach them to the old village, continue in pursuit of the buffalo longer than others who have greater attachments to their native villages.

The ravages of the smallpox, which swept off—about four years ago—400 men and women and children in proportion, reduced this nation not exceeding 300 men, and left them to the insults of their weaker neighbors, which before were glad to be on friendly terms with them.

August 15th, Wednesday, 1804,
Camp three miles N.E. of the Maha village.

I went with ten men to a creek dammed by the beavers about halfway to the village. With some small willows and bark we made a drag, and hauled up the creek, and caught 318 fish of different kinds, i.e., pike, bass, salmon, perch, red horse, small cat, and a kind of perch called silverfish on the Ohio. I caught a shrimp precisely of shape, size, and flavor of those about New Orleans and the lower part of the Mississippi, in this creek, which is only the pass or straight from

---

[7] At this period "spy" meant merely a scout. Even as late as the Civil War, the distinction between a scout (a soldier reconnoitering in uniform) and a spy (a secret agent in disguise) was not always clear. Clark had learned the word from his brother, General George Rogers Clark, whose "spies" included both scouts and spies, in the modern sense, among the latter the famous frontiersman, Simon Kenton. Sheridan's "scouts," in the Shenandoah Valley and in the pursuit of Lee to Appomattox, were almost invariably in false uniform, occasionally delivering fairly large attacks on Confederates with the Union forces in Confederate uniform—the result being most amazing confusion.

[one] beaver pond to another and is crowded with large mussels. Very fat ducks, plover of different kinds, are on those ponds as well as on the river.

In my absence, Captain Lewis sent Mr. Dorion, the Sioux interpreter, and three men to examine a fire which threw up an immense smoke from the prairies on the N.E. side of the river, and at no great distance from camp. The object of this party was to find some bands of Sioux, which the interpreter thought were near the smoke, and get them to come in. In the evening this party returned, and informed that the fire arose from some trees which had been left burning by a small party of Sioux [8] who had passed [by that place] several days. The wind, setting from that point, blew the smoke from that point over our camp. Our party all in health and spirits. The men sent to the Otos and in pursuit of the deserter, Reed, have not yet returned or joined our party.

16th August, 1804
Fishing Camp 3 miles N.E. of the Mahas.

A very cool morning, the wind as usual from the N.W. Captain Lewis took twelve men and went to the pond and creek between camp and the old village, and caught upwards of 800 fine fish: 79 pike, 8 salmon resembling trout [8 fish resembling salmon trout], 1 rock, 1 flat back, 127 buffalo and red horse, 4 bass, and 490 cats, with many small silver fish and shrimp. I had a mast made and fixed to the boat today. The party sent to the Otos not yet joined us. The wind shifted around to the S.E. Every evening a breeze rises which blows off the mosquitoes and cools the atmosphere.

17th August, 1804

A fine morning, the wind from the S.E. I collected a grass much resembling wheat in its growth, the grain like rye, and also some resembling rye and barley. A kind of timothy, the seed of which branches from the main stalk and is more like a flaxseed than that of timothy.

[8] Dorion may merely have been guessing that these Indians (whom he did not see) were Sioux. But different tribes made everyday articles very differently—moccasins, for instance. A man who knew the tribe as intimately as Dorion could identify innumerable Sioux characteristics, especially in any small objects left behind.

At six o'clock this evening, Labiche, one of the party sent to the Otos, joined and informed that the party was behind with one of the deserters, M. B. Reed, and the three principal chiefs of the Nations. La Liberté they caught, but he deceived them and got away. The object of those chiefs coming forward is to make peace with the Mahas through us. As the Mahas are not at home, this great object cannot be accomplished at this time. Set the prairies on fire to bring the Mahas and Sioux if they were near, this being the usual signal.

A cool evening; two beaver caught today.

18th August, 1804

A fine morning. Wind from the S.E. In the after part of the day, the party with the Indians arrived. We met them under a shade near the boat, and after a short talk we gave them provisions to eat and proceeded to the trial of Reed. He confessed that he "deserted and stole a public rifle, shot-pouch, powder and ball," and requested that we would be as favorable with him as we could, consistently with our oaths, which we were, and only sentenced him to run the gantlet four times through the party, and that each man with 9 switches should punish him, and for him not to be considered in future as one of the party. The three principal chiefs petitioned for pardon for this man. After we explained the injury such men could do them by false representations, and explained the customs of our country, they were all satisfied with the propriety of the sentence, and were witnesses to the punishment. After which we had some talk with the chiefs about the origin of the war between them and the Mahas, &c.

Captain Lewis's birthday. The evening was closed with an extra gill of whiskey, and a dance until 11 o'clock.

19th August, 1804

A fine morning. Wind from the S.E. Prepared a small present for the chiefs and warriors present. The main chief breakfasted with us and begged for a sun glass. Those people are all naked, covered only with breechclouts, blankets, or buffalo robes—the flesh side painted with different colors and figures. At ten o'clock we assembled the chiefs and warriors, nine in number, under an awning, and Captain Lewis and I explained the speech sent to the nation from the Council Bluffs by Mr. Faufon. The three chiefs and all the men or warriors made short speeches approving the advice and council their Great Father had sent them, and concluded by giving themselves some credit for their acts.

We then brought out the presents and exchanged The Big Horse's medal and gave him one equal to the one sent to the Little Thief, and gave all some small articles and eight carrots of tobacco. We gave one small medal to one of the chiefs and a certificate to the others, of their good intentions.

Names	Great chiefs I have
The Little Thief	mentioned before.
The Big Horse	Karkapaha—Missouri
Crows Head, or	Nenasawa—"
Black Cat, or	Sarnanono—Oto
Iron Eyes, or	Neeswarunja—"
Big Ax [Ox], or	Stargeahunja—"
Big Blue Eyes	Warsarshaco
Brave Man, or	

One of those Indians, after receiving his certificate, delivered it again to me—The Big Blue Eyes. The chief petitioned for the certificate again. We would not give the certificate, but rebuked them very roughly for having in object goods and not peace with their neighbors. This language they did not like at first, but at length all petitioned for us to give back the certificate to The Big Blue Eyes. He came forward and made a plausible excuse. I then gave the certificate to the great chief to bestow it to the most worthy. They gave it to him. We then gave them a dram and broke up the council.

The chiefs requested we would not leave them this evening. We determined to set out early in the morning. We showed them many curiosities, and the air gun, which they were much astonished at. Those people begged much for whiskey. Sergeant Floyd is taken very bad all at once with a bilious colic. We attempt to relieve him without success as yet. He gets worse and we are much alarmed at his situation. All attention to him.

20th August, Monday, 1804

Sergeant Floyd much weaker and no better. Made Mr. Faufon, the interpreter, a few presents and the Indians a canister of whiskey. We set out under a gentle breeze from the S.E., and proceeded on very well. Sergeant Floyd as bad as he can be, no pulse, and nothing will stay a moment on his stomach or bowels. Passed two islands on the S.S. Sergeant Floyd died with a great deal of composure. Before his death, he said to me, "I am going away—I want you to write me a letter." We buried him on the top of the bluff a half mile below a small river to which we gave his name. He was buried with the honors of war, much lamented. A cedar post with the name:

Sergeant C. Floyd
died here
20th of August
1804

was fixed at the head of his grave.[9] This man at all times gave us proof of his firmness, and determined resolution to do service to his country, and honor to himself. After paying all the honor to our deceased brother, we camped in the mouth of Floyd's River, about 30 yards wide. A beautiful evening.

22nd August, 1804

Set out early. Wind from the south. At three miles, we landed at a bluff where the two men sent with the horses were waiting with two deer. By examination, this bluff contained alum, copperas, cobalt, pyrites; an alum rock, soft and sand stone. Captain Lewis, in proving the quality of those minerals, was near poisoning himself by the fumes and taste of the cobalt, which had the appearance of soft isinglass. Copperas and alum are very poisonous. Above this bluff a small creek comes in from the L.S., passing under the cliff for several miles.

Captain Lewis took a dose of salts to work off the effects

[9] Floyd's body now lies in a new grave, under a monument, along the Missouri at Sioux City, Iowa. When the Missouri cut into the bank and exposed the bones, they had to be moved to the new location, which is as close as possible to the place where the expedition originally buried him. That site is now, however, in the air over the Missouri River.

of the arsenic. We camped on the S.S. Sailed the greater part of this day with a hard wind from the S.E. Great deal of elk sign and great appearance of wind from the N.W.

Ordered a vote for a sergeant to choose one of three which may be the highest number. The highest numbers are P. Gass (had 19 votes), Bratton, and Gibson.

23rd August, 1804

Set out this morning very early. The two men with the horses did not come up last night. I walked on shore and killed a fat buck. J. Fields sent out to hunt; came to the boat and informed that he had killed a buffalo in the plain ahead. Captain Lewis took twelve men and had the buffalo brought to the boat. In the next bend to the S.S., two elk swam the river, and were fired at from the boat. R. Fields came up with the horses and brought two deer. One deer killed from the boat. Several prairie wolves seen today. Saw elk standing on the sand bar. The wind blew hard and raised the sands off the bar in such clouds that we could scarcely see. This sand, being fine and very light, stuck to everything it touched, and in the plain for half a mile—the distance I was out—every spire of grass was covered with sand or dirt.

24th August, 1804

Some rain last night. A continuation this morning. We set out at the usual time and proceeded on the course of last night, to the commencement of a blue clay bluff 180 or 190 feet high on the L.S. Those bluffs appear to have been latterly on fire and at this time are too hot for a man to bear his hand in the earth at any depth. Great appearance of coal. An immense quantity of cobalt, or a crystalized substance which answers its description, is on the face of the bluff.

Great quantities of a kind of berry resembling a currant, except double the size, and grows on a bush like a privet, and the size of a damson, deliciously flavored, and makes delightful tarts. This fruit is now ripe. I took my servant [10] and a French boy and walked on shore. Killed two buck elks and a fawn, and intercepted the boat, and had all the meat butchered and in by sunset, at which time it began to rain and rained hard. Captain Lewis and myself walked out and got very wet. A cloudy, rainy night. In my absence, the boat passed a small river, called by the Indians Whitestone River. This river is about 30 yards wide, and runs through a plain or prairie in its whole course.

In a northerly direction from the mouth of this creek, in an immense plain, a high hill is situated, and appears of a conic form, and by the different nations of Indians in this quarter, is supposed to be the residence of devils: that they are in human form with remarkable large heads, and about 18 inches high, that they are very watchful, and are armed with sharp arrows with which they can kill at a great distance. They are said to kill all persons who are so hardy as to attempt to approach the hill. They state that tradition informs them that many Indians have suffered by those little people, and, among others, three Maha men fell a sacrifice to their merciless fury not many years since. So much do the Maha, Sioux, Otos, and other neighboring nations, believe this fable, that no consideration is sufficient to induce them to approach the hill.

[10] The "servant" was, of course, the slave, York. Virginians of this period and later habitually used the word "servant" instead of "slave."

Chapter III

BETWEEN THE VERMILION
AND TETON RIVERS

August 25—September 24, 1804

25th August, 1804

[Clark]

A cloudy morning. Captain Lewis and myself concluded to go and see the mound which was viewed with such terror by all the different nations in this quarter. We selected Shields, J. Fields, W. Bratton, Sergeant Ordway, J. Colter, Carr, and Corporal Warfington and Frazer, also G. Drouilliard, and dropped down to the mouth of Whitestone River, where we left the pirogue with two men; and, at 200 yards, we ascended a rising ground of about 60 feet. From the top of this high land, the country is level and open as far as can be seen, except some few rises at a great distance, and the mound which the Indians call "Mountain of little people, or spirits." This mound appears of a conic form, and is N. 20° W. from the mouth of the creek. We left the river at 8 o'clock. At 4 miles we crossed the creek, 23 yards wide, in an extensive valley, and continued on two miles further.

Our dog was so heated and fatigued, we were obliged to send him back to the creek. At 12 o'clock we arrived at the hill. Captain Lewis much fatigued from heat—the day, it being very hot, and he being in a debilitated state from the precautions he was obliged to take, to prevent the effects of the cobalt and mineral substance which had like to have poisoned him two days ago. His want of water, and several men complaining of great thirst, determined us to make for the first water, which was the creek in a bend N.E. from the mound, about three miles. After a delay of about one hour and a half to recruit our party, we set out on our return down the creek through the bottom, of about one mile in width, crossed the creek three times to the place we first struck it, where we gathered some delicious fruit, such as grapes, plums, and blue currants. After a delay of an hour, we set out on our back trail, and arrived at the pirogue at sunset. We proceeded on to the place we camped last night, and stayed all night.

This mound is situated on an elevated plain in a level and extensive prairie, bearing N. 20° W. from the mouth of Whitestone Creek nine miles. The base of the mound is a regular parallelogram, the long side of which is about 300 yards in length, the shorter 60 or 70 yards. From the longer side of the base, it rises from the north and south, with a steep ascent to the height of 65 or 70 feet, leaving a level plain on the top 12 feet in width and 90 in length. The north and south parts of this mound are joined by two regular rises, each in oval forms of half its height, forming three regular rises from the plain. The ascent of each elevated part is as sudden as the principal mound at the narrower sides of its base.

The regular form of this hill would in some measure justify a belief that it owed its origin to the hand of man; but as the earth and loose pebbles and other substances of which it was composed bore an exact resemblance to the steep ground which borders on the creek, in its neighborhood, we concluded it was most probably the production of nature.

The only remarkable characteristic of this hill, admitting it to be a natural production, is that it is insulated or separated a considerable distance from any other, which is very unusual in the natural order or disposition of the hills.

The surrounding plains are open, void of timber, and level to a great extent; hence the wind, from whatever quarter it may blow, drives with unusual force over the naked plains and against this hill. The insects of various kinds are thus involuntarily driven to the mound by the force of the wind, or fly to its leeward side for shelter. The small birds, whose food they are, consequently resort in great numbers to this place in search of them—particularly the small brown martin, of which we saw a vast number hovering on the leeward side of the hill, when we approached it in the act of catching those insects. They were so gentle that they did not quit the place until we had arrived within a few feet of them.

One evidence which the Indians give for believing this place to be the residence of some unusual spirits is that they frequently discover a large assemblage of birds about this mound. This is, in my opinion, a sufficient proof to produce in the savage mind a confident belief of all the properties which they ascribe to it.

From the top of this mound, we beheld a most beautiful landscape. Numerous herds of buffalo were seen feeding in various directions. The plain to north, northwest, and northeast extends without interruption as far as can be seen.

25th August

The boat under the command of Sergeant Pryor proceeded on in our absence (after jerking [1] the elk I killed yesterday) six miles, and camped on the larboard side. R. Fields brought in five deer. George Shannon killed an elk buck. Some rain this evening.

We set the prairies on fire as a signal for the Sioux to come to the river.

27th August, 1804

This morning the star called the morning star much larger than common. G. Drouilliard came up and informed that he could neither find Shannon nor horses. We sent Shields and J. Fields back to hunt Shannon and the horses, with directions to keep on the hills to the Grand Calumet above, on Rivière qui Court.

We set sail under a gentle breeze from the S.E. At seven miles, passed a white clay marl or chalk bluff. Under this bluff, which is extensive, I discovered large stone much like lime, encrusted with a clear substance which I believe to be cobalt; also ore is embedded in the dark earth resembling slate, but much softer. Above this bluff, we had the prairie set on fire to let the Sioux see that we were on the river, and as a signal for them to come to it.

At 2 o'clock, passed the mouth of river Jacques [or Yankton]. One Indian at the mouth of this river swam to the pirogue. We landed and two others came to us. Those Indians informed that a large camp of Sioux were on River Jacques, near the mouth. We sent Sergeant Pryor and a Frenchman with Mr. Dorion, the Sioux interpreter, to the camp with directions to invite the principal chiefs to council with us at a bluff above, called the Calumet. Two of those Indians accompanied them, and the third continued in the boat showing an inclination to continue. This boy is a

---

[1] "Jerked" meat was sliced very thin and then dried till it was hard.

Maha, and informs that his nation were gone to the Pawnees to make a peace with that nation.

28th August, 1804

Set out under a stiff breeze from the south, and proceeded on past a willow island at two miles. Several sand bars. The river wide and shallow. At four miles passed a short white bluff of about 70 or 80 feet high. Below this bluff the prairie rises gradually from the water, back to the height of the bluff, which is on the starboard side. Here the Indian who was in the boat returned to the Sioux camp on the river Jacques. Captain Lewis and myself much indisposed owing to some cause for which we cannot account. One of the pirogues ran a snag through her and was near sinking, in the opinions of the crew. We came to below the Calumet bluff and formed a camp in a beautiful plain near the foot of the high land, which rises with a gradual ascent near this bluff. I observe more timber in the valleys and on the points than usual. The pirogue which was injured, I had unloaded, and the loading put into the other pirogue, which we intended to send back, and changed the crew. After examining her and finding that she was unfit for service, determined to send her back by the party. Some load which was in the pirogue much injured.

The wind blew hard this afternoon from the south. J. Shields and J. Field, who were sent back to look for Shannon and the horses, joined us and informed that Shannon had the horses ahead and that they could not overtake him. This man not being a first-rate hunter, we determined to send one man in pursuit of him, with some provisions.

Orders, August 28th, 1804

[Orderly Book: Lewis]

The commanding officers direct that the two messes who form the crews of the pirogues shall select each one man from their mess for the purpose of cooking, and that these cooks, as well as those previously appointed to the messes of the barge crew, shall in future be exempted from mounting guard, or any detail for that duty. They are therefore no longer to be held on the roster.

M. Lewis Captain
1st. U.S. Regiment Infantry
Wm. Clark Captain &c.

29th August, 1804

[Clark]

Some rain last night and this morning. Sent on Colter with provisions in pursuit of Shannon. Had a tow rope made of elkskin. I am much engaged in writing. At four o'clock, P.M., Sergeant Pryor and Mr. Dorion, with five chiefs and about 70 men and boys, arrived on the opposite side. We sent over a pirogue, and Mr. Dorion and his son, who was trading with the Indians, came over with Sergeant Pryor, and informed us that the chiefs were there. We sent Sergeant Pryor and young Mr. Dorion with some tobacco, corn, and a few kettles for them to cook in, with directions to inform the chiefs that we would speak to them tomorrow.

Those Indians brought with them, for their own use, 2 elk and 6 deer, which the young men killed on the way from their camp, twelve miles distant.

Sergeant Pryor informs me that when they came near the Indian camp, they were met by men with a buffalo robe to carry them. Mr. Dorion informed they were not the owners of the boats and did not wish to be carried.[2] The Sioux's camps are handsome—of a conic form, covered with buffalo robes painted different colors, and all compact and handsomely arranged, covered all around. An open part in the center for the fire, with buffalo robes. Each lodge has a place for cooking, detached. The lodges contain from ten to fifteen persons. A fat dog was presented as a mark of their great respect for the party, of which they partook heartily, and thought it good and well flavored.

30th of August, 1804

A very thick fog this morning. After preparing some presents for the chiefs, which we intended to make by giving medals, and finishing a speech which we intended to give them, we sent Mr. Dorion in a pirogue for the chiefs and warriors, to a council under an oak tree, near where we had a flag flying on a high flagstaff. At 12 o'clock we met, and Captain Lewis delivered the speech; and then made one great

---

[2] To be carried in a buffalo robe was a special honor among the Sioux. It was tactless of Sergeant Pryor and Dorion to decline, but no harm seems to have been done. The two captains were later honored in the same way.

chief by giving him a medal and some clothes; one second chief and three third chiefs, in the same way. They received those things with the goods and tobacco with pleasure. To the grand chief we gave a flag, and the parole [certificate] and wampum with a hat and chief's coat. We smoked out of the pipe of peace, and the chiefs retired to a bower, made of bushes by their young men, to divide their presents, and smoke, eat, and council. Captain Lewis and myself retired to dinner, and to consult about other measures. Mr. Dorion is much displeased that we did not invite him to dine with us—which he was sorry for afterward. The Sioux are a stout, bold-looking people; the young men handsome and well made. The greater part of them make use of bows and arrows. Some few fusees [rifles] I observe among them, notwithstanding they live by the bow and arrow. They do not shoot so well as the northern Indians. The warriors are very much decorated with paint, porcupine quills and feathers, large leggings and moccasins—all with buffalo robes of different colors. The squaws wore petticoats and a white buffalo robe with the black hair turned back over their necks and shoulders.

31st of August, 1804

After the Indians got their breakfast, the chiefs met and arranged themselves in a row, with elegant pipes of peace all pointing to our seats. We came forward, and took our seats. The great chief, The Shake Hand, rose, and spoke at some length, approving what we had said, and promising to pursue the advice.

Martoree, second chief (White Crane) rose and made a short speech, and referred to the great chief, Parnarnearparbe (Struck by the Pawnees). Third chief rose and made a short speech, Areawecharche (The Half Man). Third chief rose and spoke at some length to the same purpose. The other chief said but little. One of the warriors spoke, after all were done, and promised to support the chiefs. They promised to go and see their Great Father in the spring with Mr. Dorion, and to do all things we advised them to do. And all concluded by telling the distresses of their nation by not having traders, and wished us to take pity on them. They wanted powder, ball, and a little milk. [Rum: "milk of Great Father" means spirits.]

Last night the Indians danced until late in their dances. We gave them [threw in to them as is usual] some knives, tobacco, and bells, tape, and binding, with which they were satisfied.

We gave a certificate to two men of war, attendants on the chief. Gave to all the chiefs a carrot of tobacco. Had a talk with Mr. Dorion, who agreed to stay and collect the chiefs from as many bands of Sioux as he could this fall, and bring about a peace between the Sioux and their neighbors, &c.

After dinner, we gave Mr. Peter Dorion a commission to act with a flag and some clothes and provisions and instructions to bring about a peace with the Sioux, Mahas, Pawnees, Poncas, Otos, and Missouris, and to employ any trader to take some of the chiefs of each, or as many of those nations as he could, particularly the Sioux, down to Washington. I took a vocabulary of the Sioux language, and the answer to a few queries such as referred to their situation, trade, number, war, &c. This nation is divided into twenty tribes, possessing separate interests. Collectively, they are numerous—say from two to three thousand men. Their interests are so unconnected that some bands are at war with nations with which other bands are on the most friendly terms.

This great nation, whom the French have given the nickname of Sioux, call themselves Dakota—Darcotar. Their language is not peculiarly their own, they speak a great number of words which are the same in every respect with the Maha, Ponca, Osage, and Kansas, which clearly proves that those nations, at some period not more than a century or two past, are of the same nation. Those Darcotars, or Sioux, inhabit or rove over the country on the Red River of Lake Winnipeg, St. Peters, and the west of the Mississippi, above Prairie du Chien, head of River Des Moines, and the Missouri and its waters on the N. side for a great extent. They are only at peace with eight nations, and, agreeable to their calculation, at war with twenty-odd. Their trade comes from the British, except this band and one on Des Moines who trade with the traders of St. Louis. The Sioux rove and follow the buffalo, raise no corn or anything else, the woods and prairies affording a sufficiency. They eat meat, and substitute the ground potato, which grows in the plains, for bread.

In the evening, late, we gave Mr. Dorion a bottle of whiskey, and he, with the chiefs, and his son, crossed the river and camped on the opposite bank. Soon after night, a violent wind from the N.W. with rain. The rain continued the greater part of the night. The river a-rising a little.

September 5th, 1804

Set out early. The wind blew hard from the south. Goats, turkeys seen today. Passed a large island. Opposite this island near the head, the Ponca River comes into the Missouri from the west. This river is about 30 yards wide. Dispatched two men to the Ponca village, situated in a handsome plain on the lower side of this creek, about two miles from the Missouri. The Ponca nation is small and, at this time, out in the prairies hunting the buffalo. One of the men sent to the village killed a buffalo in the town, the other a large buck near it. Some sign of the two men who are ahead.

Sept. 7th, 1804

A very cold morning. Wind S.E. Set out at daylight. We landed after proceeding 5½ miles, near the foot of a round mountain, which I saw yesterday, resembling a dome. Captain Lewis and myself walked up to the top, which forms a cone and is about 70 feet higher than the high lands around it. The base is about 300 feet. In descending this cupola, discovered a village of small animals that burrow in the ground. (Those animals are called by the French *petit chien*)[3] Killed one, and caught one alive, by pouring a great quantity of water in his hole.

We attempted to dig to the beds of one of those animals. After digging 6 feet, found, by running a pole down, that we were not halfway to his lodge. We found 2 frogs in the hole, and killed a dark rattlesnake near with a ground rat [or prairie dog] in him. Those rats are numerous. The village of those animals covered about 4 acres of ground on a gradual descent of a hill, and contains great numbers of holes on the top of which those little animals sit erect, and make a whistling noise, and, when alarmed, step into their hole. We poured into one of the holes 5 barrels of water without filling it.

Those animals are about the size of a small squirrel, shorter [or longer] and thicker, the head much resembling a squirrel in every respect, except the ears, which are shorter. His tail like a ground squirrel, which they shake, and whistle when alarmed. The toenails long. They have fine fur and the longer hair is gray. It is said that a kind of lizard, also a snake, resides with those animals. [Did not find this correct.] Camped.

9th September, 1804

Set out at sunrise, and proceeded on past the head of the island, on which we camped. Passed three sand and willow

---

[3] The "petit chien" is the prairie dog, though the interesting little beast is, of course, not a dog at all.

islands. The sand bars so numerous, it is not worth mentioning them. The river shoal or shallow. Wind S.E. Came to and
camped on a sand bar on the L.S. Captain Lewis went out to
kill a buffalo. I walked on shore all this evening with a view
to kill a goat or some prairie dogs. In the evening after the
boat landed, I directed my servant, York, with me, to kill a
buffalo near the boat, from a number then scattered in the
plains. I saw at one view, near the river, at least 500 buffalo.
Those animals have been in view all day, feeding in the
plains on the L.S. Every copse of timber appears to have elk or
deer. D. killed 3 deer, I killed a buffalo, York 2, R. Fields
one.

10th September, 1804

A cloudy, dark morning. Set out early, a gentle breeze from
the S.E. Passed two small islands on the L.S., and one on the
S.S. all in the first course at 10½ miles. Passed the lower
point of an island covered with red cedar, situated in a bend
on the L.S. This island is about 2 miles in length. Below
this on a hill on the L.S. we found the backbone of a fish,
45 feet long, tapering to the tail. Some teeth, &c. Those
joints were separated, and all petrified. Opposite this island,
1½ miles from the river on the L.S., is a large salt spring of
remarkably salt water. One other, high up the hill, ½ mile,
not so salt. We proceeded on, under a stiff breeze. Three
miles above Cedar Island, passed a large island on the S.S.
No water on that side. Several elk swam to this island.
Passed a small island near the center of the river, of a mile
in length, and camped on one above, separated from the other
by a narrow channel. Those islands are called Mud Islands.
The hunters killed 3 buffalo and one elk today. The river
is falling a little. Great number of buffalo and elk on the
hillside, feeding. Deer scarce.

Sept. 11th, 1804

A cloudy morning. Set out very early. The river wide, and
shallow; the bottom narrow, and the river crowded with sand
bars. Passed the island on which we lay, at one mile. Passed
three islands—one on the L.S., and two on the S.S. Opposite
the island on the L.S., I saw a village of barking squirrels
[prairie dogs], 970 yards long and 800 yards wide, situated on a gentle slope of a hill. Those animals are numerous.
I killed four, with a view to have their skins stuffed.
Here, the man who left us with the horses, 22 [16]
days ago, George Shannon—he started 26th August, and has

been ahead ever since—joined us, nearly starved to death. He had been twelve days without anything to eat but grapes and one rabbit, which he killed by shooting a piece of hard stick in place of a ball. This man, supposing the boat to be ahead, pushed on as long as he could. When he became weak and feeble, determined to lay by and wait for a trading boat, which is expected, keeping one horse for the last recourse. Thus a man had like to have starved to death in a land of plenty for the want of bullets or something to kill his meat.

We camped on the L.S., above the mouth of a run. A hard rain all the afternoon, and most of the night, with hard wind from the N.W. I walked on shore the fore part of this day, over some broken country, which continues about three miles back, and then is level and rich—all plains. I saw several foxes, and killed an elk and 2 deer, and squirrels. The men with me killed an elk, 2 deer, and a pelican.

September 16th, 1804

[Lewis]

This morning set out at an early hour, and came to at ½ after 7 A.M. on the larboard shore 1¼ mile above the mouth of a small creek which we named Corvus, in consequence of having killed a beautiful bird of that genus near it. We concluded to lay by at this place the balance of this day and the next, in order to dry our baggage, which was wet by the heavy showers of rain which had fallen within the last three days, and also to lighten the boat by transferring a part of her lading to the red pirogue, which we now determined to take on with us to our winter residence, wherever that might be. While some of the men were employed in the necessary labor, others were dressing skins, washing and mending their clothes, &c.

Captain Clark and myself killed each a buck immediately on landing, near our encampment. The deer were very gentle and in great numbers in this bottom, which had more timber on it than any part of the river we had seen for many days past, consisting of cottonwood, elm, some different ash, and a considerable quantity of a small species of white oak, which was loaded with acorns of an excellent flavor,[4] having very

---

[4] To the white man's palate, no species of oak produces acorns fit for human consumption. Many Indian tribes, however, dried and leached them, after which the kernel lost its bitterness and astringency and became "a nutty meat rich in oil and starch which is as nutritious as the meat of other nuts and thoroughly palatable." Such, at least, is the opinion of Fernald, Kinsey, and

little of the bitter roughness of the nuts of most species of oak.

The leaf of this oak is small, pale green, and deeply indented. It seldom rises higher than thirty feet, is much branched; the bark is rough and thick, and of a light color. The cup which contains the acorn is fringed on its edges, and embraces the nut about one-half. The acorns were now falling, and we concluded that the number of deer which we saw here had been induced thither by the acorns, of which they are remarkably fond. Almost every species of wild game is fond of the acorn—the buffalo, elk, deer, bear, turkeys, ducks, pigeons, and even the wolves feed on them.

We sent three hunters out who soon added eight deer and two buffalo to our stock of provisions. The buffalo were so poor that we took only the tongues, skins, and marrow bones. The skins were particularly acceptable as we were in want of a covering for the large pirogue to secure the baggage.

September 17th, 1804

Having for many days past confined myself to the boat, I determined to devote this day to amusing myself on shore with my gun, and view the interior of the country lying between the river and the Corvus Creek. Accordingly, before sunrise, I set out with six of my best hunters, two of whom I dispatched to the lower side of Corvus Creek, two with orders to hunt the bottoms and woodland on the river, while I retained two others to accompany me in the intermediate country.

One quarter of a mile in rear of our camp, which was situated in a fine open grove of cottonwood, passed a grove of plum trees, loaded with fruit and now ripe. Observed but little difference between this fruit and that of a similar kind common to the Atlantic states. The trees are smaller and more thickly set. This forest of plum trees garnish a plain about 20 feet more elevated than that on which we were encamped.

This plain extends back about a mile to the foot of the

Rollins in *Edible Wild Plants* (New York: Harper & Brothers, 1943, 2nd ed., 1958), p. 159. Dr. Kinsey, though more famous for other studies, was familiar with many aspects of American nature. The Pilgrim Fathers, in 1620, found baskets of roasted acorns hidden in the ground near Plymouth, Mass. (O. P. Medsger, *Edible Wild Plants*, New York: The Macmillan Company, 1942, pp. 111-112). Some Indians made acorns palatable by soaking them in water to remove tannin.

hills one mile distant, and to which it is gradually ascending. This plain extends with the same breadth from the creek below to the distance of nearly three miles above, parallel with the river, and it is entirely occupied by the burrows of the barking squirrel heretofore described. This animal appears here in infinite numbers. And the shortness and verdure of grass gave the plain the appearance, throughout its whole extent, of beautiful bowling green in fine order. Its aspect is S.E. A great number of wolves of the small kind, hawks, and some polecats were to be seen. I presume that those animals feed on this squirrel. Found the country in every direction, for about three miles, intersected with deep ravines and steep irregular hills 100 to 200 feet high. At the tops of these hills, the country breaks off as usual into a fine level plain extending as far as the eye can reach. From this plain I had an extensive view of the river below, and the irregular hills which border the opposite sides of the river and creek.

The surrounding country had been burnt about a month before, and young grass had now sprung up to a height of 4 inches, presenting the live green of the spring; to the west a high range of hills stretch across the country from N. to S., and appeared distant about 20 miles. They are not very extensive, as I could plainly observe their rise and termination. No rock appeared on them, and the sides were covered with verdure similar to that of the plains. This scenery, already rich, pleasing, and beautiful, was still further heightened by immense herds of buffalo, deer, elk, and antelopes, which we saw in every direction, feeding on the hills and plains. I do not think I exaggerate when I estimate the number of buffalo which could be comprehended at one view to amount to 3,000. My object was, if possible, to kill a female antelope, having already procured a male. I pursued my route on this plain to the west, flanked by my two hunters, until eight in the morning, when I made the signal for them to come to me, which they did shortly after.

We rested ourselves about half an hour, and regaled ourselves on half a biscuit each, and some jerks of elk, which we had taken the precaution to put in our pouches in the morning before we set out, and drank of the water of a small pool, which had collected on the plain from the rains which had fallen some days before. We had now, after various windings in pursuit of several herds of antelope which we had seen on our way, made the distance of about eight miles from our camp.

We found the antelope extremely shy and watchful, insomuch that we had been unable to get a shot at them. When at rest they generally select the most elevated point in the neighborhood, and as they are watchful and extremely quick of sight, and their sense of smelling very acute, it is almost impossible to approach them within gunshot. In short, they will frequently discover, and flee from, you at the distance of three miles.

I had this day an opportunity of witnessing the agility and the superior fleetness of this animal which was to me really astonishing. I had pursued and twice surprised a small herd of seven. In the first instance they did not discover me distinctly, and therefore did not run at full speed, though they took care before they rested to gain an elevated point where it was impossible to approach them under cover, except in one direction, and that happened to be in the direction from which the wind blew toward them. Bad as the chance to approach them was, I made the best of my way toward them, frequently peeping over the ridge with which I took care to conceal myself from their view. The male, of which there was but one, frequently encircled the summit of the hill on which the females stood in a group, as if to look out for the approach of danger. I got within about 200 paces of them when they smelled me and fled. I gained the top of the eminence on which they stood as soon as possible, from whence I had an extensive view of the country. The antelopes, which had disappeared in a steep ravine, now appeared at the distance of about three miles on the side of a ridge which passed obliquely across me, and extended about four miles.

So soon had these antelopes gained the distance at which they had again appeared to my view, I doubted at first that they were the same that I had just surprised; but my doubts soon vanished when I beheld the rapidity of their flight along the ridge before me. It appeared rather the rapid flight of birds than the motion of quadrupeds. I think I can safely venture the assertion that the speed of this animal is equal, if not superior, to that of the finest blooded courser.

21st of September, 1804

At half-past one o'clock this morning, the sand bar on which we camped began to undermine and give way, which alarmed the sergeant on guard. The motion of the boat awakened me. I got up and by the light of the moon observed that the sand had given way both above and below our camp, and was falling in fast. I ordered all hands on, as quick as possible, and pushed off. We had pushed off but a few minutes before the bank, under which the boat and pirogues lay, gave way, which would certainly have sunk both pirogues. By the time we made the opposite shore, our camp fell in.

We made a second camp for the remainder of the night, and at daylight proceeded on to the gorge of this great bend, and breakfast. We sent a man to measure (step off) the distance across the gorge. He made it 2,000 yards. The distance around is 30 miles. The hills extend through the gorge and are about 200 feet above the water. In the bend as also the opposite sides, both above and below the bend, is a beautiful inclined plain, in which there are great numbers of buffalo, elk, and goats in view, feeding and sipping on those plains. Grouse, larks, and the prairie bird are common in those plains.

We proceeded on, past a willow island below the mouth of a small river, called Tylor's River, about 35 yards wide, which comes in on the L.S. 6 miles above the gorge of the bend. At the mouth of this river, the two hunters ahead left a deer and its skin, also the skin of a white wolf. We observe an immense number of plover of different kinds collecting and taking their flight southerly; also brants, which appear to move in the same direction. The catfish are small and not so plenty as below.

The shore on each side is lined with hard rough gulley stones of different sizes, which have rolled from the hills and out of small brooks. Cedar is common here. This day is warm. The wind, which is not hard, blows from the S.E. We camped at the lower point of the Mock Island on the S.S. This now connected with the mainland; it has the appearance of once being an island detached from the mainland, covered with tall cottonwood. We saw some camps and tracks of the Sioux which appear to be old, three or four weeks ago. One Frenchman, I fear, has got an abscess on his thigh. He complains very much. We are making every exertion to relieve him.

The prairies in this quarter contain great quantities of prickly pears.

22nd of September, 1804

Passed an island situated nearest the S.S., immediately above the last, called Cedar Island. This is about 1½ miles long and nearly as wide, covered with cedar. On the south side of this island, Mr. Loisel, a trader from St. Louis, built a fort of cedar and a good house, to trade with the Sioux, and wintered last winter. About this fort, I observed a number of Indian camps in conical form.[5] They fed their horses on cotton limbs, as it appears. Here, our hunters joined us, having killed two deer and a beaver. They complain much of the mineral substances in the barren hills, over which they passed, destroying their moccasins.

We proceeded on, and camped late on the S. side, below a small island in the bend S.S., called Goat Island. The large stones which lay on the sides of the banks in several places, lay some distance in the river, under the water, and are dangerous.

I walked out this evening and killed a fine deer. The mosquitoes are very troublesome in the bottoms.

23rd of September, 1804

Set out under a gentle breeze from the S.E. Passed a small island situated in a bend to the L.S., called Goat Island. A short distance above the upper point, a creek 12 yards wide comes in on the S.S. We observed a great smoke to the S.W. I walked on shore and observed buffalo in great herds at a distance.

Passed two small willow islands with large sand bars making out from them. Passed Elk Island, about 2½ miles long and ¾ mile wide, situated near the L.S., covered with cottonwood; the red currants called by the French *gres de beuff* [*groseilles de boeuf*], and grapes, &c.

The river is nearly straight for a great distance, wide and shallow. Passed a creek on the S.S. 16 yards wide, we call Reuben Creek as R. Fields found it. Camped on the S.S., below the mouth of a creek on the L.S. Three Sioux boys came to us—swam the river and informed that the band of Sioux called the Tetons, of 80 lodges, were camped at the next creek above; and 60 lodges more a short distance above. We gave those boys two carrots of tobacco to carry to their chiefs, with directions to tell them that we would speak to them tomorrow.

Captain Lewis walked on shore this evening. R. F. killed a doe goat.

24th September, 1804

Set out early. A fair day, the wind from the E. Passed the mouth of a creek on the L.S. called Creek High Water.

---

[5] The Indian "camps" were, of course, only clusters of abandoned teepee poles. Plains Indians usually took their big teepee poles with them, wood being scarce. But where wood was plentiful, no one bothered to take them down, especially when the

Passed a large island on the L.S. about 2 miles and ½ long on which Colter had camped and killed 4 elk. The wind fair from the S.E. We prepared some clothes and a few medals for the chiefs of the Tetons' bands of Sioux, which we expect to see today at the next river. Observed a great deal of stone on the sides of the hills on the S.S. We saw one hare today. Prepared all things for action in case of necessity. Our pirogues went to the island for the meeting. Soon after, the man on shore ran up the bank and reported that the Indians had stolen the horse.

We soon after met 5 Indians, and anchored out some distance, and spoke to them. Informed them we were friends, and wished to continue so, but were not afraid of any Indians. Some of their young men had taken the horse sent by their Great Father for their chief, and we would not speak to them until the horse was returned to us again.

Passed an island on the S.S., on which we saw several elk, about 1½ miles long, called Good Humored Island. Came to about 1½ miles above, off the mouth of a small river about 70 yards wide, called by Mr. Evans the Little Missouri River. The tribes of the Sioux called the Tetons are camped about two miles up on the N.W. side; and we shall call the river after that nation, Teton. This river is 70 yards wide at the mouth of water, and has a considerable current. We anchored off the mouth.

The French pirogue came up early in the day; the other did not get up until the evening. Soon after we had come to, I went and smoked with the chiefs who came to see us here. All well. We prepare to speak with the Indians tomorrow, at which time, we are informed, the Indians will be here. The Frenchman, who had for some time been sick, began to bleed, which alarmed him. Two-thirds of our party camped on board, the remainder—with the guard—on shore.

teepee was a small, temporary shelter. In Ontario, I have often been amused to discover, while breaking my own camp in the morning, that my red brothers had selected the same camp site— and left their teepee poles—some time before.

Chapter IV

TO THE MANDAN COUNTRY

September 25—October 26, 1804

25th September

[Clark]

A fair morning. The wind from the S.E. All well. Raised a flagstaff and made an awning or shade on a sand bar in the mouth of Teton River, for the purpose of speaking with the Indians under.[1] The boat crew on board at 70 yards distance from the bar. The five Indians which we met last night continued. About 11 o'clock, the 1st and 2nd chiefs came. We gave them some of our provisions to eat. They gave us great quantities of meat, some of which was spoiled. We feel much at a loss for the want of an interpreter; the one we have can speak but little.

Met in council at 12 o'clock and, after smoking—agreeable to the usual custom—Captain Lewis proceeded to deliver a speech which we were obliged to curtail for want of a good interpreter. All our party paraded. Gave a medal to the grand chief, called in Indian Untongarsarbar, in French Boeuf Noir, Black Buffalo. Said to be a good man. 2nd chief, Tortohongar or The Partisan—bad. The 3rd is the Boeuf de Médecine, his name is Tartongarwaker. 1st considerable man, Warzinggo. 2nd considerable man, Second Bear—Matocoquepar.

Invited those chiefs on board to show them our boat, and such curiosities as were strange to them. We gave them ¼ glass of whiskey, which they appeared to be very fond of; sucked the bottle after it was out and soon began to be

[1] "For . . . speaking with the Indians under" is an example of the explorers' occasionally remarkable syntax. "Under which we could speak with the Indians" is what they are trying to say. As a matter of aboriginal diplomatic etiquette, many tribes counciled under canopies of some kind.

troublesome, one, the second chief, assuming drunkenness as a cloak for his rascally intentions. I went with those chiefs, in one of the pirogues with 5 men—3 and 2 Indians (which left the boat with great reluctance)—to shore, with a view of reconciling those men to us.

As soon as I landed the pirogue, three of their young men seized the cable of the pirogue [in which we had presents, &c.]. The chiefs' soldier [each chief has a soldier] hugged the mast, and the 2nd chief was very insolent, both in words and gestures [pretended drunkenness and staggered up against me], declaring I should not go on, stating he had not received presents sufficient from us. His gestures were of such a personal nature, I felt myself compelled to draw my sword, and made a signal to the boat to prepare for action. At this motion Captain Lewis ordered all under arms in the boat. Those with me also showed a disposition to defend themselves and me. The grand chief then took hold of the rope and ordered the young warriors away.

I felt myself warm and spoke in very positive terms.

Most of the warriors appeared to have their bows strung, and took out their arrows from the quiver. As I, being surrounded, was not permitted by them to return, I sent all the men except two interpreters to the boat. The pirogue soon returned with about 12 of our determined men ready for any event. This movement caused a number of the Indians to withdraw at a distance, leaving their chiefs and soldiers alone with me. Their treatment to me was very rough and, I think, justified roughness on my part. They all left my pirogue, and counciled with themselves. The result I could not learn, and nearly all went off after remaining in this situation some time. I offered my hand to the 1st and 2nd chiefs, who refused to receive it. I turned off and went with my men on board the pirogue. I had not proceeded more than ten paces before the 1st chief, 3rd, and 2 Brave Men waded in after me. I took them in and went on board.

We proceeded on about one mile, and anchored out off a willow island. Placed a guard on shore to protect the cooks and a guard in the boat. Fastened the pirogues to the boat. I called this island Bad Humored Island, as we were in a bad humor.

26th of September, 1804

Set out early. Proceeded on, and came to, by the wish of the chiefs, for to let their squaws and boys see the boat, and suffer them to treat us well. Great numbers of men, women, and children on the banks viewing us. These people show great anxiety. They appear sprightly. Generally ill-looking and not well made; their legs and arms small generally; high cheekbones, prominent eyes. They grease and black [paint] themselves with coal when they dress. The distinguished men make use of hawks' feathers [calumet feather adorned with porcupine quills and fastened to the top of the head and falls backward about their heads]. The men wear a robe, and each a polecat's skin, for to hold their *bois roulé* for smoking. Fond of dress and show. Badly armed with fusees, &c. The squaws are cheerful, fine-looking women, not handsome; high cheeks; dressed in skins; a petticoat and robe, which folds back over their shoulder, with long wool. Do all their laborious work, and, I may say, perfect slaves to the men, as all squaws of nations much at war, or where the women are more numerous than the men.

After coming to, Captain Lewis and 5 men went on shore with the chiefs, who appeared disposed to make up and be friendly. After Captain Lewis had been on shore about 3 hours, I became uneasy for fear of deception, and sent a sergeant to see him and know his treatment, which he reported was friendly, and they were preparing for a dance this evening. They made frequent solicitations for us to remain one night only and let them show their good disposition toward us. We determined to remain.

After the return of Captain Lewis, I went on shore. On landing, I was received on an elegant painted buffalo robe, and taken to the village by 6 men, and was not permitted to touch the ground until I was put down in the grand council house, on a white dressed robe. I saw several Maha prisoners, and spoke to the chiefs, telling them that it was necessary to give those prisoners up and become good friends with the Mahas if they wished to follow the advice of their Great Father. I was in several lodges, neatly formed, as before mentioned as to the Bois Brulé—Yankton tribe.

This house formed a ¾ circle of skins well dressed, and sewn together, under this shelter. About 70 men sat, forming a circle. In front of the chiefs, a place of 6 feet diameter was clear, and the pipe of peace raised on forked sticks, about 6 or 8 inches from the ground, under which there was swansdown scattered. On each side of this circle, two pipes, the two flags of Spain [2] and the flag we gave them in front of the grand chief. A large fire was near, in which

[2] The Spanish flags indicated that the Mexican provincial government was trying to attach these Indians to the Spanish cause. Lewis and Clark habitually tried to substitute their flag for the Spanish.

provisions were cooking. In the center, about 400 pounds of excellent buffalo beef as a present for us.

Soon after they set me down, the men went for Captain Lewis. Brought him in the same way, and placed him also by the chief. In a few minutes an old man rose and spoke, approving what we had done, and informing us of their situation, requesting us to take pity on them and which was answered. The great chief then rose with great state, speaking to the same purpose as far as we could learn, and then, with great solemnity, took up the pipe of peace and, after pointing it to the heavens, the four quarters of the globe and the earth, he made some dissertation [then made a speech], lit it and presented the stem to us to smoke. When the principal chief spoke with the pipe of peace, he took in one hand some of the most delicate parts of the dog which was prepared for the feast, and made a sacrifice to the flag.

After a smoke had taken place, and a short harangue to his people, we were requested to take the meal, and they put before us the dog which they had been cooking, and pemmican, and ground potato in several platters. Pemmican is buffalo meat dried or jerked, pounded, and mixed with grease, raw. Dog, Sioux think great dish, used on festivals. Ate little of dog—pemmican and potato good.[3] We smoked for an hour, till dark, and all was cleared away. A large fire made in the center. About ten musicians playing on tambourines [made of hoops and skin, stretched], long sticks with deer and goats' hoofs tied so as to make a jingling noise, and many others of a similar kind. Those men began to sing and beat on the tambourine. The women came forward, highly decorated in their way, with the scalps and trophies of war of their fathers, husbands, brothers, or near connections, and proceeded to dance the War Dance [women only dance, jump up and down—five or six young men selected, accompanied with songs the tambourine, making the song extempore, words and music; every now and then one of the company came out and repeated some exploit in a sort of song—this taken up by the young men, and the women dance to it] which they did with great cheerful-

---

[3] Clark ate only a little dogmeat because he could never learn to like it and throughout the expedition ate dog only when ceremonial required him to do so, as in this case, or when even roots were not available. Lewis soon came to like dogmeat as well as any other kind. The reference to pemmican, which Stefansson was later to describe as the best all-around expedition food, is interesting. It was widely used by various tribes. Admiral Byrd also used it. The various recipes seem, however, to have been very different.

ness, until about twelve o'clock, when we informed the chiefs that they must be fatigued amusing us, &c.

They then retired, and we, accompanied by four chiefs, returned to our boat. They stayed with us all night. Those people have some brave men which they make use of as soldiers. Those men attend to the policing of the village; correct all errors. I saw one of them, today, whip two squaws who appeared to have fallen out. When he approached, all about appeared to flee with great terror. At night they keep 2, 3, 4, 5 men at different distances, walking around camp, singing the occurrences of the night.

All the men on board, 100 paces from shore. Wind from the S.E., moderate. One man very sick on board with a dangerous abscess on his hip. All in spirits this evening.

In this tribe, I saw 25 squaws and boys taken 13 days ago in a battle with the Mahas. In this battle, they destroyed 40 lodges, killed 75 men, and some boys and children, and took 48 prisoners—women and boys—which they promise both Captain Lewis and myself shall be delivered up to Mr. Dorion at the Bois Brûlé tribe.[4] Those are a wretched and dejected-looking people. The squaws appear low and coarse, but this is an unfavorable time to judge of them.

27th of Sept., 1804

I rose early after a bad night's sleep. Found the chiefs all up, and the bank, as usual, lined with spectators. We gave the two great chiefs a blanket apiece, or rather, they took off, agreeable to their custom, the one they lay on; and each, one peck of corn. After breakfast, Captain Lewis and the chiefs went on shore, as a very large part of their nation was coming in, the disposition of whom I did not know. One of us being sufficient on shore, I wrote a letter to Mr. P. Dorion, and prepared a medal and some certificates, and sent to Captain Lewis. At two o'clock Captain Lewis returned with four chiefs and a Considerable Man, named Warchapa, or On His Guard. When the friends of those people (the Sioux) die, they run arrows through their flesh above and below their elbows, as a testimony of their grief.

After staying about half an hour, I went with them on shore. Those men left the boat with reluctance. I went first to the 2nd chief's lodge, where a crowd came around. After speaking on various subjects, I went to a principal man's lodge, from them to the grand chief's lodge. After a few

---

[4] The Bois Brûlé, or Brûlé Sioux, a subdivision of the Sioux tribe.

minutes, he invited me to a lodge within the circle, in which I stayed with all their principal men until the dance began, which was similar to the one of last night, performed by their women with poles in their hands, on which scalps of their enemies were hung. Some with the guns, spears, and war implements taken by their husbands, in their hands.

Captain Lewis came on shore, and we continued until we were sleepy and returned to our boat. The 2nd chief and one principal man accompanied us. Those two Indians accompanied me on board in the small pirogue; Captain Lewis, with a guard, still on shore. The man who steered, not being much accustomed to steer, passed the bow of the boat, and the pirogue came broadside against the cable and broke it, which obliged me to order, in a loud voice, all hands up and at their oars. My peremptory order to the men, and the bustle of their getting to their oars, alarmed the chiefs, together with the appearance of the men on shore as the boat turned. The chief hallooed and alarmed the camp or town, informing them that the Mahas were about, attacking them. In about ten minutes the bank was lined with men armed, the 1st chief at their head. About 200 men appeared, and after about half an hour returned, all but about 60 men, who continued on the bank all night. The chiefs continued all night with us. This alarm I, as well as Captain Lewis, considered as the signal of their intentions—which was to stop our proceeding on our journey and, if possible, rob us. We were on our guard all night. The misfortune of the loss of our anchor obliged us to lie under a falling bank much exposed to the accomplishment of their hostile intentions. Peter Cruzat, our bowman, who could speak Maha, informed us in the night that the Maha prisoners informed him we were to be stopped. We showed as little signs of a knowledge of their intentions as possible. All prepared on board for anything which might happen. We kept a strong guard all night. No sleep.

28th of September, 1804

Made many attempts in different ways to find our anchor, but could not; the sand had covered it. From the misfortune of last night, our boat was lying at shore in a very unfavorable situation. After finding that the anchor could not be found, we determined to proceed on. With great difficulty, got the chiefs out of our boat; and when we were about setting out, the class called the soldiers [5] took possession of the

---

[5] The "soldiers" were a kind of camp police.

cable. The 1st chief, who was still on board, intended to go a short distance with us. I told him the men of his nation sat on the cable. He went out and told Captain Lewis, who was at the bow, the men who sat on the rope were soldiers and wanted tobacco. Captain Lewis would not agree to be forced into anything. The 2nd chief demanded a flag and tobacco, which we refused to give, stating proper reasons to them for it. After much difficulty, which had nearly reduced us to the necessity for hostilities, I threw a carrot of tobacco to 1st chief. Took the port fire from gunner. Spoke so as to touch his pride. The chief gave the tobacco to his soldiers, and he jerked the rope from them, and handed it to the bowman. We then set out under a breeze from the S.E. About two miles up, we observed the 3rd chief on shore, beckoning to us. We took him on board. He informed us the rope was held by the order of the 2nd chief, who was a double-spoken man. Soon after, we saw a man coming full speed through the plains; left his horse, and proceeded across a sand bar near the shore. We took him on board and observed that he was the son of the chief we had on board. We sent, by him, a talk to the nation, stating the cause of our hoisting the red flag under the white. If they were for peace, stay at home and do as we had directed them. If they were for war, or were determined to stop us, we were ready to defend ourselves. We halted one hour and one-half on the S.S. and made a substitute of stones for an anchor, refreshed our men, and proceeded on about two miles higher up, and came to a very small sand bar in the middle of the river, and stayed all night. I am very unwell for want of sleep. Determined to sleep tonight if possible. The men cooked, and we rested well.

29th of September, 1804

Set out early. Some bad sand bars. Proceeded on. At 9 o'clock we observed the 2nd chief and 2 principal men, one man, and a squaw on shore. They wished to go up with us as far as the other part of their band, which, they said, was on the river ahead not far distant. We refused, stating very sufficient reasons, and were plain with them on the subject. They were not pleased. Observed that they would walk on shore to the place we intended to camp tonight. We observed it was not our wish that they should; for, if they did, we could not take them or any other Tetons on board, except the one we had now with us, who might go on shore whenever he pleased. They proceeded on. The chief on board asked for a twist of tobacco for those men. We gave him ½ of a twist, and sent one by them for that part of their band which we did not see, and continued on. Saw great numbers of elk at the mouth of a small creek—called No Timber Creek, as no timber appeared to be on it. Above the mouth of this creek, an Arikara band had a village five years ago. No remains, but the mound which surrounded the town. The 2nd chief came on the sand bar and requested we would put him across the river. I sent a pirogue and crossed him and one man to the S.S., and proceeded on, and came to on a sand bar about ½ mile on, from the main shore, and put on it two sentinels. Continued all night at anchor. We substitute large stones for anchors in place of the one we lost. All in high spirits, &c.

30th of September, 1804

Set out this morning early. Had not proceeded on far before we discovered an Indian running after us. He came up with us at 7 o'clock and requested to come on board and go up to the Arikaras. We refused to take any of that band on board. If he chose to proceed on shore it was very well. Soon after, I discovered on the hills, at a great distance, great numbers of Indians which appeared to be making to the river above us. We proceeded on under a double-reefed sail and some rain. At 9 o'clock, observed a large band of Indians, the same which I had before seen on the hills, encamping on the bank on the L.S. We came to on a sand bar, breakfasted, and proceeded on, and cast the anchor opposite their lodge, at about 100 yards distant; and informed the Indians, which we found to be a part of the band we had before seen, that we took them by the hand and sent to each chief a carrot of tobacco, as we had been treated badly by some of the band below. After staying 2 days for them, we could not delay any time, and referred them to Mr. Dorion for a full account of us, and to hear our talk sent by him to the Tetons. Those were very solicitous for us to land and eat with them, that they were friendly, &c. We apologized and proceeded on. Sent the pirogue to shore above, with the tobacco, and delivered it to a soldier of the chief with us. Several of them ran up the river. The chiefs on board threw them out a small twist of tobacco, and told them to go back and open their ears. They received the tobacco and returned to their lodges. We saw great numbers of white gulls. This day is cloudy and rainy. Refreshed the men with a glass of whiskey after breakfast.

We saw about 6 miles above, 2 Indians who came to the bank, and looked at us about ½ an hour, and went over the hills to the S.W. We proceeded on under a very stiff breeze from the S.E. The stern of the boat got fast on a log, and the boat turned and was very near filling before we got her righted, the waves being very high. The chief on board was so frightened at the motion of the boat, which in its rocking caused several loose articles to fall on the deck from the lockers, he ran off and hid himself. We landed. He got his gun and informed us he wished to return, that all things were clear for us to go on, we would not see any more Tetons, &c. We repeated to him what had been said before, and advised him to keep his men away. Gave him a blanket, a knife and some tobacco. Smoked a pipe and he set out. We also set sail, and came to at a sand bar, and camped. A very cold evening. All on guard.

Sand bars are so numerous that it is impossible to describe them, and think it unnecessary to mention them.

1st of October, 1804

The wind blew hard all last night from the S.E. Very cold. Set out early, the wind still hard. Passed a large island in the middle of the river. Opposite the lower point of this island, the Arikaras formerly lived in a large town on the L.S.— remains only a mound, circular, walls three or four feet high. Above the head of the island about two miles, we passed the River Chien, or Dog River [Cheyenne] L.S. This river comes in from the S.W. and is about 400 yards wide. The current appears gentle, throwing out but little sand, and appears to throw out but little water. The head of this river is not known. In the second range of the Côte Noire its course, generally, about east. So called from the Cheyenne Indians who live on the head of it. A part of the nation of Dog Indians live some distance up this river, the precise distance I can't learn. Above the mouth of this river, the sand bars are thick and the water shallow. The river still very wide and falling a little. We are obliged to haul the boat over a sand bar, after making several attempts to pass. The wind so hard, we came to and stayed three hours. After it slackened a little, we proceeded on round a bend, the wind, in the after part of the day, ahead. Passed a creek on the L.S. which we call the Sentinel. This part of the river has but little timber, the hills not so high, the sand bars more numerous, and river more than one mile wide, including the sand bars. Passed a small creek above the latter, which we call Lookout Creek. Continued on, with the wind immediately ahead, and came to on a large sand bar in the middle of the river. We saw a man opposite to our camp on the L.S.

which we discovered to be a Frenchman. A little off from shore, among the willows, we observed a house. We called to them to come over. A boy came in a canoe and informed that two Frenchmen were at the house with goods to trade with the Sioux, which he expected down from the Arikaras [6] every day. Several large parties of Sioux set out from the "Rees" [6] for this place to trade with those men.

This Mr. Jean Vallé informs us that he wintered last winter 300 leagues up the Cheyenne River under the Black Mountains. He informs us that this river is very rapid and difficult even for pirogues to ascend, and when rising the swells are very high. One hundred leagues up, it forks; one fork comes from the S., the other, at 40 leagues above the forks, enters the Black Mountains. The country from the Missouri to the Black Mountains is much like the country on the Missouri, less timber and a great proportion of cedar.

The Black Mountains, he says, are very high, and some parts of them have snow on them in the summer. Great quantities of pine grow on the mountains. A great noise is heard frequently on those mountains. No beaver on Dog River. On the mountains great numbers of goats, and a kind of animal with large circular horns; this animal is nearly the size of a small elk. White [7] bears are also plenty. The Cheyenne Indians are about 300 lodges. They inhabit this river principally, and steal horses from the Spanish settlements to the S.W. This excursion they make in one month.

[6] The Rees, or Rickarees, were the Arikaras. Indian pronunciations differed, and so did white men's ability to imitate their words. Some white men did not hear the initial "A" or it was not pronounced clearly. Hence the variation in the white men's names for various tribes. Thus the Mahas, Omahas, and Mahars were all one tribe; some white men did not hear the initial "O." Clark, being a Virginian, obviously did not sound his "r"; hence he usually wrote "Mahar"—and even "squar" (squaw). What happened is clear enough, but in the journals it can be rather confusing.

[7] The "white" bears were grizzlies—not polar bears on the Missouri! The first white man to leave a record of seeing this bear was David Ingram, who, in 1568 or immediately thereafter, walked a long distance from Tampico, Mexico, to an unknown point on the Atlantic coast. He had with him a few companions, two of whom were, with Ingram, the only survivors of 114 seamen whom Sir John Hawkins had to put ashore near Tampico in 1568. Ingram's description, in 1582, of "white" bears led historians to doubt his accuracy. After Ingram, there were descriptions of the *tracks* of grizzlies but not of the bears themselves. Grizzlies may, in fact, be very light in color and are sometimes called "silvertips."

The bottoms and sides of River Cheyenne are coarse gravel. This Frenchman gives an account of a white-booted turkey [prairie cock], an inhabitant of the Côte Noire.

2nd of October, 1804

A violent wind all night from the S.E. Slackened a little and we proceeded on. Mr. Jean Vallé came on board and proceeded on two miles with us. A very cold morning. Some black clouds flying. Took a meridian altitude and made the latitude 44° 19′ 36″ North. This was taken at the upper part of the gorge of the Lookout Bend, the Sentinel. Heard a shot over the hills to the L.S. during the time we were dining on a large sand bar. The after part of this day is pleasant. At two o'clock, opposite a wood on the larboard side, we observed some Indians on a hill on the S.S. One came down to the river opposite to us and fired off his gun, and beckoned to us to come to. We paid no attention to him. He followed on some distance. We spoke a few words to him. He wished us to go ashore, and to his camp, which was over the hill, and consisted of twenty lodges. We excused ourselves. Advised him to go and hear our talk of Mr. Dorion. He inquired for traders. We informed him one was in the next bend below, and parted. He returned, and we proceeded on. Passed a large island on the S.S. Here we expected the Tetons would attempt to stop us, and under that idea we prepared ourselves for action, which we expected every moment. Opposite this island, on the L.S., a small creek comes in. This island we call Island of Caution. We took in some wood on a favorable situation where we could defend our men on shore, and camped on a sand bar half a mile from the main shore. The wind changed to the N.W., and rose very high, and cold, which continued. The current of the Missouri is less rapid and contains much less sediment, of the same color.

4th of October, 1804

The wind blew all night from the N.W. Some rain. We were obliged to drop down 3 miles to get the channel sufficiently deep to pass up. Several Indians on the shore viewing of us, called to us to land. One of them gave 3 yells and skipped a ball before us. We paid no attention to him. Proceeded on and came to on the L.S. to breakfast. One of those Indians swam across to us, begged for powder. We gave him a piece of tobacco, and set him over on a sand bar, and set out. The wind hard ahead. Passed an island in the middle of the river about 3 miles in length, we call Good Hope Island. At 4 miles, passed a creek on the L.S. about 12 yards wide. Captain Lewis and 3 men walked on shore, and crossed over to an island situated on the S.S. of the current, and near the center of the river. This island is about 1½ miles long and nearly half as wide. In the center of this island was an old village of the Arikaras, called Lahoocatt. It was circular and walled, containing 17 lodges, and it appears to have been deserted about five years. The island contains but little timber. We camped on the sand bar making from this island. The day very cool.

5th of October, 1804

Frost this morning. We set out early and proceeded on. Passed a small creek on the L.S. At 7 o'clock heard some yells. Proceeded on. Saw three Indians of the Teton band. They called to us to come on shore. Begged some tobacco. We answered them as usual and proceeded on. Saw a gang of goats [*antelope*] swimming across the river, out of which we killed four. They were not fat. We came to and camped on a mud bar making from the S.S. The evening is calm and pleasant. Refreshed the men with a glass of whiskey.

6th October, 1804

A cool morning. Wind from the north. Set out early. Passed a willow island situated near the S. shore at the upper point of some timber on the S.S. Many large round stones near the middle of the river. Those stones appear to have been washed from the hills. Passed a village of about 80 neat lodges, covered with earth and picketed around.[8] Those lodges are spacious—of an octagon form, as close together as they can possibly be placed, and appear to have

---

[8] No one knows why all these Indians were away from home. Probably everybody had just gone hunting. The "lodges" were not, of course, the buffalo-hide-covered teepees of the Sioux, but the big rounded earth houses used by both Arikaras and Mandans. Like teepees, they had a hole in the center of the roof to release smoke. For some reason, no Indian ever thought of two important inventions that white men take for granted—the chimney and the wheel, though the Mayas probably used log rollers.

The camp referred to just below (Oct. 7, 1804) had been deserted permanently or for the season. The mats and canoes mentioned were probably left behind because it was easier to make new ones than to transport old ones.

been inhabited last spring. From the canoes of skins, mats, buckets, &c., found in the lodges, we are of opinion they were the Arikaras. We found squashes of three different kinds growing in the village.

One of our men killed an elk close by this village. I saw two wolves in pursuit of another, which appeared to be wounded and nearly tired. We proceeded on. Found the river shallow. We made several attempts to find the main channel between the sand bars, and were obliged at length to drag the boat over to save a league which we must return to get into the deepest channel. We have been obliged to hunt a channel for some time past, the river being divided in many places in a great number of channels. Saw geese, swan, brants, and ducks of different kinds on the sand bars today. Captain Lewis walked on shore. Saw great numbers of prairie hens. I observe but few gulls or plover in this part of the river.

7th of October, 1804

A cloudy morning. Some little rain frost last night. We set out early. Proceeded on 2 miles to the mouth of a river on the L.S., and breakfasted. This river when full is 90 yards wide. The water is at this time confined within 20 yards; the current appears gentle. This river throws out but little sand. At the mouth of this river we saw the tracks of white bear, which were very large. I walked up this river a mile. Below the mouth of this river are the remains of an Arikara village, or wintering camp fortified in a circular form of about 60 lodges, built in the same form as those passed yesterday. This camp appears to have been inhabited last winter. Many of their willow and straw mats, baskets, and buffalo-skin canoes remain entire within the camp. The Arikaras call this river Surwarkarna, or Park.

From this river, which heads in the first of the Black Mountains, we proceeded on under a gentle breeze from the S.W. At 10 o'clock, we saw 2 Indians on the S.S. They asked for something to eat.

8th of October, 1804

A cool morning. Set out early, the wind from the N.W. Proceeded on, passed the mouth of a small creek on the L.S. About 2½ miles above Grouse Island, passed a willow island which divides the current equally. Passed the mouth of a river called by the Arikaras Wetarhoo, on the L.S. This river is 120 yards wide, the water of which, at this time, is confined within 20 yards, discharging but a small quantity, throwing out mud with small proportion of sand. Great quantities of the red berries, resembling currants, are on the river at every bend. 77° 33′ 00″. Latitude from the observation of today at the mouth of this river [heads in the Black Mountains] is 45° 39′ 5″ North. Proceeded on past a small river 25 yards wide called Rampart or Beaver Dam River. This river (Maropa) is entirely choked up with mud, with a stream of one inch diameter passing through, discharging no sand. At one mile, passed the lower point of an island close on the L.S.

Two of our men discovered the Arikara village, about the center of the island on the L. side on the main shore. This island is about three miles long, separated from the L.S. by a channel about 60 yards wide, very deep. The island is covered with fields, where those people raise their corn, tobacco, beans &c. Great numbers of those people came on the island to see us pass. We passed above the head of the island, and Captain Lewis, with two interpreters and two men, went to the village. I formed a camp of the French and the guard, on shore, with one sentinel on board of the boat, at anchor. A pleasant evening. All things arranged, both for peace or war. This village is situated about the center of a large island near the L. side, and near the foot of some high, bald, uneven hills.

Several Frenchmen came up with Captain Lewis in a pirogue, one of which is a Mr. Gravelines,[9] a man well versed in the language of this nation, and gave us some information relative to the country, nation, &c.

Orders, October the 8th, 1804

[Orderly Book: Clark]

Robert Frazer [10] being regularly enlisted and having become one of the Corps of Volunteers for North-Western

---

[9] Joseph Gravelines was an employee of the trader Régis Loisel. Among the Frenchmen was probably Pierre Antoine Tabeau, who came back with Loisel a day or two later. This man, who spoke Arikara and despised the tribe, was very helpful to the explorers. Three ms. copies of his diary survived, one at the archdiocesan library at Quebec, one at the Library of Congress, and another (little known) in the Coe Collection at Yale. The Quebec copy has been lost.

[10] In other words, Frazer had decided to join the group which was to go all the way to the Pacific Coast, instead of the group which was to return to St. Louis from the Mandan country in the spring of 1805.

Discovery, he is therefore to be viewed and respected accordingly; and will be annexed to Sergeant Gass's mess.

> Wm. Clark. Capt. &c.
> Meriwether Lewis
> Capt. 1st Regiment,
> U. S. Infty.

River Maropa, 9th of October, 1804

[Clark]

A windy, rainy night, and cold—so much so we could not speak with the Indians today. The three great chiefs and many others came to see us today. We gave them some tobacco, and informed them we would speak tomorrow. The day continued cold and windy, some rain. Sorry. Canoes of skins passed down from the two villages a short distance above, and many came to view us all day, much astonished at my black servant, who did not lose the opportunity of displaying his powers, strength, &c. This nation never saw a black man before.[11]

Several hunters came in with loads of meat. I observed several canoes made of a single buffalo skin, with three squaws, cross the river today in waves as high as I ever saw on this river—quite uncomposed. I have a slight pleurisy this evening. Very cold, &c.

10th of October, 1804

A fine morning. Wind from the S.E. At about 11 o'clock the wind shifted to the N.W. We prepare all things ready to speak to the Indians. Mr. Tabeau and Mr. Gravelines came to breakfast with us. The chiefs, &c., came from the lower town, but none from the two upper towns, which are the largest. We continue to delay and wait for them. At twelve o'clock, dispatched Gravelines to invite them to come down. We have every reason to believe that a jealousy exists between the villages for fear of our making the first chief of the lower village. At one o'clock, the chiefs all assembled, and after some little ceremony, the council commenced. We

---

[11] This was the first of York's many triumphs, all the way across the continent. Indians who had hardly seen white men found it amazing that there should also be black ones. What they would have made of Orientals is hard to imagine.

informed them what we had told the others before, i.e., Otos and Sioux. Made three chiefs, one for each village. Gave them presents. After the council was over, we shot the air gun, which astonished them much. They then departed, and we rested secure all night. Those Indians were much astonished at my servant. They never saw a black man before. All flocked around him and examined him from top to toe. He carried on the joke and made himself more terrible than we wished him to do. Those Indians are not fond of spirits—liquor of any kind.

11th October, 1804

A fine morning. The wind from the S.E. At 11 o'clock we met the Grand Chief in council, and he made a short speech, thanking us for what we had given him and his nation, promising to attend to the counsel we had given him, and informed us the road was open and no one dare shut it, and we might depart at pleasure. At 1 o'clock we set out for the upper villages 3 miles distant, the grand chief and nephew on board. Proceeded on. At 1 mile, took in the 2nd chief, and came to off the second village, separated from the third by a creek. After arranging all matters, we walked up with the second chief to his village and sat, talking on various subjects, until late. We also visited the upper, or third, village—each of which gave us something to eat in their way, and a few bushels of corn, beans, &c. After being treated with every civility by those people, who are both poor and dirty, we returned to our boat at about 10 o'clock P.M., informing them, before we departed, that we would speak to them tomorrow at their separate villages. Those people gave us to eat bread made of corn and beans, also corn and beans boiled: a large bean of which they rob the mice of the prairie—who collect and discover it—which is rich and very nourishing; also squashes, &c. All tranquillity.

12th October, 1804

I rose early. After breakfast we joined the Indians who were waiting on the bank for us to come out and go and counsel. We accordingly joined them, and went to the house of the 2nd chief, Lassel, where there were many chiefs and warriors, and they made us a present of about 7 bushels of corn, a pair of leggings, a twist of their tobacco, and seeds of two kinds of tobacco. We sat some time before the council commenced. This man spoke at some length, declaring his disposition to believe and pursue our counsels, his intention of going to visit his Great Father, acknowledged the satisfaction in receiving the presents, &c., raising a doubt as to the safety in passing the nations below,[12] particularly the Sioux. Requested us to take a chief of their nation and make a good peace with the Mandans and nations above. After answering those parts of the 2nd chief's speech which required it, which appeared to give general satisfaction, we went to the village of the 3rd chief and, as usual, some ceremony took place before he could speak to us on the great subject. This chief spoke very much in the same style on nearly the same subjects as the other chief, who sat by his side, more sincerely and pleasantly. He presented us with about 10 bushels of corn, some beans and squashes, all of which we accepted with much pleasure. After we had answered his speech, and given them some account of the magnitude and power of our country, which pleased and astonished them very much, we returned to our boat. The chiefs accompanied us on board. We gave them some sugar, a little salt, and a sun glass, and set 2 on shore, and the third proceeded on with us to the Mandans. At 2˙o'clock we set out, the inhabitants of the two villages viewing us from the banks. We proceeded on about 9½ miles and camped on the S.S. at some woods. The evening clear and pleasantly cool.

The nation of the Arikaras is about 600 men (Mr. Tabeau says; I think 500 men [Mr. Tabeau is right]) able to bear arms. A great proportion of them have fusees. They appear to be peaceful. Their men tall and proportioned, women small and industrious, raise great quantities of corn, beans, simlins,[13] &c., also tobacco for the men to smoke. They collect all the wood and do the drudgery, as is common among savages.

Two villages are made up of ten [nine] different tribes of the Pawnees, who had formerly been separate, but by commotion and war with their neighbors have become reduced, and compelled to come together for protection. The corruption of the language of those different tribes has so reduced the language that the different villages do not understand all the words of the others.

[12] "Below" and "above" as here used seem a little confusing but are not really so. The chief feared the nations "below" (downstream) if he ever had to pass them on his way to Washington. He also wanted peace with the nations upstream ("above").

[13] "Simlin," or "simnel," is a Southern word for summer squash. Almost all Indians raised squash or pumpkins of one kind or another. Clark, as a Virginian, used the Southern word. Both captains wrote "evening" for "afternoon," as Virginians still do.

Those people are dirty, kind, poor, and extravagant, possessing national pride, not beggarly, receive what is given with great pleasure, live in warm houses, large and built in an octagon form, forming a cone at top which is left open for the smoke to pass. Those houses are generally 30 or 40 feet in diameter, covered with earth on poles—willows and grass to prevent the earth passing through. Those people express an inclination to be at peace with all nations. The Sioux, who trade the goods which they get of the British traders for their corn and have great influence over the Arikaras, poison their minds and keep them in perpetual dread.

A curious custom with the Sioux, as well as the Arikaras, is to give handsome squaws to those whom they wish to show some acknowledgments to. The Sioux we got clear of without taking their squaws. They followed us with squaws two days. The Arikaras we put off during the time we were at the towns, but two handsome young squaws were sent by a man to follow us. They came up this evening and persisted in their civilities.

Dress of the men of this nation is simply a pair of moccasins, leggings, flap in front, and a buffalo robe, with their hair, arms, and ears decorated.

The women wore moccasins, leggings fringed, and a shirt of goat skins, some with sleeves. This garment is long and generally white and fringed, tied at the waist, with a robe. In summer, without hair.

13th of October, 1804

One man, J. Newman, confined for mutinous expression. Set out early. Proceeded on. Passed a camp of Sioux on the S.S. Those people only viewed us and did not speak one word. The visitors of last evening, all except one, returned, which is the brother of the chief we have on board.

Passed a creek about 15 yards wide on the L.S. We call after the second chief, Pocasse, or "Hay." Nearly opposite this creek, a few miles from the river, on the S.S., are two stones resembling human persons and one resembling a dog, situated in the open prairie. To those stones the Arikaras pay great reverence and make offerings whenever they pass (information of the chief and interpreter). Those people have a curious tradition of those stones. One was a man in love, one a girl whose parents would not let them marry. The man, as is customary, went off to mourn. The female followed. The dog went to mourn with them. All turned to stone gradually, commencing at the feet. Those people fed on grapes until they turned, and the woman has a bunch of grapes yet in her hand. On the river near the place those are said to be situated, we obtained a greater quantity of fine grapes than I ever saw at one place.

We tried the prisoner Newman last night by 9 of his peers. They did "sentence him 75 lashes and disbanded from the party." [14]

14th of October, 1804

Some rain last night. All wet and cold. We set out early. The rain continued all day. At [blank] miles we passed a creek on the L.S., 15 yards wide. This creek we call after the 3rd chief, Piaheto, or Eagle's Feather. At 1 o'clock we halted on a sand bar, and, after dinner, executed the sentence of the court-martial so far as giving the corporal punishment; and proceeded on a few miles. The wind ahead from N.E. Camped in a cove of the bank on the S.S. immediately opposite our camp on the L.S. I observe an ancient fortification, the walls of which appear to be 8 or 10 feet high, most of it washed in. The evening wet and disagreeable. The river something wider. More timber on the banks.

The punishment of this day alarmed the Indian chief very much. He cried aloud, or affected to cry. I explained the cause of the punishment and the necessity for it. He also thought examples were necessary, and he himself had made them by death. His nation never whipped even their children, from their birth.

15th of October, 1804

Rained all last night. We set out early and proceeded on. At 3 miles passed an Indian camp, of Arikara hunters, on the

---

[14] Though "disbanded from the party"—in other words, dishonorably discharged—Newman had to be taken along or he would have died or been killed by Indians. Lewis's note in the Orderly Book says: "The commanding officers further direct that John Newman in future be attached to the mess and crew of the red pirogue as a laboring hand on board the same and that he be deprived of his arms and accouterments and not be permitted the honor of mounting guard till further orders. The commanding officers further direct that, in lieu of the guard duty from which Newman has been exempted by virtue of this order, he shall be exposed to such drudgeries as they may think proper to direct from time to time, with a view to the general relief of the detachment."

S.S. We halted above, and about 30 of the Indians came over in their canoes of skins. We ate with them. They gave us meat. In return, we gave fish hooks, and some beads. About a mile higher, we came to on the L.S. At the camp of the Arikaras of about 8 lodges, we also ate and they gave some meat. We proceeded on. Saw numbers of Indians on both sides, passing a creek. Saw many curious hills, high, and much the resemblance of a house with a hipped roof, like ours. At 12 o'clock it cleared away, and the evening was pleasant. Wind from the N.E. At sunset we arrived at a camp of Arikaras of 10 lodges on the S.S. We came to, and camped near them. Captain Lewis and myself went with the chief who accompanies us to the huts of several of the men, all of whom smoked and gave us something to eat, also some meat to take away. Those people were kind and appeared to be much pleased at the attention paid them.

Those people are much pleased with my black servant. Their women very fond of caressing our men, &c.

16th of October, 1804

Some rain this morning. Two young squaws very anxious to accompany us. We set out with our chief on board, by name Arketarnashar, or Chief of the Town. Captain Lewis and the Indian chief walked on shore. Soon after, I discovered great numbers of goats in the river, and Indians on the shore on each side. As I approached, or got nearer, I discovered boys in the water killing the goats with sticks and hauling them to shore. Those on the banks shot them with arrows, and as they approached the shore, would turn them back. Of this gang of goats I counted 58 which they had killed on the shore. One of our hunters out with Captain Lewis killed three goats. We passed the camp on the S.S., and proceeded ½ mile, and camped on the L.S. Many Indians came to the boat to see. Some came across late at night. As they approached, they hallooed and sang. After staying a short time, two went for some meat, and returned in a short time with fresh and dried buffalo, also goat. Those Indians stayed all night. They sang, and were very merry the greater part of the night.

17th of October, 1804

Set out early. A fine morning. The wind from the N.W. After breakfast, I walked on shore with the Indian chief and interpreters. Saw buffalo, elk, and great numbers of goats in large gangs. (I am told by Mr. G. that those animals winter in the Black Mountains to feed on timber, &c.) And this is about the season they cross from the east of the Missouri to go to that mountain. They return in the spring and pass the Missouri in great numbers, to the plains. This chief tells me of a number of their traditions about turtles, snakes, &c., and the power of a particular rock or cove on the next river, which informs of everything. None of those, I think, worth while mentioning. The wind so hard ahead, the boat could not move after 10 o'clock. Captain Lewis took the altitude of the sun, Latitude 46° 23' 57". I killed 3 deer, and the hunters with me killed 3 also. The Indian shot one but could not get it. I scaffolded up the deer, and returned and met the boat after night, on the L.S., about 6 miles above the place we camped last night. One of the men saw a number of snakes. Captain Lewis saw a large beaver house S.S. I caught a whippoorwill, small and not common. The leaves are falling fast. The river wide and full of sand bars. Great numbers of very large stones on the sides of the hills, and some rock of a brownish color in the L. bend below this.

Great numbers of goats are flocking down to the S. side of the river, on their way to the Black Mountains, where they winter. Those animals return in the spring in the same way, and scatter in different directions.

18th of October, 1804

Set out early. Proceeded on. At 6 miles, passed the mouth of Le Boulet, or Cannon Ball River, about 140 yards wide on the L.S. This river heads in the Côte Noire or Black Mountains. A fine day. Above the mouth of the river, great numbers of stone, perfectly round, with fine grit, are in the bluff and on the shore. The river takes its name from those stones, which resemble cannon balls. The water of this river is confined within 40 yards. We met two Frenchmen in a pirogue, descending from hunting, and complained of the Mandans robbing them of four traps, their furs, and several other articles. Those men were in the employ of our Arikara interpreter, Mr. Gravelines. They turned and followed us.

Note: The Arikaras are not fond of spirituous liquors, nor do they appear to be fond of receiving any or thankful for it. They say we are no friends or we would not give them what makes them fools.

20th of October, 1804

Set out early this morning and proceeded on. The wind

from the S.E. After breakfast I walked out on the L. side to see those remarkable places pointed out by Evans.[15] I saw an old remains of a village, covering 6 or 8 acres, on the side of a hill which the chief with Tooné tells me that nation lived in. Two villages, one on each side of the river, and the troublesome Sioux caused them to move about 40 miles higher up, where they remained a few years, and moved to the place they now live. Passed a small creek on the S.S. and one on the L.S. Passed an island covered with willows lying in the middle of the river. No current on the L.S. Camped on the L.S. above a bluff containing coal of an inferior quality. This bank is immediately above the old village of the Mandans. The country is fine, the high hills at a distance with gradual ascents. I killed 3 deer. The timber, confined to the bottoms as usual, is much larger than below. Great numbers of buffalo, elk, and deer, goats. Our hunters killed 10 deer and a goat today, and wounded a white bear. I saw several fresh tracks of those animals which are 3 times as large as a man's track. The wind hard all day from the N.E. and E. Great numbers of buffalo swimming the river. I observe near all large gangs of buffalo, wolves, and when the buffalo move, those animals follow, and feed on those that are killed by accident, or those that are too poor, or fat, to keep up with the gang.

21st October, 1804

A very cold night. Wind hard from the N.E. Some rain in the night which froze as it fell. At daylight it began to snow and continued all the fore part of the day. Passed, just above our camp, a small river on the L.S., called by the Indians, Chisschetar. This river is about 38 yards wide, containing a good deal of water. Some distance up this river is situated a stone which the Indians have great faith in, and say they see, painted on the stone, all the calamities and good fortune to happen to the nation, and parties who visit it. A tree, an oak, which stands alone near this place— about 2 miles off—in the open prairie, which has withstood the fire, they pay great respect to: Make holes and tie strings through the skin of their necks and around this tree, to

---

[15] John Evans (sometimes referred to as Lewis Evans) was a young Welshman who had come to America to investigate the legend of "Welsh Indians." He reached the Mandan country a few years before Lewis and Clark and had made a map of the Missouri as far as the Mandan country. President Jefferson provided Lewis with a copy of this map before the expedition started.

make them brave. [Captain Clark saw this tree.] All this is the information of Tooné (Is a Whippoorwill), the chief of the Arikaras, who accompanied us to the Mandans. At 2 miles, passed the second village of the Mandans, which was in existence at the same time with the first. This village is at the foot of a hill on the S.S. in a beautiful and extensive plain, at this time covered with buffalo. Nearly opposite is another village in a bottom, the other side of the Missouri. I killed a fine buffalo. We camped on the L.S., below an old Mandan village, having passed another up a creek 3 miles below on the S.S. Very cold. Ground covered with snow. One otter killed.

Last night at 1 o'clock, I was violently and suddenly attacked with the rheumatism in the neck, which was so violent I could not move. Captain Lewis applied a hot stone wrapped in flannel, which gave me some temporary ease. We set out early; the morning cold. At 7 o'clock, we came to at a camp of Teton Sioux on the L.S. Those people, 12 in number, were naked, and had the appearance of war. We have every reason to believe that they are going, or have been, to steal horses from the Mandans. They tell two stories. We gave them nothing. After taking breakfast, proceeded on. My neck is yet very painful, at times—spasms. Passed old Mandan village, near which we lay—another at 4 miles; one at 8 miles at mouth of large creek 4 miles farther, all on larboard side. The mounds, 9 in number, along river within 20 miles; the fallen-down earth of the houses, some teeth and bones of men and animals mixed in these villages. Human skulls are scattered in these villages.

Camped on the L. side. Passed an island situated on the L. side, at the head of which we passed a bad place, and Mandans' village S.S., 2 miles above. The hunters killed a buffalo bull. They say out of about 300 buffalo which they saw, they did not see one cow. Great deal of beaver sign. Several caught every night.

23rd of October, 1804

A cloudy morning. Some snow. Set out early. Passed five lodges which were deserted, the fires yet burning. We suppose those were the Indians who robbed the 2 French trappers a few days ago. Those 2 men are now with us, going up with a view to getting their property from the Indians, through us. Cold and cloudy. Camped on the L.S. of the river.

24th October, 1804

Set out early. A cloudy day. Some little snow in the

morning. I am something better of the rheumatism in my neck. A beautiful country on both sides of the river: the bottoms covered with woods. We have seen no game on the river today, a proof of the Indians hunting in the neighborhood. Passed an island on the S.S., made by the river cutting through a point, by which the river is shortened several miles. On this island we saw one of the grand chiefs of the Mandans, with five lodges, hunting. This chief met the chief of the Arikaras who accompanied us, with great cordiality and ceremony. Smoked the pipe, and Captain Lewis, with the interpreter, went with the chiefs to his lodges at 1 mile distant. After his return, we admitted the grand chief and his brother for a few minutes on our boat. Proceeded on a short distance, and camped on the S.S., below the old village of the Mandans and Arikaras. Soon after our landing, 4 Mandans came from a camp above. The Arikaras' chief went with them to their camp.

25th of October, 1804

A cold morning. Set out early under a gentle breeze from the S.E. by E. Proceeded on. Passed the 3rd old village of the Mandans which has been deserted for many years. This village was situated on an eminence of about 40 feet above the water on the L.S. Back for several miles is a beautiful plain. At a short distance above this old village, on a continuation of the same eminence, was situated the Arikaras' village. Two old villages of Arikaras, one on top of high hill, the second below, in the bottom, which have been evacuated only six [five] years. About 3 or 4 miles above Arikaras' villages are 3 old villages of Mandans near together. Here they lived when the Arikaras came for protection—afterward moved where they now live. Above this village, a large and extensive bottom for several miles in which the squaws raised their corn. But little timber near the villages. On the S.S., below, is a point of excellent timber, and in the point several miles above is fine timber.

Several parties of Mandans rode to the river on the S.S. to view us. Indeed they are continually in sight, satisfying their curiosities as to our appearance, &c. We are told that the Sioux have latterly fallen in with and stolen the horses of the Big Bellies [Gros Ventres]. On their way home they fell in with the Assiniboines, who killed them and took the horses. A Frenchman has latterly been killed by the Indians, on the track to the trading establishment on the Assiniboine River in the north of this place (or British fort). This Frenchman has lived many years with the Mandans.

We were frequently called on to land and talk to parties of the Mandans on the shore.

Wind shifted to the S.W. at about 11 o'clock, and blew hard until 3 o'clock. Clouded up. River full of sand bars, and we are at a great loss to find the channel of the river. Frequently run on the sand bars, which delays us much. Passed a very bad riffle of rocks in the evening, by taking the L.S. of a sand bar, and camped on a sand point on the S.S. opposite a high hill on the L.S. Several Indians came to see us this evening—among others, the son of the great chief of the Mandans—mourning for his father. This man has his two little fingers off. On inquiring the cause, was told it was customary for this nation to show their grief by some testimony of pain, and that it was not uncommon for them to take off 2 smaller fingers on the hand, at the second joints, and sometimes more, with other marks of savage affection.

The wind blew very hard this evening from the S.W. Very cold. R. Fields with the rheumatism in his neck. P. Cruzat with the same complaint in his legs. The party otherwise is well. As to myself, I feel but slight symptoms of that disorder at this time.

26th of October, 1804

Set out early. Wind from the S.W. Proceeded on. Saw numbers of the Mandans on shore. We set the Arikara chief on shore and we proceeded on to the camp of two of their grand chiefs, where we delayed a few minutes, with the chiefs, and proceeded on, taking two of their chiefs on board, and some of the heavy articles of his household, such as earthen pots and corn. Proceeded on. At this camp saw a Mr. McCracken,[16] Englishman from the N.W. [Hudson's Bay] Company. This man came nine days ago to trade for horses and buffalo robes—one other man came with him. The Indians continued on the banks all day. But little wood on this part of the river. Many sand bars and bad places. Water much divided between them.

We came to and camped on the L.S. about ½ a mile below the first Mandan town on the L.S. Soon after our arrival, many men, women and children flocked down to see us. Captain Lewis walked to the village with the principal chiefs and our interpreters. My rheumatic complaint increasing, I could

---

[16] Hugh McCracken was a North-West Company trader, not a Hudson's Bay man. He had first visited the Mandans with David Thompson nine years earlier.

not go. If I had been well, only one would have left the boat and party until we knew the disposition of the Indians. I smoked with the chiefs who came after. Those people appeared much pleased with the corn mill which we were obliged to use, and was fixed in the boat.

Chapter V

AMONG THE MANDANS
October 27—December 27, 1804

27th of October, 1804. Mandans.

[Clark]

We set out early. Came to at the village on the L.S. This village is situated on an eminence about 50 feet above the water in a handsome plain. It contains [blank] houses [1] in a kind of picket work. The houses are round and very large, containing several families, and also their horses, which are tied on one side of the entrance. A description of those houses will be given hereafter. I walked up and smoked a pipe with the chiefs of the village. They were anxious that I would stay and eat with them. My indisposition prevented my eating, which displeased them, until a full explanation took place. I returned to the boat and sent two carrots of tobacco for them to smoke, and proceeded on. Passed the second village, and camped opposite the village of the Wetersoons, or Ahwahharways, which is situated on an eminence in a plain on the L.S. This village is small and contains but few inhabitants. Above this village, also above the Knife River on the same side of the Missouri, the Big Bellies' towns are situated. A further description will be given hereafter, as also of the town of the Mandans on this side of the river, i.e., S. side.

A fine warm day. We met with a Frenchman, by the name of Jussome,[2] whom we employ as an interpreter. This

[1] The number is left blank in the official journals. However, Sergeant Patrick Gass, who was also keeping a journal, says there were forty or fifty houses.

[2] René Jussome was not a trader but a typical "squaw man," who had been living among the Indians for the last fifteen years. One indignant Canadian called him an "old sneaking cheat,"

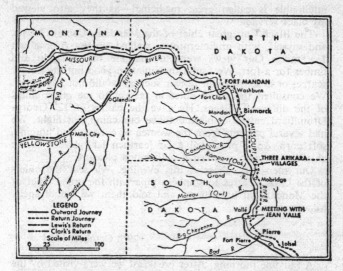

man has a wife and children in the village. Great numbers on both sides flocked down to the bank to view us as we passed. Captain Lewis, with the interpreter, walked down to the village below our camp. After delaying one hour, he returned and informed me the Indians had returned to their village, &c. We sent three twists of tobacco by three young men to the three villages above, inviting them to come down and counsel with us tomorrow. Many Indians came to view us. Some stayed all night in the camp of our party. We procured some information of Mr. Jussome, about the chiefs of the different nations.

28th of October, 1804

A windy day, fair and clear. Many of the Gros Ventres— or Big Bellies—and Wetersoons came to see us and hear the council. The wind being so violently hard from the S.W. prevented our going into council. Indeed the chiefs of the Mandans from the lower village could not cross. We made up the presents, and entertained several of the curious chiefs who wished to see the boat, which was very curious to them, viewing it as great medicine [whatever is mysterious or un-

---

but men who fled white society were rarely admirable characters. As he spoke Mandan, Lewis and Clark found him useful.

intelligible is called great medicine]—as they also viewed my black servant.

The Black Cat, great chief of the Mandans, Captain Lewis, and myself, with an interpreter, walked up the river about 1½ miles. Our views were to examine the situation and timber for a fort. We found the situation good but the timber scarce; or at least, small timber such as would not answer us. We consulted the grand chief in respect to the other chiefs of the different villages. He gave the names of 12. George Drouilliard caught 2 beaver above our camp last night. We had several presents from the women of corn, boiled hominy, soft corn, &c. I presented a jar [earthen jar, glazed] to the chief's wife, who received it with much pleasure.

Our men very cheerful this evening. We sent the chiefs of the Gros Ventres to smoke a pipe with the grand chief of the Mandans in his village, and told them we would speak tomorrow.

29th October, 1804

A fair fine morning. After breakfast we were visited by the old chief of the Big Bellies. This man was old and had transferred his power to his son, who was then out at war against the Snake Indians, who inhabit the Rocky Mountains. At 10 o'clock the S.W. wind rose very high. We collected the chiefs and commenced a council, under an awning and our sails stretched around to keep out as much wind as possible. We delivered a long speech, the substance of which was similar to what we had delivered to the nations below.

The old chief of the Gros Ventres was very restless before the speech was half ended; observed that he could not wait long, that his camp was exposed to the hostile Indians, &c. He was rebuked by one of the chiefs for his uneasiness at such a time as the present. At the end of the speech, we mentioned the Arikara who accompanied us to make a firm peace. They all smoked with him. I gave this chief a dollar of the American coin, as a medal, with which he was much pleased. In council, we presented him with a certificate of his sincerity and good conduct, &c. We also spoke about the fur which was taken from two Frenchmen by a Mandan, and informed of our intentions of sending back the French hands.

After the council, we gave the presents with much ceremony, and put the medals on the chiefs we intended to make, viz., one for each town, to whom we gave coats, hats, and flags; one grand chief to each nation, to whom we gave medals with the President's likeness. In council, we requested them to give us an answer tomorrow, or as soon as possible, on some points which required their deliberation. After the council was over, we shot the air gun, which appeared to astonish the natives much. The greater part then retired soon after.

The Arikara chief, Arketarnashar, came to me this evening and tells me that he wishes to return to his village and nation. I put him off, saying tomorrow we would have an answer to our talk to their satisfaction and send by him a string of wampum informing what had passed here. An iron, or steel, corn mill which we gave to the Mandans was very thankfully received. The prairie was set on fire (or caught by accident) by a young man of the Mandans. The fire went with such velocity that it burned to death a man and woman, who could not get to any place of safety. One man, a woman, and child much burned, and several narrowly escaped the flame.

A boy half white was saved unhurt in the midst of the flame. These ignorant people say this boy was saved by the Great Medicine Spirit because he was white. The cause of his being saved was a green buffalo skin thrown over him by his mother, who perhaps had more foresight for the protection of her son, and less for herself, than those who escaped the flame. The fire did not burn under the skin, leaving the grass around the boy. This fire passed our camp last night about eight o'clock, P.M. It went with great rapidity and looked tremendous.

We sent the presents intended for the grand chief of the Minnetaree, or Big Belly, and the presents, flag, and wampum by the old chief, and those intended for the chief of the lower village by a young chief.

30th October, 1804

Two chiefs came to have some talk: one the principal of the lower village, the other the one who thought himself the principal man, and requested to hear some of the speech that was delivered yesterday. They were gratified; and we put the medal on the neck of The Big White, to whom we had sent clothes yesterday, and a flag. Those men did not return from hunting in time to join the council. They were well pleased. (Second of those is a Cheyenne.) I took 8 men in a small pirogue and went up the river as far as the first island, about 7 miles, to see if a situation could be got on it for our winter quarters. Found the wood on the island, as also on the point above, so distant from the water that I did not think

that we could get a good wintering ground there; and as all
the white men here informed us that wood was scarce, as
well as game above, we determined to drop down a few miles
near wood and game.

On my return, found many Indians at our camp. Gave the
party a dram. They danced, as is very common in the evening, which pleased the savages much. Wind S.E.

31st of October, 1804

A fine morning. The chief of the Mandans sent a second
chief to invite us to his lodge to receive some corn and hear
what he had to say. I walked down and, with great ceremony, was seated on a robe by the side of the chief. He
threw a handsome robe over me, and after smoking the pipe
with several old men around, the chief spoke:

Said he believed what we had told them, and that peace
would be general, which not only gave him satisfaction but
all his people: they could now hunt without fear, and their
women could work in the fields without looking every moment for the enemy; and put off their moccasins at night.
[Sign of peace: undress.] As to the Arikaras, we will show
you that we wish peace with all, and do not make war on
any without cause. That chief—pointing to the second—and
some brave men will accompany the Arikara chief now
with you to his village and nation, to smoke with that people. When you came up, the Indians in the neighboring villages, as well as those out hunting, when they heard of you,
had great expectations of receiving presents. Those hunting,
immediately on hearing, returned to the village; and all were
disappointed, and some dissatisfied. As to himself, he was
not much so; but his village was. He would go and see his
Great Father, &c.

He had put before me two of the steel traps which were
robbed from the French a short time ago, and about twelve
bushels of corn, which were brought and put before me by the
women of the village. After the chief finished and smoked
in great ceremony, I answered the speech, which satisfied
them very much, and returned to the boat. Met the principal
chief of the third village, and the Little Crow, both of whom
I invited into the cabin, and smoked and talked with for
about one hour.

Soon after those chiefs left us, the grand chief of the
Mandans came, dressed in the clothes we had given, with his
two small sons, and requested to see the men dance, which
they very readily gratified him in. The wind blew hard all the

after part of the day from the N.E., and continued all night to blow hard from that point. In the morning it shifted N.W. Captain Lewis wrote to the N.W. Company's agent on the Assiniboine River [fort, &c., there, about 150 miles hence] about nine days' march north of this place.

1st of November, 1804

The wind hard from the N.W. Mr. McCracken, a trader, set out at 7 o'clock, to the fort on the Assiniboine. By him sent a letter (enclosing a copy of the British Minister's protection) to the principal agent of the Company.

At about 10 o'clock, the chiefs of the lower village came, and after a short time informed us they wished we would call at their village and take some corn; that they would make peace with the Arikaras; they never made war against them but after the Arikaras killed their chiefs. They killed them like birds, and were tired of killing them, and would send a chief and some brave men to the Arikaras to smoke with that people.

In the evening we set out, and fell down to the lower village, where Captain Lewis got out and continued at the village until after night. I proceeded on, and landed on the S.S. at the upper point of the first timber on the starboard side. After landing and continuing all night, dropped down to a proper place to build. Captain Lewis came down after night, and informed me he intended to return the next morning, by the particular request of the chiefs.

We passed the villages on our descent, in view of great numbers of the inhabitants.

2nd November, 1804

This morning at daylight, I went down the river with 4 men, to look for a proper place to winter. Proceeded down the river three miles, and found a place well supplied with wood, and returned. Captain Lewis went to the village to hear what they had to say, and I fell down, and formed a camp, near where a small camp of Indians were hunting. Cut down the trees around our camp. In the evening, Captain Lewis returned with a present of 11 bushels of corn. Our Arikara chief set out, accompanied by one chief of Mandans and several brave men of Minnetarees and Mandans. He called for some small article which we had promised, but as I could not understand him, he could not get it. [Afterward he did get it.] The wind from the S.E. A fine day. Many Indians to view us today.

4th November, 1804

A fine morning. We continued to cut down trees and raise our houses. A Mr. Charbonneau,[3] interpreter for the Gros Ventre nation, came to see us, and informed that he came down with several Indians from a hunting expedition up the river, to hear what we had told the Indians in council. This man wished to hire as an interpreter. The wind rose this evening from the east, and clouded up. Great numbers of Indians pass, hunting, and some on the return.

5 November, 1804

I rose very early and commenced raising the two ranges of huts. The timber large and heavy, all to carry on hand sticks,[4] cottonwood, and elm, some ash, small. Our situation sandy. Great numbers of Indians pass to and from hunting. A camp of Mandans a few miles below us. Caught, within two days, 100 goats, by driving them in a strong pen, directed by a bush fence widening from the pen, &c. The greater part of this day cloudy, wind moderate from the N.W. I have the rheumatism very bad. Captain Lewis writing all day. We are told by our interpreter that four Assiniboine Indians have arrived at the camp of the Gros Ventres, and fifty lodges are coming.

6th November, 1804. Fort Mandan

Last night late we were awakened by the sergeant of the guard to see a northern light,[5] which was light, but not red, and appeared to darken and sometimes nearly obscured, and open. Divided about 20 degrees above horizon—various shapes—considerable space. Many times appeared in light streaks, and at other times a great space light, and containing floating columns, which appeared to approach each other and retreat, leaving the lighter space at no time of the same appearance.

---

[3] "Mr. Charbonneau" was Toussaint Charbonneau, husband of the famous Sacagawea, and of another Shoshone girl as well.

[4] Hand sticks were apparently stout sticks thrust under a log, one at each end. With two men on each stick, four men would be able to carry a log.

[5] The northern lights were an unusual phenomenon to the Virginian officers, neither of whom had been very far north of the Ohio River in cold weather.

This morning I rose at daylight. The clouds to the north appeared black. At eight o'clock the wind began to blow hard from the N.W., and cold; and continued all day. Mr. Joe Gravelines, our Arikara interpreter, Paul Primaut, La-Jeunesse,[6] and two French boys who came with us, set out in a small pirogue, on their return to the Arikara nation and the Illinois. Mr. Gravelines has instructions to take on the Arikaras in the spring, &c. Continue to build the huts out of cotton [wood] timber, this being the only timber we have.

7th November, 1804

A temperate day. We continued to build our hut. Cloudy and foggy all day.

8th Nov., 1804

A cloudy morning. Jussome, our Mandan interpreter, went to the village. On his return he informed us that three Englishmen had arrived from the Hudson's Bay Company, and would be here tomorrow. We continued to build our huts. Many Indians come to see us, and bring their horses to graze near us.

9th Nov., 1804

A very hard frost this morning. We continue to build our cabins under many disadvantages. Day cloudy. Wind from the N.W. Several Indians pass with flying news [reports]. We got a white weasel—tail excepted, which was black at the end—of an Indian. Captain Lewis walked to the hill about ¾ of a mile. We are situated in a point of the Missouri, north side, in a cottonwood timber. This timber is tall and heavy, containing an immense quantity of water; brittle and soft. Fine food for horses to winter, as is said by the Indians. The Mandans graze their horses in the day on grass, and at night, give them a stick [an armful] of cottonwood boughs to eat. Horses, dogs, and people all pass the night in the same lodge, or round house, covered with earth, with a fire in the

---

[6] Gravelines had been employed to take an Arikara chief to Washington. Primaut is unknown. Baptiste La Jeunesse was the "patroon" in charge of the red pirogue.

middle. Great number of wild geese passed to the south. Flew very high.

10th November, 1804

Rose early. Continued to build our fort. Numbers of Indians came to see us. A chief, half Pawnee, came and brought a side of buffalo. In return, we gave some few small things to himself and wife and son. He crossed the river in the buffalo-skin canoe, and the squaw took the boat on her back, and proceeded on to the town—3 miles. The day raw and cold. Wind from the N.W. The geese continue to pass in gangs, as also brants, to the south. Some ducks also pass.

11th November, 1804. Fort Mandan

A cold day. Continued to work at the Fort. Two men cut themselves with an ax. The large ducks pass to the south. An Indian gave me several rolls of parched meat. Two squaws of the Rock Mountains, purchased from the Indians by a Frenchman—Charbonneau—came down.[7] The Mandans out hunting the buffalo.

12th November, 1804

A very cold night. Early this morning, The Big White, principal chief of the lower village of the Mandans, came down. He packed about 100 pounds of fine meat on his squaw for us. We made some small presents to the squaw and child, gave a small ax with which she was much pleased. Three men sick with the [blank in MS.]. Several. Wind changeable. Very cold evening. Freezing all day. Some ice on the edges of the river.

Swans passing to the south. The hunters we sent down the river to hunt have not returned.

The Mandans speak a language peculiar to themselves, very much [blank in MS.]. They can raise about 350 men; the Wetersoons or Mahas, 80; and the Big Bellies, or Minnetarees, about 600 or 650 men. The Mandans and Sioux have the same word for water. The Big Bellies or Minnetarees and Raven [Wetersoon, as also the Crow or Raven]

---

[7] Charbonneau had bought the captive girls to marry them —he was always marrying somebody.

Indians speak nearly the same language, and the presumption is they were originally the same nation. The Raven Indians have 400 lodges and about 1,200 men, and follow the buffalo, or hunt for their subsistence in the plains, and on the Côte Noire and Rocky Mountains, and are at war with the Sioux and Snake Indians.

The Big Bellies and Wetersoons are at war with the Snake Indians and Sioux, and were at war with the Arikaras until we made peace a few days past. The Mandans are at war with all who make war [on them—at present with the Sioux] only, and wish to be at peace with all nations. Seldom the aggressors.

14th of November, 1804. Fort Mandan

A cloudy morning. Ice running very thick. River rose ½ inch last night. Some snow falling. Only two Indians visited us today, owing to a dance at the village last night in concluding a ceremony of adoption, and interchange of property, between the Assiniboines, Crees, and the nations of this neighborhood. We sent one man by land on horseback to know the reason of the delay of our hunters. This evening, 2 Frenchmen who were trapping below came up with 20 beaver. We are compelled to use our pork, which we do sparingly, for fear of some failure in procuring a sufficiency from the woods.

15th of November, 1804

A cloudy morning. The ice runs much thicker than yesterday. At 10 o'clock, George Drouilliard and the Frenchman we dispatched yesterday came up from the hunters who are encamped about 30 miles below. After about one hour, we dispatched a man, with orders to the hunters to proceed on without delay through the floating ice. We sent by the man, tin, to put on the parts of the pirogue exposed to the ice, and a tow rope. The wind changeable. All hands work at their huts until 1 o'clock at night. Swans passing to the south—but few waterfowls to be seen. Not one Indian came to our fort today.

16th November, 1804

A very white frost; all the trees all covered with ice. Cloudy. All the men move into the huts, which are not finished. Several Indians came to camp today. The Assiniboines are at the Big Belly camp. Some trouble likely to take place between them, from the loss of horses, &c., as is said by an old Indian who visited us, with four buffalo robes and corn to trade for a pistol, which we did not let him have. Men employed until late in daubing their huts. Some horses sent down to stay in the woods near the fort, to prevent the Assiniboines stealing them.

19th Nov.

A cold day. The ice continues to run. Our pirogue of hunters arrived with 32 deer, 12 elk, and a buffalo. All of this meat we had hung up in a smokehouse, a timely supply. Several Indians here all day. The wind blew hard from the N.W. by W. Our men move into their huts. Several little Indian anecdotes told me today.

20th November, 1804

Captain Lewis and myself move into our hut. A very hard wind from the W. All the after part of the day, a temperate day. Several Indians came down to eat fresh meat. Three chiefs from the second Mandan village stayed all day. They are very curious in examining our works.

21st Nov.

A fine day. Dispatched a pirogue, and collected stone for our chimneys. Some wind from the S.W. Arranged our different articles. Many Indians visited us today. George Drouilliard hurt his hand very bad. All the party in high spirits. The river clear of ice, and rising a little.

22nd of November, 1804

A fine morning. Dispatched a pirogue and 5 men under the direction of Sergeant Pryor, to the second village, for 100 bushels of corn in ears, which Mr. Jussome let us have. [Did not get more than 30 bushels.] I was alarmed about 10 o'clock by the sentinel, who informed that an Indian was about to kill his wife, in the interpreter's fire [i.e., lodge] about 60 yards below the works. I went down and spoke to the fellow about the rash act he was likely to commit, and forbade any act of the kind near the Fort.

Some misunderstanding took place between this man and his wife, about 8 days ago, and she came to this place, and continued with the squaws of the interpreters. [He might lawfully have killed her for running away.] Two days ago, she returned to the village. In the evening of the same day, she came to the interpreter's fire, apparently much beaten and stabbed in 3 places. We directed that no man of this party have any intercourse with this woman under the penalty of punishment. He, the husband, observed that one of our sergeants slept with his wife, and if he wanted her he would give her to him.

We directed the sergeant (Ordway) to give the man some articles, at which time I told the Indian that I believed not one man of the party had touched his wife except the one he had given the use of her for a night, in his own bed [8]; no man of the party should touch his squaw, or the wife of any Indian, nor did I believe they touched a woman if they knew her to be the wife of another man, and advised him to take his squaw home and live happily together in future. At this time the grand chief of the nation arrived, and lectured him, and they both went off, apparently dissatisfied.

24th of November, 1804

A warm day. Several men with bad colds. We continued to cover our huts with hewed puncheons.[9] Finished a cord to draw our boat out on the bank. This is made of 9 strands of elk skin.

25th of Nov., 1804

Capt. Lewis and 2 interpreters and 6 men set out to see the Indians in the different towns and camps in this neighborhood. We continue to cover and daub our huts.

27th of November, 1804

A cloudy morning after a very cold night. The river crowded with floating ice. Captain Lewis returned from the

[8] Among these Indians, as among some other primitive peoples, a husband had a perfect right to give (or sell) his wife's favors to anyone he pleased. Surreptitious adultery was an offense, which the husband might punish, practically as he pleased. But a squaw who yielded to another at her husband's order was merely doing her duty as a wife.

[9] A puncheon was a log hewn flat on one side, for use as a floor or ceiling board, bench, or table. "Daubing" meant filling the interstices between rough logs (which, of course, could never be made to join closely) with mud. Log houses were still being built, and both Lewis and Clark were familiar with the usual terms of log architecture.

·villages with two chiefs, Marnohtoh and Mannessurree, and a considerable man with the party who accompanied him. The Minnetarees, or Big Bellies, were alarmed at the tales told them by the Mandans, viz., that we intended to join the Sioux to cut them off in the course of the winter. Many circumstances combined to give force to those reports, i.e., the movements of the interpreters and their families to the Fort, the strength of our work, &c. All those reports were contradicted by Captain Lewis with a conviction on the minds of the Indians of the falsity of those reports.

The Indians in all the towns and camps treated Captain Lewis and the party with great respect, except one of the principal chiefs, Marparpaparrapasatoo, or Horned Weasel, who did not choose to be seen by the Captain, and left word that he was not at home, &c. Seven traders arrived from the fort on the Assiniboine from the N.W. Company, one of which, LaFrance, took upon himself to speak unfavorably of our intentions, &c. The principal, Mr. Larocque, and Mr. McKenzie [10] were informed of the conduct of their interpreter and the consequences, if they did not put a step to unfavorable and ill-founded assertions, &c.

28th Nov., 1804

A cold morning. Wind from the N.W. River full of floating ice. Began to snow at 7 o'clock, A.M., and continued all day. At eight o'clock, the Posscossohe, Black Cat, grand chief of the Mandans, came to see us. After showing these chiefs many things which were curiosities to them, and giving a few presents of curious handkerchiefs, arm bands, and paint, with a twist of tobacco, they departed at 1 o'clock much pleased. At parting we had some little talk on the subject of the British trader, Mr. Larocque giving medals and flags, and told those chiefs to impress it on the minds of their nations that those symbols were not to be received by any from them, without they wished to incur the pleasure of their Great American Father. A very disagreeable day. No work done today. River fell 1 inch today.

[10] Antoine Larocque, Charles McKenzie, and Baptiste LaFrance were Canadian traders who, with four voyageurs, had come overland from Canada. Lewis let them use Charbonneau as interpreter, having first stipulated that the man was not to translate any remark unfavorable to the United States. Canadian traders at this time were much alarmed at the prospect of the business rivalry of American traders, who did, in fact, follow the Lewis and Clark Expedition, as the Canadians had feared.

29th November, 1804

A very cold windy day. Wind from the N.W. by W. Some snow last night. The depth of the snow is various in the woods, about 13 inches. The river closed at the village above, and fell last night two feet. Mr. Larocque and one of his men came to visit us. We informed him what we had heard of his intentions of making chiefs, &c., and forbade him to give medals or flags to the Indians. He denied having any such intention. We agreed that one of our interpreters should speak for him on condition he did not say anything more than what tended to trade alone. He gave fair promises, &c.

Sergeant Pryor, in taking down the mast, put his shoulder out of place. We made four trials before we replaced it. A cold afternoon. Wind as usual N.W. River began to rise a little.

30th of November, 1804

This morning at 8 o'clock, an Indian called from the other side, and informed that he had something of consequence to communicate. We sent a pirogue for him, and he informed us as follows: "Five men of the Mandan nation, out hunting in a S.W. direction about eight leagues, were surprised by a large party of Sioux and Pawnees. One man was killed and two wounded with arrows, and 9 horses taken; 4 of the Wetersoon nation were missing, and they expected to be attacked by the Sioux, &c." We thought it well to show a disposition to aid and assist them against their enemies, particularly those who came in opposition to our councils. And I determined to go to the town with some men and, if the Sioux were coming to attack the nation, to collect the warriors from each village and meet them. Those ideas were also those of Captain Lewis.

I crossed the river in about an hour after the arrival of the Indian express with 23 men including the interpreters, and flanked the town and came up on the back part. The Indians, not expecting to receive such strong aid in so short a time, were much surprised, and a little alarmed at the formidable appearance of my party. The principal chiefs met me some distance from the town (say 200 yards) and invited me in to town. I ordered my party into different lodges, &c. I explained to the nation the cause of my coming in this formidable manner to their town was to assist and chastise the enemies of our dutiful children. I requested the grand chief to repeat the circumstances as they happened, which he did, as was mentioned by the express in the morning.

I then informed them that if they would assemble their warriors and those of the different towns, I would go to meet the army of Sioux, &c., and chastise them for taking the blood of our dutiful children, &c. After a conversation of a few minutes among themselves, one chief—The Big Man, a Cheyenne—said they now saw that what we had told them was the truth: that when we expected the enemies of their nation were coming to attack them, or had spilled their blood, we were ready to protect them, and kill those who would not listen to our good talk. His people had listened to what we had told them, and fearlessly went out to hunt in small parties believing themselves to be safe from the other nations, and were killed by the Pawnees and Sioux.

"I knew," said he, "that the Pawnees were liars, and told the old chief who came with you (to confirm a peace with us) that his people were liars and bad men, and that we killed them like the buffalo—when we pleased. We had made peace several times and your nation has always commenced the war. We do not want to kill you, and will not suffer you to kill us or steal our horses. We will make peace with you as our two fathers have directed, and they shall see that we will not be the aggressors. But we fear the Arikaras will not be at peace long. My father, those are the words I spoke to the Arikaras in your presence. You see they have not opened their ears to your good counsels, but have spilled our blood.

"Two Arikaras, whom we sent home this day, for fear of our people's killing them in their grief, informed us when they came here several days ago, that two towns of the Arikaras were making their moccasins, and that we had best take care of our horses, &c. Numbers of Sioux were in their towns and, they believed, not well disposed toward us. Four of the Wetersoons are now absent. They were to have been back in 16 days; they have been out 24. We fear they have fallen. My father, the snow is deep and it is cold. Our horses cannot travel through the plains. Those people who have spilt our blood have gone back. If you will go with us in the spring after the snow goes off, we will raise the warriors of all the towns and nations around about us, and go with you."

I told this nation that we should be always willing and ready to defend them from the insults of any nation who would dare to come to do them injury, during the time we remained in their neighborhood, and requested that they would inform us of any party who might at any time be discovered by their patrols or scouts. I was sorry that the snow in the plains had fallen so deep since the murder of the young chief by the Sioux as prevented their horses from traveling. I wished to meet those Sioux and all others who will not open their ears, but make war on our dutiful children, and let you see that the warriors of your Great Father will chastise the enemies of his dutiful children the Mandans, Wetersoons, and Minnetarees, who have opened their ears to his advice. You say that the Pawnees or Arikaras were with the Sioux. Some bad men may have been with the Sioux. You know there are bad men in all nations. Do not get mad with the Arikaras until we know if those bad men are countenanced by their nation, and we are convinced those people do not intend to follow our counsels. You know that the Sioux have great influence over the Arikaras, and perhaps have led some of them astray. You know that the Arikaras are dependent on the Sioux for their guns, powder, and ball; and it was policy in them to keep on as good terms as possible with the Sioux until they had some other means of getting those articles, &c. You know yourselves that you are compelled to put up with little insults from the Crees and Assiniboines (or Stone Indians) because if you go to war with those people, they will prevent the traders in the north from bringing you guns, powder, and ball, and by that means distress you very much. But when you will have certain supplies from your Great American Father of all those articles, you will not suffer any nation to insult you, &c.

After about two hours' conversation on various subjects, all of which tended toward their situation, &c., I informed them I should return to the Fort. The chief said they all thanked me very much for the fatherly protection which I showed toward them; that the village had been crying all the night and day for the death of the brave young man who fell, but now they would wipe away their tears and rejoice in their father's protection, and cry no more.

I then paraded and crossed the river on the ice, and came down on the north side. The snow so deep, it was very fatiguing. Arrived at the Fort after night, gave a little taffee [11] [dram] to my party. A cold night. The river rose to

---

[11] "Taffee," or "taffia," was a local rum, which frontiersmen drank when they could get nothing else. The other Lieutenant William Clark, cousin of the explorer, testified at a court-martial during the Revolution that his commanding officer, a certain Captain George, drank too much at night "during the time the Taffia lasted." In this Revolutionary command, the quartermaster was issuing two quarts a day to each officer! Lewis and Clark were always careful to issue a very small liquor ration.

its former height. The chief frequently thanked me for coming to protect them; and the whole village appeared thankful for that measure.

1st of December, 1804

Wind from the N.W. All hands engaged in getting pickets, &c. At 10 o'clock, the half-brother of the man who was killed came and informed us that, after my departure last night, six Chiens [Cheyennes]—so called by the French— or Sharha Indians, had arrived with a pipe, and said that their nation was at one day's march and intended to come and trade, &c. Three Pawnees had also arrived from the nation. Their nation was then within 3 days' march, and were coming on to trade with us. Three Pawnees accompanied these Cheyennes. The Mandans call all Arikaras Pawnees; they don't use the name of Arikaras, but the Arikaras call themselves Arikaras. The Mandans apprehended danger from the Sharhas, as they were at peace with the Sioux; and wished to kill them and the Arikaras (or Pawnees), but the chiefs informed the nation it was our wish that they should not be hurt and forbid their being killed, &c. We gave a little tobacco, &c., and this man departed, well satisfied with our counsels and advice to him.

In the evening a Mr. G. Henderson arrived, in the employ of the Hudson's Bay Company, sent to trade with the Gros Ventres, or Big Bellies, so called by the French traders.

3rd December, 1804

A fine morning. The after part of the day cold and windy, the wind from the N.W. The father of the Mandan who was killed came and made us a present of some dried pumpkins and a little pemmican. We made him some small presents, for which he was much pleased.

7th of December, 1804

A very cold day. Wind from the N.W. The Big White, grand chief of the first village, came and informed us that a large drove of buffalo was near, and his people were waiting for us to join them in a chase. Captain Lewis took 15 men and went out and joined the Indians who were, at the time he got up, killing the buffalo, on horseback with arrows, which they did with great dexterity. His party killed 10 buffalo, five of which we got to the fort by the assistance of a horse, in addition to what the men packed on their backs. One cow was killed on the ice. After drawing her out of a vacancy in the ice in which she had fallen, we butchered her at the fort. Those we did not get in were taken by the Indians under a custom which is established among them, i.e., any person seeing a buffalo lying, without an arrow sticking in him or some particular mark, takes possession. Many times, as I am told, a hunter who kills many buffalo in a chase only gets a part of one. All meat which is left out all night falls to the wolves, which are in great numbers, always in the neighborhood of the buffaloes. The river closed, opposite the Fort, last night—1½ inches thick. The thermometer stood this morning at 1 degree below zero. Three men were frostbitten badly today.

9th December, 1804

The thermometer stood this morning at 7 degrees above zero. Wind from the E. Captain Lewis took 18 men and 4 horses [3 hired, 1 bought] and went out to send in the meat killed yesterday, and kill more. The sun shone today clear. Both interpreters went to the villages today. At 12 o'clock, two chiefs came, loaded with meat; one with a dog and sleigh also loaded with meat. Captain Lewis sent 4 horses loaded with meat. He continued at the hunting camp near which they killed 9 buffalo.

10th Dec., 1804. Fort Mandan

A very cold day. The thermometer today at 10 and 11 degrees below zero. Captain Lewis returned today at 12 o'clock, leaving 6 men at the camp to prepare the meat for to pack. Four horse loads came in. Captain Lewis had a cold. Disagreeable last night in the snow, on a cold point with one small blanket. The buffalo crossed the river below in immense herds without breaking in. Only 2 buffalo killed today, one of which was too poor to skin. The men who were frostbitten are getting better. The river rose 1½ inch. Wind north.

16th December, 1804

A clear cold morning. The thermometer at sunrise stood

at 22 degrees below zero. A very singular appearance of the moon last night, as she appeared through the frosty atmosphere. Mr. Heney [12] from the establishment on the river Assiniboine, with a letter from Mr. Charles Chaboillez, one of the Company, arrived in six days. Mr. C., in his letter, expressed a great anxiety to serve us in anything in his power.

A root described by Mr. Heney for the cure of a mad dog.

Mr. Larocque, a clerk of the N.W. Company, and Mr. George Bunch, a clerk of the Hudson's Bay Company, accompanied Mr. Heney from the village.

17th December, 1804

A very cold morning. The thermometer stood at 45 degrees below zero. We found Mr. Heney a very intelligent man, from whom we obtained some sketches of the country between the Mississippi and Missouri, and some sketches from him which he had obtained from the Indians to the west of this place, also the names and characters of the Sioux, &c. About 8 o'clock P.M., the thermometer fell to 74 degrees below the freezing point. The Indian chiefs sent word that buffalo were in our neighborhood, and if we would join them in the morning, they would go and kill them.

18th December, 1804

The thermometer the same as last night. Messrs. Heney and Larocque left us for the Gros Ventres' camp. Sent out seven men to hunt for the buffalo. They found the weather too cold, and returned. Several Indians came who had set out with a view to kill buffalo. The river rose a little. I employ myself making a small map of connection, &c. Sent Jussome to the main chief of the Mandans to know the cause of his detaining or taking a horse of Charbonneau's, our Big Belly interpreter, which, we found, was through the rascality of

---

[12] Hugh Heney had been a partner of the St. Louis trader Régis Loisel, and may still have been a partner at this time. Tabeau, who assisted the expedition among the Arikaras, was a Loisel employee. Chaboillez was agent for the North-West Company on the Assiniboine River. He had obviously been alerted by Larocque and had come down to the Mandans to see what the Americans were doing.

Needless to say, there is no herb whose root cures hydrophobia.

one LaFrance, a trader from the N.W. Company, who told this chief that Charbonneau owed him a horse—to go and take him. He did so, agreeable to an Indian custom. He gave up the horse.

19th December, 1804

The wind from the S.W. The weather moderated a little. I engage myself in connecting the country,[13] from information. River rose a little.

21st December, 1804

A fine day; warm, and wind from the N.W. by W. The Indian whom I stopped from committing murder on his wife, through jealousy of one of our interpreters, came and brought his two wives, and showed great anxiety to make up with the man with whom his jealousy sprang. A woman brought a child with an abscess on the lower part of the back, and offered as much corn as she could carry for some medicine. Captain Lewis administered, &c.

25th December, Christmas, 1804

I was awakened before day by a discharge of three platoons from the party, and the French. The men merrily disposed. I gave them all a little taffia and permitted three cannon fired at the raising of our flag. Some men went out to hunt, and the others to dancing and continued until 9 o'clock P.M., when the frolic ended, &c.

---

[13] By "connecting the country," Clark means posting new information on his map. His originals are now in the Yale University Library.

Chapter VI

LEAVING THE MANDANS

December 28, 1804—March 21, 1805

Fort Mandan on the N.E. bank
of the Missouri, 1,600 miles up,
January the 1st, 1805

[Clark]

The day was ushered in by the discharge of two cannon.
We suffered 16 men with their music to visit the first village
for the purpose of dancing, by—as they said—the particular
request of the chiefs of that village. About 11 o'clock, I
with an interpreter and two men, walked up to the village.
My views were to allay some little misunderstanding which
had taken place through jealousy and mortification as to
our treatment toward them. I found them much pleased at
the dancing of our men. I ordered my black servant to dance,
which amused the crowd very much, and somewhat astonished them that so large a man should be active, &c. I went
into the lodges of all the men of note, except two, who I
heard had made some expressions not favorable toward us,
in comparing us with the traders of the north. Those chiefs
observed to us that what they said was in jest and laughter.

2nd of January, 1805

A snowy morning. A party of men go to dance at the
second village. Captain Lewis and the interpreter visit the
second village, and return in the evening. Some snow today.
Very cold in the evening.

5th of January, 1805

A cold day. Some snow. Several Indians visit us with their

axes, to get them mended. I employ myself drawing a connection of the country from what information I have received. A buffalo dance (or medicine) for three nights past, in the first village. A curious custom: The old men arrange themselves in a circle, and after smoking a pipe which is handed them by a young man dressed up for the purpose, the young men who have their wives back of the circle go each to one of the old men and, with a whining tone, request the old man to take his wife, who presents herself naked, except a robe, and sleep with her. The girl then takes the old man (who very often can scarcely walk) and leads him to a convenient place for the business, after which they return to the lodge. If the old man (or a white man) returns to the lodge without gratifying the man and his wife, he offers her again and again. It is often the case that, after the second time without kissing, the husband throws a new robe over the old man, &c., and begs him not to despise him and his wife. We sent a man to this medicine dance last night, and they gave him four girls. All this is to cause the buffalo to come near, so that they may kill them.[1]

10th of January, 1805

Last night was excessively cold. The mercury this morning stood at 40 degrees below zero, which is 72 degrees below freezing point. We had one man out last night who returned about 8 o'clock this morning. The Indians of the lower village turned out to hunt for a man and a boy who had not returned from the hunt of yesterday, and borrowed a sleigh to bring them in, expecting to find them frozen to death. About 10 o'clock, the boy—about 13 years of age—came to the Fort with his feet frozen. He had lain out last night without fire, with only a buffalo robe to cover him. The dress which he wore was a pair of antelope leggings, which is very thin, and moccasins. We had his feet put in cold water, and they are coming to. Soon after the arrival of the boy, a man came in who had also stayed out without fire, and very thinly

---

[1] This was an ordinary primitive fertility rite, but it naturally made the Mandan camps popular among white traders. The prim David Thompson in 1797 described the Mandan girls as "a sett of handsome tempting women," and Clark in his later years described them as "the handsomest women in the world." Other American soldiers joined in the fertility rites, besides the man Clark mentions, and were, says a trader who was also present, "untiringly zealous in attracting the cow." Whatever the cause, the buffalo appeared promptly in the following season.

clothed. This man was not in the least injured. Customs, and the habits of those people, have inured them to bear more cold than I thought it possible for man to endure. Sent out 3 men to hunt elk, below, about 7 miles.

13th of January, 1805

A cold, clear day. Great numbers of Indians move down the river to hunt. Those people kill a number of buffalo near their villages and save a great proportion of the meat. Their custom of making this article of life general [2] leaves them more than half of their time without meat. Their corn and beans, &c., they keep for the summer, and as a reserve in case of an attack from the Sioux, of which they are always in dread, and seldom go far to hunt except in large parties. About ½ the Mandan nation passed today, to hunt on the river below. They will stay out some days. Mr. Charbonneau, our interpreter, and one man who accompanied him to some lodges of the Minnetarees near the Turtle Hill, returned, both frozen in their faces. Charbonneau informs me that the clerk of the Hudson's Bay Company, with the Minnetarees, has been speaking some few expressions unfavorable toward us, and that it is said the N.W. Company intends building a fort at the Minnetarees. He saw the Grand Chief of the Big Bellies, who spoke slightingly of the Americans, saying if we would give our great flag to him he would come to see us.

14th of January, 1805

This morning early a number of Indians, men, women, children, dogs, &c., passed down on the ice to join those that passed yesterday. We sent Sergeant Pryor and five men with those Indians to hunt. Several men with the venereal, caught from the Mandan women. One of our hunters, sent out several days ago, arrived and informs that one man—Whitehouse—is frostbitten and can't walk home.

16th January, 1805

About thirty Mandans came to the fort today; 6 chiefs.

---

[2] It was a matter of pride, among many tribes, for a hunter to be generous with his kill, if others lacked meat. A successful hunter's family might, therefore, as Clark suggests, suffer from sharing with other members of the tribe.

Those Minnetarees told them they were liars; had told them
if they came to the fort the white men would kill them.
They had been with them all night, smoked the pipe and
have been treated well, and the whites had danced for them,
observing the Mandans were bad, and ought to hide themselves. One of the first war chiefs of the Big Bellies' nation
came to see us today, with one man and his squaw to wait
on him. Requested that she might be used for the night. His
wife handsome. We shot the air gun and gave two shots with
the cannon, which pleased them very much. The Little Crow,
second chief of the lower village, came and brought us corn,
&c. Four men of ours, who had been hunting, returned; one
frosted.

This war chief gave us a chart, in his way, of the Missouri.
He informed us of his intentions of going to war in the
spring against the Snake Indians. We advised him to look
back at the number of nations who had been destroyed by
war, and reflect upon what he was about to do; observing, if
he wished, the happiness of his nation, he would be at
peace with all. By that, by being at peace, and having plenty
of goods amongst them, and a free intercourse with those
defenseless nations, they would get, on easy terms, a greater
number of horses; and that nation would increase. If he
went to war against those defenseless people, he would displease his Great Father, and he would not receive that protection and care from him, as other nations who listened
to his word. This chief, who is a young man 26 years old,
replied that if his going to war against the Snake Indians
would be displeasing to us, he would not go.

7th February, 1805

[Lewis]

This morning was fair. Thermometer at 18 degrees above
zero. Much warmer than it has been for some days. Wind
S.E. Continue to be visited by the natives. The sergeant of
the guard reported that the Indian women (wives to our interpreters) were in the habit of unbarring the fort gate at any
time of night and admitting their Indian visitors. I therefore
directed a lock to be put to the gate, and ordered that no
Indian but those attached to the garrison should be permitted
to remain all night within the fort, or admitted during the
period which the gate had been previously ordered to be
kept shut, which was from sunset until sunrise.

9th February, 1805

This morning fair and pleasant. Wind from the S.E. Visited by Mr. McKenzie, one of the N.W. Company's clerks. This evening, a man by the name of Howard, whom I had given permission to go to the Mandan village, returned after the gate was shut, and rather than call to the guard to have it opened, scaled the works. An Indian who was looking on, shortly after followed his example. I convinced the Indian of the impropriety of his conduct, and explained to him the risk he had run of being severely treated. The fellow appeared much alarmed. I gave him a small piece of tobacco, and sent him away. Howard I had committed to the care of the guard, with a determination to have him tried by a court-martial for this offense. This man is an old soldier, which still heightens this offense.

11th February, 1805

The party that were ordered last evening set out early this morning. The weather was fair and cold. Wind N.W. About five o'clock this evening, one of the wives of Charbonneau was delivered of a fine boy.[3] It is worthy of remark that this was the first child which this woman had born, and as is common in such cases her labor was tedious and the pain violent. Mr. Jussome informed me that he had frequently administered a small portion of the rattle of the rattlesnake, which he assured me had never failed to produce the desired effect—that of hastening the birth of the child. Having the rattle of a snake by me, I gave it to him, and he administered two rings of it to the woman, broken in small pieces with the fingers, and added to a small quantity of water. Whether this medicine was truly the cause or not, I shall not undertake to determine. But I was informed that she had not taken it more than ten minutes, before she brought forth. Perhaps this remedy may be worthy of future experiments, but I must confess that I want faith as to its efficacy.

[3] The mother was, of course, Sacagawea, and the child she now bore was the indestructible baby that the Lewis and Clark Expedition carried across the continent and back. The ground-up rattlesnake rattle, being merely chitin, had no therapeutic value, but it may have had some use as a faith cure.

12th February, 1805

This morning was fair though cold. Thermometer 14 degrees below zero. Wind S.E. Ordered the blacksmith to shoe the horses, and some others to prepare some gears in order to send them down with three sleighs to join the hunting party, and transport the meat which they may have procured, to this place. The men whom I had sent for the meat left by Charbonneau did not return until 4 o'clock this evening.

Drouilliard arrived with the horses about the same time. The horses appeared much fatigued. I directed some bran be given them, moistened with a little water, but to my astonishment found that they would not eat it, but preferred the bark of the cottonwood, which forms the principal article of food usually given them by their Indian masters in the winter season. For this purpose, they cause the tree to be felled by their women, and the horses feed on the boughs and bark of their tender branches. The Indians in our neighborhood are frequently pilfered of their horses by the Arikaras, Sioux, and Assiniboines, and therefore make it an invariable rule to put their horses in their lodges at night. In this situation, the only food of the horses consists of a few sticks of the cottonwood, from the size of a man's finger to that of his arm.

21st February, 1805

[Clark]

A delightful day. Put out our clothes to sun. Visited by The Big White and Big Man. They informed me that several men of their nation were gone to consult their medicine stone, about 3 days' march to the southwest, to know what was to be the result of the ensuing year. They have great confidence in this stone, and say that it informs them of everything which is to happen, and visit it every spring and sometimes in the summer. "They, having arrived at the stone, give it smoke, and proceed to the woods at some distance to sleep. The next morning, return to the stone, and find marks white and raised on the stone, representing the peace or war which they are to meet with, and other changes which they are to meet." This stone has a level surface about 20 feet in circumference, thick and porous, and no doubt has some mineral qualities affected by the sun.

The Big Bellies have a stone to which they ascribe nearly the same virtues.

Captain Lewis returned with 2 sleighs loaded with meat. After finding that he could not overtake the Sioux war party, (who had in their way destroyed all the meat at one deposit which I had made, and burned the lodges), determined to proceed on to the lower deposit which he found had not been observed by the Sioux. He hunted two days; killed 36 deer and 14 elk, several of them so meager that they were unfit for use. The meat which he killed and that in the lower deposit, amounting to about 3,000 pounds, was brought up on two sleighs; one, drawn by 16 men, had about 2,400 pounds on it.

25th of February, 1805

We fixed a windlass and drew up the two pirogues on the upper bank, and attempted the boat; but the rope, which we had made of elk skins, proved too weak, and broke several times. Night coming on obliged us to leave her in a situation but little advanced. We were visited by the Black Moccasin, chief of the little village of the Big Bellies, the chief of the Shoe Indians, and a number of others. Those chiefs gave us some meat which they packed on their wives; and one requested an ax to be made for his son, Mr. Root Bunch, one of the under traders for the Hudson's Bay Company. One of the Big Bellies asked leave for himself and his two wives to stay all night, which was granted. Also two boys stayed all night, one the son of The Black Cat.

This day has been exceedingly pleasant.

26th February, 1805

A fine day. Commenced very early in making preparations for drawing up the boat on the bank. At sunset, by repeated exertions the whole day, we accomplished this troublesome task. Just as we were fixed for hauling the boat, the ice gave way near us for about 100 yards in length. A number of Indians here today to see the boat rise on the bank.

28th of February, 1805

A fine morning. Two men of the N.W. Company arrived with letters, and sackacomah [sacacommis], also a root and top of a plant, presented by Mr. Heney, for the cure of mad dogs, snakes, &c., and to be found and used as follows, viz., "this root is found on the high lands and ascent of hills. The way of using it is to scarify the part when bitten; to chew or pound an inch, or more if the root is small, and apply it to the bitten part, renewing it twice a day. The bitten person is not to chew or swallow any of the root, for it might have contrary effect."

Sent out 16 men to make four pirogues. Those men returned in the evening, and informed that they found trees they thought would answer.

Mr. Gravelines, two Frenchmen, and two Indians arrived from the Arikara nation, with letters from Mr. Anthony Tabeau [*Pierre Antoine Tabeau*], informing us of the peaceable dispositions of that nation toward the Mandans and Minnetarees, and their avowed intentions of pursuing our counsels and advice. They express a wish to visit the Mandans, and to know if it will be agreeable to them to admit the Arikaras to settle near them, and join them against their common enemy, the Sioux. We mentioned this to the Mandans, who observed they had always wished to be at peace and good neighbors with the Arikaras, and it is also the sentiment of all the Big Bellies and Shoe nations.

Mr. Gravelines informs that the Sissetons and the 3 upper bands of the Tetons, with the Yanktons of the north, intend to come to war in a short time against the nations in this quarter, and will kill every white man they see. Mr. Tabeau also informs that Mr. Cameron of St. Peters has put arms into the hands of the Sioux, to revenge the death of 3 of his men killed by the Chippewas, latterly; and that the band of Tetons which we saw is disposed to do as we have advised them, through the influence of their chief, Black Buffalo.

Mr. Gravelines further informs that the party which robbed us of the two horses latterly, were all Sioux—106 in number. They called at the Arikaras on their return. The Arikaras, being displeased at their conduct, would not give then anything to eat, that being the greatest insult they could possibly offer them, and upbraided them.

9th of March, 1805

A cloudy, cold, and windy morning. Wind from the north. I walked up to see the party that is making pirogues, about 5 miles above this. The wind hard and cold. On my way up, I met Le Borgne, main chief of the Minnetarees, with four Indians on their way to see us. I requested him to proceed on to the Fort, where he would find Captain Lewis. I should be there myself in the course of a few hours. Sent the interpreter back with him, and proceeded on myself to the canoes. Found them nearly finished. The timber very bad. After visiting all the pirogues, where I found a number of Indians, I went to the upper Mandan village and smoked a pipe (the greatest mark of friendship and attention) with the chief, and returned. On my return, found the Minnetaree chief about to set out on his return to his village, having received of Captain M. Lewis, a medal, gorget, arm bands, a flag shirt, scarlet, &c., for which he was much pleased. Those things were given in place of sundry articles sent to him which, he says, he did not receive. Two guns were fired for this great man.

11th of March, 1805

We have every reason to believe that our Minnetaree interpreter (whom we intended to take, with his wife, as an interpreter through his wife, to the Snake [*Shoshone*] Indians, of which nation she is) has been corrupted by the [blank in MS.] Company.[4] Some explanation has taken place which clearly proves to us the fact. We give him tonight to reflect, and determine whether or not he intends to go with us, under the regulations stated.

12th

A fine day. Some snow last night. Our interpreter, Charbonneau, determines on not proceeding with us as an interpreter under the terms mentioned yesterday. He will not agree to work, let our situation be what it may, nor stand guard, and, if miffed with any man, he wishes to return when he pleases, also [*to*] have the disposal of as much provisions as he chooses to carry. Inadmissible. And we suffer him to be off the engagement, which was only verbal.

[4] The appearance of Lewis and Clark greatly disturbed the Canadian fur traders, who feared American competition, of which they correctly believed the expedition was a forerunner. Hence this covert effort to make difficulties. The blank in the MS. evidently means that the explorers were not sure which fur company was responsible, the Hudson's Bay Company or the North-West Company.

17th of March

A windy day. Attempted to air our goods, &c. Mr. Charbonneau sent a Frenchman of our party [to say] that he was sorry for the foolish part he had acted, and if we pleased, he would accompany us agreeable to the terms we had proposed, and do everything we wished him to do, &c. He had requested me some [*sic*], through our French interpreter, two days ago, to excuse his simplicity, and take him into the service. After he had taken his things across the river, we called him in and spoke to him on the subject. He agreed to our terms, and we agreed that he might go on with us.

Chapter *VII*

TO THE YELLOWSTONE
March 22—April 27, 1805

29th [28th] of March, [Thursday], 1805

[Clark]

The ice has stopped running, owing to some obstacle above. Repaired the boat and pirogues, and preparing to set out. But few Indians visited us today. They are now attending on the river bank to catch the floating buffalo.

30th [29th] of March, 1805

The obstacle broke away above, and the ice came down in great quantities. The river rose 13 inches the last 24 hours. I observed extraordinary dexterity of the Indians in jumping from one cake of ice to another, for the purpose of catching the buffalo as they float down. Many of the cakes of ice which they pass over are not two feet square. The plains are on fire in view of the Fort, on both sides of the river. It is said to be common for the Indians to burn the plains near their villages, every spring, for the benefit of their horses, and to induce the buffalo to come near them.

31st [30th] of March, 1805

Sergeant Ordway now here. Cloudy day. Several gangs of geese and ducks pass up the river. But a small portion of ice floating down today. But few Indians visited us today. All the party in high spirits. They pass but few nights without amusing themselves dancing, possessing perfect harmony and good understanding toward each other. Generally healthy except venereal complaints, which are very common among the natives, and the men catch it from them.

April the 1st, 1805

The fore part of today hail, rain, with thunder and lightning. The rain continued with intermissions all day. It is worthy of remark that this is the first rain which has fallen since we have been here, or since the 15 of October last, except a few drops at two or three different times. Had the boat, pirogues, and canoes all put into the water.

Fort Mandan, April 7th, 1805

[Lewis]

Having on this day at 4 P.M. completed every arrangement necessary for our departure, we dismissed the barge and crew, with orders to return without loss of time to St. Louis. A small canoe with two French hunters accompanied the barge. These men had ascended the Missouri with us the last year as *engagés*. The barge crew consisted of six soldiers and two [blank space in MS.] Frenchmen. Two Frenchmen and an Arikara Indian also take their passage in her as far as the Arikara villages, at which place we expect Mr. Tabeau to embark, with his peltry, who, in that case, will make an addition of two, perhaps four, men to the crew of the barge.

We gave Richard Warfington, a discharged corporal, the charge of the barge and crew, and confided to this care likewise our dispatches to the government, letters to our private friends, and a number of articles to the President of the United States. One of the Frenchmen, by the name of Joseph Gravelines, an honest, discreet man, and an excellent boatman, is employed to conduct the barge as a pilot. We have therefore every hope that the barge and, with her, our dispatches will arrive safe at St. Louis. Mr. Gravelines, who speaks the Arikara language extremely well, has been employed to conduct a few of the Arikara chiefs to the seat of government, who have promised us to descend in the barge to St. Louis with that view.

At the same moment that the barge departed from Fort Mandan, Captain Clark embarked with our party and proceeded up the river. As I had used no exercise for several weeks, I determined to walk on shore as far as our encampment of this evening. Accordingly I continued my walk on the north side of the river about six miles, to the upper village of the Mandans, and called on The Black Cat, or Posecopsehá, the Great Chief of the Mandans. He was not at home. I rested myself a few minutes and, finding that the party had not arrived, I returned about two miles and joined them at their encampment on the N. side of the river opposite the lower Mandan village.

Our party now consisted of the following individuals: [1]

Sergeants:	John Ordway
	Nathaniel Pryor
	Patrick Gass
Privates:	William Bratton
	John Colter
	Reuben Fields
	Joseph Fields
	John Shields
	George Gibson
	George Shannon
	John Potts
	John Collins
	Joseph Whitehouse
	Richard Windsor
	Alexander Willard
	Hugh Hall
	Silas Goodrich
	Robert Frazer
	Peter Cruzat
	John Baptiste Lepage
	Francis Labiche
	Hugh McNeil
	William Warner
	Thomas P. Howard
	Peter Wiser
	John B. Thompson

Interpreters: George Drouilliard and Toussaint Charbonneau; also a black man by the name of York, servant to Captain

[1] Though some of these men had been court-martialed, their officers evidently believed in them, for they retained them. Lewis says specifically that he believed in the sincerity of Newman's repentance; but mutiny was too serious an offense to overlook, and he was sent back from the Mandan village.

Clark; an Indian woman, wife to Charbonneau, with a young child; and a Mandan man who had promised us to accompany us as far as the Snake Indians, with a view to bring about a good understanding and friendly intercourse between that nation and his own, the Minnetarees and Amahamis.

Our vessels consisted of six small canoes and two large pirogues. This little fleet, although not quite so respectable as that of Columbus or Captain Cook, was still viewed by us with as much pleasure as those deservedly famed adventurers ever beheld theirs, and, I daresay, with quite as much anxiety for their safety and preservation. We were now about to penetrate a country at least two thousand miles in width, on which the foot of civilized man had never trod. The good or evil it had in store for us was for experiment yet to determine, and these little vessels contained every article by which we were to expect to subsist or defend ourselves. However, as the state of mind in which we are, generally gives the coloring to events, when the imagination is suffered to wander into futurity, the picture which now presented itself to me was a most pleasing one.

Entertaining as I do the most confident hope of succeeding in a voyage which had formed a darling project of mine for the last ten years, I could but esteem this moment of my departure as among the most happy of my life. The party are in excellent health and spirits, zealously attached to the enterprise, and anxious to proceed. Not a whisper or murmur of discontent to be heard among them, but all act in unison and with the most perfect harmony.

April 13th

Being disappointed in my observations of yesterday for longitude, I was unwilling to remain at the entrance of the river another day for that purpose, and therefore determined to set out early this morning, which we did accordingly. The wind was in our favor after 9 A.M., and continued favorable until 3 P.M. We therefore hoisted both the sails in the white pirogue, consisting of a small square sail and spritsail, which carried her at a pretty good gait until about 2 in the afternoon, when a sudden squall of wind struck us and turned the pirogue so much on the side as to alarm Charbonneau, who was steering at the time.

In this state of alarm, he threw the pirogue with her side to the wind, when the spritsail, jibing, was as near oversetting the pirogue as it was possible to have missed. The wind, however, abating for an instant, I ordered Drouilliard to the helm and the sails to be taken in, which was instantly executed, and the pirogue, being steered before the wind, was again placed in a state of security.

This accident was very near costing us dearly. Believing this vessel to be the most steady and safe, we had embarked on board of it our instruments, papers, medicine, and the most valuable part of the merchandise which we had still in reserve as presents for the Indians. We had also embarked on board ourselves, with three men who could not swim and the squaw with the young child, all of whom, had the pirogue overset, would most probably have perished, as the waves were high, and the pirogue upwards of 200 yards from the nearest shore. However, we fortunately escaped, and pursued our journey under the square sail, which, shortly after the accident, I directed to be again hoisted.

Our party caught 3 beaver last evening, and the French hunters, 7. As there was much appearance of beaver just above the entrance of the Little Missouri, these hunters concluded to remain some days. We therefore left them without the expectation of seeing them again. Just above the entrance of the Little Missouri, the Great Missouri is upwards of a mile in width, though immediately at the entrance of the former it is not more than 200 yards wide and so shallow that the canoes passed it with setting poles.

At the distance of 9 miles, passed the mouth of a creek on the starboard side which we called Onion Creek from the quantity of wild onions which grow in the plains on its borders. Captain Clark, who was on shore, informed me that this creek was 16 yards wide a mile and a half above its entrance, discharges more water than creeks of its size usually do in this open country, and that there was not a stick of timber of any description to be seen on its borders, or the level plain country through which it passes.

Saw some buffalo and elk at a distance today, but killed none of them. We found a number of carcasses of the buffalo lying along shore, which had been drowned by falling through the ice in winter, and lodged on shore by the high water when the river broke up about the first of this month. We saw also many tracks of the white bear of enormous size, along the river shore and about the carcasses of the buffalo, on which I presume they feed.

We have not as yet seen one of these animals, though their tracks are so abundant and recent. The men, as well as ourselves, are anxious to meet with some of these bear. The Indians give a very formidable account of the strength and ferocity of this animal, which they never dare to attack but in parties of six, eight, or ten persons; and are even then frequently defeated with the loss of one or more of their party.

The savages attack this animal with their bows and arrows and the indifferent guns with which the traders furnish them. With these they shoot with such uncertainty and at so short a distance that, unless shot through head or heart, wound not mortal, they frequently miss their aim and fall a sacrifice to the bear. Two Minnetarees were killed during the last winter in an attack on a white bear. This animal is said more frequently to attack a man on meeting with him, than to flee from him. When the Indians are about to go in quest of the white bear, previous to their departure they paint themselves and perform all those superstitious rites commonly observed when they are about to make war upon a neighboring nation.

April 14th, 1805

One of the hunters saw an otter last evening and shot at it, but missed it. A dog came to us this morning, which we supposed to have been lost by the Indians who were recently encamped near the lake that we passed yesterday. The mineral appearances of salts, coal, and sulphur, together with burned hills and pumice stone, still continue. While we remained at the entrance of the Little Missouri, we saw several pieces of pumice stone floating down that stream, a considerable quantity of which had lodged against a point of driftwood a little above its entrance.

Captain Clark walked on shore this morning, and on his return informed me that he had passed through the timbered bottoms on the N. side of the river, and had extended his walk several miles back on the hills. In the bottom lands he had met with several uninhabited Indian lodges built with the boughs of the elm, and in the plains he met with the remains of two large encampments of a recent date, which from the appearance of some hoops of small kegs seen near them, we concluded that they must have been the camps of the Assiniboines, as no other nation who visit this part of the Missouri ever indulge themselves with spirituous liquor. Of this article the Assiniboines are passionately fond, and we are informed that it forms their principal inducement to furnish the British establishments on the Assiniboine River with the dried and pounded meat and grease which they do.

The mineral appearances still continue. Considerable

quantities of bituminous water, about the color of strong lye, trickle down the sides of the hills. This water partakes of the taste of Glauber salts and slightly of alum. While the party halted to take dinner today, Captain Clark killed a buffalo bull. It was meager, and we therefore took the marrowbones and a small proportion of the meat only.

. Near the place we dined, on the larboard side, there was a large village of burrowing squirrels. I have remarked that these animals generally select a southeasterly exposure for their residence, though they are sometimes found in the level plains. Passed an island above which two small creeks fall in on the larboard side; the upper creek largest, which we called Charbonneau's Creek, after our interpreter, who encamped several weeks on it with a hunting party of Indians. This was the highest point to which any white man had ever ascended, except two Frenchmen—one of whom, Lepage, was now with us—who, having lost their way, had straggled a few miles farther, though to what place precisely I could not learn. I walked on shore above this creek and killed an elk, which was so poor that it was unfit for use. I therefore left it, and joined the party at their encampment on the starboard shore a little after dark. On my arrival, Captain Clark informed me that he had seen two white bear pass over the hills shortly after I fired, and that they appeared to run nearly from the place where I shot.

April 15th, 1805

Set out at an early hour this morning. I walked on shore, and Captain Clark continued with the party, it being an invariable rule with us not to be both absent from our vessels at the same time. I passed through the bottoms of the river on the starboard side. They were partially covered with timber, were extensive, level, and beautiful. In my walk, which was about 6 miles, I passed a small rivulet of clear water making down from the hills, which, on tasting, I discovered to be in a small degree brackish. It possessed less of the Glauber salts, or alum, than those little streams from the hills usually do.

In a little pond of water, formed by this rivulet where it entered the bottom, I heard the frogs crying for the first time this season. Their note was the same as that of the small frogs which are common to the lagoons and swamps of the United States. I saw greater quantities of geese feeding in the bottoms, of which I shot one. Saw some deer and elk, but they were remarkably shy. I also met with great numbers of grouse or prairie hens, as they are called by the English traders of the N.W. These birds appeared to be mating; the note of the male is kuck, kuck, kuck, coo, coo, coo. The first part of the note both male and female use when flying. The male also drums with his wings, something like the pheasant, but by no means as loud. After breakfast, Captain Clark walked on the starboard shore.

April 22nd, 1805

Set out at an early hour this morning. Proceeded pretty well until breakfast, when the wind became so hard ahead that we proceeded with difficulty even with the assistance of our towlines. The party halted, and Captain Clark and myself walked to the White Earth River, which approaches the Missouri very near this place, being about 4 miles above its entrance. We found that it contained more water than streams of its size generally do at this season. The water is much clearer than that of the Missouri. The banks of the river are steep and not more than ten or twelve feet high. The bed seems to be composed of mud altogether.

The salts which have been before mentioned as common on the Missouri appear in great quantities along the banks of this river, which are in many places so thickly covered with it that they appear perfectly white. Perhaps it has been from this white appearance of its banks that the river has derived its name. This river is said to be navigable nearly to its source, which is at no great distance from the Saskatchewan, and I think from its size, the direction which it seems to take, and the latitude of its mouth, that there is very good ground to believe that it extends as far north as latitude 50°. This stream passes through an open country generally.

The broken hills of the Missouri, about this place, exhibit large irregular and broken masses of rock and stone; some of which, though 200 feet above the level of the water, seem at some former period to have felt its influence, for they appear smooth as if worn by the agitation of the water. This collection consists of white and gray granite, a brittle black rock, flint, limestone, freestone, some small specimens of an excellent pebble and occasionally broken strata of a stone which appears to be petrified wood. It is of a black color, and makes excellent whetstones. Coal or carbonated wood, pumice stone, lava, and other mineral appearances still continue. The coal appears to be of better quality. I exposed a specimen of it to the fire, and found that it burned tolerably well; it afforded but little flame or smoke, but produced a hot and lasting fire.

I ascended to the top of the cut bluff this morning, from whence I had a most delightful view of the country, the whole of which, except the valley formed by the Missouri, is void of timber or underbrush, exposing to the first glance of the spectator immense herds of buffalo, elk, deer, and antelopes feeding in one common and boundless pasture. We saw a number of beaver feeding on the bark of the trees along the verge of the river, several of which we shot. Found them large and fat.

Walking on shore this evening, I met with a buffalo calf which attached itself to me, and continued to follow close at my heels, until I embarked and left it. It appeared alarmed at my dog, which was probably the cause of its so readily attaching itself to me. Captain Clark informed me that he saw a large drove of buffalo pursued by wolves today; that they at length caught a calf which was unable to keep up with the herd. The cows only defend their young so long as they are able to keep up with the herd, and seldom return any distance in search of them.

April 26th, 1805

This morning I dispatched Joseph Field up the Yellowstone River with orders to examine it as far as he could conveniently and return the same evening. Two others were directed to bring in the meat we had killed last evening, while I proceeded down the river with one man in order to take a view of the confluence of this great river with the Missouri, which we found to be two miles distant, on a direct line N.W., from our encampment. The bottom land on the lower side of the Yellowstone River near its mouth, for about one mile in width, appears to be subject to inundation, while that on the opposite side of the Missouri and the point formed by the junction of these rivers is of the common elevation, say from 12 to 18 feet above the level of the water, and of course not liable to be overflowed except in extreme high water, which does not appear to be very frequent. There is more timber in the neighborhood of the junction of these rivers, and on the Missouri as far below as the White Earth River, than there is on any part of the Missouri above the entrance of the Cheyenne River to this place.

About 12 o'clock I heard the discharge of several guns at the junction of the rivers, which announce to me the arrival of the party with Captain Clark. I afterwards learned that they had fired on some buffalo which they met with at that place, and of which they killed a cow and several calves—the latter now fine veal. I dispatched one of the men to Captain Clark requesting him to send up a canoe to take down the meat we had killed, and our baggage, to his encampment, which was accordingly complied with.

After I had completed my observations in the evening, I walked down and joined the party at their encampment on the point of land formed by the junction of the rivers. Found them all in good health, and much pleased at having arrived at this long-wished-for spot. And, in order to add in some measure to the general pleasure which seemed to pervade our little community, we ordered a dram to be issued to each person. This soon produced the fiddle, and they spent the evening with much hilarity, singing and dancing, and seemed as perfectly to forget their past toils as they appeared regardless of those to come!

In the evening, the man I had sent up the river this morning returned, and reported that he had ascended it about eight miles on a straight line; that he had found it crooked, meandering from side to side of the valley formed by it, which is from four to five miles wide. The current of the river, gentle; and its bed much interrupted and broken by sandbars. At the distance of five miles, he passed a large island well covered with timber; and three miles higher, a large creek falls in on the S.E. side, above a high bluff in which there are several strata of coal. The country bordering on this river, as far as he could perceive—like that of the Missouri—consisted of open plains. He saw several of the big-horned animals in the course of his walk, but they were so shy that he could not get a shot at them. He found a large horn of one of these animals, which he brought with him. The bed of the Yellowstone River is entirely composed of sand and mud, not a stone of any kind to be seen in it near its entrance.

Captain Clark measured these rivers just above their confluence: found the bed of the Missouri 520 yards wide, the water occupying 330. Its channel deep. The Yellowstone River,[2] including its sand bar, 858 yards, of which the water

[2] The expedition made no further exploration of the Yellowstone until Clark passed through the lower valley on the return journey. Even he, however, missed the picturesque country now included in the national park. This was discovered later by John Colter, one of the enlisted men of the expedition, after he had left it to return to the wilds. His subsequent accounts of the

occupied 297 yards. The deepest part, 12 feet. It was falling at this time and appeared to be nearly at its summer tide.

The Indians inform that the Yellowstone River is navigable for pirogues and canoes nearly to its source in the Rocky Mountains, and that in its course, near these mountains, it passes within less than half a day's march of a navigable part of the Missouri. Its extreme sources are adjacent to those of the Missouri, River Platte, and I think probably with some of the south branch of the Columbia River.

April 27th, 1805

This morning I walked through the point formed by the junction of the rivers. The woodland extends about a mile when the rivers approach each other within less than half a mile. Here a beautiful level, low plain commences, and extends up both rivers for many miles, widening as the rivers recede from each other, and extending back half a mile to a plain about 12 feet higher than itself. The low plain appears to be a few inches higher than high-water mark and, of course, will not be liable to be overflowed; though where it joins the high plain, a part of the Missouri, when at its greatest height, passes through a channel 60 or 70 yards wide, and falls into the Yellowstone River.

On the Missouri, about 2½ miles from the entrance of the Yellowstone River and between this high and low plain, a small lake is situated, about 200 yards wide, extending along the edge of the high plain, parallel with the Missouri about one mile. On the point of the high plain, at the lower extremity of this lake, I think would be the most eligible site for an establishment. Between this low plain and the Yellowstone River, there is an extensive body of timbered land extending up the river for many miles. This site recommended is about 400 yards distant from the Missouri, and about double that distance from the River Yellowstone. From it, the high plain, rising very gradually, extends back about three miles to the hills, and continues with the same width between these hills and the timbered land on the Yellowstone River, up that stream, for seven or eight miles; and is one of the handsomest plains I ever beheld.

On the Missouri side, the hills circumscribe its width, and at the distance of three miles up that river from this site,

wonders he had seen were skeptically received, and the Yellowstone National Park was for some time known as "Colter's Hell."

it is not more than 400 yards wide. Captain Clark thinks that the lower extremity of the low plain would be most eligible for this establishment. It is true that it is much nearer both rivers and might answer very well, but I think it rather too low to venture a permanent establishment, particularly if built of brick or other durable materials at any considerable expense. For, so capricious and versatile are these rivers, that it is difficult to say how long it will be until they direct the force of their currents against this narrow part of the low plain, which, when they do, must shortly yield to their influence. In such case, a few years only would be necessary for the annihilation of the plain, and with it the fortification.

I continued my walk on shore. At 11 A.M. the wind became very hard from N.W., insomuch that the pirogues and canoes were unable either to proceed or pass the river to me. I was under the necessity, therefore, of shooting a goose and cooking it for my dinner. The wind abated about 4 P.M., and the party proceeded, though I could not conveniently join them until night.

Although the game is very abundant and gentle, we only kill as much as is necessary for food. I believe that two good hunters could conveniently supply a regiment with provisions. For several days past, we have observed a great number of buffalo lying dead on the shore; some of them entire, and others partly devoured by the wolves and bear. Those animals either drowned during the winter in attempting to pass the river on the ice, or by swimming across, at present, to bluff banks where they are unable to ascend and, feeling themselves too weak to return, remain and perish for the want of food. In this situation we met with several little parties of them.

Beaver are very abundant. The party kill several of them every day. The eagles, magpies, and geese have their nests in trees adjacent to each other. The magpie particularly appears fond of building near the eagle, as we scarcely see an eagle's nest unaccompanied with two or three magpie's nests within a short distance. The bald eagles are more abundant here than I ever observed them in any part of the country.

Chapter VIII

FROM THE YELLOWSTONE TO THE MUSSELSHELL

April 28—May 19, 1805

April 29th, 1805

[Lewis]

Set out this morning at the usual hour. The wind was moderate. I walked on shore with one man. About 8 A.M. we fell in with two brown or yellow [white] bear, both of which we wounded. One of them made his escape; the other, after my firing on him, pursued me 70 or 80 yards but fortunately had been so badly wounded that he was unable to pursue so closely as to prevent my charging my gun. We again repeated our fire, and killed him. It was a male, not fully grown. We estimated his weight at 300 pounds, not having the means of ascertaining it precisely.

The legs of this bear are somewhat longer than those of the black, as are its talons and tusks incomparably larger and longer. The testicles, which in the black bear are placed pretty well back between the thighs and contained in one pouch like those of the dog and most quadrupeds, are, in the yellow or brown bear, placed much further forward, and are suspended in separate pouches, from two to four inches asunder. Its color is yellowish brown; the eyes small, black, and piercing. The front of the forelegs near the feet is usually black. The fur is finer, thicker, and deeper than that of the black bear. These are all the particulars in which this animal appeared to me to differ from the black bear. It is a much more furious and formidable animal, and will frequently pursue the hunter when wounded. It is astonishing to see the wounds they will bear before they can be put to death. The Indians may well fear this animal, equipped as they generally are with their bows and arrows or indifferent fusees; but in the hands of skillful riflemen, they are by no means as formidable or dangerous as they have been presented.

Game is still very abundant. We can scarcely cast our eyes in any direction without perceiving deer, elk, buffalo, or antelopes. The quantity of wolves appears to increase in the same proportion. They generally hunt in parties of six, eight, or ten. They kill a great number of the antelopes at this season. The antelopes are yet meager, and the females are big with young. The wolves take them most generally in attempting to swim the river. In this manner, my dog caught one, drowned it, and brought it on shore. They are but clumsy swimmers, though on land, when in good order, they are extremely fleet and durable.

We have frequently seen the wolves in pursuit of the antelope in the plains. They appear to decoy a single one from a flock, and then pursue it, alternately relieving each other, until they take it. On joining Captain Clark, he informed me that he had seen a female and fawn of the big-horned animal;[1] that they ran for some distance with great apparent ease along the side of the river bluff where it was almost perpendicular. Two of the party fired on them while in motion, without effect. We took the flesh of the bear on board and proceeded. Captain Clark walked on shore this evening; killed a deer, and saw several of the big-horned animals.

May 3rd, 1805

The morning being very cold, we did not set out as early as usual. Ice formed on a kettle of water, ¼ of an inch thick. The snow has melted generally in the bottoms, but the hills still remain covered. On the larboard side, at the distance of 2 miles, we passed a curious collection of bushes which had been tied up in the form of a fascine, and standing on end in the open bottom, it appeared to be about 30 feet high and ten or twelve feet in diameter. This we supposed to have been placed there by the Indians, as a sacrifice for some purpose. The wind continued to blow hard from the west, but not so strong as to compel us to lay by.

Captain Clark walked on shore and killed an elk, which he caused to be butchered by the time I arrived with the party. Here we halted and dined, it being about 12 o'clock—our

---

[1] The "big-horned animals" were bighorns, or Rocky Mountain sheep, also called bighorn sheep. At one time called *Ovis cervina*, these are now *Ovis canadensis*. There are several subspecies.

usual time of halting for that purpose. After dinner, Captain Clark pursued his walk while I continued with the party, it being a rule which we had established never to be absent at the same time from the party.

We saw vast quantities of buffalo, elk, deer—principally of the long-tail kind—antelope or goats, beaver, geese, ducks, brant, and some swan. Near the entrance of the river mentioned in the 10th course [2] of this day, we saw an unusual number of porcupines, from which we determined to call the river after that animal, and accordingly denominated it Porcupine River. This stream discharges itself into the Missouri on the starboard side, 2,000 miles above the mouth of the latter. It is a beautiful bold, running stream, 40 yards wide at its entrance. The water is transparent, it being the first of this description that I have yet seen discharge itself into the Missouri.

May 4th, 1805

We were detained this morning until about 9 o'clock in order to repair the rudder irons of the red pirogue, which were broken last evening in landing. We then set out, the wind hard against us. I walked on shore this morning. The weather was more pleasant, the snow had disappeared. The frost seems to have affected the vegetation much less than could have been expected. The leaves of the cottonwood, the grass, the box alder, willow, and the yellow flowering pea seem to be scarcely touched. The rosebushes and honeysuckle seem to have sustained the most considerable injury. The country on both sides of the Missouri continues to be open, level, fertile, and beautiful as far as the eye can reach— which, from some of the eminences, is not short of 30 miles. The river bottoms are very extensive and contain a much greater proportion of timber than usual. The fore part of this day, the river was bordered with timber on both sides, a circumstance which is extremely rare, and the first which has occurred of anything like the same extent since we left the Mandans. In the after part of the day, we passed an extensive beautiful plain on the starboard side which gradually ascended from the river. I saw immense quantities of buffalo in

[2] The "course" was the exact direction of the boat as shown by compass bearings, as in any other navigation. As the river forced frequent changes of course, the journals usually record a series of "courses" each day, together with an estimate of the length of each. The "10th course" was the tenth compass bearing for the day.

every direction, also some elk, deer, and goats. Having an abundance of meat on hand, I passed them without firing on them. They are extremely gentle; the bull buffalo, particularly, will scarcely give way to you. I passed several in the open plain within fifty paces. They viewed me for a moment as something novel, and then very unconcernedly continued to feed. Captain Clark walked on shore this evening, and did not rejoin us until after dark. He struck the river several miles above our camp and came down to us. We saw many beaver, some of which the party shot. We also killed two deer today. Much sign of the brown bear. Passed several old Indian hunting camps in the course of the day.

May 5th, 1805

A fine morning. I walked on shore until after 8 A.M., when we halted for breakfast, and in the course of my walk killed a deer, which I carried about a mile and a half to the river. It was in good order. Soon after setting out, the rudder irons of the white pirogue were broken by her running foul on a sawyer.[3] She was, however, refitted in a few minutes with some tugs of rawhide and nails. As usual, saw a great quantity of game today: buffalo, elk, and goats or antelopes feeding in every direction. We kill whatever we wish. The buffalo furnish us with fine veal and fat beef. We also have venison and beaver tails when we wish them. The flesh of the elk and goat is less esteemed, and certainly is inferior. We have not been able to take any fish for some time past. The country is, as yesterday, beautiful in the extreme. We saw the carcasses of many buffalo lying dead along the shore, partially devoured by the wolves and bear.

Captain Clark found a den of young wolves in the course of his walk today, and also saw a great number of those animals. They are very abundant in this quarter, and are of two species: The small wolf, or burrowing dog of the prairies, are the inhabitants almost invariably of the open plains. They usually associate in bands of ten or twelve, some-

---

[3] "Sawyers," in river parlance, were snags, often whole trees, with one end sunk to the bottom, while the other end "sawed" up and down with the current. Other and more dangerous snags were completely under water. "Sawyers" were dreaded because they might rise suddenly under, or immediately in front of, a boat. Large snags of all kinds would tear the bottom out of a large steamboat and sink her; they were sometimes responsible for the loss of many lives. Though there were as yet no steamboats on western rivers, the snags were nearly as dangerous to ordinary riverboats.

times more, and burrow near some pass or place much frequented by game. Not being able alone to take a deer or goat, they are rarely ever found alone but hunt in bands. They frequently watch and seize their prey near their burrows. In these burrows they raise their young, and to them they also resort when pursued.

When a person approaches them, they frequently bark—their note being precisely that of the small dog. They are of an intermediate size, between that of the fox and dog. Very active, fleet, and delicately formed; the ears large, erect, and pointed; the head long and pointed more like that of the fox; tail long and bushy; the hair and fur also resembles the fox, though [*it*] is much coarser and inferior. They are of a pale, reddish-brown color, the eye of a deep sea-green color, small and piercing. Their talons are rather longer than those of the ordinary wolf, or that common to the Atlantic states, none of which are to be found in this quarter nor, I believe, above the River Platte.

The large wolf found here is not as large as those of the Atlantic states. They are lower and thicker-made, shorter-legged. Their color, which is not affected by the seasons, is a gray or blackish-brown and every intermediate shade from that to a cream-colored white. These wolves resort to the woodlands and are also found in the plains, but never take refuge in the ground or burrow, so far as I have been able to inform myself.

We scarcely see a gang of buffalo without observing a parcel of those faithful shepherds on their skirts, in readiness to take care of the maimed [*and*] wounded. The large wolf never barks, but howls as those of the Atlantic states do.

Captain Clark and Drouilliard killed the largest brown bear this evening which we have yet seen. It was a most tremendous-looking animal, and extremely hard to kill. Notwithstanding he had five balls through his lungs and five others in various parts, he swam more than half the distance across the river, to a sandbar, and it was at least twenty minutes before he died. He did not attempt to attack, but fled, and made the most tremendous roaring from the moment he was shot. We had no means of weighing this monster. Captain Clark thought he would weigh 500 pounds. For my own part, I think the estimate too small by 100 pounds. He measured 8 feet 7½ inches from the nose to the extremity of the hind feet; 5 feet 10½ inches around the breast; 1 foot 11 inches around the middle of the arm; and 3 feet 11 inches around the neck. His talons, which were five in number on each foot, were 4⅜ inches in length. He was in good order.

We therefore divided him among the party, and made them boil the oil and put it in a cask for future use. The oil is as hard as hog's lard when cool—much more so than that of the black bear.

This bear differs from the common black bear in several respects: its talons are much longer and more blunt; its tail shorter; its hair, which is of a reddish or bay brown, is longer, thicker, and finer than that of the black bear; his liver, lungs, and heart are much larger, even in proportion with his size. The heart, particularly, was as large as that of a large ox. His maw was also ten times the size of black bear, and was filled with flesh and fish. His testicles were pendent from the belly and placed four inches asunder in separate bags or pouches. This animal also feeds on roots and almost every species of wild fruit.

May 6th, 1805

Saw a brown bear swim the river above us; he disappeared before we could get in reach of him. I find that the curiosity of our party is pretty well satisfied with respect to this animal. The formidable appearance of the male bear killed on the 5th, added to the difficulty with which they die, even when shot through the vital parts, has staggered the resolution of several of them [*i.e., the men.*] Others, however, seem keen for action with the bear. I expect these gentlemen will give us some amusement shortly as they [the bears] soon begin now to copulate. Saw a great quantity of game of every species common here. Captain Clark walked on shore and killed two elk. They were not in very good order; we therefore took a part of the meat only. It is now only amusement for Captain Clark and myself to kill as much meat as the party can consume. I hope it may continue thus through our whole route, but this I do not much expect. Two beaver were taken in traps this morning, and one since shot by one of the party. Saw numbers of these animals peeping at us as we passed, out of their holes which they form of a cylindrical shape, by burrowing in the face of the abrupt banks of the river.

May the 8th, 1805

[Clark]

A very black cloud to the S.W. We set out under a gentle breeze from the N.E. About 8 o'clock began to rain but not sufficient to wet. We passed the mouth of a large river on the starboard side, 150 yards wide, and appears to be navigable.

The country through which it passes, as far as could be seen from the top of a very high hill on which I was, is a beautiful level plain. This river forks about N.W. from its mouth 12 or 15 miles. One fork runs from the north and the other to the west of N.W. The water of this river will justify a belief that it has its source at a considerable distance, and waters a great extent of country.

We are willing to believe that this is the river the Minnetarees call The River Which Scolds at All Others. The country on the larboard side is high, and broken with much stone scattered on the hills.

In walking on shore with the interpreter and his wife, the squaw gathered, on the sides of the hills, wild licorice, and the white apple,[4] so called by the *engagés*, and gave me to eat. The Indians of the Missouri make great use of the white apple dressed in different ways.

Saw great numbers of buffalo, elk, antelope, and deer, also black-tailed deer, beaver, and wolves. I killed a beaver which I found on the bank, and a wolf. The party killed three beaver, one deer. I saw where an Indian had taken the hair off a goat skin a few days past. Camped early on the larboard side. The river we passed today we call Milk River from the peculiar whiteness of its water, which precisely resembles tea with a considerable mixture of milk.

May 10th, 1805

[Lewis]

Boils and abscesses have been very common with the party. Bratton is now unable to work, with one on his hand. Sore eyes continue also to be common to all of us in a greater or less degree. For the abscesses, I use emollient poultices, and for sore eyes a solution of white vitriol and the sugar of lead.

May 11th, 1805

About 5 P.M. my attention was struck by one of the party

---

[4] The "white apple," also called *pomme blanche* and *pomme de prairie* by the Canadian *voyageurs,* has been identified as *Psoralea esculenta* (Pursch). It is described in Gray's Manual as having "a tuberous or turnip-shaped farinaceous root." It was, of course, not an apple but one of the Leguminosae (pulse, pea, or bean family). "Wild licorice" was almost certainly *Glycyrrhiza lepidota,* of the same family, which grows in this area. This has a root with a taste like licorice. Indians roasted it and for many years white men chewed it.

running at a distance toward us, and making signs and hallooing as if in distress. I ordered the pirogues to put to, and waited until he arrived. I now found that it was Bratton, the man with the sore hand whom I had permitted to walk on shore. He arrived so much out of breath that it was several minutes before he could tell what had happened. At length he informed me that in the woody bottom on the larboard side, about 1½ miles below us, he had shot a brown bear which immediately turned on him and pursued him a considerable distance, but he had wounded it so badly that it could not overtake him.

I immediately turned out with seven of the party in quest of this monster. We at length found his trail and pursued him about a mile, by the blood, through very thick brush of rosebushes and the large-leafed willow. We finally found him concealed in some very thick brush, and shot him through the skull with two balls.

We proceeded to dress him as soon as possible. We found him in good order. It was a monstrous beast, not quite so large as that we killed a few days past but in all other respects much the same. The hair is remarkably long, fine, and rich, though he appears partially to have discharged his winter coat.

We now found that Bratton had shot him through the center of the lungs, notwithstanding which, he had pursued him near half a mile and had returned more than double that distance, and with his talons had prepared himself a bed in the earth about 2 feet deep and five long, and was perfectly alive when we found him, which could not have been less than two hours after he received the wound.

These bears, being so hard to die,[5] rather intimidate us all. I must confess that I do not like the gentlemen and had rather fight two Indians than one bear. There is no other chance to conquer them by a single shot but by shooting them through the brains, and this becomes difficult in consequence of two large muscles which cover the sides of the forehead, and the sharp projection of the center of the frontal bone, which is also of a pretty good thickness. The fleece and skin were as much as two men could possibly carry.

By the time we returned, the sun had set, and I determined to remain here all night, and directed the cooks to

[5] The words "hard to die," which Lewis here applies to the grizzly, have a pathetic interest. He used them of himself a few years later, as he lay dying (whether murdered or a suicide no one knows, despite opinions expressed by many), at Grinder's Stand, on the Natchez Trace, at what is now Hohenwald, Tenn.

render the bear's oil and put it in the kegs, which was done. There was about eight gallons of it.

May 12th, 1805

Set out at an early hour, the weather clear and calm. I walked on shore this morning for the benefit of exercise which I much wanted, and also to examine the country and its productions. In these excursions I most generally went alone, armed with my rifle and espontoon.[6] Thus equipped, I feel myself more than an equal match for a brown bear, provided I get him in open woods or near the water, but feel myself a little diffident with respect to an attack in the open plains. I have therefore come to a resolution to act on the defensive only should I meet these gentlemen in the open country.[7]

I ascended the hills and had a view of a rough and broken country on both sides of the river. On the north side, the summits of the hills exhibit some scattering pine and cedar; on the south side, the pine has not yet commenced, though there is some cedar on the face of the hills and in the little ravines. The chokecherry also grows here in the hollows and at the heads of the gullies. The chokecherry has been in bloom since the ninth inst. This growth has frequently made its appearance on the Missouri from the neighborhood of the Bald-pated Prairie to this place.

May 14th, 1805

In the evening, the men in two of the rear canoes discovered a large brown bear lying in the open grounds about 300 paces from the river, and six of them went out to attack him —all good hunters. They took the advantage of a small eminence which concealed them, and got within 40 paces of

[6] The espontoon, or spontoon, a kind of halberd—spear and ax combined—was regulation equipment for junior officers and, like the ceremonial saber, occasionally turned out to be a rather practical weapon.

[7] Lewis was learning about grizzlies fast. It is amusing to compare the precautions he now took with the confidence he had expressed a few days earlier (April 29).

Bear's oil was a much used edible fat for many years. The Cherokees liked the oil of the black bear—of which a single animal might yield 15 gallons. Oil from Plains grizzlies was sold in New Orleans for many years. Indians sometimes flavored bear's oil with sassafras. An eighteenth-century white traveler remarks that it was "sweet and wholesome" and never cloyed the palate.

him, unperceived. Two of them reserved their fires as had been previously concerted; the four others fired nearly at the same time, and put each his bullet through him. Two of the balls passed through the bulk of both lobes of his lungs. In an instant, this monster ran at them with open mouth. The two who had reserved their fires discharged their pieces at him as he came toward them. Both of them struck him —one only slightly, and the other, fortunately, broke his shoulder. This, however, only retarded his motion for a moment.

The men, unable to reload their guns, took to flight. The bear pursued, and had very nearly overtaken them before they reached the river. Two of the party betook themselves to a canoe, and the others separated and concealed themselves among the willows, [and] reloaded their pieces; each discharged his piece at him as they had an opportunity. They struck him several times again, but the guns served only to direct the bear to them. In this manner he pursued two of them, separately, so close that they were obliged to throw away their guns and pouches, and throw themselves into the river, although the bank was nearly twenty feet perpendicular. So enraged was this animal that he plunged into the river only a few feet behind the second man he had compelled to take refuge in the water.

When one of those who still remained on shore shot him through the head and finally killed him, they then took him on shore and butchered him, when they found eight balls had passed through him in different directions. The bear being old, the flesh was indifferent. They therefore only took the skin and fleece; the latter made us several gallons of oil. It was after the sun had set before these men came up with us, where we had been halted by an occurrence which I have now to recapitulate, and which, although happily passed without ruinous injury, I cannot recollect but with the utmost trepidation and horror. This is the upsetting and narrow escape of the white pirogue.

It happened, unfortunately for us this evening, that Charbonneau was at the helm of this pirogue instead of Drouilliard, who had previously steered her. Charbonneau cannot swim, and is perhaps the most timid waterman in the world. Perhaps it was equally unlucky that Captain Clark and myself were both on shore at that moment, a circumstance which rarely happened, and though we were on the shore opposite to the pirogue, were too far distant to be heard, or to do more than remain spectators of her fate. In this pirogue were embarked our papers, instruments, books, medicine, a great part of our merchandise—and, in short, almost every article indispensably necessary to further the view or ensure the success of the enterprise in which we are now launched to the distance of 2,200 miles.

Suffice it to say that the pirogue was under sail when a sudden squall of wind struck her obliquely and turned her considerably. The steersman, alarmed, instead of putting her before the wind, luffed her up into it. The wind was so violent that it drew the brace of the squaresail out of the hand of the man who was attending it, and instantly upset the pirogue, and would have turned her completely topsy-turvy had it not have been for the resistance made by the awning against the water.

In this situation, Captain Clark and myself both fired our guns to attract the attention, if possible, of the crew, and ordered the halyards to be cut and the sail hauled in, but they did not hear us. Such was their confusion and consternation at this moment that they suffered the pirogue to lie on her side for half a minute before they took the sail in. The pirogue then righted but had filled within an inch of the gunwales.

Charbonneau, still crying to his God for mercy, had not yet recollected the rudder, nor could the repeated orders of the bowsman, Cruzat, bring him to his recollection until he threatened to shoot him instantly if he did not take hold of the rudder and do his duty.

The waves by this time were running very high, but the fortitude, resolution, and good conduct of Cruzat saved her. He ordered 2 of the men to throw out the water with some kettles that fortunately were convenient, while himself and two others rowed her ashore, where she arrived scarcely above the water. We now took every article out of her and laid them to drain as well as we could for the evening, bailed out the canoe, and secured her.

There were two other men besides Charbonneau on board who could not swim and who, of course, must also have perished had the pirogue gone to the bottom.

While the pirogue lay on her side, finding I could not be heard, I, for a moment, forgot my situation, and involuntarily dropped my gun, threw aside my shot pouch, and was in the act of unbuttoning my coat, before I recollected the folly of the attempt I was about to make, which was to throw myself into the river and endeavor to swim to the pirogue. The pirogue was three hundred yards distant, the waves so high that a person [8] could scarcely live in any sit-

[8] Lewis wrote that a "perogue [sic] could scarcely live in any situation," but this appears to be a slip of the pen for "a

uation, the water excessively cold, and the stream rapid. Had I undertaken this project, therefore, there was a hundred to one but what I should have paid the forfeit of my life for the madness of my project, but this—had the pirogue been lost—I should have valued but little.

After having all matters arranged for the evening as well as the nature of circumstances would permit, we thought it a proper occasion to console ourselves and cheer the spirits of our men, and accordingly took a drink of grog, and gave each man a gill of spirits.

May 16th

This morning was fair and the day proved favorable to our operations. By 4 o'clock in the evening, our instruments, medicine, merchandise, provisions, etc., were perfectly dried, repacked, and put on board the pirogue. The loss we sustained was not so great as we had at first apprehended. Our medicine sustained the greatest injury, several articles of which were entirely spoiled, and many others considerably injured. The balance of our losses consisted of some garden seeds, a small quantity of gunpowder, and a few culinary articles which fell overboard and sank. The Indian woman, to whom I ascribe equal fortitude and resolution with any person on board at the time of the accident, caught and preserved most of the light articles which were washed overboard.

All matters being now arranged for our departure, we lost no time in setting out. Proceeded on tolerably well about seven miles and encamped on the starboard side.

In the early part of the day, two of our men fired on a panther, a little below our encampment, and wounded it. They informed us that it was very large, had just killed a deer, partly devoured it, and was in the act of concealing the balance as they discovered him.

We caught two antelopes at our encampment in attempting to swim the river. These animals are but lean as yet, and of course not very pleasant food. I walked on shore this evening and killed a buffalo cow and calf; we found the calf most excellent veal.

The country on either side of the river is broken, and hills much higher than usual. The bottoms now become narrow and the timber more scant. Some scattering pine and cedar on the steep declivities of the hills. This morning a white bear tore Labiche's coat which he had left in the plains.

---

person." The pirogue would have been all right with proper handling, and the cold of the water would not have affected it.

Friday, May 17th

The party with me killed a female brown bear. She was but meager, and appeared to have suckled young very recently. Captain Clark narrowly escaped being bitten by a rattlesnake in the course of his walk. The party killed one this evening at our encampment which, he informed me, was similar to that he had seen. This snake is smaller than those common to the Middle Atlantic States, being about 2 feet 6 inches long. It is of a yellowish-brown color on the back and sides, variegated with one row of oval spots of a dark-brown color lying transversely over the back from the neck to the tail, and two other rows of small circular spots of the same color which garnish the sides along the edge of the scuta. Its belly contains 176 scuta on the belly and 17 on the tail.

We were roused late at night by the sergeant of the guard and warned of the danger we were in from a large tree that had taken fire and which leaned immediately over our lodge. We had the lodge removed, and a few minutes after, a large proportion of the top of the tree fell on the place the lodge had stood. Had we been a few minutes later, we should have been crushed to atoms. The wind blew so hard that, notwithstanding the lodge was fifty paces distant from the fire, it sustained considerable injury from the burning coals which were thrown on it. The party were much harassed also by this fire, which communicated to a collection of fallen timber and could not be extinguished.

May 18th, 1805

[Lewis]

The wind blew hard this morning from the west. We were enabled to employ our tow line [9] the greater part of the day and therefore proceeded on tolerably well. There are now but few sandbars. The river is narrow and current gentle. The timber consists of a few cottonwood trees along the verge of the river; the willow has in great measure disap-

---

[9] Towing was often necessary on western rivers, especially if the wind was wrong or the current too swift for oars. The "tow rope," often called the cord, or "cordelle," was attached to the bow of the riverboat and the boat was then hauled by manpower. The use of horses or mules, as on an ordinary canal boat, was quite impossible, since there was no tow path and the banks were often muddy and full of trees or thickets, not to mention snakes. At times, the men on the rope had to wade through the water along the bank.

peared. In the latter part of the day the hills widened, the bottoms became larger and contained more timber. Captain Clark in the course of his walk this evening killed four deer, two of which were the black-tailed, or mule, deer. The skins are now good. They have not yet produced their young. We saw a number of buffalo, elk, deer, and antelope.

May 19th, 1805

The last night was disagreeably cold. We were unable to set out until 8 o'clock A.M. in consequence of a heavy fog which obscured the river in such a manner that we could not see our way. This is the first we have experienced in anything like so great a degree. There was also a fall of dew last evening, which is the second we have experienced since we have entered this extensive open country. At eight we set out and proceeded as yesterday, by means of the cord principally. The hills are high and the country similar to that of yesterday. Captain Clark walked on shore with two of the hunters and killed a brown bear. Notwithstanding that it was shot through the heart, it ran at its usual pace nearly a quarter of a mile before it fell. One of the party wounded a beaver, and my dog, as usual, swam in to catch it. The beaver bit him through the hind leg and cut the artery. It was with great difficulty that I could stop the blood. I fear it will yet prove fatal to him.[10]

This afternoon the river was crooked, rapid, and containing more sawyers [11] than we have seen in the same place since we left the entrance of the River Platte. Captain Clark, in the course of his walk, killed three deer and a beaver. I also walked on shore this evening a few miles and killed an elk, a buck, and a beaver. The party killed and caught 4 other beaver and 3 deer.

---

[10] As Lewis's Newfoundland was still with the expedition on the return journey, the beaver's bite was evidently less serious than his owner feared.

[11] The Platte River was so full of snags, mudflats, and mud, with so little water that the frontier joke was that it ran with its bottom uppermost. Hence Lewis's comment. It was also described as "too thick to drink, too thin to walk on."

Chapter **IX**

FROM THE MUSSELSHELL
TO MARIA'S RIVER

May 20—June 7, 1805

May 20th, 1805

[Lewis]

At 11 A.M., we arrived at the entrance of a handsome bold river, which discharges itself into the Missouri on the larboard side. This stream we take to be that called by the Minnetarees the Musselshell River. If it be the same, of which I entertain but little doubt, it takes its rise, by their information, in the first chain of the Rocky Mountains, at no great distance from the Yellowstone River, from whence in its course to this place it passes through a high and broken country, pretty well timbered, particularly on its borders, and interspersed with handsome fertile plains and meadows.

May 22nd, 1805

We have caught but few fish since we left the Mandans. They do not bite freely. What we took were the white cat of 2 to 5 pounds. I presume that fish are scarce in this part of the river. We encamped earlier this evening than usual in order to render the oil of a bear which we killed. I do not believe that the black bear, common to the lower part of this river and the Atlantic states, exists in this quarter. We have neither seen one of them nor their tracks, which would be easily distinguished by its shortness of talons when compared with the brown grizzly, or white bear. I believe that it is the same species or family of bears which assumes all those colors at different ages and seasons of the year.

May 25th, 1805

The two canoes which we left behind yesterday to bring on the meat did not arrive this morning until 8 A.M., at which time we set out. The wind being against us, we did not proceed with so much ease or expedition as yesterday. We employed the towline principally, which the banks favored the use of. The current was strong, particularly around the points against which the current happened to set, and at the entrances of the little gullies from the hills, these rivulets having brought down considerable quantities of stone, and deposited it at their entrances, forming partial barriers to the water of the river to the distance of 40 or 50 feet from the shore. Around these, the water ran with great violence and compelled us, in some instances, to double our force in order to get a pirogue or canoe by them.

May 25th, 1805

[Clark]

In my walk of this day, I saw mountains on either side of the river at no great distance. Those mountains appeared to be detached, and not ranges as laid down by the Minnetarees. I also think I saw a range of high mountains at a great distance to the south-southwest but am not certain, as the horizon was not clear enough to view it with certainty.

May 26th, 1805

We set out early and proceeded as yesterday. Wind from the S.W. The river enclosed with very high hills on either side. I took one man and walked out this morning, and ascended the high country to view the mountains which I thought I saw yesterday. From the first summit of the hill I could plainly see the mountains on either side, which I saw yesterday, and at no great distance from me. Those on the starboard side are an irregular range, the two extremities of which bore west and N. west from me. Those mountains on the larboard side appeared to be several detached knobs or mountains rising from a level open country, at different distances from me, from southwest to southeast.

On one, the most southwesterly of those mountains, there appeared to be snow. I crossed a deep hollow and ascended a part of the plain elevated much higher than where I first viewed the above mountains. From this point, I beheld the Rocky Mountains for the first time, with certainty. I could only discover a few of the most elevated points above the horizon, the most remarkable of which, by my pocket compass, I found bore S. 60 W. Those points of the Rocky Mountains were covered with snow, and the sun shone on it in such a manner as to give me a most plain and satisfactory view.

Whilst I viewed those mountains, I felt a secret pleasure in finding myself so near the head of the—heretofore conceived—boundless Missouri. But when I reflected on the difficulties which this snowy barrier would most probably throw in my way to the Pacific Ocean, and the sufferings and hardships of myself and party in them, it in some measure counterbalanced the joy I had felt in the first moments in which I gazed on them. But, as I have always held it little short of criminality to anticipate evils, I will allow it to be a good, comfortable road until I am compelled to believe otherwise.

The high country in which we are at present, and have been passing for some days, I take to be a continuation of what the Indians, as well as the French *engagés*, call the Black Hills.[1] This tract of country, so called, consists of a collection of high, broken, and irregular hills, and short chains of mountains, sometimes 100 miles in width, and again becoming much narrower, but always much higher than the country on either side. They commence about the head of the Kansas River, and to the west of that river, near the Arkansas River, from whence they take their course, a little to the west of N.W., approaching the Rocky Mountains obliquely, passing the River Platte near the forks, and intercepting the Yellowstone River near the bend of that river, and passing the Missouri at this place, and probably continuing to swell the country as far north as the Saskatchewan River, though they are lower here than they are described to the south, and may therefore terminate before they reach the Saskatchewan. The Black Hills, in their course northerly, appear to approach more nearly the Rocky Mountains.

[1] Not, of course, identical with the modern Black Hills.

May 28th, 1805

[Lewis]

This morning we set forward at an early hour; the weather dark and cloudy, the air smoky, had a few drops of rain. We employed the cord, generally, to which we also gave the assistance of the pole at the riffles and rocky points. These are as numerous, and many of them much worse than those we passed yesterday. Around those points the water drives with great force, and we are obliged, in many instances, to steer our vessels through the apertures formed by the points of large, sharp rocks which reach a few inches above the surface of the water. Here, should our cord give way, the bow is instantly driven outward by the stream and the vessel thrown with her side on the rocks, where she must inevitably overset or perhaps be dashed to pieces. Our ropes are but slender—all of them, except one, being made of elk skin and much worn—frequently wet, and, exposed to the heat of the weather, are weak and rotten. They have given way several times in the course of the day, but happily at such places that the vessel had room to wheel free of the rocks and therefore escaped injury. With every precaution we can take, it is with much labor and infinite risk that we are enabled to get around these points.

Found a new Indian lodge pole today which had been brought down by the stream. It was worn at one end as if dragged by dogs or horses. A football also, and several other articles, were found, which have been recently brought down by the current. These are strong evidences of Indians being on the river above us, and probably at no great distance. The football is such as I have seen among the Minnetarees, and therefore think it most probable that they are a band of the Minnetarees of Fort de Prairie.

May 29th, 1805

Last night we were all alarmed by a large buffalo bull which swam over from the opposite shore and, coming along the side of the white pirogue, climbed over it to land. He, then alarmed, ran up the bank in full speed directly toward the fires, and was within 18 inches of the heads of some of the men who lay sleeping, before the sentinel could alarm him or make him change his course. Still more alarmed, he now took his direction immediately toward our lodge, passing between 4 fires, and within a few inches of the heads of one range of the men as they yet lay sleeping.

When he came near the tent, my dog saved us by causing him to change his course a second time, which he did by turning a little to the right, and was quickly out of sight, leaving us by this time all in an uproar with our guns in our hands, inquiring of each other the cause of the alarm, which, after a few moments, was explained by the sentinel. We were happy to find no one hurt.

The next morning we found that the buffalo, in passing the pirogue, had trodden on a rifle which belonged to Captain Clark's black man, who had negligently left her in the pirogue. The rifle was much bent. He had also broken the spindle, pivot, and shattered the stock of one of the blunderbusses on board. With this damage I felt well content—happy, indeed, that we had sustained no further injury. It appears that the white pirogue, which contains our most valuable stores, is attended by some evil genius.

This morning we set out at an early hour and proceeded as usual by the cord. At the distance of 2½ miles, passed a handsome river which discharged itself on the larboard side. I walked on shore and ascended this river about a mile and a half in order to examine it. I found this river about 100 yards wide from bank to bank, the water occupying about 75 yards. The bed was formed of gravel and mud, with some sand. It appeared to contain much more water than the Musselshell River; was more rapid, but equally navigable. There were no large stones or rocks in its bed to obstruct the navigation. The banks were low, yet appeared seldom to overflow. The water of this river is clearer, much, than any we have met with.

Great abundance of the Argalia or big-horned animals [2] in the high country through which this river passes. Captain Clark, who ascended this river much higher than I did, has thought proper to call it Judith's River. [3] The bottoms of this stream, as far as I could see, were wider and contained more timber than the Missouri. Here I saw some box alder intermixed with the cottonwood willow; rosebushes and

[2] By "argal," or "argalia," Clark means the bighorn, or Rocky Mountain sheep. This was correct enough under the zoological nomenclature of his day. In our times, the name "argal" is applied only to *Ovis ammon*, an Asiatic species in the same genus as the bighorn.

[3] Clark named this river in honor of Julia Hancock, whom he married soon after the expedition returned. Julia was usually called "Judy," and Clark supposed her name was Judith.

honeysuckle, with some red willow, constitute the under-growth.

On the Missouri, just above the entrance of the Big Horn (Judith) River, I counted the remains of the fires of 126 Indian lodges which appeared to be of very recent date, perhaps 12 or 15 days. Captain Clark also saw a large encampment just above the entrance of this river on the starboard side of rather older date; probably they were the same Indians. The Indian woman with us examined the moccasins which we found at these encampments and informed us that they were not of her nation, the Snake Indians. But she believed they were some of the Indians who inhabit the country on this side of the Rocky Mountains and north of the Missouri, and I think it most probable that they were the Minnetarees of Fort de Prairie.

At the distance of 6½ miles from our encampment of last night, we passed a very bad rapid to which we gave the name of the Ash Rapid, from a few trees of that wood growing near them. This is the first ash I have seen for a great distance. At this place, the hills again approach the river closely on both sides, and the same scene which we had on the 27th and 28th in the morning, again presents itself, and the rocky points and riffles rather more numerous and worse. There was but little timber. Salts, coal, &c., still appear.

Today we passed, on the starboard side, the remains of a vast many [*meaning a great many*] mangled carcasses of buffalo, which had been driven over a precipice of 120 feet by the Indians, and perished. The water appeared to have washed away a part of this immense pile of slaughter, and still there remained the fragments of at least a hundred carcasses. They created a most horrid stench. In this manner, the Indians of the Missouri destroy vast herds of buffalo at a stroke. For this purpose, one of the most active and fleet young men is selected and disguised in a robe of buffalo skin, having also the skin of the buffalo's head with the ears and horns fastened on his head in form of a cap. Thus caparisoned, he places himself at a convenient distance between a herd of buffalo and a precipice proper for the purpose, which happens in many places on this river for miles together. The other Indians now surround the herd on the back and flanks and, at a signal agreed on, all show themselves at the same time moving forward toward the buffalo.

The disguised Indian or decoy has taken care to place himself sufficiently near the buffalo to be noticed by them when they take to flight, and running before them, they follow him in full speed to the precipice; the cattle behind driving those in front over and, seeing them go, do not look or hesitate about following until the whole are precipitated down the precipice, forming one common mass of dead and mangled carcasses. The decoy, in the meantime, has taken care to secure himself in some cranny or crevice of the cliff which he has previously prepared for that purpose.

The part of the decoy, I am informed, is extremely dangerous. If they are not very fleet runners, the buffalo tread them underfoot and crush them to death, and sometimes drive them over the precipice also, where they perish in common with the buffalo. We saw a great many wolves in the neighborhood of these mangled carcasses. They were fat and extremely gentle. Captain Clark, who was on shore, killed one of them with his espontoon.

Just above this place we came to for dinner, opposite the entrance of a bold running river 40 yards wide which falls in on the larboard side. This stream we called Slaughter River. Its bottoms are but narrow and contain scarcely any timber. Our situation was a narrow bottom on the starboard, possessing some cottonwood. Soon after we landed it began to blow and rain, and as there was no appearance of even wood enough to make our fires for some distance above, we determined to remain here until the next morning, and accordingly fixed our camp and gave each man a small dram. Notwithstanding the allowance of spirits we issued did not exceed one-half gill per man, several of them were considerably affected by it. Such is the effect of abstaining for some time the use of spirituous liquors. They were all very merry. The hunters killed an elk this evening, and Captain Clark killed two beaver.

May 31st, 1805

The obstructions of rocky points and riffles still continue as yesterday. At those places the men are compelled to be in the water even to their armpits, and the water is yet very cold, and so frequent are those points that they are one-fourth of their time in the water. Added to this, the banks and bluffs along which they are obliged to pass are so slippery, and the mud so tenacious, that they are unable to wear their moccasins, and in that situation, dragging the heavy burden of a canoe, and walking occasionally for several hundred yards over the sharp fragments of rocks which tumble from the cliffs and garnish the borders of the river. In short, their labor is incredibly painful and great, yet those faithful fellows bear it without a murmur. The towrope of the white pirogue—the only one, indeed, of hemp, and that on which we most depended—gave way today at a bad point. The pirogue swung and but slightly touched a rock, yet was very near oversetting. I fear her evil genius will play so many pranks with her that she will go to the bottom one of these days.

Captain Clark walked on shore this morning but found it so excessively bad that he shortly returned. At 12 o'clock M. we came to for refreshment and gave the men a dram, which they received with much cheerfulness—and well deserved.

The hills and river cliffs which we passed today exhibit a most romantic appearance. The bluffs of the river rise to the height of from two to three hundred feet, and in most places perpendicular. They are formed of remarkable white sandstone which is sufficiently soft to give way readily to the impression of water.

Two or three thin horizontal strata of white freestone, on which the rains or water make no impression, lie imbedded in these cliffs of soft stone, near the upper part of them. The earth on the top of these cliffs is a dark rich loam which, forming a gradually ascending plain, extends back from ½ a mile to a mile, where the hills commence and rise abruptly to a height of about 300 feet more. The water, in the course of time, in descending from those hills and plains, on either side of the river, has trickled down the soft sand cliffs and worn it into a thousand grotesque figures which, with the help of a little imagination, and an oblique view, at a distance are made to represent elegant ranges of lofty freestone buildings, having their parapets well stocked with statuary.

Columns of various sculpture, both grooved and plain, are also seen supporting long galleries in front of those buildings. In other places, on a much nearer approach and with the help of less imagination, we see the remains or ruins of elegant buildings: some columns standing and almost entire, with their pedestals and capitals; others retaining their pedestals but deprived by time or accident of their capitals; some lying prostrate and broken; others in the form of vast pyramids of conic structure bearing a series of other pyramids on their tops, becoming less as they ascend and finally terminating in a sharp point. Niches and alcoves of various forms and sizes are seen at different heights as we pass.

June 2, 1805

Game becoming more abundant this morning, I thought it best now to lose no time or suffer an opportunity to escape in providing the necessary quantity of elk skins to cover my leather boat, which I now expect I shall be obliged to use shortly. Accordingly, I walked on shore most of the day with some of the hunters for that purpose, and killed 6 elk, 2 buffalo, 2 mule deer, and a bear. These animals were all in good order. We therefore took as much of the meat as our canoes and pirogues could conveniently carry.

The bear was very near catching Drouilliard. It also pursued Charbonneau,[4] who fired his gun in the air as he ran but fortunately eluded the vigilance of the bear, by secreting himself very securely in the bushes, until Drouilliard finally killed it by a shot in the head—the only shot, indeed, that will conquer the ferocity of those tremendous animals.

June 3rd, 1805

This morning early we passed over and formed a camp on the point formed by the junction of two large rivers. An interesting question was now to be determined: Which of these rivers was the Missouri, or that which the Minnetarees call Amahte Arzzha, or Missouri, and which they had described to us as approaching very near to the Columbia River? To mistake the stream at this period of the season—two months of the traveling season having now elapsed—and to ascend such stream to the Rocky Mountains or perhaps much farther before we could inform ourselves whether it did approach the Columbia or not, and then be obliged to return and take the other stream, would not only lose us the whole of this season but would probably so dishearten the party that it might defeat the expedition altogether.

Convinced we were that the utmost circumspection and caution was necessary in deciding on the stream to be taken. To this end, an investigation of both streams was the first thing to be done—to learn their widths, depths, comparative rapidity of their currents, and thence the comparative bodies

---

[4] This incident is just one more example of the feckless Charbonneau's inadequacy to all emergencies. The man had only two virtues: he was a good cook and he was married to Sacagawea. Throughout the journey he continued to make trouble by losing his head in emergencies.

of water furnished by each. Accordingly, we dispatched two light canoes with three men in each up those streams. We also sent out several small parties by land, with instructions to penetrate the country as far as they conveniently can, permitting themselves to return this evening, and endeavor, if possible, to discover the distant bearing of those rivers by ascending the rising grounds. Between the time of my A.M. and meridian, Captain Clark and myself strolled out to the top of the heights in the fork of these rivers, from whence we had an extensive and most enchanting view. The country, in every direction around us, was one vast plain in which innumerable herds of buffalo were seen, attended by their shepherds, the wolves. The solitary antelope, which now had their young, were distributed over its face. Some herds of elk were also seen. The verdure perfectly clothed the ground. The weather was pleasant and fair. To the south we saw a range of lofty mountains which we supposed to be a continuation of the S. mountains, stretching themselves from S.E. to N.W., terminating abruptly about S. west from us. These were partially covered with snow. Behind these mountains, and at a great distance, a second and more lofty range of mountains appeared to stretch across the country in the same direction with the others, reaching from west, to the N. of N.W., where their snowy tops lost themselves beneath the horizon. This last range was perfectly covered with snow. The direction of the rivers could be seen but little way, soon losing the break of their channels to our view in the common plain.

On our return to camp, we bore a little to the left and discovered a handsome little river falling into the N. fork on larboard side about 1½ miles above our camp. This little river has as much timber in its bottoms as either of the larger streams. There are a great number of prickly pears in these plains. The chokecherry grows here in abundance, both in the river bottoms and in the steep ravines along the river bluffs. Saw the yellow and red currants, not yet ripe; also the gooseberry, which begins to ripen. The wild rose, which grows here in great abundance in the bottoms of all these rivers, is now in full bloom, and adds not a little to the beauty of the scenery.

We took the width of the two rivers, found the left-hand or S. fork 372 yards, and the N. fork 200. The north fork is deeper than the other, but its current not so swift. Its waters run in the same boiling and rolling manner which has uniformly characterized the Missouri throughout its whole course so far. Its waters are of a whitish brown color, very thick and turbid, also characteristic of the Missouri, while the south fork is perfectly transparent, runs very rapid, but with a smooth, unruffled surface, its bottom composed of round and flat smooth stones like most rivers issuing from a mountainous country. The bed of the N. fork composed of some gravel but principally mud.

In short, the air and character of this river is so precisely that of the Missouri below that the party with very few exceptions have already pronounced the N. fork to be the Missouri. Myself and Captain Clark, not quite so precipitate, have not yet decided, but if we were to give our opinions I believe we should be in the minority.

Certain it is that the north fork gives the coloring matter and character which is retained from hence to the Gulf of Mexico. I am confident that this river rises in and passes a great distance through an open plain country. I expect that it has some of its sources on the eastern side of the Rocky Mountains, south of the Saskatchewan, but that it does not penetrate the first range of these mountains, and that much the greater part of its sources are in a northwardly direction toward the lower and middle parts of the Saskatchewan in the open plains. Convinced I am that, if it penetrated the Rocky Mountains to any great distance, its waters would be clearer, unless it should run an immense distance indeed after leaving those mountains through these level plains in order to acquire its turbid hue. What astonishes us a little is that the Indians, who appeared to be so well acquainted with the geography of this country, should not have mentioned this river on [the] right hand, if it be not the Missouri. The River That Scolds at All Others, as they call it— if there is in reality such a one—ought, agreeably to their account, to have fallen in a considerable distance below. And, on the other hand, if this right-hand or north fork be the Missouri, I am equally astonished at their not mentioning the south fork, which they must have passed in order to get to those large falls which they mention on the Missouri. Thus have our cogitating faculties been busily employed all day.

Those who have remained at camp today have been busily engaged in dressing skins for clothing, notwithstanding that many of them have their feet so mangled and bruised with the stones and rough ground over which they passed barefoot that they can scarcely walk or stand. At least, it is with great pain they do either. For some days past, they were unable to wear their moccasins. They have fallen off considerably, but notwithstanding the difficulties past or those which seem now to menace us, they still remain perfectly cheerful.

In the evening, the parties whom we had sent out returned, agreeably to instructions. The parties who had been sent up the rivers in canoes informed that they ascended some distance and had then left their canoes and walked up the rivers a considerable distance farther, barely leaving themselves time to return. The north fork was not so rapid as the other and afforded the easiest navigation, of course. Six [7] feet appeared to be the shallowest water of the S. branch, and 5 feet that of the N. Their accounts were by no means satisfactory, nor did the information we acquired bring us nigher to the decision of our question, or determine us which stream to take.

Joseph and Reuben Fields reported that they had been up the south fork about seven miles on a straight course, somewhat N. of W., and that there the little river which discharges itself into the north fork just above us, was within 100 yards of the S. fork; that they came down this little river and found it a bold running stream about 40 yards wide, containing much timber in its bottom, consisting of the narrow- and wide-leafed cottonwood with some birch and box alder, undergrowth willows, rosebushes, currants, &c. They saw a great number of elk on this river, and some beaver.

Those accounts being by no means satisfactory as to the fundamental point, Captain Clark and myself concluded to set out early the next morning with a small party each, and ascend these rivers until we could perfectly satisfy ourselves of the one which it would be most expedient for us to take on our main journey to the Pacific. Accordingly, it was agreed that I should ascend the right-hand fork and he the left. I gave orders to Sergeant Pryor, Drouilliard, Shields, Windsor, Cruzat, and Lepage, to hold themselves in readiness to accompany me in the morning. Captain Clark also selected Reuben and Joseph Fields, Sergeant Gass, Shannon, and his black man, York, to accompany him. We agreed to go up those rivers one day and a half's march, or further if it should appear necessary to satisfy us more fully of the point in question. The hunters killed 2 buffalo, 6 elk, and 4 deer today. The evening proved cloudy. We took a drink of grog this evening and gave the men a dram, and made all matters ready for an early departure in the morning. I had now my sack and blanket wrapped in readiness to swing on my back, which is the first time in my life that I had ever prepared a burden of this kind, and I am fully convinced that it will not be the last.

June 4th, 1805

This morning early, Captain Clark departed, and at the same time I passed the right-hand fork opposite to our camp below a small island. From hence, I steered N. 30 W. 4½ to a commanding eminence. Here I took the following bearings of the mountains which were in view: The North Mountains appear to change their direction from that of being parallel with the Missouri, turning to the north and terminating abruptly, their termination bearing N. 48° E., distant, by estimate, 30 miles. The South Mountains appear to turn to the S., also terminating abruptly, their extremity bearing S. 8° W., distant 25 miles. The Barn Mountain, a lofty mountain so-called from its resemblance to the roof of a large barn, is a separate mountain, and appears rather to the right of, and retreating from, the extremity of the S. Mountains. This bore S. 38° W., distant 35 miles. The north fork, which I am now ascending, lies to my left and appears to make a considerable bend to the N.W. On its western border, a range of hills about 10 miles long appear to lie parallel with the river, and from hence bear N. 60° W. To the N. of this range of hills, an elevated point of the river bluff on its larboard side bore N. 72° W., distant 12 miles. To this last object I now directed my course through a high, level, dry, open plain. The whole country, in fact, appears to be one continued plain to the foot of the mountains or as far as eye can reach. Ths soil appears dark, rich, and fertile, yet the grass is by no means as high nor does it look so luxuriant as I should have expected. It is short, just sufficient to conceal the ground. Great abundance of prickly pears, which are extremely troublesome, as the thorns very readily pierce the foot through the moccasin. They are so numerous that it requires one-half of the traveler's attention to avoid them.

June 5th, 1805

[Clark]

Some little rain and snow last night. The mountains to our S.E. covered with snow this morning. Air very cold, and raining a little. We saw 8 buffalo opposite. They made two attempts to cross, the water being so swift they could not. About the time we were setting out, three white bear approached our camp. We killed the three and ate part of one; and set out, and proceeded on N. 20° W., 11 miles. Struck the river at many places in this distance, to a ridge on the N. side from the top of which I could plainly see a mountain to the south and west covered with snow, at a long distance. The mountains opposite to us, to the S.E., are also covered with snow this morning. A high ridge from those mountains approaches the river on the S.E. side, forming some cliffs of hard dark stone. From the ridge at which place I struck the river last, I could discover that the river ran west of south a long distance, and has a strong rapid current. As this river continued its width, depth, and rapidity, and the course west of south, going up further would be useless. I determined to return. I accordingly set out through the plain on a course N. 30° E. on my return and struck the little river, at 20 miles, passing through a level plain. At the little river we killed 2 buck elk and dined on their marrowbones. Proceeded on a few miles and camped, having killed 2 deer which were very fat. Some few drops of rain today; the evening fair, wind hard from the N.E. I saw great numbers of elk and white-tailed deer, some beaver, antelope, mule deer, and wolves, and one bear on this little river. Marked my name in a tree N. side near the ridge where the little river breaks through.

June 6th, 1805

[Lewis]

I now became well convinced that this branch of the Missouri had its direction too much to the north for our route to the Pacific, and therefore determined to return the next day after taking an observation of the ⊙'s meridian altitude in order to fix the latitude of the place. The fore part of the last evening was fair, but in the latter part of the night clouded up and continued so with short intervals of sunshine until a little before noon, when the whole horizon was overcast, and I, of course, disappointed in making the observation which I much wished.

I had sent Sergeant Pryor and Windsor, early this morning, with orders to proceed up the river to some commanding eminence and take its bearing as far as possible. In the meantime, the four others and myself were busily engaged in making two rafts on which we purposed descending the river. We had just completed this work when Sergeant Pryor and Windsor returned, it being about noon. They reported that they had proceeded from hence S. 70 W. 6 miles to the summit of a commanding eminence from whence the river on their left was about 2½ miles distant; that a point of its larboard bluff, which was visible, bore S. 80° W., distant about 15 miles; that the river on their left bent gradually around to this point, and from thence seemed to run northwardly.

We now took dinner and embarked with our plunder and five elk skins on the rafts, but were soon convinced that this mode of navigation was hazardous, particularly with those rafts, they being too small and slender. We wet a part of our baggage and were near losing one of our guns. I therefore determined to abandon the rafts and return as we had come—by land. I regretted much being obliged to leave my elk skins, which I wanted to assist in forming my leather boat, those we had prepared at Fort Mandan being injured in such manner that they would not answer.

We again swung our packs and took our way through the open plains for about 12 miles, when we struck the river. The wind blew a storm from N.E., accompanied by frequent showers of rain. We were wet and very cold. Continued our route down the river only a few miles before the abruptness of the cliffs and their near approach to the river compelled us to take the plains and once more face the storm. Here we bore rather too much to the north, and it was late in the evening before we reached the river.

In our way, we killed two buffalo and took with us as much of the flesh as served us that night and a part of the next day. We encamped a little below the entrance of the large dry creek called Lark Creek, having traveled but 23 miles since noon. It continues to rain and we have no shelter; an uncomfortable night's rest is the natural consequence.

June 6th, 1805

[Clark]

A cloudy, cold, raw day. Wind hard from the N.E. We set out early and traveled down the little river which was immediately in our course. On this river we killed 7 deer for their skins. The bottoms of this little river are, in every respect (except in extent), like the large bottoms of the Missouri below the forks, containing a great proportion of a kind of cottonwood with a leaf resembling a wild cherry. I also observed wild tansy on this little river in great quantities. We halted at 12 o'clock and ate a part of a fat buck. After dinner we ascended the plain, at which time it began to rain, and continued all day. At 5 o'clock, we arrived at our camp on the point, where I expected to meet Captain Lewis. He did not return this evening. Myself and party much fatigued, having walked constantly as hard as we could march over a dry hard plain, descending and ascending the steep river hills and gullies. In my absence the party had killed an elk and two buffalo. I sent out for the meat, a part of which was brought in. Nothing remarkable had transpired at camp in my absence.

June 7th, 1805

[Lewis]

It continued to rain almost without intermission last night, and, as I expected, we had a most disagreeable and restless night. Our camp possessing no allurements, we left our watery beds at an early hour and continued our route down the river. It still continues to rain—the wind hard from N.E., and cold; the ground remarkably slippery, insomuch that we were unable to walk on the sides of the bluffs where we had passed as we ascended the river. Notwithstanding the rain that has now fallen, the earth of these bluffs is not wet to a greater depth than 2 inches. In its present state it is precisely like walking over frozen ground which is thawed to a small depth, and slips equally bad. This clay not only appears to require more water to saturate it, as I before observed, than any earth I ever observed, but when saturated it appears, on the other hand, to yield its moisture with equal difficulty.

In passing along the face of one of these bluffs today, I slipped at a narrow pass about 30 yards in length, and but for a quick and fortunate recovery by means of my espontoon, I should have been precipitated into the river down a craggy precipice of about ninety feet. I had scarcely reached a place on which I could stand with tolerable safety, even with the assistance of my espontoon, before I heard a voice behind me cry out, "Good God, Captain, what shall I do?"

On turning about, I found it was Windsor, who had slipped and fallen about the center of this narrow pass, and was lying prostrate on his belly, with his right-hand arm and leg over the precipice while he was holding on with the left arm and foot as well as he could, which appeared to be with much difficulty. I discovered his danger, and the trepidation which he was in gave me still further concern, for I expected every instant to see him lose his strength and slip off.

Although much alarmed at his situation, I disguised my feelings and spoke very calmly to him, and assured him that he was in no kind of danger—to take the knife out of his belt behind him with his right hand, and dig a hole with it in the face of the bank to receive his right foot, which he did, and then raised himself to his knees.

I then directed him to take off his moccasins and to come forward on his hands and knees, holding the knife in one hand and the gun in the other. This he happily effected, and escaped. Those who were some little distance behind, returned by my orders and waded the river at the foot of the bluff, where the water was breast deep. It was useless, we knew, to attempt the plains on this part of the river in consequence of the numerous steep ravines which intersected, and which were quite as bad as the river bluffs. We therefore continued our route down the river, sometimes in the mud and water of the bottom lands, at others in the river to our breasts, and when the water became so deep that we could not wade, we cut footsteps in the face of the steep bluffs with our knives and proceeded. We continued our disagreeable march through the rain, mud, and water until late in the evening, having traveled only about 18 miles, and encamped in an old Indian stick lodge which afforded us a dry and comfortable shelter.

Chapter X

GREAT FALLS OF THE MISSOURI

June 8—June 20, 1805

June 8th, 1805

[Lewis]

It continued to rain moderately all last night. This morning was cloudy until about ten o'clock, when it cleared off and became a fine day. We breakfasted, and set out about sunrise and continued our route down the river bottoms through the mud and water as yesterday, though the road was somewhat better than yesterday, and we were not so often compelled to wade in the river. We passed some dangerous and difficult bluffs. The river bottoms affording all the timber which is to be seen in the country, they are filled with innumerable little birds that resort thither, either for shelter or to build their nests. When sun began to shine today, these birds appeared to be very gay and sang most enchantingly. I observed among them the brown thrush, robin, turtledove, linnet, goldfinch, the large and small blackbird, wren, and several other birds of less note. Some of the inhabitants of the prairies also take refuge in these woods at night, or from a storm.

The whole of my party to a man, except myself, were fully persuaded that this river was the Missouri. But, being fully of opinion that it was neither the main stream, nor that which it would be advisable for us to take, I determined to give it a name, and in honor of Miss Maria W———d, called it Maria's River. It is true that the hue of the waters of this turbulent and troubled stream but illy comport with the pure, celestial virtues and amiable qualifications of that lovely fair one.[1] But, on the other hand,

[1] Maria, "that lovely fair one," remains a mystery. Lewis often, rather halfheartedly, imagined himself in love, but it is impossible to identify most of the girls.

it is a noble river—one destined to become, in my opinion, an object of contention between the two great powers of America and Great Britain with respect to the adjustment of the northwesterly boundary of the former. And that it will become one of the most interesting branches of the Missouri in a commercial point of view I have but little doubt, as it abounds with animals of the fur kind, and most probably furnishes a safe and direct communication to that productive country of valuable furs exclusively enjoyed at present by the subjects of His Britannic Majesty. In addition to which, it passes through a rich, fertile, and one of the most beautifully picturesque countries that I ever beheld, through the wide expanse of which innumerable herds of living animals are seen, its borders garnished with one continued garden of roses, while its lofty and open forests are the habitation of myriads of the feathered tribes who salute the ear of the passing traveler with their wild and simple yet sweet and cheerful melody.

I arrived at camp about 5 o'clock in the evening much fatigued, where I found Captain Clark and the balance of the party waiting our return with some anxiety for our safety, having been absent near two days longer than we had engaged to return. On our way to camp we had killed 4 deer and two antelopes, the skins of which, as well as those we killed while on the route, we brought with us. Maria's River may be stated generally from sixty to a hundred yards wide, with a strong and steady current and possessing 5 feet of water in the most shallow parts.

I now gave myself this evening to rest from my labors, took a drink of grog, and gave the men who had accompanied me each a dram. Captain Clark plotted the courses of the two rivers as far as we had ascended them. I now began more than ever to suspect the veracity of Mr. Fidler,[2] or the correctness of his instruments. For I see that Arrowsmith, in his late map of N. America, has laid down a remarkable mountain in the chain of the Rocky Mountains, called the Tooth, nearly as far south as latitude 45°, and this is said to be from the discoveries of Mr. Fidler. We are now within a hundred miles of the Rocky Mountains, and I find from my observation of the 3rd inst. that the latitude of this place is 47° 24′ 12″ 8. The river must, therefore, turn much to the south between this and the Rocky Mountains to have permitted Mr. Fidler to have passed along

---

[2] Peter Fidler was an early eighteenth-century explorer, a Hudson's Bay Company man, who had approached the eastern edges of the Rockies at some points.

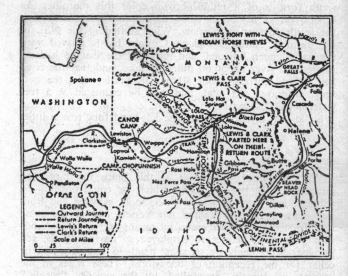

the eastern border of these mountains as far S. as nearly 45° without even seeing it. But from hence, as far as Captain Clark had ascended the S. fork or Missouri, being the distance of 55 miles (45 miles in a straight line), its course is S. 29° W., and it still appeared to bear considerably to the W. of south as far as he could see it. I think, therefore, that we shall find that the Missouri enters the Rocky Mountains to the north of 45°.[3]

June 8th, 1805

[Clark]

Rained moderately all the last night and some this morning until 10 o'clock. I am somewhat uneasy for Captain Lewis and party as days have now passed the time he was to have returned. I had all the arms put in order and permitted several men to hunt, aired and dried our stores, &c. The rivers at this point have fallen 6 inches since our arrival. At 10 o'clock cleared away and became fair. The wind all the morning from the S.W., and hard. The water of the

[3] The Missouri River doesn't "enter" the Rockies, it emerges from them; but Lewis was really thinking of his own party, which did enter the Rockies along the course of the river—well north of 45°.

south fork is of a reddish-brown color this morning; the other river of a whitish color, as usual. The mountains to the south covered with snow. Wind shifted to the N.E. in the evening. About 5 o'clock Captain Lewis arrived with the party, much fatigued, and informed me that he had ascended the river about 60 miles by land, and that the river had a bold current about 80 or 100 yards wide; the bottoms of gravel and mud, and may be estimated at 5 feet water in shoalest parts.

Some rain in the evening. The left-hand fork rose a little.

June 9th, 1805

[Lewis]

We determined to deposit at this place the large red pirogue, all the heavy baggage which we could possibly do without, and some provision—salt, tools, powder and lead, &c.—with a view to lighten our vessels and at the same time to strengthen their crews by means of the seven hands who have been heretofore employed in navigating the red pirogue. Accordingly we set some hands to digging a hole or cellar for the reception of our stores. These holes in the ground, or deposits, are called, by the *engagés*, "caches." On inquiry I found that Cruzat was well acquainted with this business and therefore left the management of it entirely to him. Today we examined our maps and compared the information, derived as well from them as from the Indians, and fully settled in our minds the propriety of adopting the south fork for the Missouri, as that which it would be most expedient for us to take.

The information of Mr. Fidler, incorrect as it is, strongly argued the necessity of taking the south fork, for if he has been along the eastern side of the Rocky Mountains as far as even latitude 47°, which I think fully as far south as he ever was in that direction, and saw only small rivulets making down from those mountains, the presumption is very strong that those little streams do not penetrate the Rocky Mountains to such distance as would afford rational grounds for a conjecture that they had their sources near any navigable branch of the Columbia. And if he has seen those rivulets as far south as 47°, they are most probably the waters of some northern branch of the Missouri or south fork, probably the river called by the Indians Medicine River. We therefore cannot hope by going northwardly of this place, being already in latitude 47° 24″, to find a stream between this place and the Saskatchewan which does penetrate the Rocky Mountains and which, agreeably to the information of the Indians with respect to the Missouri, does possess a navigable current some distance in those mountains. The Indian information also argued strongly in favor of the south fork. They informed us that the water of the Missouri was nearly transparent at the Great Falls [*Montana*] (this is the case with the water of the south fork); that the falls lay a little to the south of sunset from them (this is also probable, as we are only a few minutes [4] north of Fort Mandan, and the south fork bears considerably south from hence to the mountains); and that falls are below the Rocky Mountains and near the northern termination of one range of those mountains. A range of mountains which appear behind the S. mountains (and which appear to terminate S.W. from this place and on this side of the unbroken chain of the Rocky Mountains) gives us hope that this part of their information is also correct, and there is sufficient distance between this and the mountains for many—and I fear, for us, much too many—falls.

Another impression on my mind is that, if the Indians had passed any stream as large as the south fork on their way to the Missouri, they would not have omitted mentioning it. And the south fork, from its size and complexion of its waters, must enter the Rocky Mountains and, in my opinion, penetrates them to a great distance, or else whence such an immense body of water as it discharges? It cannot proceed from the dry plains to the N.W. of the Yellowstone River on the east side of the Rocky Mountains, for those numerous large dry channels which we witnessed on that side as we ascended the Missouri forbid such a conjecture. And that it should take its sources to the N.W. under those mountains, the travels of Mr. Fidler forbid us to believe.

Those ideas as they occurred to me I endeavored to impress on the minds of the party—all of whom, except Captain Clark, being still firm in the belief that the N. fork was the Missouri and that which we ought to take. They said, very cheerfully, that they were ready to follow us anywhere we thought proper to direct; but that they still thought that the other was the river, and that they were afraid that the south fork would soon terminate in the mountains and leave us at a great distance from the Columbia.

Cruzat, who had been an old Missouri navigator and who, from his integrity, knowledge, and skill as a waterman, had

---

[4] Lewis inadvertently makes this sound like a measurement of time. He means, of course, the geographical minute, or one-sixtieth of a degree.

acquired the confidence of every individual of the party, declared it as his opinion that the N. fork was the true genuine Missouri and could be no other.

Finding them so determined in this belief, and wishing, if we were in an error, to be able to detect it and rectify it as soon as possible, it was agreed between Captain Clark and myself that one of us should set out with a small party by land up the south fork, and continue our route up it until we found the falls or reached the snowy mountains, by which means we should be enabled to determine this question pretty accurately.

This expedition I preferred undertaking, as Captain Clark is the best waterman, &c., and determined to set out the day after tomorrow. I wished to make some further observations at this place, and as we had determined to leave our blacksmith's bellows and tools here, it was necessary to repair some of our arms, and particularly my air gun, the main spring of which was broken, before we left this place. These and some other preparations will necessarily detain us two, perhaps three, days.

I felt myself very unwell this morning, and took a portion of salts, from which I feel much relief this evening.

The cache being completed, I walked to it and examined its construction. It is in a high plain about 40 yards distant from a steep bluff of the south branch on its northern side. The situation a dry one, which is always necessary. A place being fixed on for a cache, a circle about 20 inches in diameter is first described; the turf or sod of this circle is carefully removed, being taken out as entire as possible in order that it may be replaced in the same situation when the cache is filled and secured. This circular hole is then sunk perpendicularly to the depth of one foot—if the ground be not firm, somewhat deeper. They then begin to work it out wider as they proceed downward, until they get it about six or seven feet deep, giving it nearly the shape of the kettle, or lower part of a large still. Its bottom is also somewhat sunk in the center.

The dimensions of the cache are in proportion to the quantity of articles intended to be deposited. As the earth is dug, it is handed up in a vessel and carefully laid on a skin or cloth, and then carried to some place where it can be thrown in such manner as to conceal it, usually into some running stream where it is washed away and leaves no traces which might lead to the discovery of the cache.

Before the goods are deposited, they must be well dried. A parcel of small dry sticks are then collected, and with them a floor is made, three or four inches thick, which is then covered with some dry hay or a raw hide well dried. On this, the articles are deposited, taking care to keep them from touching the walls by putting other dry sticks between as you stow away the merchandise. When nearly full, the goods are covered with a skin, and earth thrown in and well rammed until, with the addition of the turf first removed, the hole is on a level with the surface of the ground. In this manner, dried skins or merchandise will keep perfectly sound for several years.

The traders of the Missouri, particularly those engaged in the trade with the Sioux, are obliged to have frequent recourse to this method in order to avoid being robbed.

Most of the men are busily engaged dressing skins for clothing. In the evening, Cruzat gave us some music on the violin and the men passed the evening in dancing, singing, &c., and were extremely cheerful.

June 10th, 1805

[Lewis]

The day being fair and fine, we dried all our baggage and merchandise. Shields renewed the mainspring of my air gun. We have been much indebted to the ingenuity of this man on many occasions. Without having served any regular apprenticeship to any trade, he makes his own tools, principally, and works extremely well in either wood or metal, and in this way has been extremely serviceable to us, as well as being a good hunter and an excellent waterman.

In order to guard against accidents, we thought it well to conceal some ammunition here, and accordingly buried a tin canister of 4 lbs. of powder and an adequate quantity of lead near our tent; a canister of 6 lbs. lead and an axe, in a thicket up the S. fork, three hundred yards distant from the point. We concluded that we still could spare more ammunition for this deposit. Captain Clark was therefore to make a further deposit in the morning. In addition to one keg of 20 lbs. and an adequate proportion of lead which had been laid by to be buried in the large cache, we now selected the articles to be deposited in this cache which consisted of two best falling axes, one auger, a set of planes, some files, blacksmith's bellows, and hammers, stake, tongs, &c., 1 keg of flour, 2 kegs of parched meal, 2 kegs of pork, 1 keg of salt, some chisels, a cooper's awl, some tin cups, 2 muskets, 3 brown bearskins, beaver skins, horns of the big-horned animal, a part of the men's robes, clothing, and all their superfluous baggage of every description, and beaver traps.

We drew up the red pirogue into the middle of a small island at the entrance of Maria's River, and secured and made her fast to the trees to prevent the high floods from carrying her off. Put my brand on several trees standing near her, and covered her with brush to shelter her from the effects of the sun. At 3 P.M. we had a hard wind from the S.W., which continued about an hour, attended with thunder and rain. As soon as the shower had passed over, we drew out our canoes, corked, repaired, and loaded them. I still feel myself somewhat unwell with the dysentery, but determined to set out in the morning up the south fork, or Missouri, leaving Captain Clark to complete the deposit, and follow me by water with the party. Accordingly, gave orders to Drouilliard, Joseph Fields, Gibson, and Goodrich to hold themselves in readiness to accompany me in the morning. Sacagawea, our Indian woman, is very sick this evening. Captain Clark bled her. The night was cloudy with some rain.

This morning I felt much better but somewhat weakened by my disorder. At 8 A.M., I swung my pack and set forward with my little party. Proceeded to the point where Rose [Tansy] River, a branch of Maria's River, approaches the Missouri so nearly. From this height we discovered a herd of elk on the Missouri, just above us, to which we descended and soon killed four of them. We butchered them and hung up the meat and skins in view of the river in order that the party might get them.

I determined to take dinner here, but before the meal was prepared I was taken with such violent pain in the intestines that I was unable to partake of the feast of marrowbones. My pain still increased, and toward evening was attended with a high fever. Finding myself unable to march, I determined to prepare a camp of some willow boughs and remain all night. Having brought no medicine with me, I resolved to try an experiment with some simples; and the chokecherry which grew abundantly in the bottom first struck my attention.

I directed a parcel of the small twigs to be gathered, stripped of their leaves, cut into pieces of about two inches in length, and boiled in water until a strong black decoction of an astringent bitter taste was produced. At sunset I took a pint of this decoction, and about an hour after repeated the dose. By 10 in the evening, I was entirely relieved from pain, and in fact, every symptom of the disorder forsook me. My fever abated, a gentle perspiration was produced, and I had a comfortable and refreshing night's rest.

Goodrich, who is remarkably fond of fishing, caught several dozen fish of two different species—one about 9 inches long, of white color, round, and in form and fins resembling the white chub common to the Potomac. The other species is precisely the form and about the size of the well-known fish called the hickory shad, or old wife.[5]

June 12th, 1805

[Lewis]

This morning I felt myself quite revived, took another portion of my decoction, and set out at sunrise. I now bore out from the river in order to avoid the steep ravines of the river, which usually make out in the plain to the distance of one or two miles. After gaining the level plain, my course was a little to the west of S.W. Having traveled about 12 miles by 9 in the morning, the sun became warm, and I bore a little to the south in order to gain the river, as well to obtain water to allay my thirst as to kill something for breakfast. For the plain through which we had been passing possesses no water, and is so level that we cannot approach the buffalo within shot before they discover us and take to flight. We arrived at the river about 10 A.M. having traveled about 15 miles. At this place there is a handsome open bottom with some cottonwood timber. Here we met with two large bear and killed them both at the first fire, a circumstance which, I believe, has never happened with the party in killing the brown bear before. We dressed the bear, breakfasted on a part of one of them, and hung the meat and skins on the trees out of the reach of the wolves. I left a note on a stick near the river for Captain Clark, informing him of my progress, &c. After refreshing ourselves about two hours, we again ascended the bluffs and gained the high plain. Saw a great number of burrowing squirrels in the plains today, also wolves, antelopes, mule deer, and immense herds of buffalo. We passed a ridge of land considerably higher than the adjacent plain on either side. From this height, we had a most beautiful and picturesque view of the Rocky Mountains which were perfectly covered with snow, and reaching from S.E. to the N. of N.W. They appear to be formed of several ranges, each succeeding range rising higher than the preceding one, until

---

[5] The first is probably a pike perch (*Stizostedion canadense*), the second, one of the Missouri herrings (*Hyodon alosoides*). "Old wife" is probably a confusion with "alewife," a common fish of the eastern coast and rivers.

the most distant appear to lose their snowy tops in the clouds. This was an august spectacle and still rendered more formidable by the recollection that we had them to pass. We traveled about twelve miles when we again struck the Missouri at a handsome little bottom of cottonwood timber, and although the sun had not yet set, I felt myself somewhat weary, being weakened, I presume, by my late disorder, and therefore determined to remain here during the balance of the day and night, having marched about 27 miles today. On our way, in the evening, we had killed a buffalo, an antelope, and three mule deer, and taken a sufficient quantity of the best of the flesh of these animals for three meals, which we had brought with us. This evening I ate very heartily, and after penning the transactions of the day, amused myself catching those white fish mentioned yesterday. They are here in great abundance. I caught upwards of a dozen in a few minutes.

June 12th, 1805

[Clark]

Saw a number of rattlesnakes today. One of the men caught one by the head, in catching hold of a bush on which his head lay reclined. Three canoes were in great danger today; one dipped water, another very near turning over, &c. At 2 o'clock P.M. a few drops of rain. I walked through a point and killed a buck elk and deer, and we camped on the starboard side. The interpreter's woman very sick. One man has a felon rising on his hand; the other, with the toothache, has taken cold in the jaw, &c.

June 13th, 1805

[Lewis]

This morning we set out about sunrise after taking breakfast off our venison and fish. We again ascended the hills of the river and gained the level country. Fearing that the river bore to the south, and that I might pass the Falls if they existed between this and the snowy mountains, I altered my course nearly to the south and proceeded through the plain. I sent Fields on my right and Drouilliard and Gibson on my left, with orders to kill some meat and join me at the river, where I should halt for dinner.

I had proceeded on this course about two miles with Goodrich at some distance behind me, when my ears were saluted with the agreeable sound of a fall of water, and advancing a little further, I saw the spray rise above the plain like a column of smoke, which would frequently disappear again in an instant, caused, I presume, by the wind which blew pretty hard from the S.W. I did not, however, lose my direction to this point, which soon began to make a roaring too tremendous to be mistaken for any cause short of the Great Falls of the Missouri. Here I arrived about 12 o'clock, having traveled, by estimate, about 15 miles. I hurried down the hill, which was about 200 feet high and difficult of access, to gaze on this sublimely grand spectacle.

I took my position on the top of some rocks about 20 feet high opposite the center of the Falls. This chain of rocks appears once to have formed a part of those over which the waters tumbled, but in the course of time has been separated from it to the distance of 150 yards, lying parallel to it, and an abutment against which the water, after falling over the precipice, beats with great fury. This barrier extends on the right to the perpendicular cliff which forms that border of the river, but to the distance of 120 yards next to the cliff it is but a few feet above the level of the water, and here the water in very high tides appears to pass in a channel of 40 yards next to the higher part of the ledge of rocks. On the left, it extends within 80 or 90 yards of the larboard cliff, which is also perpendicular. Between this abrupt extremity of the ledge of rocks and the perpendicular bluff, the whole body of water passes with incredible swiftness.

Immediately at the cascade, the river is about 300 yards wide. About 90 or 100 yards of this, next the larboard bluff, is a smooth even sheet of water falling over a precipice of at least 80 feet; the remaining part, about 200 yards wide, on my right, forms the grandest sight I ever beheld. The height of the fall is the same as the other, but the irregular and somewhat projecting rocks below receive the water in its passage down, and break it into a perfect white foam which assumes a thousand forms in a moment, sometimes flying up in jets of sparkling foam to the height of fifteen or twenty feet, which are scarcely formed before large rolling bodies of the same beaten and foaming water are thrown over and conceal them. In short, the rocks seem to be most happily fixed to present a sheet of the whitest beaten froth for 200 yards in length and about 80 feet perpendicular.

The water, after descending, strikes against the abutment before mentioned, or that on which I stand, and seems to reverberate, and being met by the more impetuous current, they roll and swell into half-formed billows of great height which rise and again disappear in an instant. The abutment of rock defends a handsome little bottom of about three acres which is diversified and agreeably shaded with some cottonwood trees.

In the lower extremity of the bottom there is a very thick grove of the same kind of trees which are small. In this wood, there are several Indian lodges formed of sticks. A few small cedar grow near the ledge of rocks where I rest. Below the point of these rocks, at a small distance, the river is divided by a large rock which rises several feet above the water, and extends downward with the stream for about 20 yards. About a mile before the water arrives at the pitch, it descends very rapidly, and is confined on the larboard side by a perpendicular cliff of about 100 feet. On the starboard side it is also perpendicular for about three hundred yards above the pitch, where it is then broken by the discharge of a small ravine, down which the buffalo have a large beaten road to the water, for it is but in very few places that these animals can obtain water near this place, owing to the steep and inaccessible banks. I see several skeletons of the buffalo lying in the edge of the water near the starboard bluff which I presume have been swept down by the current and precipitated over this tremendous fall.

About 300 yards below me, there is another abutment of solid rock with a perpendicular face and about 60 feet high, which projects from the starboard side at right angles to the distance of 134 yards, and terminates the lower part nearly of the bottom before mentioned, there being a passage around the end of this abutment, between it and the river, of about 20 yards. Here the river again assumes its usual width, soon spreading to near 300 yards but still continuing its rapidity. From the reflection of the sun on the spray or mist which arises from these Falls, there is a beautiful rainbow produced which adds not a little to the beauty of this majestically grand scenery.

After writing this imperfect description, I again viewed the Falls, and was so much disgusted with the imperfect idea which it conveyed of the scene, that I determined to draw my pen across it and begin again; but then reflected that I could not perhaps succeed better than penning the first impressions of the mind. I wished for the pencil of Salvator Rosa, a Titian, or the pen of [James] Thomson, that I might be enabled to give to the enlightened world some just idea of this truly magnificent and sublimely grand object which has, from the commencement of time, been concealed from the view of civilized man. But this was fruitless and vain. I most sincerely regretted that I had not brought a camera obscura with me, by the assistance of which even I could have hoped to have done better, but alas, this was also out of my reach.

I therefore, with the assistance of my pen only, endeavored to trace some of the stronger features of this scene by the assistance of which, and my recollection aided by some able pencil, I hope still to give to the world some faint idea of an object which at this moment fills me with such pleasure and astonishment; and which of its kind, I will venture to assert, is second to but one in the known world.

I retired to the shade of a tree, where I determined to fix my camp for the present, and dispatch a man in the morning to inform Captain Clark and the party of my success in finding the Falls, and settle in their minds all further doubts as to the Missouri. The hunters now arrived, loaded with excellent buffalo meat, and informed me that they had killed three very fat [*buffalo*] cows about ¾ of a mile from hence. I directed them, after they had refreshed themselves, to go back and butcher them and bring another load of meat each to our camp, determining to employ those who remained with me in drying meat for the party against their arrival. In about two hours, or at 4 o'clock P.M., they set out on this duty, and I walked down the river about three miles to discover, if possible, some place to which the canoes might arrive, or at which they might be drawn on shore in order to be taken by land above the falls, but returned without effecting either of these objectives.

The river was one continued scene of rapids and cascades, which I readily perceived could not be encountered with our canoes, and the cliffs still retained their perpendicular structure, and were from 150 to 200 feet high. In short, the river appears here to have worn a channel in the process of time through a solid rock.

On my return, I found the party at camp. They had butchered the buffalo and brought in some more meat, as I had directed. Goodrich had caught half a dozen very fine trout and a number of both species of the white fish. These trout (caught in the Falls) are from sixteen to twenty-three inches in length, precisely resemble our mountain or speckled trout in form and the position of their fins, but the specks on these are of a deep black instead of the red or gold color of those common to the U. States. These are furnished long sharp teeth on the palate and tongue, and have generally a small dash of red on each side behind the front ventral fins. The flesh is of a pale yellowish red or, when in good order, of a rose red.

I am induced to believe that the brown, the white, and the grizzly bear of this country are the same species, only differing in color from age or more probably from the same natural cause that many other animals of the same family differ in color. One of those which we killed yesterday was of a cream-colored white, while the other in company with it was of the common bay or reddish brown, which seems to be the most usual color of them. The white one appeared from its talons and teeth to be the youngest; it was smaller than the other, and although a monstrous beast, we supposed that it had not yet attained its growth, and that it was a little upwards of two years old. The young cubs which we have killed have always been of a brownish-white, but none of them as white as that we killed yesterday. One other that we killed some time since had a white stripe or list of about eleven inches wide entirely around his body just behind the shoulders, and was much darker than these bear usually are.

My fare is really sumptuous this evening: Buffalo's humps, tongues, and marrowbones, fine trout, parched meal, pepper and salt, and a good appetite. The last is not considered the least of the luxuries.

June 13th, 1805

[Clark]

A fair morning. Some dew this morning. The Indian woman very sick. I gave her a dose of salts. We set out early. At a mile and ½, passed a small rapid stream on the larboard side, which heads in a mountain to the S.E., 12 or 15 miles, which at this time is covered with snow. We call this stream Snow River, as it is the conveyance of the melted snow from that mountain at present. Numbers of geese and goslings. The geese cannot fly at this season. Gooseberries are ripe and in great abundance. The yellow currant is also common, not yet ripe. Killed a buffalo and camped on the larboard side, near an old Indian fortified camp. One man sick, and three with swellings. The Indian woman very sick.

June 14th, 1805

[Lewis]

This morning at sunrise I dispatched Joseph Fields with a letter to Captain Clark, and ordered him to keep sufficiently near the river to observe its situation in order that he might be enabled to give Captain Clark an idea of the point at which it would be best to halt to make our portage. I set one man preparing a scaffold and collecting wood to dry the meat. Sent the others to bring in the balance of the buffalo meat, or at least the part which the wolves had left us, for those fellows are ever at hand, and ready to partake with us the moment we kill a buffalo. And there is no means of putting the meat out of their reach in those plains. The two men, shortly after, returned with the meat and informed me that the wolves had devoured the greater part of the meat.

About ten o'clock this morning, while the men were engaged with the meat, I took my gun and espontoon and thought I would walk a few miles and see where the rapids terminated above, and return to dinner. Accordingly, I set out and proceeded up the river about S.W. After passing one continued rapid and three small cascades of about four or five feet each at the distance of about five miles, I arrived at a fall of about 19 feet. The river is here about 400 yards wide. This pitch, which I called the Crooked Falls, occupies about three-fourths of the width of the river, commencing on the south side, extends obliquely upward about 150 yards, then, forming an acute angle, extends downward nearly to the commencement of four small islands lying near the N. shore. Among these islands and between them and the lower extremity of the perpendicular pitch, being a distance of 100 yards or upwards, the water glides down the side of a sloping rock with a velocity almost equal to that of its perpendicular descent. Just above this rapid the river makes a sudden bend to the right, or northwardly.

I should have returned from hence; but, hearing a tremendous roaring above me, I continued my route across the point of a hill a few hundred yards further, and was again presented by one of the most beautiful objects in nature—a cascade of about fifty feet perpendicular stretching at right angles across the river from side to side to the distance of at least a quarter of a mile. Here the river pitches over a shelving rock, with an edge as regular and as straight as if formed by art, without a niche or break in it. The water descends in one even and uninterrupted sheet to the bottom, where, dashing against the rocky bottom, it rises into foaming billows of great height and rapidly glides away, hissing, flashing, and sparkling as it departs. The spray rises, from one extremity to the other, to 50 feet. I now thought that if a skillful painter had been asked to make a beautiful cascade, he would most probably have presented the precise image of this one. Nor could I for some time determine on which of those two great cataracts to bestow the palm—on this, or that which I had discovered yesterday. At length I determined between these two great rivals for glory, that this was *pleasingly beautiful,* while the other was *sublimely grand.*

I had scarcely unfixed my eyes from this pleasing object before I discovered another fall above at the distance of half a mile. Thus invited, I did not once think of returning, but hurried thither to amuse myself with this newly discovered object. I found this to be a cascade of about 14 feet, possessing a perpendicular pitch of about 6 feet. This was tolerably regular, stretching across the river, from bank to bank, where it was about a quarter of a mile wide. In any other neighborhood but this, such a cascade would probably be extolled for its beauty and magnificence, but here I passed it by with but little attention, determining, as I had proceeded so far, to continue my route to the head of the rapids if it should even detain me all night. At every rapid, cataract, and cascade I discovered that the bluffs grew lower, or that the bed of the river rose nearer to a level with the plains.

Still pursuing the river, with its course about S.W., passing a continuous scene of rapids and small cascades, at the distance of 2½ miles I arrived at another cataract of 26 feet. This is not immediately perpendicular. A rock about ⅓ of its descent seems to protrude to a small distance and receives the water in its passage downward and gives a curve to the water, though it falls mostly with a regular and smooth sheet.

The river is near six hundred yards wide at this place: a beautiful level plain on the S. side only a few feet above the level of the pitch; on the N. side, where I am, the country is more broken, and immediately behind me, near the river, a high hill. Below this fall, at a little distance, a beautiful little island, well timbered, is situated about the middle of the river. In this island, on a cottonwood tree, an eagle has placed her nest. A more inaccessible spot I believe she could not have found, for neither man nor beast dare pass those gulfs which separate her little domain from the shores. The water is also broken in such manner as it descends over this pitch that the mist or spray rises to a considerable height. This fall is certainly much the greatest I ever beheld except those two which I have mentioned. It is incomparably a greater cataract and a more noble, interesting object than the celebrated falls of Potomac or Schuylkill, &c.

Just above this is another cascade of about 5 feet, above which the water, as far as I could see, began to abate of its velocity, and I therefore determined to ascend the hill behind me, which promised a fine prospect of the adjacent country; nor was I disappointed at my arrival at its summit. From hence, I overlooked a most beautiful and extensive plain reaching from the river to the base of the snow-clad mountains to the S. and S.West. I also observed the Missouri, stretching its meandering course to the south through this plain to a great distance, filled to its even and grassy brim. Another large river flowed in on its western side, about four miles above me, and extended itself through a level and fertile valley of three miles in width, a great distance to the N.W., rendered more conspicuous by the timber which garnished its borders. In these plains, and more particularly in the valley just below me, immense herds of buffalo are feeding. The Missouri, just above this hill, makes a bend to the south, where it lies a smooth, even, and unruffled sheet of water, nearly a mile in width, bearing on its watery bosom vast flocks of geese which feed at pleasure in the delightful pasture on either border. The young geese are now completely feathered except the wings which, both in the young and old, are yet deficient.

After feasting my eyes on this ravishing prospect and resting myself a few minutes, I determined to proceed as far as the river which I saw discharge itself on the west side of the Missouri, convinced that it was the river which the Indians call Medicine River, and which they informed us fell into the Missouri just above the falls. I descended the hill and directed my course to the bend of the Missouri, near which there was a herd of at least a thousand buffalo. Here I thought it would be well to kill a buffalo and leave him until my return from the river, and if I then found that I had not time to get back to camp this evening, to remain all night here—there being a few sticks of driftwood lying along the shore which would answer for my fire, and a few scattering cottonwood trees a few hundred yards below, which would afford me at least the semblance of a shelter. Under this impression, I selected a fat buffalo and shot him very well, through the lungs.

While I was gazing attentively on the poor animal discharging blood in streams from his mouth and nostrils, expecting him to fall every instant, and having entirely forgotten to reload my rifle, a large white—or rather, brown—bear had perceived and crept on me within twenty steps before I discovered him. In the first moment, I drew up my gun to shoot but at the same instant recollected that she was not loaded, and that he was too near for me to hope to perform this operation before he reached me, as he was then briskly advancing on me. It was an open level plain, not a bush within miles nor a tree within less than three hundred yards of me. The river bank was sloping and not more than three feet above the level of the water. In short, there was no place by means of which I could conceal myself from this monster until I could charge my rifle.

In this situation, I thought of retreating in a brisk walk as fast as he was advancing until I could reach a tree about 300 yards below me, but I had no sooner turned myself about but he pitched at me, open-mouthed and full speed. I ran about 80 yards, and found he gained on me fast. I then ran into the water. The idea struck me to get into the water to such depth that I could stand and he would be obliged to swim, and that I could, in that situation, defend myself with my espontoon. Accordingly, I ran hastily into the water about waist deep and faced about and presented the point of my espontoon.

At this instant, he arrived at the edge of the water within about twenty feet of me. The moment I put myself in this attitude of defense, he suddenly wheeled about as if frightened, declined the combat on such unequal grounds, and retreated with quite as great precipitation as he had just before pursued me. As soon as I saw him run off in that manner, I returned to the shore and charged my gun, which I had still retained in my hand throughout this curious adventure. I saw him run through the level open plain about three miles, till he disappeared in the woods on Medicine River. During the whole of this distance he ran at full speed, sometimes appearing to look behind him as if he expected pursuit.

I now began to reflect on this novel occurrence and endeavored to account for this sudden retreat of the bear. I at first thought that perhaps he had not smelled me before he arrived at the water's edge so near me, but I then reflected that he had pursued me for about 80 or 90 yards before I took to the water, and on examination saw the ground torn with his talons immediately on the impression of my steps; and the cause of his alarm still remains with me mysterious and unaccountable. So it was; and I felt myself not a little gratified that he had declined the combat. My gun reloaded, I felt confidence once more in my strength, and determined not to be thwarted in my design of visiting Medicine River, but determined never again to suffer my piece to be longer empty than the time she necessarily required to charge her.

I passed through the plain nearly in the direction which the bear had run to Medicine River. Found it a handsome stream, about 200 yards wide, with a gentle current, apparently deep. Its waters clear, and banks, which were formed principally of dark brown and blue clay, were about the height of those of the Missouri, or from 3 to 5 feet. Yet they had not the appearance of ever being overflowed, a circumstance which I did not expect so immediately in the neighborhood of the mountains, from whence I should have supposed that sudden and immense torrents would issue at certain seasons of the year. But the reverse is absolutely the case. I am therefore compelled to believe that the snowy mountains yield their waters slowly, being partially affected every day by the influence of the sun only, and never suddenly melted down by hasty showers of rain.

Having examined Medicine River, I now determined to return, having by my estimate about 12 miles to walk. I looked at my watch and found it was half after six P.M. In returning through the level bottom of Medicine River, and about 200 yards distant from the Missouri, my direction led me directly to an animal that I at first supposed was a wolf. But on nearer approach, or about sixty paces distant, I discovered that it was not. Its color was a brownish yellow. It was standing near its burrow, and when I approached it thus nearly, it crouched itself down like a cat, looking immediately at me as if it designed to spring on me. I took aim at it and fired. It instantly disappeared in its burrow. I loaded my gun, and examined the place, which was dusty, and saw the track, from which I am still further convinced that it was of the tiger kind.[7] Whether I struck it or not, I could not determine, but I am almost confident that I did. My gun is true, and I had a steady rest by means of my espontoon, which I have found very serviceable to me in this way, in the open plains.

It now seemed to me that all the beasts of the neighborhood had made a league to destroy me, or that some fortune was disposed to amuse herself at my expense, for I had not proceeded more than 300 yards from the burrow of this tiger cat, before three bull buffalo, which were feeding with a large herd about half a mile from me on my left, separated from the herd and ran full speed toward me. I thought at least to give them some amusement, and altered my direction to meet them. When they arrived within a hundred yards they made a halt, took a good view of me, and retreated with precipitation. I then continued my route homeward, passed the buffalo which I had killed, but did not think it prudent to remain all night at this place, which

[7] The animal "of the tiger kind" was probably either a wolverine (*Gulo luscus*) or a cougar (*Felis concolor*, also called *Felis cougar*). Neither beast is considered aggressively dangerous today, though all animals were bolder before the introduction of firearms. Either might fight if it were cornered or thought it was cornered. Lewis was probably a bit nervous after his encounter with the grizzly.

really, from the succession of curious adventures, wore the impression on my mind of enchantment. At some times, for a moment, I thought it might be a dream, but the prickly pears which pierced my feet very severely once in a while, particularly after it grew dark, convinced me that I was really awake, and that it was necessary to make the best of my way to camp.

It was some time after dark before I returned to the party. I found them extremely uneasy for my safety. They had formed a thousand conjectures, all of which equally forboding my death, which they had so far settled among them that they had already agreed on the route which each should take in the morning to search for me. I felt myself much fatigued, but ate a hearty supper and took a good night's rest. The weather being warm, I had left my leather over-shirt and had worn only a yellow flannel one.

June 14th, 1805

[Clark]

A fine morning. The Indian woman complaining all night, and excessively bad this morning. Her case is somewhat dangerous. Two men with the toothache, 2 with tumors, and one man with a tumor and a slight fever. Passed the camp Captain Lewis made the first night, at which place he had left part of two bears, their skins, &c. Three men with tumors went on shore and stayed out all night. One of them killed 2 buffalo, a part of which we made use of for breakfast.

The current excessively rapid, more so as we ascend. We find great difficulty in getting the pirogue and canoes up in safety. Canoes take in water frequently.

At 4 o'clock this evening, Joe Fields returned from Captain Lewis with a letter for me. Captain Lewis dates his letter from the Great Falls of the Missouri, which, Fields informs me, is about 20 miles in advance and about 10 miles above the place I left the river the time I was up last week. Captain Lewis informs me that those falls in part answer the description given of them by the Indians, much higher; the eagle's nest which they describe is there. From those signs, he is convinced of this being the river the Indians call the Missouri.

He intends examining the river above, until my arrival at a point from which we can make a portage, which he is apprehensive will be at least 5 miles, and both above and below there are several small pitches and swift troubled water. We made only 10 miles today, and camped on the larboard side. Much hard slate in the cliffs and but a small quantity of timber.

June 15th, 1805

[Lewis]

This morning the men again were sent to bring in some more meat which Drouilliard had killed yesterday and continued the operation of drying it. I amused myself in fishing and sleeping away the fatigues of yesterday. I caught a number of very fine trout, which I made Goodrich dry. Goodrich also caught about two dozen and several small cat [*i.e., fish*] of a yellow color, which would weigh about 4 pounds. The tail was separated with a deep angular notch like that of the white cat of the Missouri, from which indeed they differed only in color.

When I awoke from my sleep today, I found a large rattlesnake coiled on the leaning trunk of a tree under the shade of which I had been lying at the distance of about ten feet from him. I killed the snake and found that he had 176 scuta on the abdomen and 17 half-formed scuta on the tail. It was of the same kind which I had frequently seen before. They do not differ in their colors from the rattlesnake common to the Middle Atlantic States, but considerably in the form and figures of those colors.

This evening after dark, Joseph Fields returned and informed me that Captain Clark had arrived with the party at the foot of a rapid about 5 miles below which he did not think proper to ascend, and would wait my arrival there. I had discovered from my journey yesterday that a portage on this side of the river will be attended by much difficulty in consequence of several deep ravines which intersect the plains nearly at right angles with the river to a considerable distance, while the south side appears to be a delightful smooth, unbroken plain. The bearings of the river also make it probable that the portage will be shorter on that side than on this. I directed Fields to return early in the morning to Captain Clark and request him to send up a party of men for the dried meat which we had made. I find a very heavy dew on the grass about my camp every morning, which no doubt proceeds from the mist of the falls, as it takes place nowhere in the plains nor on the river, except here.

June the 15th, 1805

[Clark]

A fair morning, and warm. We set out at the usual time

and proceeded on with great difficulty, as the river is more rapid. We can hear the falls this morning very distinctly. Our Indian woman sick and low-spirited. I gave her the bark and applied it externally to her region, which revived her much.

The current excessively rapid and difficult to ascend. Great numbers of dangerous places, and the fatigue which we have to encounter is incredible: the men in the water from morning until night, hauling the cord and boats, walking on sharp rocks and round slippery stones which alternately cut their feet and throw them down. Notwithstanding all this difficulty, they go with great cheerfulness. Added to those difficulties, the rattlesnakes are innumerable and require great caution to prevent being bitten.

We passed a small river on the larboard side about 30 yards wide, very rapid, which heads in the mountains to the S.E. I went up this river 5 miles. It has some timber in its bottoms and a fall of 15 feet at one place. Above this river, the bluffs are of red earth mixed with strata of black stone. Below this little river, we passed a white clay which mixes with water like flour in every respect.

The Indian woman much worse this evening. She will not take any medicine. Her husband petitions to return, &c. River more rapid.

June 16th, 1805

[Lewis]

J. Fields set out early on his return to the lower camp. At noon the men arrived, and shortly after, I set out with them to rejoin the party. We took with us the dried meat, consisting of about 600 pounds, and several dozen of dried trout. About 2 P.M., I reached the camp.

Found the Indian woman extremely ill and much reduced by her indisposition. This gave me some concern, as well for the poor object herself—then with a young child in her arms—as from the consideration of her being our only dependence for a friendly negotiation with the Snake Indians, on whom we depend for horses to assist us in our portage from the Missouri to the Columbia River.

I now informed Captain Clark of my discoveries with respect to the most proper side for our portage, and of its great length, which I could not estimate at less than 16 miles. Captain Clark had already sent two men this morning to examine the country on the south side of the river. He now passed over with the party to that side, and fixed a camp about a mile below the entrance of a creek where there was a sufficient quantity of wood for fuel, an article which can be obtained but in few places in this neighborhood.

After discharging the loads, four of the canoes were sent back to me, which, by means of strong ropes, we hauled above the rapids, and passed over to the south side, from whence, the water not being rapid, we can readily convey them into the creek by means of which we hope to get them on the high plain with more ease. One of the small canoes was left below this rapid in order to pass and repass the river for the purpose of hunting, as well as to procure the water of the sulphur spring, the virtues of which I now resolved to try on the Indian woman. The water to all appearance is precisely similar to that of Bowyer's Sulphur Spring in Virginia.

Captain Clark determined to set out in the morning to examine the country and survey the portage and discover the best route. As the distance was too great to think of transporting the canoes and baggage on the men's shoulders, we selected six men and ordered them to look out some timber this evening and early in the morning to set about making a parcel of truck wheels in order to convey our canoes and baggage over the portage.

We determined to leave the white pirogue at this place and substitute the iron boat, and also to make a further deposit of a part of our stores. In the evening, the men who had been sent out to examine the country returned and made a very unfavorable report. They informed us that the creek just above us, and two deep ravines still higher up, cut the plain between the river and mountain in such a manner that, in their opinions, a portage for the canoes on this side was impracticable.

Good or bad, we must make the portage. Notwithstanding this report, I am still convinced from the view I had of the country the day before yesterday that a good portage may be had on this side—at least much better than on the other, and much nearer also.

I found that two doses of barks and opium, which I had given her [*Sacagawea*] since my arrival, had produced an alteration in her pulse for the better. They were now much fuller and more regular. I caused her to drink the mineral water altogether. When I first came down, I found that her pulse was scarcely perceptible—very quick, frequently irregular, and attended with strong nervous symptoms, that of the twitching of the fingers and leaders of the arm. Now the pulse had become regular, much fuller, and a gentle perspiration had taken place. The nervous symptoms have also in a great measure abated, and she feels herself much freer from pain. She complains principally of the lower region of the abdomen. I therefore continued the cataplasms of barks and laudanum which had been previously used by my friend Captain Clark. I believe her disorder originated principally from an obstruction of the menses in consequence of taking cold.

I determined to remain at this camp in order to make some celestial observations, restore the sick woman, and have all matters in a state of readiness to commence the portage immediately on the return of Captain Clark.

June 17th, 1805

[Lewis]

Captain Clark set out early this morning with five men to examine the country and survey the river and portage, as had been concerted last evening. I set six men at work to prepare four sets of truck wheels with couplings, tongues and bodies, that they might either be used without the bodies for transporting our canoes, or with them in transporting our baggage. I found that the elk skins I had prepared for my boat were insufficient to complete her, some of them having become damaged by the weather and being frequently wet. To make up this deficiency, I sent out two hunters this morning to hunt elk.

The balance of the party I employed first in unloading the white pirogue, which we intend leaving at this place, and bringing the whole of our baggage together and arranging it in proper order near our camp. This duty being completed, I employed them in taking five of the small canoes up the creek, which we now call Portage Creek, about 1¾ miles. Here I had them taken out and laid in the sun to dry.

From this place there is a gradual ascent to the top of the high plain, to which we can now take them with ease. The bluffs of this creek below and those of the river above its entrance are so steep that it would be almost impracticable to have gotten them on the plain.

We found much difficulty in getting the canoes up this creek to the distance we were compelled to take them, in consequence of the rapids and rocks which obstruct the channel of the creek. One of the canoes overset and was very near injuring 2 men essentially. Just above the canoes, the creek has a perpendicular fall of 5 feet and the cliffs again become very steep and high. We were fortunate enough to find one cottonwood tree, just below the entrance of Portage Creek, that was large enough to make our carriage wheels about 22 inches in diameter. Fortunate I say, because I do not believe that we could find another of the same size, perfectly sound, within 20 miles of us. The cottonwood which we are obliged to employ in the other parts of the work is extremely illy calculated for it, being soft and brittle.

We have made two axletrees of the mast of the white pirogue, which I hope will answer tolerably well, though it is rather small. The Indian woman much better today. I have still continued the same course of medicine. She is free from pain, clear of fever, her pulse regular, and eats as heartily as I am willing to permit her, of broiled buffalo well seasoned with pepper and salt, and rich soup of the same meat. I think, therefore, that there is every rational hope of her recovery.

Saw a vast number of buffalo feeding in every direction around us in the plains, others coming down in large herds to water at the river. The fragments of many carcasses of these poor animals daily pass down the river, thus mangled, I presume, in descending those immense cataracts above us. As the buffalo generally go in large herds to water, and the passages to the river about the falls are narrow and steep, the hinder part of the herd press those in front out of their depth, and the water instantly takes them over the cataracts, where they are instantly crushed to death without the possibility of escaping. In this manner, I have seen ten or a dozen disappear in a few minutes. Their mangled carcasses lie along the shores below the falls in considerable quantities and afford fine amusement for the bear, wolves, and birds of prey. This may be one reason—and I think not a bad one, either—that the bear are so tenacious of their right of spoil in this neighborhood.

June 17th, 1805

[Clark]

A fine morning. Wind as usual. Captain Lewis with the party unloaded the pirogue, and he determined to keep the party employed in getting the loading to the creek about one mile over a low hill, in my absence on the portage.

I set out with 5 men at 8 o'clock, and proceeded on up the creek some distance, to examine that and, if possible, ascend that sufficiently high, that a straight course to the mouth of Medicine River would head the two ravines. The creek I found confined, rapid, and shallow, generally passed through an open rolling prairie, so as to head the two ravines.

After heading two, we steered our course so as to strike the river below the great pitch. On our course to the river, crossed a deep ravine near its mouth, with steep cliffs. This ravine had running water which was very fine. The river at this place is narrow, and confined in perpendicular cliffs of 170 feet. From the tops of those cliffs, the country rises with a steep ascent for about 250 feet more.

We proceeded up the river, passing a succession of rapids and cascades, to the Falls, which we had heard for several miles, making a deadly sound. I beheld those cataracts with astonishment. The whole of the water of this great river confined in a channel of 280 yards and pitching over a rock of 97 feet ¾ of an inch. From the foot of the Falls rises a continued mist which is extended for 150 yards down and to near the top of the cliffs on L. side.

The river below is confined in a narrow channel of 93 yards, leaving a small bottom of timber on the starboard side which is defended by a rock, ranging crosswise the river a little below the chute. A short distance below this cataract a large rock divides the stream. In descending the cliffs to take the height of the fall, I was near slipping into the water, at which place I must have been sucked under in an instant, and with difficulty and great risk I ascended again, and descended the cliff lower down (but few places can be descended to the river), and took the height with as much accuracy as possible, with a spirit level, &c. Dined at a fine spring 200 yards below the pitch, near which place 4 cotton willow trees grew. On one of them I marked my name, the date, and height of the falls. We then proceeded on up the river, passing a continued cascade and rapid to a fall of 19 feet at 4 small islands. This fall is diagonally across the river from the larboard side, forming an angle of ¾ of the width for the larboard, from which side it pitches for ⅔ of that distance. On the starboard side is a rapid decline. Below this chute, a deep ravine falls in, in which we camped for the night, which was cold.

The mountains in every direction have snow on them. The plain to our left is level. We saw one bear and innumerable numbers of buffalo. I saw 2 herds of those animals watering immediately above a considerable rapid. They descended by a narrow pass, &c., the bottom small. The river forced those forward into the water, some of which were taken down in an instant, and seen no more. Others made shore with difficulty. I beheld 40 or 50 of those swimming at the same time. Those animals in this way are lost, and accounts for the number of buffalo carcasses below the rapids.

June 18th, 1805

[Lewis]

This morning I employed all hands in drawing the pirogue on shore in a thick bunch of willow bushes some little distance below our camp. Fastened her securely, drove out the plugs of the gauge holes of her bottom, and covered her with bushes and driftwood to shelter her from the sun. I now selected a place for a cache and set three men at work to complete it and employed all others—except those about the wagons—in overhauling, airing, and repacking our Indian goods, ammunition, provision, and stores of every description which required inspection. Examined the frame of my iron boat and found all the parts complete except one screw, which the ingenuity of Shields can readily replace—a resource which we have very frequent occasion for.

About twelve o'clock, the hunters returned. They had killed ten deer but no elk. I begin to fear that we shall have some difficulty in procuring skins for the boat. I would prefer those of the elk because I believe them more durable and strong than those of the buffalo, and that they will not shrink so much in drying.

We saw a herd of buffalo come down to water at the sulphur spring this evening. I dispatched some hunters to kill some of them, and a man also for a cask of mineral water. The hunters soon killed two of them, in fine order, and returned with a good quantity of the flesh, having left the remainder in a situation that it will not spoil provided the wolves do not visit it. The wagons are completed this evening, and appear as if they would answer the purpose very well if the axletrees prove sufficiently strong. The wind blew violently this evening, as they frequently do in this open country where there is not a tree to break or oppose their force.

The Indian woman is recovering fast. She sat up the greater part of the day, and walked out for the first time since she arrived here. She eats heartily, and is free from fever or pain. I continue same course of medicine and regimen except that I added one dose of 15 drops of the oil of vitriol today, about noon.

June 18th, 1805

[Clark]

We set out early and arrived at the second great cataract

about 200 yards above the last, of 19 feet pitch. This is one of the grandest views in nature, and by far exceeds anything I ever saw: the Missouri falling over a shelving rock for 47 feet 8 inches, with a cascade, &c., of 14 feet 7 inches above the chute, for ¼ mile. I descended the cliff below this cataract with ease, measured the height of the perpendicular fall of 47 feet 8 inches, at which place the river is 473 yards wide, as also the height of the cascade, &c. A continual mist quite across this fall.

After which, we proceeded on up the river a little more than a mile to the largest fountain or spring I ever saw, and doubt if it is not the largest in America known. This water boils up from under the rocks near the edge of the river and falls immediately into the river eight feet, and keeps its color for ½ a mile, which is immensely clear and of a bluish cast.

Proceeded on up the river past a succession of rapids to the next great fall of 26 feet 5 inches, river 580 yards wide. This fall is not entirely perpendicular. A short bench gives a curve to the water as it falls. A beautiful small island at the foot of this fall near the center of the channel, covered with trees.

This evening one man, A. Willard, going for a load of meat at 170 yards distance on an island, was attacked by a white bear, and very near being caught. Pursued within 40 yards of camp, where I was, with one man. I collected three others of the party and pursued the bear (who had pursued my track from a buffalo I had killed on the island at about 300 yards distance and chanced to meet Willard), for fear of his attacking one man, Colter, at the lower point of the island. Before we had got down, the bear had alarmed the man and pursued him into the water. At our approach he retreated, and we relieved the man in the water. I saw the bear, but the bushes were so thick that I could not shoot him, and it was nearly dark. The wind from the S.W. and cool. Killed a beaver and an elk for their skins this evening.

June 19th, 1805

[Lewis]

This morning I sent over several men for the meat which was killed yesterday. A few hours after, they returned with it; the wolves had not discovered it. I also dispatched George Drouilliard, Reuben Fields, and George Shannon on the north side of the Missouri with orders to proceed to the entrance of Medicine River, and endeavor to kill some elk in that neighborhood. As there is more timber on that river than the Missouri, I expect that the elk are more plenty. The cache completed today. The wind blew violently the greater part of the day.

The Indian woman was much better this morning. She walked out and gathered a considerable quantity of the white apples, of which she ate so heartily in their raw state, together with a considerable quantity of dried fish without my knowledge, that she complained very much and her fever again returned. I rebuked Charbonneau severely for suffering her to indulge herself with such food, he being privy to it and having been previously told what she must only eat. I now gave her broken doses of diluted niter until it produced perspiration, and at 10 P.M., 30 drops of laudanum, which gave her a tolerable night's rest.

Chapter XI

PORTAGING AMONG THE GRIZZLY BEARS

June 21—July 14, 1805

June 21st, 1805

[Lewis]

This morning I employed the greater part of the men in transporting a part of the baggage over Portage Creek to the top of the high plain about three miles in advance on the portage. I also had one canoe carried on truck wheels to the same place and put the baggage in it, in order to make an early start in the morning, as the route of our portage is not yet entirely settled, and it would be inconvenient to remain in the open plain all night at a distance from water, which would probably be the case if we did not set out early, as the latter part of the route is destitute of water for about 8 miles.

Having determined to go to the upper part of the portage tomorrow, in order to prepare my boat and receive and take care of the stores as they were transported, I caused the iron frame of the boat and the necessary tools, my private baggage, and instruments to be taken as a part of this load; also the baggage of Joseph Fields, Sergeant Gass, and John Shields, whom I had selected to assist me in constructing the leather boat.

Three men were employed today in shaving the elk skins which had been collected for the boat. The balance of the party were employed in cutting the meat we had killed yesterday into thin flitches and drying it, and in bringing in the balance of what had been left over the river with three men last evening. I readily perceive several difficulties in preparing the leather boat, which are the want of convenient and proper timber, bark, skins, and above all, that of pitch to pay her seams, a deficiency that I really know not how to surmount, unless it be by means of tallow and pounded charcoal, which mixture has answered a very good purpose on our wooden canoes heretofore.

June 22nd, 1805

This morning early, Captain Clark and myself with all the party except Sergeant Ordway, Charbonneau, Goodrich, York, and the Indian woman, set out to pass the portage with the canoe and baggage to the Whitebear Island, where we intend that this portage shall end. Captain Clark piloted us through the plains. About noon we reached a little stream about 8 miles on the portage, where we halted and dined. We were obliged here to renew both axletrees and the tongues and horns of one set of wheels, which took us no more than 2 hours. These parts of our carriage had been made of cottonwood and one axletree of an old mast, all of which proved deficient and had broken down several times before we reached this place. We have now renewed them with the sweet willow and hope that they will answer better. After dark, we had reached within half a mile of our intended camp when the tongues gave way and we were obliged to leave the canoe. Each man took as much of the baggage as he could carry on his back and proceeded to the river, where we formed our encampment, much fatigued. The prickly pears were extremely troublesome to us, sticking our feet through our moccasins.

June 23rd, 1805

This morning early, I selected a place for the purpose of constructing my boat, near the water under some shady willows. Captain Clark had the canoe and baggage brought up, after which we breakfasted and nearly consumed the meat which he had left here. He now set out on his return with the party. I employed the three men with me in the forenoon clearing away the brush and forming our camp, and putting the frame of the boat together.

This being done, I sent Shields and Gass to look out for the necessary timber, and with J. Fields descended the river in the canoe to the mouth of Medicine River, in search of the hunters whom I had dispatched thither on the 19th inst., and from whom we had not heard a sentence. I entered the mouth of Medicine River and ascended it about half a mile, when we landed and walked up the starboard side, frequently whooping as we went on in order to find the hunters. At length, after ascending the river about five miles, we found Shannon, who had passed the Medicine River and fixed his camp on the larboard side, where he had killed seven deer and several buffalo, and dried about 600 pounds of buffalo meat; but had killed no elk.

Shannon could give me no further account of R. Fields and Drouilliard than that he had left them about noon on the 19th at the Great Falls and had come on to the mouth of Medicine River to hunt elk as he had been directed, and never had seen them since. The evening being now far spent, I thought it better to pass the Medicine River and remain all night at Shannon's camp. I passed the river on a raft which we soon constructed for the purpose.

June 23rd, 1805

[Clark]

A cloudy morning. Wind from the S.E. After getting the canoe to camp and the articles left in the plains, we ate breakfast of the remaining meat found in camp, and I, with the party, the truck wheels, and poles to stick up in the prairie as a guide, set out on our return. We proceeded on, and measured the way, which I straightened considerably from that I went on yesterday, and arrived at our lower camp in sufficient time to take up two canoes on the top of the hill from the creek. Found all safe at camp. The men mended their moccasins with double soles to save their feet from the prickly pear, which abounds in the prairies, and the hard ground, which in some and many places is so hard as to hurt the feet very much. The immense number of buffalo, after the last rain, have trod the flat places in such a manner as to leave it uneven, and that has dried and is worse than frozen ground.

June 24th, 1805

[Lewis]

Supposing that Drouilliard and R. Fields might possibly be still higher up Medicine River, I dispatched J. Fields up the river with orders to proceed about four miles and then return, whether he found them or not, and join Shannon at this camp. I set out early and walked down the southwest side of the river, and sent Shannon down the opposite side, to bring the canoe over to me and put me across the Missouri. Having landed on the larboard side of the Missouri, I sent Shannon back with the canoe to meet J. Fields and bring the dried meat at that place to the camp at Whitebear Island, which he accomplished, and arrived with Fields this morning.

The party also arrived this evening with two canoes from the lower camp. They were wet and fatigued. Gave them a dram. R. Fields came with them and gave me an account of his and Drouilliard's hunt, and informed me that Drouilliard was still at their camp with the meat they had dried. The iron frame of my boat is 36 feet long, 4½ feet in the beam, and 26 inches in the hold.

This morning early, Captain Clark had the remaining canoe drawn out of the water, and divided the remainder of our baggage into three parcels, one of which he sent today by the party with two canoes. The Indian woman is now perfectly recovered. Captain Clark came a few miles this morning to see the party under way and returned. On my arrival at the upper camp this morning, I found that Sergeant Gass and Shields had made but slow progress in collecting timber for the boat. They complained of great difficulty in getting straight, or even tolerably straight, sticks 4½ feet long. We were obliged to make use of the willow and box alder, the cottonwood being too soft and brittle. I kept one of them collecting timber while the other shaved and fitted them. I have found some pine logs among the driftwood near this place, from which I hope to obtain as much pitch as will answer to pay the seams of the boat. I directed Frazer to remain in order to sew the hides together and form the covering for the boat.

June 25th, 1805

This morning early I sent the party back to the lower camp; dispatched Frazer down with the canoe for Drouilliard and the meat he had collected, and Joseph Fields up the Missouri to hunt elk. At eight o'clock, sent Gass and Shields over to the large island for bark and timber.

About noon Fields returned and informed me that he had seen two white bear near the river a few miles above and, in attempting to get a shot at them, had stumbled upon a third, which immediately made at him, being only a few steps distant; that in running in order to escape from the bear he had leaped down a steep bank of the river on a stony bar, where he fell, cut his hand, bruised his knees, and bent his gun; that fortunately for him the bank hid him from the bear when he fell; and that by that means he had escaped. This man has been truly unfortunate with these bear. This is the second time that he has narrowly escaped from them.

The party that returned this evening to the lower camp reached it in time to take one canoe on the plain and prepare their baggage for an early start in the morning, after which such as were able to shake a foot amused themselves in dancing on the green to the music of the violin, which Cruzat plays extremely well. Captain Clark somewhat unwell today. He made Charbonneau cook for the party against their return.

It is worthy of remark that the winds are sometimes so strong in these plains that the men informed me that they hoisted a sail in the canoe and it had driven her along on the truck wheels. This is really sailing on dry land.

June 26th, 1805

Set Frazer to work to sew the skins together for the covering of the boat. Shields and Gass I sent over the river to search a small timbered bottom on that side, opposite to the islands, for timber and bark. And to myself I assign the duty of cook [1] as well for those present as for the party which I expect again to arrive this evening from the lower camp. I collected my wood and water, boiled a large quantity of excellent dried buffalo meat, and made each man a large suet dumpling by way of a treat.

About 4 P.M., Shields and Gass returned with a better supply of timber than they had yet collected, though not by any means enough. They brought some bark, principally of the cottonwood, which I found was too brittle and soft for the purpose. For this article, I find my only dependence is the sweet willow, which has a tough and strong bark.

Shields and Gass had killed seven buffalo in their ab-

---

[1] The spectacle of a captain dutifully cooking for his men was never equaled till *H.M.S. Pinafore*, but it is a good illustration of the informality of the expedition's discipline, which was nevertheless excellent. Note that both officers were at the same time serving as medical men.

The folding boat, *Experiment*, was to be built on a special collapsible framework of Lewis's own design. It was the worst failure of the expedition, not because the design was impractical but because none of the numerous preliminary studies for the expedition had shown the lack of suitable covering material. During his eastern service, Lewis had, of course, seen only bark-covered canoes.

sence, the skins of which and a part of the best of the meat they brought with them. If I cannot procure a sufficient quantity of elk skins, I shall substitute those of the buffalo. Late in the evening, the party arrived with two more canoes and another portion of the baggage.

Whitehouse, one of them, much heated and fatigued on his arrival, drank a very hearty draught of water and was taken almost instantly extremely ill. His pulse was full, and I therefore bled him plentifully, from which he felt great relief. I had no other instrument with which to perform this operation but my penknife; however, it answered very well. The wind being from S.E. today and favorable, the men made considerable progress by means of their sails.

At the Lower Camp. The party set out very early from this place, and took with them two canoes and a second allotment of baggage, consisting of parched meal, pork, powder, lead, axes, tools, biscuit, portable soup, some merchandise, and clothing. Captain Clark gave Sergeant Pryor a dose of salts this morning, and employed Charbonneau in rendering the buffalo tallow which had been collected there. He obtained a sufficient quantity to fill three empty kegs.

Captain Clark also selected the articles to be deposited in the cache, consisting of my desk—which I had left for that purpose and in which I had left some books, my specimens of plants, minerals, &c., collected from Fort Mandan to that place—also 2 kegs of pork, ½ a keg of flour, two blunderbusses, ½ a keg of fixed ammunition, and some other small articles belonging to the party which could be dispensed with. Deposited the swivel and carriage under the rocks, a little above the camp, near the river.

June 27th, 1805

At 1 P.M. a cloud arose to the southwest, and shortly after came on, attended with violent thunder, lightning, and hail. Soon after this storm was over, Drouilliard and J. Fields returned. They were about 4 miles above us during the storm. The hail was of no uncommon size where they were.[2]

[2] The hail *was* of uncommon size where the main party happened to be. Sergeant Patrick Gass's diary says that some of the hailstones measured seven inches in circumference. The ground was covered as if with snow. Allowing for a certain exaggeration in Gass's statements, one must believe it was a very serious storm, though neither Lewis nor Clark devotes much space to it.

June 28th, 1805

Set Drouilliard to shaving the elk skins, Fields to make the cross stays for the boat, Frazer and Whitehouse continue their operation with the skins, Shields and Gass finish the horizontal bars of the sections, after which I sent them in search of willow bark, a sufficient supply of which they now obtained to line the boat.

Expecting the party this evening, I prepared a supper for them, but they did not arrive. Not having quite enough elk skins, I employed three buffalo hides to cover one section. Not being able to shave these skins, I had them singed pretty closely with a blazing torch. I think they will answer tolerably well.

The white bear have become so troublesome to us that I do not think it prudent to send one man alone on an errand of any kind, particularly where he has to pass through the brush. We have seen two of them on the large island opposite to us today, but are so much engaged that we could not spare the time to hunt them, but will make a frolic of it when the party returns, and drive them from these islands. They come close around our camp every night but have never yet ventured to attack us, and our dog gives us timely notice of their visits. He keeps constantly patrolling all night. I have made the men sleep with their arms by them as usual, for fear of accidents.

June 29th, 1805

Not having seen the large fountain of which Captain Clark spoke, I determined to visit it today, as I could better spare this day from my attention to the boat than probably any other when the work would be further advanced. Accordingly, after setting the hands at their several employments, I took Drouilliard and set out for the fountain, and passed through a level beautiful plain for about six miles, when I reached the break of the river hills. Here we were overtaken by a violent gust of wind and rain from the S.W., attended with thunder and lightning. I expected a hailstorm probably from this cloud and therefore took refuge in a little gully, where there were some broad stones with which I purposed protecting my head if we should have a repetition of the scene of the 27th. But fortunately, we had but little hail and that not large. I sat very composedly for about an hour without shelter and took a copious drenching of rain.

After the shower was over I continued my route to the fountain, which I found much as Captain Clark had described, and think it may well be retained on the list of prodigies of this neighborhood, toward which Nature seems to have dealt with a liberal hand; for I have scarcely experienced a day since my first arrival in this quarter without experiencing some novel occurrence among the party or witnessing the appearance of some uncommon object. I think this fountain the largest I ever beheld, and the handsome cascade which it affords over some steep and irregular rocks in its passage to the river adds not a little to its beauty. It is about 25 yards from the river, situated in a pretty little level plain, and has a sudden descent of about 6 feet in one part of its course. The water of this fountain is extremely transparent and cold, nor is it impregnated with lime or any other extraneous matter which I can discover, but is very pure and pleasant. Its waters mark their passage, as Captain Clark observes, for a considerable distance down the Missouri, notwithstanding its rapidity and force. The water of the fountain boils up with such force near its center that its surface in that part seems even higher than the surrounding earth, which is a firm handsome turf of fine green grass.

June 29th, 1805

[Clark]

Finding that the prairie was so wet as to render it impossible to pass on to the end of the portage, determined to send back to the top of the hill at the creek for the remaining part of the baggage left at that place yesterday, leaving one man to take care of the baggage at this place, I determined to proceed on to the falls and take the river. Accordingly, we all set out. I took my servant and one man. Charbonneau, our interpreter, and his squaw accompanied. Soon after I arrived at the falls, I perceived a cloud which appeared black and threatened immediate rain. I looked out for a shelter but could see no place without being in great danger of being blown into the river if the wind should prove as turbulent as it is at some times.

About ¼ of a mile above the falls, I observed a deep ravine in which were shelving rocks under which we took shelter near the river, and placed our guns, the compass, &c., under a shelving rock on the upper side of the creek, in a place which was very secure from rain. The first shower was moderate, accompanied with a violent wind, the effects of which we did not feel. Soon after, a torrent of rain and hail fell, more violent than ever I saw before. The rain fell like one volley of water falling from the heavens and gave us time only to get out of the way of a torrent of water which was pouring down the hill into the river with immense force, tearing everything before it, taking with it large rocks and mud.

I took my gun and shot pouch in my left hand and with the right scrambled up the hill, pushing the interpreter's wife—who had her child in her arms—before me, the interpreter himself making attempts to pull up his wife by the hand, much scared and nearly without motion. We at length reached the top of the hill safely, where I found my servant in search of us, greatly agitated for our welfare. Before I got out of the bottom of the ravine, which was a flat dry rock when I entered it, the water was up to my waist and wet my watch. I scarcely got out before it rose 10 feet deep with a torrent which was terrible to behold, and by the time I reached the top of the hill, at least 15 feet water. I directed the party to return to the camp, at the run, as fast as possible to get to our load, where clothes could be got to cover the child, whose clothes were all lost; and the woman, who was but just recovering from a severe indisposition and was wet and cold, I was fearful of a relapse. I caused her, as also the others of the party, to take a little spirits, which my servant had in a canteen, which revived them very much. On arrival at the camp on the willow run, met the party, who had returned in great confusion to the run, leaving their loads in the plain, the hail and wind being so large and violent in the plains, and them naked; they were much bruised, and some nearly killed—one knocked down three times—and others without hats or anything on their heads, bloody and complained very much. I refreshed them with a little grog.

June 30th, 1805

I set four men to make new axletrees and repair the carriages, others to take the load across the river, which had fallen and is about 3 feet water. Men complain of being sore this day, dull and lolling about. The two men dispatched in search of the articles lost yesterday returned and brought the compass, which they found in the mud and stones near the mouth of the ravine. No other articles found. The place I sheltered under filled up with huge rocks. I set the party out at 11 o'clock to take a load to the 6-mile stake and return this evening, and I intend to take on the balance to the river tomorrow if the prairie will permit. At 3 o'clock a storm of wind from the S.W., after which we had a clear evening. Great numbers of buffalo in every direction. I think 10,000 may be seen in a view.

July 1st, 1805

[Lewis]

This morning I set Frazer and Whitehouse to sewing the leather on the sides of the sections of the boat; Shields and J. Fields to collect and split light wood and prepare a pit to make tar. Gass I set to work to make the way strips out of some willow limbs, which, though indifferent, were the best which could be obtained. Drouilliard and myself completed the operation of rendering the tallow. We obtained about 100 pounds.

By evening the skins were all attached to their sections, and I returned them again to the water. All matters were now in readiness to commence the operation of putting the parts of the boat together in the morning. The way strips are not yet ready but will be done in time, as I have obtained the necessary timber. The difficulty in obtaining the necessary materials has retarded my operations in forming this boat—extremely tedious and troublesome. And as it was a novel piece of mechanism to all who were employed, my constant attention was necessary to every part of the work. This, together with the duties of chief cook, has kept me pretty well employed.

At 3 P.M., Captain Clark arrived with the party, all very much fatigued. He brought with him all the baggage except what he had deposited yesterday at the six-mile stake, for which the party were too much fatigued to return this evening. We gave them a dram, and suffered them to rest from their labors this evening. I directed Bratton to assist in making the tar tomorrow, and selected several others to assist in putting the boat together. The day has been warm and the mosquitoes troublesome, of course. The bear were about our camp all last night. We have therefore determined to beat up their quarters tomorrow, and kill them or drive them from their haunts about this place.

July 2nd, 1805

[Lewis]

After I had completed my observation of equal altitudes today, Captain Clark, myself, and 12 men passed over to the large islands to hunt bear. The brush in that part of it where the bear frequent is an almost impenetrable thicket of the broad-leafed willow. This brush we entered in small parties of three or four together and searched in every part. We found only one, which made at Drouilliard, and he shot him in the breast at the distance of about 20 feet. The ball fortunately passed through his heart. The stroke knocked the bear down and gave Drouilliard time to get out of his sight. The bear changed his course. We pursued him about 100 yards by the blood and found him dead. We searched the thicket in every part but found no other, and therefore returned. This was a young male and would weigh about 400 pounds.

July 4th, 1805

[Lewis]

Yesterday we permitted Sergeant Gass, McNeal, and several others who had not yet seen the Falls to visit them. No appearance of tar yet, and I am now confident that we shall not be able to obtain any—a serious misfortune. I employed a number of hands on the boat today, and by 4 P.M. in the evening completed her except the most difficult part of the work—that of making her seams secure. I had her turned up and some small fires kindled underneath to dry her.

Captain Clark completed a draft of the river from Fort Mandan to this place which we intend depositing at this place in order to guard against accidents. Not having seen the Snake Indians or knowing in fact whether to calculate on their friendship or hostility, we have conceived our party sufficiently small, and therefore have concluded not to dispatch a canoe with a part of our men to St. Louis as we had intended early in the spring.

We fear also that such a measure might possibly discourage those who would in such case remain, and might possibly hazard the fate of the expedition. We have never once hinted to any one of the party that we had such a scheme in contemplation, and all appear perfectly to have made up their minds to succeed in the expedition or perish in the attempt. We all believe that we are now about to enter on the most perilous and difficult part of our voyage, yet I see no one repining. All appear ready to meet those difficulties which await us with resolution and becoming fortitude.

The mountains to the N.W. and W. of us are still entirely covered, are white, and glitter with the reflection of the sun. I do not believe that the clouds which prevail at this season of the year reach the summits of those lofty mountains; and if they do, the probability is that they deposit snow only, for there has been no perceptible diminution of the snow which they contain since we first saw them. I have thought it probable that these mountains might have derived their appellation of "Shining Mountains" from their glittering appearance when the sun shines in certain directions on the snow which covers them.

July 5th, 1805

This morning I had the boat removed to an open situation, scaffolded her off the ground, turned her keel to the sun, and kindled fires under her to dry her more expeditiously. I then set a couple of men to pounding charcoal to form a composition with some beeswax which we have and buffalo tallow, now my only hope and resource for paying my boat. I sincerely hope it may answer, yet I fear it will not. The boat in every other respect completely answers my most sanguine expectation. She is not yet dry, and eight men can carry her with the greatest ease. She is strong and will carry at least 8,000 pounds with her set of hands. Her form is as complete as I could wish it. The stitches begin to gape very much since she has begun to dry. I am now convinced this would not have been the case had the skins been sewed with a sharp point only and the leather not cut by the edges of a sharp needle.

July 9th, 1805

The wind continued violent until late in the evening, by which time we discovered that a greater part of the composition had separated from the skins, and left the seams of the boat exposed to the water, and she leaked in such manner that she would not answer. I need not add that this circumstance mortified me not a little; and to prevent her leaking without pitch was impossible with us, and to obtain this article was equally impossible, therefore the evil was irreparable. I now found that the section formed of the buffalo hides on which some hair had been left, answered much the best purpose. This leaked but little, and the parts which were well covered with hair about ⅛ of an inch in length retained the composition perfectly and remained sound and dry. From these circumstances I am persuaded that had I formed her with buffalo skins, singed not quite as close as I had done those I employed, she would have answered even with this composition. But to make any further experiments in our present situation seemed to me madness. The buffalo had principally deserted us, and the season was now advancing fast. I therefore relinquished all further hope of my favorite boat, and ordered her to be sunk in the water, that the skins might become soft in order the better to take her to pieces tomorrow, and deposited the iron frame at this place as it could probably be of no further service to us.

July 12th, 1805

I feel excessively anxious to be moving on. The canoes were detained by the wind until 2 P.M., when they set out and arrived at this place so late that I thought it best to detain them until morning. Bratton came down today for a couple of axes, which I sent by him. He returned immediately. Sergeant Gass and party joined Captain Clark at 10 A.M. Captain Clark kept all the men with him busily engaged—some in drying meat, others in hunting, and as many as could be employed about the canoes.

July 13th, 1805

We eat an immensity of meat. It requires 4 deer, an elk and a deer, or one buffalo, to supply us plentifully 24 hours. Meat now forms our food principally, as we reserve our flour, parched meal, and corn as much as possible for the Rocky Mountains, which we are shortly to enter, and where, from the Indian account, game is not very abundant.

Chapter **XII**

THREE FORKS OF THE MISSOURI

July 15—July 27, 1805

July 15th, 1805

[Lewis]

We arose very early this morning, assigned the canoes their loads, and had it put on board. We now found our vessels, eight in number, all heavily laden, notwithstanding our several deposits; though it is true we have now a considerable stock of dried meat and grease. We find it extremely difficult to keep the baggage of many of our men within reasonable bounds; they will be adding bulky articles of but little use or value to them.

At 10 A.M., we once more saw ourselves fairly under way, much to my joy, and I believe that of every individual who compose the party. I walked on shore and killed two elk, near one of which the party halted and dined. We took the skins, marrowbones, and a part of the flesh of these elk. In order to lighten the burden of the canoes, I continued my walk all the evening, and took our only invalids, Potts and Lepage, with me.

July 18th, 1805

Set out early this morning. Previous to our departure, saw a large herd of the big-horned animals on the immensely high and nearly perpendicular cliff opposite to us. On the face of this cliff they walked about and bounded from rock to rock with apparent unconcern where it appeared to me that no quadruped could have stood, and from which, had they made one false step, they must have been precipitated at least 500 feet. This animal appears to frequent such precipices and cliffs, where in fact they are perfectly secure from the pursuit of the wolf, bear, or even man himself.

As we were anxious now to meet with the Shoshones, or Snake Indians, as soon as possible, in order to obtain information relative to the geography of the country, and also, if necessary, some horses, we thought it better for one of us —either Captain Clark or myself—to take a small party and proceed on up the river some distance, before the canoes, in order to discover them should they be on the river, before the daily discharge of our guns, which was necessary in procuring subsistence for the party, should alarm and cause them to retreat to the mountains and conceal themselves, supposing us to be their enemies who visit them usually by way of this river. Accordingly, Captain Clark set out this morning after breakfast with Joseph Field, Potts, and his servant York.

July 20th, 1805

[Clark]

A fine morning. We proceeded on through a valley, leaving the river about 6 miles to our left, and fell into an Indian road which took us to the river above the mouth of a creek, 18 miles. The mosquitoes very troublesome. My man York nearly tired out. The bottoms of my feet blistered. I observe a smoke rise to our right, up the valley of the last creek, about 12 miles distant. The cause of this smoke I can't account for certainly, though think it probable that the Indians have heard the shooting of the party below, and set the prairies or valley on fire to alarm their camps, supposing our party to be a war party coming against them. I left signs to show the Indians if they should come on our trail that we were not their enemies. Camped on the river. The feet of the men with me so stuck with prickly pear and cut with stones that they were scarcely able to march at a slow gait this afternoon.

July 21st, 1805

[Lewis]

Set out early this morning and passed a bad rapid where the river enters the mountain, about 1 mile from our camp of last evening. The cliffs high, and covered with fragments of broken rocks. The current strong. We employed the tow-rope principally, and also the poles, as the river is not now so deep but rather wider and much more rapid. Our progress was therefore slow and laborious. We saw three swans this morning, which, like the geese, have not yet recovered the feathers of the wings and could not fly. We killed two of them; the third escaped by diving and passed down with the current. They had no young ones with them, therefore presume they do not breed in this country. These are the first we have seen on the river for a great distance. We daily see great numbers of geese with their young which are perfectly feathered except the wings, which are deficient in both young and old. My dog caught several today, as he frequently does.

July 22nd, 1805

The Indian woman recognizes the country and assures us that this is the river on which her relations live, and that the Three Forks are at no great distance.[1] This piece of information has cheered the spirits of the party, who now begin to console themselves with the anticipation of shortly seeing the head of the Missouri, yet unknown to the civilized world. The large creek which we passed on starboard, 15 yards, we call White Earth Creek from the circumstance of the natives procuring a white paint on this creek.

July 23rd, 1805

I ordered the canoes to hoist their small flags in order that, should the Indians see us, they might discover that we were not Indians, nor their enemies. We made great use of our setting poles and cords, the use of both which the river and banks favored. Most of our small sockets were lost, and the stones were so smooth that the points of their poles slipped in such manner that it increased the labor of navigating the canoes very considerably. I recollected a parcel of gigs which

---

[1] Sacagawea was a valuable member of the expedition. Her mere presence, with her baby, was a guarantee to strange Indians that this was not a war party. Without her services as Shoshone translator, the expedition would have failed. But this passage shows clearly that she did not "guide Lewis and Clark across the continent," as popular tradition has it. This is one of several occasions when she was of some small use a guide. It is too bad she has always been given credit for guiding the explorers—which she almost never did—and not at all for her help among the Shoshones—which saved everything. Note, however, that she again supplies geographical information on the 24th.

I had brought on, and made the men each attach one of these to the lower ends of their poles with strong wire, which answered the desired purpose.

July 24th, 1805

[Lewis]

The valley through which the river passed today is much as that of yesterday, nor is there any difference in the appearance of the mountains. They still continue high and seem to rise in some places like an amphitheater, one range above another, as they recede from the river, until the most distant and lofty have their tops clad with snow. The adjacent mountains commonly rise so high as to conceal the more distant and lofty mountains from our view.

I fear every day that we shall meet with some considerable falls or obstruction in the river notwithstanding the information of the Indian woman to the contrary, who assures us that the river continues much as we see it. I can scarcely form an idea of a river running to great extent through such a rough, mountainous country without having its stream intercepted by some difficult and dangerous rapids or falls. We daily pass a great number of small rapids or riffles, which descend one, two, or three feet in 150 yards, but we are rarely incommoded with fixed or standing rocks, and although strong rapid water, they are nevertheless quite practicable and by no means dangerous.

This morning Captain Clark set out early and pursued the Indian road, which took him up a creek some miles. About 10 A.M., he discovered a horse about six miles distant, on his left. He changed his route toward the horse. On approaching him, he found the horse in fine order but so wild he could not get within less than several hundred paces of him. He still saw much Indian sign, but none of recent date. From this horse he directed his course obliquely to the river, where, on his arrival, he killed a deer and dined.

July 25th, 1805

[Clark]

A fine morning. We proceeded on a few miles to the Three Forks of the Missouri. Those three forks are nearly of a size. The north fork appears to have the most water and must be considered as the one best calculated for us to ascend. Middle fork is quite as large—about 90 yards wide. The south fork is about 70 yards wide, and falls in about 400 yards below the middle fork. Those forks appear to be very rapid, and contain some timber in their bottoms which are very extensive.

On the north side the Indians have latterly set the prairies on fire—the cause I can't account for. I saw one horse-track going up the river, about four or 5 days past.

After breakfast—which we made on the ribs of a buck killed yesterday—I wrote a note informing Captain Lewis the route I intended to take, and proceeded on up the main north fork through a valley, the day very hot.

About 6 or 8 miles up the north fork, a small rapid river falls in on the larboard side, which affords a great deal of water, and appears to head in the snow mountains to the S.W. This little river falls into the Missouri by three mouths, having separated after it arrives in the river bottoms, and contains, as also all the water courses in this quarter, immense numbers of beaver and otter. Many thousand inhabit the river and creeks near the Three Forks (Philosopher's River). We camped on the same side. We ascended starboard 20 miles on a direct line up the N. fork. Charbonneau, our interpreter, nearly tired out; one of his ankles failing him. The bottoms are extensive and tolerable land covered with tall grass and prickly pears. The hills and mountains are high, steep, and rocky. The river very much divided by islands.

July 26th, 1805

[Lewis]

The high lands are thin, meager soil, covered with dry, low sedge and a species of grass, also dry, the seeds of which are armed with a long, twisted, hard beard at the upper extremity, while the lower point is a sharp, subulate, firm point beset at its base with little stiff bristles standing with their points in a contrary direction to the subulate point, to which they answer as a barb and serve also to press it forward when once entered a small distance. These barbed seeds penetrate our moccasins and leather leggings and give us great pain until they are removed. My poor dog suffers with them excessively. He is constantly biting and scratching himself as if in a rack of pain.

The prickly pear also grow here as abundantly as usual. There is another species of the prickly pear of a globular form, composed of an assemblage of little conic leaves springing from a common root, to which their small points are attached as a common center; and the base of the cone forms the apex of the leaf, which is garnished with a circular range of sharp thorns, quite as stiff and more keen than the more common species with the flat leaf, like the cochineal plant.

On entering this open valley, I saw the snow-clad tops of distant mountains before us. The timber and mountains much as heretofore. Saw a number of beaver today and some otter; killed one of the former, also four deer. Found a deer's skin which had been left by Captain Clark, with a note informing me of his having met with a horse, but had seen no fresh appearance of the Indians.

July 26th, 1805

[Clark]

I determined to leave Charbonneau and one man who had sore feet to rest, and proceed on with the other two to the top of a mountain 12 miles distant, west, and from thence view the river and valleys ahead. We, with great difficulty and much fatigue, reached the top at 11 o'clock. From the top of this mountain I could see the course of the north fork [of the Missouri] about ten miles, meandering through a valley, but could discover no Indians or sign which was fresh. I could also see some distance up the small river below, and also the middle fork. After satisfying myself, returned to the two men by an old Indian path.

On this path, and in the mountain, we came to a spring of excessive cold water, which we drank rather freely of, as we were almost famished. Notwithstanding the precautions of wetting my face, hands, and feet, I soon felt the effects of the water. We continued through a deep valley without a tree to shade us, scorching with heat, to the men who had killed a poor deer. I was fatigued. My feet with several blisters, and stuck with prickly pears.

July 27th, 1805

[Lewis]

Ascended the S.W. fork 1¾ miles and encamped at a larboard bend in a handsome, level, smooth plain just below a bayou, having passed the entrance of the middle fork at ½ a mile. Here I encamped to wait the return of Captain Clark, and to give the men a little rest, which seemed absolutely necessary to them. At the junction of the S.W. and middle forks, I found a note which had been left by Captain Clark informing me of his intended route, and that he would join me at this place, provided he did not fall in with any fresh sign of Indians, in which case he intended to pursue until he overtook them, calculating on my taking the S.W. fork, which I most certainly prefer, as its direction is much more promising than any other.

Believing this to be an essential point in the geography of this western part of the continent, I determined to remain at all events until I obtained the necessary data for fixing its latitude, longitude, &c. After fixing my camp, I had the canoes all unloaded and the baggage stowed away and securely covered on shore, and then permitted several men to hunt.

I walked down to the middle fork and examined and compared it with the S.W. fork, but could not satisfy myself which was the largest stream of the two; in fact they appeared as if they had been cast in the same mold, there being no difference in character or size. Therefore, to call either of these streams the Missouri would be giving it a preference which its size does not warrant, as it is not larger than the other. They are each 90 yards wide. In these meadows I saw a number of the mallard duck with their young, which are now nearly grown.

Captain Clark arrived very sick, with a high fever on him, and much fatigued and exhausted. He informed me that he was very sick all last night, had a high fever and frequent chills and constant aching pains in all his muscles. This morning, notwithstanding his indisposition, he pursued his intended route to the middle fork, about 8 miles, and finding no recent sign of Indians, rested about an hour, and came down the middle fork to this place.

Captain Clark thought himself somewhat bilious and had not had a passage for several days. I prevailed on him to take a dose of Rush's pills, which I have always found sovereign in such cases, and to bathe his feet in warm water and rest himself. Captain Clark's indisposition was a further inducement for my remaining here a couple of days. I therefore informed the men of my intention, and they put their deer skins in the water in order to prepare them for dressing tomorrow.

We begin to feel considerable anxiety with respect to the Snake Indians. If we do not find them or some other nation who have horses, I fear the successful issue of our voyage will be very doubtful, or at all events much more difficult in its accomplishment. We are now several hundred miles within the bosom of this wild and mountainous country, where game may rationally be expected shortly to become scarce and subsistence precarious without any information with respect to the country, not knowing how far these mountains continue, or where to direct our course to pass them to advantage or intercept a navigable branch of the Columbia; or even were we on such an one, the probability is that we should not find any timber within these mountains large enough for canoes, if we judge from the portion of them through which we have passed.

However, I still hope for the best, and intend taking a tramp myself in a few days to find these yellow [2] gentlemen if possible. My two principal consolations are that from our present position it is impossible that the S.W. fork can head with the waters of any other river but the Columbia, and that if any Indians can subsist in the form of a nation in these mountains with the means they have of acquiring food, we can also subsist.

---

[2] Eighteenth- and early nineteenth-century settlers often referred to Indians as "yellow," rather than "red." At Daniel Boone's settlement in Revolutionary Kentucky, they were sometimes called "the yellow boys."

Chapter XIII

THREE FORKS
TO BEAVER'S HEAD
July 28—August 10, 1805

July 28th, 1805

[Lewis]

My friend Captain Clark was very sick all last night but feels himself somewhat better this morning, since his medicine has operated. I dispatched two men early this morning up the S.E. fork to examine the river, and permitted sundry others to hunt in the neighborhood of this place. Both Captain Clark and myself corresponded in opinion with respect to the impropriety of calling either of these streams the Missouri, and accordingly agreed to name them after the President of the United States and the Secretaries of the Treasury and State, having previously named one river in honor of the Secretaries of War and Navy.

In pursuance of this resolution, we called the S.W. fork —that which we meant to ascend—Jefferson's River, in honor of that illustrious personage, Thomas Jefferson [the author of our enterprise]. The middle fork we called Madison's River, in honor of James Madison; and the S.E. fork we called Gallatin's River, in honor of Albert Gallatin. The two first are 90 yards wide, and the last is 70 yards. All of them run with great velocity and throw out large bodies of water. Gallatin's River is rather more rapid than either of the others, is not quite as deep, but from all appearances may be navigated to a considerable distance.

Captain Clark, who came down Madison's River yesterday and has also seen Jefferson's some distance, thinks Madison's rather the most rapid, but it is not as much so, by any means, as Gallatin's. The beds of all these streams are formed of smooth pebble and gravel, and their waters perfectly transparent; in short, they are three noble streams. I had all our baggage spread out to dry this morning, and the day proving warm, I had a small bower or booth erected for the comfort of Captain Clark. Our leather lodge, when exposed to the sun, is excessively hot.

Our present camp is precisely on the spot that the Snake Indians were encamped at the time the Minnetarees of the Knife River first came in sight of them five years since. From hence they retreated about three miles up Jefferson's River and concealed themselves in the woods. The Minnetarees pursued, attacked them, killed four men, four women, a number of boys, and made prisoners of all the females and four boys. Sacagawea, our Indian woman, was one of the female prisoners taken at that time, though I cannot discover that she shows any emotion of sorrow in recollecting this event, or of joy in being again restored to her native country. If she has enough to eat and a few trinkets to wear, I believe she would be perfectly content anywhere.

August 3rd, 1805

Captain Clark set out this morning as usual. He walked on shore a small distance this morning and killed a deer. In the course of his walk he saw a track which he supposed to be that of an Indian from the circumstance of the large toes turning inward. He pursued the track and found that the person had ascended a point of a hill from which his camp of the last evening was visible. This circumstance also confirmed the belief of its being an Indian who had thus discovered them, and ran off.

August 6th, 1805

We set out this morning very early on our return to the Forks. Having nothing to eat, I sent Drouilliard to the woodlands to my left in order to kill a deer; sent Sergeant Gass to the right with orders to keep sufficiently near to discover Captain Clark and the party should they be on their way up that stream; and, with Charbonneau, I directed my course to the main Forks through the bottom, directing the others to meet us there.

About five miles above the Forks, I heard the whooping of the party to my left and changed my route toward them. On my arrival, found that they had taken the rapid fork and learned from Captain Clark that he had not found the note which I had left for him at that place and the reasons which had induced him to ascend this stream. It was easiest and more in our direction, and appeared to contain as much water. He had, however, previously to my coming up with him, met Drouilliard, who informed him of the state of the two rivers and was on his return.

One of their canoes had just overset and all the baggage wet—the medicine box, among other articles—and several articles lost, a shot pouch and horn with all the implements for one rifle lost and never recovered. I walked down to the point where I waited their return.

On their arrival, found that two other canoes had filled with water and wet their cargoes completely. Whitehouse had been thrown out of one of the canoes as she swung in a rapid current, and the canoe had rubbed him and pressed him to the bottom as she passed over him, and had the water been two inches shallower must inevitably have crushed him to death. Our parched meal, corn, Indian presents, and a great part of our most valuable stores were wet and much damaged on this occasion. To examine, dry, and arrange our stores was the first object. We therefore passed over to the larboard side, opposite to the entrance of the rapid fork, where there was a large gravelly bar that answered our purposes. Wood was also convenient and plenty. Here we fixed our camp and unloaded all our canoes, and opened, and exposed to dry, such articles as had been wet.

A part of the load of each canoe consisted of the leaden canisters of powder, which were not in the least injured, though some of them had remained upwards of an hour under water. About 20 pounds of powder which we had in a tight keg, or at least one which we thought sufficiently so, got wet and entirely spoiled. This would have been the case with the other had it not been for the expedient which I had fallen on of securing the powder by means of the lead, having the latter formed into canisters which were filled with the necessary proportion of powder to discharge the lead when used, and those canisters well secured with corks and wax.

Shannon had been dispatched up the rapid fork this morning to hunt by Captain Clark before he met with Drouilliard or learned his mistake in the rivers. When he returned, he sent Drouilliard in search of him, but he rejoined us this evening and reported that he had been several miles up the river and could find nothing of him. We had the trumpet sounded and fired several guns, but he did not join us this evening. I am fearful he is lost again. This is the same man who was separated from us fifteen days as we came up the Missouri, and subsisted nine days of that time on grapes only.

Whitehouse is in much pain this evening with the injury one of his legs sustained from the canoe today, at the time it upset and swung over him. Captain Clark's ankle is also very painful to him. We should have given the party a day's rest somewhere near this place had not this accident happened, as I had determined to take some observations to fix the latitude and longitude of these forks. Our merchandise, medicine, &c., are not sufficiently dry this evening. We covered them securely for the evening. Captain Clark had ascended the river about nine miles from this place on course of S 30° W before he met with Drouilliard.

We believe that the N.W. or rapid fork is the drain of the melting snows of the mountains, and that it is not as long as the middle fork, and does not at all seasons of the year supply anything like as much water as the other, and that about this season it rises to its greatest height. This last appears from the apparent bed of the river, which is now overflowed, and the water in many places spreads through old channels which have their bottoms covered with grass that has grown this season, and is such as appears on the parts of the bottom not inundated. We therefore determined that the middle fork was that which ought of right to bear the name we had given to the lower portion, or River Jefferson; and called the bold, rapid, and clear stream Wisdom; and the more mild and placid one which flows in from the S.E. Philanthropy, in commemoration of two of those cardinal virtues which have so eminently marked that deservedly celebrated character through life.

August 7th, 1805

[Lewis]

At one o'clock all our baggage was dry. We therefore packed it up, reloaded the canoes, and the party proceeded with Captain Clark up Jefferson's River. I remained with Sergeant Gass to complete the observation of equal altitudes and joined them in the evening at their camp. We have not heard anything from Shannon yet; we expect that he has pursued Wisdom River upwards for some distance, probably killed some heavy animal, and is awaiting our arrival. The large biting fly, or hare fly as they are sometimes called, are very troublesome to us. I observe two kinds of them—a large black species, and a small brown species with a green head.

August 8, 1805

The Indian woman recognized the point of a high plain to our right, which, she informed us, was not very distant from the summer retreat of her nation, on a river beyond the mountains which runs to the west. This hill, she says, her nation calls the Beaver's Head, from a conceived resemblance of its figure to the head of that animal. She assures us that we shall either find her people on this river, or on the river immediately west of its source, which, from its present size, cannot be very distant.

As it is now all-important with us to meet with those people as soon as possible, I determined to proceed tomorrow with a small party to the source of the principal stream of this river and pass the mountains to the Columbia, and down that river until I found the Indians. In short, it is my resolution to find them or some others who have horses, if it should cause me a trip of one month. For, without horses we shall be obliged to leave a great part of our stores, of which it appears to me that we have a stock already sufficiently small for the length of the voyage before us.[1]

August 9th, 1805

The morning was fair and fine; we set out at an early hour and proceeded on very well. I walked on shore across the land to a point which I presumed they would reach by 8 A.M., our usual time of halting. The party did not arrive, and I returned about a mile and met them. Here they halted and we breakfasted. While we halted here, Shannon arrived and informed us that, having missed the party the day on which he set out, he had returned the next morning to the place from whence he had set out and, not finding them, that he had supposed that they were above him; that he had then marched one day up Wisdom River, by which

[1] This is the first hint of what Sacagawea's real service was to be. Again she gives a little geographical information. But the important problem now is horses; and it was the meeting with Sacagawea's own band—a meeting she now predicts and at which she would soon serve as translator—that provided the horses with which to cross the Rockies.

time he was convinced that they were not above him, as the river could not be navigated; he had then returned to the Forks and pursued us up this river. He had lived very plentifully this trip, but looked a good deal worried with his march.

Chapter *XIV*

REACHING THE GREAT DIVIDE

August 11—August 16, 1805

August 11th, 1805

[Lewis]

We set out very early this morning, but the track which we had pursued last evening soon disappeared. I therefore resolved to proceed to the narrow pass on the creek, about 10 miles west, in hopes that I should again find the Indian road at that place. Accordingly, I passed the river, which was about 12 yards wide and barred in several places entirely across by beaver dams, and proceeded through the level plain directly to the pass. I now sent Drouilliard to keep near the creek to my right and Shields to my left, with orders to search for the road, which if they found, they were to notify me by placing a hat on the muzzle of their gun. I kept McNeal with me.

After having marched in this order for about five miles, I discovered an Indian on horseback about two miles distant, coming down the plain toward us. With my glass, I discovered from his dress that he was of a different nation from any that we had yet seen, and was satisfied of his being a Shoshone. His arms were a bow and quiver of arrows, and he was mounted on an elegant horse without a saddle, and a small string which was attached to the under jaw of the horse which answered as a bridle. I was overjoyed at the sight of this stranger, and had no doubt of obtaining a friendly introduction to his nation, provided I could get near enough to him to convince him of our being white men. I therefore proceeded toward him at my usual pace.

When I had arrived within about a mile, he made a halt,

which I did also; and unloosing my blanket from my pack, I made him the signal of friendship known to the Indians of the Rocky Mountains and those of the Missouri—which is, by holding the mantle or robe in your hands at two corners and then throwing it up in the air higher than the head, bringing it to the earth as if in the act of spreading it, thus repeating three times. This signal of the robe has arisen from a custom among all those nations of spreading a robe or skin for their guests to sit on when they are visited.

This signal had not the desired effect. He still kept his position, and seemed to view Drouilliard and Shields, who were now coming in sight on either hand, with an air of suspicion. I would willingly have made them halt, but they were too far distant to hear me, and I feared to make any signal to them lest it should increase the suspicion in the mind of the Indian of our having some unfriendly design upon him.

I therefore hastened to take out of my sack some beads, a looking glass, and a few trinkets, which I had brought with me for this purpose and, leaving my gun and pouch with McNeal, advanced unarmed toward him. He remained in the same steadfast posture until I arrived in about 200 paces of him, when he turned his horse about and began to move off slowly from me.

I now called to him in as loud a voice as I could command, repeating the word *tab-ba-bone,* which, in their language, signifies *"white man."* [2] But, looking over his shoulder, he still kept his eye on Drouilliard and Shields, who were still advancing, neither of them having sagacity enough to recollect the impropriety of advancing when they saw me thus in parley with the Indian. I now made a signal to these men to halt. Drouilliard obeyed; but Shields, who after-

---

[2] Lewis could hardly have chosen a worse word. In modern Shoshone, *tai-va-vone* means "a stranger" or "an enemy," the two being in early days nearly the same thing. Lewis can have learned the word only from Sacagawea, who spoke Shoshone and Minnetaree. He probably asked one of his French-speaking men to ask Charbonneau in French the Shoshone word for white man. Charbonneau would then have asked Sacagawea in Minnetaree for the Shoshone word. It is very likely that at that time there *was* no Shoshone word for "white man," whom the tribe rarely, if ever, saw. Sacagawea did the best she could. A white man certainly was a *tai-va-vone,* or *tab-ba-bone,* a stranger. When Lewis rushed forward shouting that he was a stranger or an enemy, the already suspicious Shoshone warrior naturally galloped back to camp to spread the alarm.

ward told me that he did not observe the signal, still kept on.

The Indian halted again, and turned his horse about as if to wait for me, and I believe he would have remained until I came up with him had it not been for Shields, who still pressed forward. When I arrived within about 150 paces, I again repeated the word, *tab-ba-bone*, and held up the trinkets in my hands, and stripped up my shirt sleeve to give him an opportunity of seeing the color of my skin, and advanced leisurely toward him. But he did not remain until I got nearer than about 100 paces, when he suddenly turned his horse about, gave him the whip, leaped the creek, and disappeared in the willow brush in an instant; and with him vanished all my hopes of obtaining horses for the present.

I now felt quite as much mortification and disappointment as I had pleasure and expectation at the first sight of this Indian. I felt sorely chagrined at the conduct of the men, particularly Shields, to whom I principally attributed this failure in obtaining an introduction to the natives. I now called the men to me and could not forbear upbraiding them a little for their want of attention, and imprudence, on this occasion.

They had neglected to bring my spyglass, which in haste I had dropped in the plain with the blanket where I made the signal before mentioned. I sent Drouilliard and Shields back to search it. They soon found it and rejoined me.

We now set out on the track of the horse, hoping, by that means, to be led to an Indian camp, the trail of inhabitants of which—should they abscond—we should probably be enabled to pursue to the body of the nation, to which they would most probably fly for safety. This route led us across a large island framed by nearly an equal division of the creek in this bottom. After passing to the open ground on the N. side of the creek, we observed that the track made out toward the high hills about 3 miles distant in that direction.

I thought it probable that their camp might probably be among those hills and that they would reconnoiter us from the tops of them, and that if we advanced hastily toward them that they would become alarmed and probably run off. I therefore halted in an elevated situation near the creek, had a fire kindled of willow brush, cooked and took breakfast. During this leisure, I prepared a small assortment of trinkets consisting of some moccasin awls, a few strands of several kinds of beads, some paint, a looking glass, &c., which I attached to the end of a pole and planted it near our fire in order that, should the Indians return in search of us, they might from this token discover that we were friendly, and white persons. Before we had finished our meal a heavy shower of rain came on with some hail, which continued about 20 minutes and wet us to the skin.

After this shower we pursued the track of the horse, but as the rain had raised the grass which he had trodden down, it was with difficulty that we could follow it. We pursued it, however, about 4 miles—it turning up the valley to the left under the foot of the hills. We passed several places where the Indians appeared to have been digging roots today, and saw the fresh tracks of 8 or ten horses, but they had been wandering about in such a confused manner that we not only lost track of the horse which we had been pursuing but could make nothing of them. In the head of this valley we passed a large bog covered with tall grass and moss in which were a great number of springs of cold pure water. We now turned a little to the left along the foot of the high hills and arrived at a small branch on which we encamped for the night, having traveled in different directions about 20 miles and about 10 from the camp of last evening on a direct line. After meeting with the Indian today, I fixed a small flag of the U.S. to a pole which I made McNeal carry, and planted in the ground where we halted or encamped.

August 12, 1805

This morning I sent Drouilliard out as soon as it was light, to try and discover what route the Indians had taken. He followed the track of the horse we had pursued yesterday to the mountain where it had ascended, and returned to me in about an hour and a half.

I now determined to pursue the base of the mountains which form this cove to the S.W. in the expectation of finding some Indian road which leads over the mountains. Accordingly, I sent Drouilliard to my right and Shields to my left with orders to look out for a road, or the fresh tracks of horses, either of which we should first meet with, I had determined to pursue. At the distance of about 4 miles, we passed 4 small rivulets near each other on which we saw some recent bowers or small conic lodges formed with willow brush. Near them the Indians had gathered a number of roots, from the manner in which they had torn up the ground.

Near this place, we fell in with a large and plain Indian

road, which came into the cove from the northeast and led along the foot of the mountains to the southwest, obliquely approaching the main stream, which we had left yesterday. This road we now pursued to the southwest. At 5 miles it passed a stout stream which is a principal fork of the main stream and falls into it just above the narrow pass between the two cliffs before mentioned, which we now saw below us. Here we halted and breakfasted on the last of our venison, having yet a small piece of pork in reserve. After eating, we continued our route through the low bottom of the main stream along the foot of the mountains on our right. The valley for 5 miles farther in a southwest direction was from 2 to 3 miles wide.

At the distance of 4 miles further, the road took us to the most distant fountain of the waters of the mighty Missouri in search of which we have spent so many toilsome days and restless nights. Thus far I had accomplished one of those great objects on which my mind has been unalterably fixed for many years. Judge, then, of the pleasure I felt in allaying my thirst with this pure and ice-cold water which issues from the base of a low mountain or hill of a gentle ascent for ½ a mile. The mountains are high on either hand, leave this gap at the head of this rivulet through which the road passes. Here I halted a few minutes and rested myself. Two miles below, McNeal had exultingly stood with a foot on each side of this little rivulet and thanked his God that he had lived to bestride the mighty, and heretofore deemed endless, Missouri.

After refreshing ourselves, we proceeded on to the top of the dividing ridge, from which I discovered immense ranges of high mountains still to the west of us, with their tops partially covered with snow. I now descended the mountain about ¾ of a mile, which I found much steeper than on the opposite side, to a handsome bold running creek of cold, clear water. Here I first tasted the water of the great Columbia River.[3]

After a short halt of a few minutes, we continued our march along the Indian road which led us over steep hills and deep hollows to a spring on the side of a mountain where we found a sufficient quantity of dry willow brush for fuel. Here we encamped for the night. As we had killed

[3] He was, in fact, tasting the water of a tributary (Lemhi River) of a tributary (Salmon River) of a tributary (Snake River) of the Columbia. But it was water from the Columbia River system, which would eventually flow into the Columbia itself—or would have, if Lewis hadn't drunk it.

nothing during the day, we now boiled and ate the remainder of our pork, having yet a little flour and parched meal. At the creek on this side of the mountain I observed a species of deep purple currant, lower in its growth, the stem more branched, and leaf doubly as large as that of the Missouri. The leaf is covered on its under disk with a hairy pubescence. The fruit is of the ordinary size and shape of the currant and is supported in the usual manner, but is acid and very inferior in point of flavor.

This morning Captain Clark set out early. Found the river shoaly, rapid, shallow, and extremely difficult. The men in the water almost all day. They are getting weak, sore, and much fatigued. They complained of the fatigue to which the navigation subjected them and wished to go by land. Captain Clark encouraged them and pacified them. One of the canoes was very near oversetting in a rapid today. They proceeded but slowly.

August 13th, 1805

We had proceeded about four miles through a wavy plain parallel to the valley or river bottom when, at the distance of about a mile, we saw two women, a man, and some dogs on an eminence immediately before us. They appeared to view us with attention, and two of them, after a few minutes, sat down as if to wait our arrival. We continued our usual pace toward them. When we had arrived within half a mile of them, I directed the party to halt, and leaving my pack and rifle, I took the flag, which I unfurled, and advanced singly toward them. The women soon disappeared behind the hill. The man continued until I arrived within a hundred yards of him and then likewise, absconded, though I frequently repeated the word *tab-ba-bone* sufficiently loud for him to have heard it.

I now hastened to the top of the hill where they had stood but could see nothing of them. The dogs were less shy than their masters; they came about me pretty close. I therefore thought of tying a handkerchief about one of their necks, with some beads and other trinkets, and then let them loose to search their fugitive owners, thinking by this means to convince them of our pacific disposition toward them. But the dogs would not suffer me to take hold of them. They also soon disappeared.

I now made a signal for the men to come on. They joined me and we pursued the back track of these Indians, which led us along the same road which we had been traveling.

The road was dusty and appeared to have been much traveled lately both by men and horses. We had not continued our route more than a mile when we were so fortunate as to meet with three female savages. The short and steep ravines which we passed concealed us from each other until we arrived within 30 paces. A young woman immediately took to flight. An elderly woman and a girl of about 12 years old remained. I instantly laid by my gun and advanced toward them. They appeared much alarmed but saw that we were too near for them to escape by flight. They therefore seated themselves on the ground, holding down their heads as if reconciled to die, which they expected no doubt would be their fate.

I took the elderly woman by the hand and raised her up, repeated the word *tab-ba-bone*, and stripped up my shirt sleeve to show her my skin to prove to her the truth of the assertion that I was a white man, for my face and hands, which have been constantly exposed to the sun, were quite as dark as their own. They appeared instantly reconciled; and the men coming up, I gave these women some beads, a few moccasin awls, some pewter looking glasses, and a little paint. I directed Drouilliard to request the old woman to recall the young woman, who had run off to some distance by this time, fearing she might alarm the camp before we approached and might so exasperate the natives that they would perhaps attack us without inquiring who we were.

The old woman did as she was requested, and the fugitive soon returned, almost out of breath. I bestowed an equivalent portion of trinkets on her with the others. I now painted their tawny cheeks with some vermilion, which, with this nation, is emblematic of peace. After they had become composed, I informed them by signs that I wished them to conduct us to their camp; that we were anxious to become acquainted with the chiefs and warriors of their nation. They readily obeyed, and we set out, still pursuing the road down the river.

We had marched about 2 miles when we met a party of about 60 warriors, mounted on excellent horses, who came in nearly full speed. When they arrived, I advanced toward them with the flag, leaving my gun with the party about 50 paces behind me. The chief and two others, who were a little in advance of the main body, spoke to the women, and they informed them who we were and exultingly showed the presents which had been given them. These men then advanced and embraced me very affectionately in their way, which is by putting their left arm over your right shoulder, clasping your back, while they apply their left cheek to yours, and frequently vociferate the word *âh-hí-e, âh-hí-e*—that is, "I am much pleased; I am much rejoiced." Both parties now advanced, and we were all caressed and besmeared with their grease and paint until I was heartily tired of the national hug.

I now had the pipe lit and gave them smoke. They seated themselves in a circle around us and pulled off their moccasins, before they would receive or smoke the pipe. This is a custom among them, as I afterward learned, indicative of a sacred obligation of sincerity in their profession of friendship, given by the act of receiving and smoking the pipe of a stranger; which is as much as to say, that they wish they may always go barefoot if they are not sincere—a pretty heavy penalty, if they are to march through the plains of their country! After smoking a few pipes with them, I distributed some trifles among them with which they seemed much pleased, particularly with the blue beads and vermilion.

I now informed the chief that the object of our visit was a friendly one, that after we would reach his camp I would undertake to explain to him fully those objects—who we were, from whence we had come, and whither we were going; that, in the meantime, I did not care how soon we were in motion, as the sun was very warm and no water at hand. They now put on their moccasins, and the principal chief, Cameâhwait, made a short speech to the warriors. I gave him the flag which, I informed him, was an emblem of peace among white men, and now that it had been received by him it was to be respected as the bond of union between us. I desired him to march on, which he did, and we followed him. The dragoons moved on in squadron in our rear.

After we had marched about a mile in this order, he halted them and gave a second harangue, after which six or eight of the young men rode forward to their encampment, and no further regularity was observed in the order of march.

I afterwards understood that the Indians we had first seen this morning had returned and alarmed the camp. These men had come out armed *cap à pie* for action, expecting to meet with their enemies, the Minnetarees of Fort de Prairie, whom they call Pahkees. They were armed with bows, arrows, and shields, except three whom I observed with small pieces such as the North-West Company furnish the natives with, which they had obtained from the Rocky Mountain Indians on the Yellowstone River, with whom they are at peace.

On our arrival at their encampment on the river in a handsome level and fertile bottom, at the distance of 4 miles from where we had first met them, they introduced us to a lodge made of willow brush and an old leather lodge, which had been prepared for our reception by the young men which the chief had dispatched for that purpose. Here we were seated on green boughs and the skins of antelopes. One of the warriors then pulled up the grass in the center of the lodge, forming a small circle about 2 feet in diameter.

The chief next produced his pipe and native tobacco and began a long ceremony of the pipe, when we were requested to take off our moccasins, the chief having previously taken off his, as well as all the warriors present. This we complied with. The chief then lit his pipe at the fire, kindled in this little magic circle, and, standing on the opposite side of the circle, uttered a speech of several minutes in length, at the conclusion of which he pointed the stem to the four cardinal points of the heavens, first beginning at the east and ending with the north. He now presented the pipe to me as if desirous that I should smoke, but when I reached my hand to receive it, he drew it back and repeated the same ceremony three times, after which he pointed the stem first to the heavens, then to the center of the magic circle, smoked himself with three whiffs, and held the pipe until I took as many as I thought proper. He then held it to each of the white persons and then gave it to be consumed by his warriors.

This pipe was made of a dense semitransparent green stone, very highly polished, about 2½ inches long and of an oval figure, the bowl being in the same direction with the stem. A small piece of burned clay is placed in the bottom of the bowl to separate the tobacco from the end of the stem and is of an irregularly rounded figure not fitting the tube perfectly close in order that the smoke may pass. This is the form of the pipe. Their tobacco is of the same kind as that used by the Minnetarees, Mandans, and Arikaras of the Missouri. The Shoshones do not cultivate this plant, but obtain it from the Rocky Mountain Indians and some of the bands of their own nation who live further south. I now explained to them the objects of our journey, &c.

All the women and children of the camp were shortly collected about the lodge to indulge themselves with looking at us, we being the first white persons they had ever seen. After the ceremony of the pipe was over, I distributed the remainder of the small articles I had brought with me, among the women and children. By this time it was late in the evening and we had not tasted any food since the evening before. The chief informed us that they had nothing but berries to eat and gave us some cakes of serviceberries and chokecherries which had been dried in the sun. Of these I made a hearty meal and then walked to the river, which I found about 40 yards wide, very rapid, clear, and about 3 feet deep. The banks low and abrupt as those of the upper part of the Missouri, and the bed formed of loose stones and gravel. Cameâhwait informed me that this stream discharged itself into another doubly as large, at the distance of half a day's march, which came from the S.W. But, he added on further inquiry, that there was but little more timber below the junction of those rivers than I saw here, and that the river was confined between inaccessible mountains, was very rapid and rocky insomuch that it was impossible for us to pass either by land or water down this river to the great lake where the white men lived, as he had been informed. This was unwelcome information but I still hoped that this account had been exaggerated with a view to detain us among them. As to timber, I could discover not any that would answer the purpose of constructing canoes, or, in short, more than was barely necessary for fuel.

On my return to my lodge, an Indian called me into his bower and gave me a small morsel of the flesh of an antelope, boiled, and a piece of a fresh salmon roasted, both of which I ate with a very good relish. This was the first salmon I had seen, and perfectly convinced me that we were on the waters of the Pacific Ocean. The course of this river is a little to the north of west as far as I can discover it, and is bounded on each side by a range of high mountains, though those on the east side are lowest and more distant from the river.

This evening, the Indians entertained us with their dancing nearly all night. At 12 o'clock I grew sleepy and retired to rest, leaving the men to amuse themselves with the Indians. I observe no essential difference between the music and manner of dancing among this nation and those of the Missouri. I was several times awakened in the course of the night by their yells, but was too much fatigued to be deprived of a tolerable sound night's repose.

August 14th

In order to give Captain Clark time to reach the forks of Jefferson's River, I concluded to spend this day at the Shoshone camp and obtain what information I could with respect to the country. As we had nothing but a little flour and parched meal to eat, except the berries with which the Indians furnished us, I directed Drouilliard and Shields to hunt a few hours and try to kill something. The Indians furnished them with horses, and most of their young men also turned out to hunt.

The game which they principally hunt is the antelope, which they pursue on horseback and shoot with their arrows. This animal is so extremely fleet and durable that a single horse has no possible chance to overtake them or run them down. The Indians are therefore obliged to have recourse to stratagem when they discover a herd of the antelope. They separate and scatter themselves to the distance of five or six miles in different directions around them, generally selecting some commanding eminence for a stand. Some one, or two, now pursue the herd at full speed over the hills, valleys, gullies, and the sides of precipices that are tremendous to view. Thus, after running them from five to six or seven miles, the fresh horses that were in waiting head them [*off*] and drive them back, pursuing them as far or perhaps further quite to the other extreme of the hunters, who now in turn pursue on their fresh horses, thus worrying the poor animal down and finally killing them with their arrows. Forty or fifty hunters will be engaged for half a day in this manner and perhaps not kill more than two or three antelopes.

They have but few elk or black-tailed deer, and the common red deer they cannot take as they secrete themselves in the brush when pursued, and they have only the bow and arrow, which is a very slender dependence for killing any game except such as they can run down with their horses. I was very much entertained with a view of this Indian chase. It was after a herd of about 10 antelope, and about 20 hunters. It lasted about 2 hours, and a considerable part of the chase in view from my tent. About 1 A.M., the hunters returned, had not killed a single antelope, and their horses foaming with sweat. My hunters returned soon after and had been equally unsuccessful. I now directed McNeal to make me a little paste with the flour and added some berries to it, which I found very palatable.

The means I had of communicating with these people was by way of Drouilliard, who understood perfectly the common language of gesticulation, or signs, which seems to be universally understood by all the nations we have yet seen. It is true that this language is imperfect and liable to error, but it is much less so than would be expected. The strong parts of the ideas are seldom mistaken.

I [4] now prevailed on the chief to instruct me with respect

[4] This passage appears in the Journals for August 14, 1805. However, Clark, probably when preparing the manuscript for

to the geography of his country. This he undertook very cheerfully by delineating the rivers on the ground, but I soon found that his information fell far short of my expectation or wishes. He drew the river on which we now are [i.e., the Lemhi], to which he placed two branches just above us, which he showed me, from the openings of the mountains, were in view. He next made it discharge itself into a large river which flowed from the S.W. about ten miles below us, then continued this joint stream in the same direction of this valley, or N.W., for one day's march, and then inclined it to the west for two more days' march. Here he placed a number of heaps of sand on each side, which, he informed me, represented the vast mountains of rock eternally covered with snow through which the river passed. That the perpendicular, and even jutting, rocks so closely hemmed in the river that there was no possibility of passing along the shore; that the bed of the river was obstructed by sharp pointed rocks, and the rapidity of the stream such that the whole surface of the river was beaten into perfect foam, as far as the eye could reach. That the mountains were also inaccessible to man or horse. He said that, this being the state of the country in that direction, himself nor none of his nation had ever been farther down the river than these mountains. I then inquired the state of the country on either side of the river, but he could not inform me. He said there was an old man of his nation a day's march below who could probably give me some information of the country to the northwest and referred me to an old man then present for that to the southwest.

I now told Cameâhwait that I wished him to speak to his people and engage them to go with me tomorrow to the forks of Jefferson's River, where our baggage was by this time arrived with another chief and a large party of white men, who would wait my return at that place; that I wished them to take with them about thirty spare horses to transport our baggage to this place, where we would then remain some time among them and trade with them for horses, and finally concert our future plans for getting on to the ocean and of the trade which would be extended to them, after our return to our homes.

He complied with my request and made a lengthy harangue

Biddle's edition, added a memorandum: "This part to come in the 20th, related to Captain C. thro' the interpreter." Lewis, however, enters it as if "I" were himself. This is certainly correct on the 14th, since he and Chief Cameâhwait did not meet Clark till the 16th. It is probable, however, that the same facts were later "related to Captain C. thro' the interpreter."

to his village. He returned in about an hour and a half and informed me that they would be ready to accompany me in the morning. I promised to reward them for their trouble. Drouilliard, who had had a good view of their horses, estimated them at 400. Most of them are fine horses. Indeed, many of them would make a figure on the south side of James River, or the land of fine horses. I saw several with Spanish brands on them, and some mules, which they informed me that they had also obtained from the Spaniards. I also saw a bridle bit of Spanish make, and sundry other articles, which I have no doubt were obtained from the same source.

Notwithstanding the extreme poverty of those poor people, they are very merry. They danced again this evening until midnight. Each warrior keeps one or more horses tied by a cord to a stake near his lodge both day and night, and are always prepared for action at a moment's warning. They fight on horseback altogether. I observe that the large flies are extremely troublesome to the horses as well as ourselves.

This morning being cold, and the men stiff and sore from the exertions of yesterday, Captain Clark did not set out this morning until 7 A.M. The river was so crooked and rapid that they made but little way. At one mile, he passed a bold running stream on starboard, which heads in a mountain to the north, on which there is snow. This we called Track Creek. It is 4 yards wide and 3 feet deep. At 7 miles, passed a stout stream which heads in some springs under the foot of the mountains on larboard. The river near the mountain they found one continued rapid, which was extremely laborious and difficult to ascend. This evening Charbonneau struck his Indian woman, for which Captain Clark gave him a severe reprimand. Joseph and Reuben Fields killed 4 deer and an antelope. Captain Clark killed a buck. Several of the men have lamed themselves by various accidents in working the canoes through this difficult part of the river, and Captain Clark was obliged personally to assist them in this labor.

August 15th, 1805

This morning I arose very early and as hungry as a wolf. I had eaten nothing yesterday except one scant meal of the flour and berries except the dried cakes of berries, which did not appear to satisfy my appetite as they appeared to do those of my Indian friends. I found on inquiry of McNeal that we had only about two pounds of flour remaining. This I directed him to divide into two equal parts and to cook the one half this morning in a kind of pudding with the berries as he had done yesterday, and reserve the balance for the evening. On this new-fashioned pudding four of us breakfasted, giving a pretty good allowance also to the chief, who declared it the best thing he had tasted for a long time. He took a little of the flour in his hand, tasted and examined it very scrutinously, and asked me if we made it of roots. I explained to him the manner in which it grew.

I hurried the departure of the Indians. The chief addressed them several times before they would move. They seemed very reluctant to accompany me. I at length asked the reason and he told me that some foolish persons among them had suggested the idea that we were in league with the Pahkees and had come on in order to decoy them into an ambuscade, where their enemies were waiting to receive them; but that, for his part, he did not believe it. I readily perceived that our situation was not entirely free from danger, as the transition from suspicion to the confirmation of the fact would not be very difficult in the minds of these ignorant people who have been accustomed from their infancy to view every stranger as an enemy.

I told Cameâhwait that I was sorry to find that they had put so little confidence in us, that I knew they were not acquainted with white men and therefore could forgive them. That among white men it was considered disgraceful to lie, or entrap an enemy by falsehood. I told him if they continued to think thus meanly of us, that they might rely on it that no white men would ever come to trade with them, or bring them arms and ammunition; and that, if the bulk of his nation still entertained this opinion, I still hoped that there were some among them that were not afraid to die— that were men, and would go with me and convince themselves of the truth of what I had asserted; that there was a party of white men waiting my return, either at the forks of Jefferson's River or a little below, coming on to that place in canoes loaded with provisions and merchandise.

He told me, for his own part, he was determined to go, that he was not afraid to die. I soon found that I had touched him on the right string. To doubt the bravery of a savage is at once to put him on his mettle. He now mounted his horse and harangued his village a third time, the purport of which, as he afterwards told me, was to inform them that he would go with us and convince himself of the truth or falsity of what we had told him [even] if he was certain he should be killed; that he hoped there were some of them who heard him were not afraid to die with him, and if there were to let him see them mount their horses and prepare to set out.

Shortly after this harangue, he was joined by six or eight only, and with these I smoked a pipe, and directed the men to put on their packs, being determined to set out with them while I had them in the humor.

At half after 12, we set out. Several of the old women were crying and imploring the Great Spirit to protect their warriors as if they were going to inevitable destruction. We had not proceeded far before our party was augmented by ten or twelve more, and before we reached the creek which we had passed in the morning of the 13th, it appeared to me that we had all the men of the village and a number of women with us. This may serve in some measure to illustrate the capricious disposition of those people, who never act but from the impulse of the moment. They were now very cheerful and gay, and two hours ago they looked as surly as so many imps of Saturn [*sic*]. When we arrived at the spring on the side of the mountain where we had encamped on the 12th, the chief insisted on halting to let the horses graze, with which I complied, and gave the Indians smoke. They are excessively fond of the pipe, but have it not much in their power to indulge themselves with even their native tobacco, as they do not cultivate it themselves. After remaining about an hour, we again set out, and by engaging to make compensation to four of them for their trouble, obtained the privilege of riding with an Indian myself, and a similar situation for each of my party. I soon found it more tiresome riding without stirrups than walking, and of course chose the latter, making the Indian carry my pack. About sunset, we reached the upper part of the level valley of the cove which we now called Shoshone Cove.

August 16th, 1805

I sent Drouilliard and Shields before, this morning, in order to kill some meat, as neither the Indians nor ourselves had anything to eat. I informed the chief of my view in this measure, and requested that he would keep his young men with us lest by their whooping and noise they should alarm the game and we should get nothing to eat. But so strongly were their suspicions excited by this measure that two parties of discovery immediately set out, one on each side of the valley, to watch the hunters, as I believe to see whether they had not been sent to give information of their approach to an enemy that they still persuaded themselves were lying in wait for them. I saw that any further effort to prevent their going would only add strength to their suspicions and therefore said no more.

After the hunters had been gone about an hour, we set out. We had just passed through the narrows when we saw one of the spies coming up the level plain under whip. The chief paused a little and seemed somewhat concerned. I felt a good deal so myself, and began to suspect that by some unfortunate accident, perhaps some of their enemies had straggled hither at this unlucky moment. But we were all agreeably disappointed, on the arrival of the young man, to learn that he had come to inform us that one of the white men had killed a deer.

In an instant, they all gave their horses the whip, and I was taken nearly a mile before I could learn what were the tidings. As I was without stirrups, and an Indian behind me, the jostling was disagreeable. I therefore reined up my horse, and forbade the Indian to whip him, who had given him the lash at every jump for a mile, fearing he should lose a part of the feast. The fellow was so uneasy that he left me the horse, dismounted, and ran on foot at full speed, I am confident, a mile. When they arrived where the deer was, which was in view of me, they dismounted and ran in, tumbling over each other like a parcel of famished dogs, each seizing and tearing away a part of the intestines which had been previously thrown out by Drouilliard, who killed it.

The scene was such, when I arrived, that had I not had a pretty keen appetite myself, I am confident I should not have tasted any part of the venison shortly. Each one had a piece of some description, and all eating most ravenously. Some were eating the kidneys, the milt, and liver, and the blood running from the corners of their mouths. Others were in a similar situation with the paunch and guts, but the exuding substance from their lips, in this case, was of a different description. One of the last who attracted my attention particularly had been fortunate in his allotment, or rather active in the division. He had provided himself with about nine feet of the small guts, one end of which he was chewing on, while with his hands he was squeezing the contents out of the other. I really did not, until now, think that human nature ever presented itself in a shape so nearly allied to the brute creation. I viewed these poor starved devils with pity and compassion. I directed McNeal to skin the deer and reserved a quarter; the balance I gave the chief to be divided among his people. They devoured the whole of it nearly, without cooking.

I now bore obliquely to the left in order to intercept the creek where there was some brush to make a fire, and arrived at this stream, where Drouilliard had killed a second deer. Here nearly the same scene was enacted. A fire being kindled, we cooked and ate, and gave the balance of the two deer to the Indians, who ate the whole of them, even to the soft parts of the hoofs. Drouilliard joined us at breakfast with a third deer. Of this I reserved a quarter, and gave the balance to the Indians.

They all appeared now to have filled themselves, and were in a good humor. This morning early, soon after the hunters set out, a considerable part of our escort became alarmed and returned, 28 men and three women only continued with us. After eating, and suffering the horses to graze about 2 hours, we renewed our march, and toward evening arrived at the lower part of the cove. Shields killed an antelope on the way, a part of which we took and gave the remainder to the Indians. Being now informed of the place at which I expected to meet Captain Clark and the party, they insisted on making a halt, which was complied with.

We now dismounted, and the chief, with much ceremony, put tippets about our necks such as they themselves wore. I readily perceived that this was to disguise us and owed its origin to the same cause already mentioned. To give them further confidence, I put my cocked hat with feather on the chief, and my over-shirt being of the Indian form, my hair disheveled and skin well browned with the sun, I wanted no further addition to make me a complete Indian in appearance. The men followed my example, and we were soon completely metamorphosed. I again repeated to them the possibility of the party not having arrived at the place where I expected they were, but assured them they could not be far below, lest by not finding them at the forks their suspicions might arise to such heights as to induce them to return precipitately.

We now set out and rode briskly within sight of the forks, making one of the Indians carry the flag, that our own party should know who we were. When we arrived in sight at the distance of about two miles, I discovered to my mortification that the party had not arrived, and the Indians slackened their pace. I now scarcely knew what to do, and feared every moment when they would halt altogether. I now determined to restore their confidence, cost what it might, and therefore gave the chief my gun, and told him that if his enemies were in those bushes before him that he could defend himself with that gun, that for my own part I was not afraid to die, and if I deceived him he might make what use of the gun he thought proper, or in other words that he might shoot me. The men also gave their guns to other Indians, which seemed to inspire them with more confidence. They sent their spies before them at some distance, and when I drew near the place I thought of the notes which I had left, and directed Drouilliard to go with an Indian man and bring them to me, which he did, the Indian seeing him take the notes from the stake on which they had been placed.

I now had recourse to a stratagem in which I thought myself justified by the occasion, but which I must confess sat a little awkward. It had its desired effect. After reading the notes, which were the same I had left, I told the chief that when I had left my brother chief with the party below where the river entered the mountain, we both agreed not to bring the canoes higher up than the next forks of the river above us, wherever this might happen; that there he was to await my return, should he arrive first; and that in the event of his not being able to travel as fast as usual from the difficulty of the water, he was to send up to the first forks above him and leave a note informing me where he was; that this note was left here today; and that he informed me that he was just below the mountains and was coming on slowly up, and added that I should wait here for him; but, if they did not believe me, that I should send a man at any rate to the chief, and they might also send one of their young men with him; that myself and two others would remain with them at this place.

This plan was readily adopted, and one of the young men offered his services. I promised him a knife and some beads as a reward for his confidence in us. Most of them seemed satisfied, but there were several that complained of the chief's exposing them to danger unnecessarily and said that we told different stories; in short, a few were much dissatisfied. I wrote a note to Captain Clark by the light of some willow brush, and directed Drouilliard to set out early, being confident that there was not a moment to spare.

We finally lay down, and the chief placed himself by the side of my mosquito bier. I slept but little, as might be well expected, my mind dwelling on the state of the expedition which I have ever held in equal estimation with my own existence, and the fate of which appeared at this moment to depend in a great measure upon the caprice of a few savages, who are ever as fickle as the wind.

I had mentioned to the chief several times that we had with us a woman of his nation who had been taken prisoner by the Minnetarees, and that by means of her I hoped to explain myself more fully than I could do [by] signs. Some of the party had also told the Indians that we had a man with us who was black and had short curling hair. This had excited their curiosity very much, and they seemed quite as anxious to see this monster as they were the merchandise which we had to barter for their horses.

Chapter *XV*

ACROSS THE ROCKY MOUNTAINS
August 17—September 22, 1805

August 17th, 1805

[Lewis]

This morning I arose very early and dispatched Drouilliard and the Indian down the river. Sent Shields to hunt. I made McNeal cook the remainder of our meat, which afforded a slight breakfast for ourselves and the chief. Drouilliard had been gone about two hours when an Indian, who had straggled some little distance down the river, returned and reported that the white men were coming, that he had seen them just below. They all appeared transported with joy, and the chief repeated his fraternal hug. I felt quite as much gratified at this information as the Indians appeared to be. Shortly after, Captain Clark arrived with the interpreter, Charbonneau, and the Indian woman, who proved to be a sister of the chief Cameâhwait.

The meeting of those people was really affecting, particularly between Sacagawea and an Indian woman who had been taken prisoner at the same time with her, and who had afterwards escaped from the Minnetarees and rejoined her nation.

At noon the canoes arrived, and we had the satisfaction once more to find ourselves all together, with a flattering prospect of being able to obtain as many horses shortly as would enable us to prosecute our voyage by land should that by water be deemed inadvisable.

We now formed our camp just below the junction of the forks on the larboard side in a level, smooth bottom covered with a fine turf of greensward. Here we unloaded our canoes and arranged our baggage on shore. Formed a canopy of one of our large sails and planted some willow brush in the ground to form a shade for the Indians to sit under while we spoke to them, which we thought it best to do this evening.

Accordingly, about 4 P.M., we called them together and through the medium of Labiche, Charbonneau, and Sacagawea, we communicated to them fully the objects which had brought us into this distant part of the country, in which we took care to make them a conspicuous object of our own good wishes and the care of our government. We made them sensible of their dependence on the will of our government for every species of merchandise as well for their defense and comfort; and apprised them of the strength of our government and its friendly dispositions toward them. We also gave them as a reason why we wished to penetrate the country as far as the ocean to the west of them was to examine and find out a more direct way to bring merchandise to them. That as no trade could be carried on with them before our return to our homes, that it was mutually advantageous to them as well as to ourselves that they should render us such aids as they had it in their power to furnish in order to hasten our voyage and, of course, our return home: that such were their horses to transport our baggage, without which we could not subsist; and that a pilot to conduct us through the mountains was also necessary if we could not descend the river by water. But that we did not ask either their horses or their services without giving a satisfactory compensation in return. That at present we wished them to collect as many horses as were necessary to transport our baggage to their village on the Columbia, where we would then trade with them at our leisure for such horses as they could spare us. They appeared well pleased with what had been said. The chief thanked us for friendship toward himself and nation and declared his wish to serve us in every respect; that he was sorry to find that it must yet be some time before they could be furnished with firearms, but said they could live as they had done heretofore until we brought them as we had promised. He said they had not horses enough with them at present to remove our baggage to their village over the mountain, but that he would return tomorrow and encourage his people to come over with their horses, and that he would bring his own and assist us. This was complying with all we wished at present. We next inquired who were chiefs among them. Cameâhwait pointed out two others, who, he said, were chiefs. We gave him a medal of the small size with the likeness of Mr. Jefferson, the President of the United States, in relief on one side, and clasped hands with a pipe and tomahawk on the other. To the other chiefs we gave each a small medal which were struck in the Presidency of George

Washington, Esq. We also gave small medals of the last description to two young men who, the first chief informed us, were good young men and much respected among them.

Captain Clark and myself now concerted measures for our future operations; and it was mutually agreed that he should set out tomorrow morning with eleven men, furnished with axes and other necessary tools for making canoes, their arms, accouterments, and as much of their baggage as they could carry, also to take the Indians, Charbonneau, and the Indian woman with him. That on his arrival at the Shoshone camp, he was to leave Charbonneau and the Indian woman to hasten the return of the Indians with their horses to this place, and to proceed himself with the eleven men down the Columbia in order to examine the river; and, if he found it navigable and could obtain timber, to set about making canoes immediately. In the meantime, I was to bring on the party and baggage to the Shoshone camp, calculating that by the time I should reach that place, he would have sufficiently informed himself with respect to the state of the river, &c., to determine us whether to prosecute our journey from thence by land or water.

August 17th, 1805

[Clark]

We set out at 7 o'clock and proceeded on to the forks. I had not proceeded on one mile before I saw, at a distance, several Indians on horseback coming toward me. The interpreter and squaw, who were before me at some distance, danced for the joyful sight, and she made signs to me that they were her nation. As I approached nearer them, discovered one of Captain Lewis's party with them dressed in their dress. They met me with great signs of joy. As the canoes were proceeding on nearly opposite me, I turned those people and joined Captain Lewis, who had camped with 16 of those Snake Indians at the forks 2 miles in advance. Those Indians sang all the way to their camp, where the others had provided a kind of shade of willows stuck up in a circle.

The three chiefs with Captain Lewis met me with great cordiality, embraced, and took a seat on a white robe. The main chief immediately tied to my hair six small pieces of shells, resembling pearl, which are highly valued by those people, and are procured from the nations residing near the seacoast. We then smoked in their fashion, without shoes.

Captain Lewis informed me he found those people on the

Columbia [1] River about 40 miles from the forks. At that place there was a large camp of them. He had persuaded those with him to come and see that what he said was the truth. They had been under great apprehension all the way, for fear of their being deceived. The Great Chief of this nation proved to be the brother of the woman with us, and is a man of influence, sense, and easy and reserved manners. Appears to possess a great deal of sincerity. The canoes arrived and unloaded. Everything appeared to astonish those people—the appearance of the men, their arms, the canoes, the clothing, my black servant, and the sagacity of Captain Lewis's dog. We spoke a few words to them in the evening respecting our route, intentions, our want of horses, &c., and gave them a few presents and medals. We made a number of inquiries of those people about the Columbia River, [2] the country, game, &c. The account they gave us was very unfavorable; that the river abounded in immense falls—one, particularly, much higher than the Falls of the Missouri, and at the place, the mountains closed so close that it was impracticable to pass, and that the ridge continued on each side of perpendicular cliffs impenetrable, and that no deer, elk, or any game was to be found in that country. Added to that, they informed us that there was no timber on the river sufficiently large to make small canoes. This information, if true, is alarming. I determined to go in advance and examine the country.

August 18th, 1805

[Lewis]

This morning, while Captain Clark was busily engaged in preparing for his route, I exposed some articles to barter with the Indians for horses, as I wished a few at this moment to relieve the men who were going with Captain Clark from the labor of carrying their baggage, and also one to keep here in order to pack the meat to camp which the hunters might kill. I soon obtained three very good horses, for which I gave a uniform coat, a pair of leggings, a few handkerchiefs, three knives, and some other small articles, the whole of which did not cost more than about $20 in the United States. The Indians seemed quite as well pleased with their bargain as I was. The men also purchased one for an old checked shirt, a pair of old leggings, and a knife. Two of

[1] Actually the Lemhi River, a tributary of the Columbia.

[2] By "Columbia River," Clark means either the Lemhi, where he then was, or perhaps the entire Columbia basin.

those I purchased, Captain Clark took on with him. At 10 A.M., Captain Clark departed with his detachment and all the Indians, except 2 men and 2 women, who remained with us.

This day I completed my thirty-first year, and conceived that I had, in all human probability, now existed about half the period which I am to remain in this sublunary world.[3] I reflected that I had as yet done but little, very little, indeed, to further the happiness of the human race, or to advance the information of the succeeding generation. I viewed with regret the many hours I have spent in indolence, and now sorely feel the want of that information which those hours would have given me had they been judiciously expended. But, since they are past and cannot be recalled, I dash from me the gloomy thought, and resolve in future to redouble my exertions and at least endeavor to promote those two primary objects of human existence, by giving them the aid of that portion of talents which Nature and fortune have bestowed on me; or, in future, to live *for mankind*, as I have heretofore lived *for myself*.

August 19th, 1805

This morning I arose at daylight and sent out three hunters. Some of the men who were much in want of leggings and moccasins I suffered to dress some skins; the others I employed in repacking the baggage, making pack saddles, etc. We took up the net this morning, but caught no fish. The frost which perfectly whitened the grass this morning had a singular appearance to me at this season. This evening I made a few of the men construct a seine of willow brush, which we hauled, and caught a large number of fine trout and a kind of mullet, about 16 inches long, which I had not seen before.

August 20th, 1805

This morning I sent out the two hunters, and employed the balance of the party pretty much as yesterday. I walked down the river about ¾ of a mile and selected a place near the river bank, unperceived by the Indians, for a cache which

---

[3] Sadly enough, Lewis lived only four of his self-alloted thirty-one years. Without being in the least conclusive on the point of whether he was murdered or was a suicide, this entry suggests that he was not given to contemplating self-destruction.

I set three men to make, and directed the sentinel to discharge his gun if he perceived any of the Indians going down in that direction, which was to be a signal for the men at work on the cache to desist and separate, lest these people should discover our deposit, and rob us of the baggage we intend leaving here.

By evening the cache was completed, unperceived by the Indians; and all our packages made up. The packsaddles and harness are not yet completed. In this operation, we find ourselves at a loss for nails and boards. For the former, we substitute thongs of rawhide, which answer very well, and for the latter [had] to cut off the blades of our oars and use the plank of some boxes which have heretofore held other articles, and put those articles into sacks of rawhide which I have had made for the purpose. By this means I have obtained as many boards as will make 20 saddles, which I suppose will be sufficient for our present exigencies. The Indians with us behave themselves extremely well.

This morning, Captain Clark set out at 6 in the morning, and soon after arrived near their camp, they [the Shoshones] having removed about 2 miles higher up the river than the camp at which they were when I first visited them. The chief requested a halt, which was complied with, and a number of the Indians came out from the village and joined them. After smoking a few pipes with them, they all proceeded to the village, where Captain Clark was conducted to a large lodge prepared in the center of the encampment for himself and party. Here they gave him one salmon and some cakes of dried berries. He now repeated to them what had been said to them in council at this place, which was repeated to the village by the chief. When he had concluded this address, he requested a guide to accompany him down the river, and an elderly man was pointed out by the chief who consented to undertake this task. This was the old man of whom Cameâhwait had spoken as a person well acquainted with the country to the north of this river.

August 21st, 1805

The party pursued their several occupations, as yesterday. By evening I had all the baggage, saddles, and harnesses completely ready for a march. After dark, I made the men take the baggage to the cache and deposit it. I believe we have been unperceived by the Indians in this movement.

This morning early, Captain Clark resumed his march.

At the distance of five miles, he arrived at some brush lodges of the Shoshones inhabited by about seven families. Here he halted.

August 22nd, 1805

This morning early, I sent a couple of men to complete the covering of the cache, which could not be done well last night in the dark. They soon accomplished their work and returned. Late last night Drouilliard returned with a fawn he had killed, and a considerable quantity of Indian plunder.

The anecdote with respect to the latter is perhaps worthy of relation. He informed me that, while hunting upon the cove yesterday, about 12 o'clock he came suddenly upon an Indian camp at which there were a young man, an old man, and a boy and three women; they seemed but little surprised at seeing him, and he rode up to them and dismounted, turning his horse out to graze. These people had just finished their repast on some roots. He entered into conversation with them by signs, and after about 20 minutes one of the women spoke to the others of the party, and they all went immediately and collected their horses, brought them to camp, and saddled them. At this moment, he thought he would also set out and continue his hunt, and accordingly walked to catch his horse at some little distance, and neglected to take up his gun, which he left at camp.

The Indians, perceiving him at the distance of fifty paces, immediately mounted their horses, the young man took the gun, and the whole of them left their baggage, and laid whip to their horses, directing their course to the pass of the mountains. Finding himself deprived of his gun, he immediately mounted his horse and pursued.

After running them about 10 miles, the horses of two of the women nearly gave out and the young fellow with the gun, from their frequent cries, slackened his pace and, being on a very fleet horse, rode around the women at a little distance. At length Drouilliard overtook the women and by signs convinced them that he did not wish to hurt them. They then halted, and the young fellow approached still nearer. He asked him for his gun, but the only part of the answer which he could understand, was "Pahkee," which he knew to be the name by which they called their enemies.

Watching his opportunity when the fellow was off his guard, he suddenly rode alongside of him, seized his gun, and wrested it out of his hands. The fellow, finding Drouilliard too strong for him and discovering that he must yield the gun, had presence of mind to open the pan and cast the priming before he let the gun escape from his hands. Now finding himself divested of the gun, he turned his horse about and laid whip, leaving the women to follow him as well as they could. Drouilliard now returned to the place they had left their baggage and brought it with him to my camp.

At 11 A.M. Charbonneau, the Indian woman, Cameâhwait, and about 50 men, with a number of women and children, arrived. They encamped near us. After they had turned out their horses and arranged their camp, I called the chiefs and warriors together and addressed them; gave them some further presents, particularly the second and third chiefs, who, it appeared, had agreeably to their promise exerted themselves in my favor.

August 23rd, 1805

I wished to have set out this morning, but the chief requested that I would wait until another party of his nation arrived which he expected today. To this I consented from necessity, and therefore sent out the hunters. I also laid up the canoes this morning in a pond near the forks; sunk them in the water and weighted them down with stone, after taking out the plugs of the gage holes in their bottoms,[4] hoping by this means to guard against both the effects of high water and that of the fire which is frequently kindled in these plains by the natives. The Indians have promised to do them no intentional injury, and I believe they are too lazy at any rate to give themselves the trouble to raise them from their present situation in order to cut or burn them.

At three P.M. the expected party of Indians arrived, about 50 men, women, and children. There was a good deal of anxiety on the part of some of those who had promised to assist me over the mountains; I felt some uneasiness on this subject, but as they still said they would return with me as they had promised, I said nothing to them but resolved to set out in the morning as early as possible.

Captain Clark set out this morning very early and proceeded but slowly in consequence of the difficulty of his road, which lay along the steep side of a mountain over large irregular and broken masses of rocks which had tumbled from the upper part of the mountain. It was with much risk and pain that the horses could get on. At the distance of four miles, he arrived at the river, and the rocks here were

---

[4] The gage holes in the bottom of the canoe made it easy to drain them when they were hauled ashore and also easy, as in this case, to sink them for security.

so steep and jutted into the river in such manner that there was no other alternative but passing through the river. This he attempted with success, though the water was so deep for a short distance as to swim the horses and was very rapid.

He continued his route one mile along the edge of the river under this steep cliff to a little bottom, below which the whole current of the river beat against the starboard shore on which he was, and which was formed of a solid rock perfectly inaccessible to horses. Here also the little track, which he had been pursuing, terminated. He therefore determined to leave the horses and the majority of the party here and, with his guide and three men, to continue his route down the river still further, in order more fully to satisfy himself as to its practicability.

Accordingly, he directed the men to hunt and fish at this place until his return. They had not killed anything today but one goose, and the balance of the little provision they had brought with them, as well as the five salmon they had procured yesterday, were consumed last evening. There was, of course, no inducement for his halting at any time, at this place.

After a few minutes, he continued his route, clambering over immense rocks and along the sides of lofty precipices on the border of the river to the distance of 12 miles.

He saw some late appearance of Indians having been encamped, and the tracks of a number of horses. Captain Clark halted here about 2 hours, caught some small fish on which, with the addition of some berries, they dined. The river, from the place at which he left the party to his present station, was one continued rapid, in which there were five shoals, neither of which could be passed with loaded canoes, nor even run with empty ones. At those several places, therefore, it would be necessary to unload and transport the baggage for a considerable distance over steep and almost inaccessible rocks where there was no possibility of employing horses for the relief of the men. The canoes would next have to be let down by cords, and even with this precaution, Captain Clark conceived there would be much risk of both canoes and men.

After dinner, Captain Clark continued his route down the river and at ½ a mile passed another creek not so large as that just mentioned, or about 5 yards wide. Here his guide informed him that by ascending this creek some distance, they would have a better road, and would cut off a considerable bend which the river made to the south. Accordingly, he pursued a well-beaten Indian track, which led up this creek about six miles, then, leaving the creek on the right, he passed over a ridge; and at the distance of a mile, arrived at the river where it passes through a well-timbered bottom of about eighty acres of land. They passed this bottom and ascended a steep and elevated point of a mountain from whence the guide showed him the break of the river through the mountains for about 20 miles further. This view was terminated by one of the most lofty mountains, Captain Clark informed me, he had ever seen which was perfectly covered with snow.

Captain Clark, being now perfectly satisfied as to the impracticability of this route either by land or water, informed the old man that he was convinced of the veracity of his assertions and would now return to the village from whence they had set out, where he expected to meet myself and party.

August 24th, 1805

As the Indians who were on their way down the Missouri had a number of spare horses with them, I thought it probable that I could obtain some of them and therefore desired the chief to speak to them and inform me whether they would trade. They gave no positive answer but requested to see the goods which I was willing to give in exchange. I now produced some battle axes which I had made at Fort Mandan, with which they were much pleased. Knives also seemed in great demand among them. I soon purchased three horses and a mule.

I had now nine horses and a mule, and two which I had hired made twelve. These I had loaded, and the Indian women took the balance of the baggage. I had given the interpreter some articles with which to purchase a horse for the woman, which he had obtained. At twelve o'clock we set out, and passed the river below the forks, directing our route toward the cove along the track formerly mentioned. Most of the horses were heavily laden, and it appears to me that it will require at least 25 horses to convey our baggage along such roads as I expect we shall be obliged to pass in the mountains. I had now the inexpressible satisfaction to find myself once more under way with all my baggage and party.

August 24th, 1805

[Clark]

I wrote a letter to Captain Lewis informing him of the prospects before us and information received of my guide which I thought favorable, &c., and stating two plans, one of which for us to pursue, &c., and dispatched one man and horse, and directed the party to get ready to march back. Every man appeared disheartened from the prospects of the river, and nothing to eat. I set out late and camped 2 miles above. Nothing to eat but chokecherries and red haws, which act in different ways so as to make us sick. Dew very heavy, my bedding wet. In passing around a rock, the horses were obliged to go deep into the water.

The plan I stated to Captain Lewis—if he agrees with me we shall adopt—is: to procure as many horses (one for each man if possible) and to hire my present guide, whom I sent on to him to interrogate through the interpreter, and proceed on by land to some navigable part of the Columbia River, or to the ocean, depending on what provisions we can procure by the gun added to the small stock we have on hand, depending on our horses as the last resort.

A second plan: to divide the party; one part to attempt this difficult river with what provisions we have; and the remainder to pass by land on horseback, depending on our guns &c., for provisions, &c., and come together occasionally on the river. The first of which I would be most pleased with, &c.

August 25th, 1805

[Lewis]

Some time after we had halted, Charbonneau mentioned to me, with apparent unconcern, that he expected to meet all the Indians from the camp on the Columbia tomorrow on their way to the Missouri. Alarmed at this information, I asked why he expected to meet them. He then informed me that the first chief had dispatched some of his young men this morning to this camp requesting the Indians to meet them tomorrow, and that himself and those with him would go on with them down the Missouri, and consequently leave me and my baggage on the mountain or thereabouts.

I was out of patience with the folly of Charbonneau, who had not sufficient sagacity to see the consequences which would inevitably flow from such a movement of the Indians. Although he had been in possession of this information since early in the morning, when it had been communicated to him by his Indian woman, yet he never mentioned it until the afternoon. I could not forbear speaking to him with some degree of asperity on this occasion.

I saw that there was no time to be lost in having those orders countermanded, or that we should not in all probability obtain any more horses or even get my baggage to the waters of the Columbia. I therefore called the three chiefs together and, having smoked a pipe with them, I asked them if they were men of their word, and whether I could depend on the promises they had made me. They readily answered in the affirmative. I then asked them if they had not promised to assist me with my baggage to their camp on the other side of the mountains, or to the place at which Captain Clark might build the canoes, should I wish it. They acknowledged that they had.

I then asked them why they had requested their people on the other side of the mountain to meet them tomorrow on the mountain, where there would be no possibility of our remaining together for the purpose of trading for their horses as they had also promised. That if they had not promised to have given me their assistance in transporting my baggage to the waters on the other side of the mountain, that I should not have attempted to pass the mountains, but would have returned down the river and that, in that case, they would never have seen any more white men in their country. That if they wished the white men to be their friends and to assist them against their enemies by furnishing them with arms, and keeping their enemies from attacking them, that they must never promise us anything which they did not mean to perform. That when I had first seen them they had doubted what I told them about the arrival of the party of white men in canoes, that they had been convinced that what I told them on that occasion was true; why then would they doubt what I said on any other point? I told them that they had witnessed my liberality in dividing the meat which my hunters killed with them; and that I should continue to give such of them as assisted me a part of whatever we had ourselves to eat; and finally concluded by telling them if they intended to keep the promises they had made me, to dispatch one of their young men immediately with orders to their people to remain where they were until our arrival.

The two inferior chiefs said that they wished to assist me and be as good as their word, and that they had not sent for their people, that it was the first chief who had done so, and they did not approve of the measure. Cameâhwait remained silent for some time. At length, he told me that he knew he had done wrong; but that he had been induced to that measure from seeing all his people hungry; but, as he had promised to give me his assistance, he would not in future be worse than his word. I then desired him to send immediately and countermand his orders. Accordingly, a young man was sent for this purpose and I gave him a handkerchief to engage him in my interest.

August 26th, 1805

We collected our horses and set out at sunrise. We soon arrived at the extreme source of the Missouri. Here I halted a few minutes. The men drank of the water and consoled themselves with the idea of having at length arrived at this long-wished-for point. From hence we proceeded to a fine spring on the side of the mountain, where I had lain the evening before I first arrived at the Shoshone camp. Here I halted to dine, and graze our horses, there being fine green grass on that part of the hillside which was moistened by the water of the spring, while the grass on the other parts was perfectly dry and parched with the sun. I directed a pint of corn to be given each Indian who was engaged in transporting our baggage, and about the same quantity to each of the men, which they parched, pounded, and made into soup. One of the women who had been assisting in the transportation of the baggage halted at a little run about a mile behind us, and sent on the two pack horses which she had been conducting by one of her female friends. I inquired of Cameâhwait the cause of her detention and was informed by him, in an unconcerned manner, that she had halted to bring forth a child and would soon overtake us. In about an hour the woman arrived with her newborn babe and passed us on her way to the camp, apparently as well as she ever was.

Cameâhwait requested that we would discharge our guns when we arrived in sight of the village. Accordingly, when I arrived on an eminence above the village in the plain, I drew up the party at open order in a single rank, and gave them a running fire, discharging two rounds. They appeared much gratified with this exhibition. We then proceeded to the village or encampment of brush lodges, 32 in number. I found Colter here, who had just arrived with a letter from Captain Clark, in which Captain Clark had given me an account of his peregrination and the description of the river and country as before detailed. From this view of the subject I found it a folly to think of attempting to descend this river in canoes, and therefore determined to commence the purchase of horses in the morning from the Indians in order to carry into execution the design we had formed of passing the Rocky Mountains.

I now informed Cameâhwait of my intended expedition overland to the great river which lay in the plains beyond the mountains, and told him that I wished to purchase 20 horses of himself and his people to convey our baggage. He observed that the Minnetarees had stolen a great number of their horses this spring but hoped his people would spare me the number I wished. I also asked another guide; he observed that he had no doubt but the old man who was with Captain Clark would accompany us if we wished him and that he was better informed of the country than any of them. Matters being thus far arranged, I directed the fiddle to be played and the party danced very merrily, much to the amusement and gratification of the natives, though I must confess that the state of my own mind at this moment did not well accord with the prevailing mirth.

September 2nd, 1805

[Clark]

A cloudy morning. Rained some last night. We set out early and proceeded on up the [Fish] creek, crossed a large fork from the right and one from the left, and at 8 [7½] miles left the road on which we were pursuing and which leads over to the Missouri, and proceeded up a west fork [of Fish Creek] without a road. Proceeded on through thickets in which we were obliged to cut a road, over rocky hillsides where our horses were in perpetual danger of slipping to their certain destruction, and up and down steep hills where several horses fell. Some turned over and others slipped down steep hillsides. One horse crippled, and two gave out. One load left about two miles back, the horse on which it was carried, crippled.

September 3rd, 1805

A cloudy morning. Horses very stiff. Sent two men back with the horse on which Captain Lewis rode, for the load left back last night—which detained us until 8 o'clock, at which time we set out. The country is timbered with pine generally. The bottoms have a great variety of shrubs, and the fir trees in great abundance. Hills high and rocky on each side. In the after part of the day, the high mountains closed the creek on each side and obliged us to take on the steep sides of those mountains—so steep that the horses could scarcely keep from slipping down. Several slipped and injured themselves very much. At dusk it began to snow; at 3 o'clock some rain. The mountains [we had passed] to the east covered with snow. We met with a great misfortune in having our last thermometer broken by accident. This day we passed over immense hills, and some of the worst roads that ever horses passed. Our horses frequently fell. Snow about 2 inches deep when it began to rain, which terminated in a sleet storm.

Sept. 15th, 1805

We set out early, the morning cloudy, and proceeded on down the right side of Kooskooskee River,[5] over steep points, rocky and bushy as usual, for 4 miles to an old Indian fishing place. Here the road leaves the river to the left and ascends a mountain, winding in every direction to get up the steep ascents and to pass the immense quantity of falling timber which had been falling from different causes—i.e., fire and wind—and has deprived the greater part of the southerly sides of this mountain of its green timber.

Four miles up the mountain I found a spring and halted for the rear to come up, and to let our horses rest and feed. In about 2 hours, the rear of the party came up much fatigued, and horses more so. Several horses slipped and rolled down steep hills, which hurt them very much. The one which carried my desk and small trunk turned over and rolled down a mountain for 40 yards and lodged against a tree. Broke the desk; the horse escaped and appeared but little hurt. Some others very much hurt.

September 18th, 1805

[Lewis]

Captain Clark set out this morning to go ahead with six hunters. There being no game in these mountains, we concluded it would be better for one of us to take the hunters and hurry on to the level country ahead and there hunt and provide some provisions, while the other remained with and brought on the party. The latter of these was my part. Accordingly, I directed the horses to be gotten up early, being determined to force my march as much as the abilities of our horses would permit. The negligence of one of the party (Willard), who had a spare horse, in not attending to him and bringing him up last evening, was the cause of our detention this morning until ½ after eight A.M., when we set out. I sent Willard back to search for his horse, and proceeded on with the party. At four in the evening, he overtook us

---

[5] The Kooskooskee is the modern Clearwater. At this time the river had no English name, as no white man had ever seen it.

without the horse. We marched 18 miles this day and encamped on the side of a steep mountain. We suffered for water this day, passing one rivulet only. We were fortunate in finding water in a steep ravine about ½ mile from our camp. This morning we finished the remainder of our last colt.[6] We dined and supped on a scant proportion of portable soup, a few canisters of which, a little bear's oil, and about 20 pounds of candles form our stock of provision, the only resources being our guns and pack horses. The first is but a poor dependence in our present situation, where there is nothing upon earth except ourselves and a few small pheasants, small gray squirrels, and a blue bird of the vulture kind about the size of a turtledove or jaybird. Our route lay along the ridge of a high mountain. Course S. 20 W. 18 miles. Used the snow for cooking.

18th Sept. 1805

[Clark]

A fair morning. Cold. I proceeded on in advance with six hunters. Made 32 miles and encamped on a bold running creek passing to the left, which I call Hungry Creek, as at that place we had nothing to eat.

September 19th, 1805

[Lewis]

Set out this morning a little after sunrise and continued our route about the same course of yesterday, or S. 20 W. for 6 miles, when the ridge terminated and we, to our inexpressible joy, discovered a large tract of prairie country lying to the S.W., and widening as it appeared to extend to the W. Through that plain the Indian informed us that the Columbia River—of which we were in search—ran.

After leaving the ridge, we ascended and descended several steep mountains in the distance of 6 miles further when we struck a creek about 15 yards wide, our course being S. 35 W. The road was excessively dangerous along this creek, being a narrow rocky path, generally on the side of a steep precipice, from which, in many places, if either man or horse were precipitated, they would inevitably be dashed to pieces. Frazer's horse fell from this road in the evening, and rolled with his load near a hundred yards into the creek. We all expected that the horse was killed, but to our astonishment,

---

[6] When food shortage forced the expedition to eat horses, they began with the colts, as least valuable, on September 14.

when the load was taken off him, he arose to his feet and appeared to be but little injured. In 20 minutes he proceeded with his load. This was the most wonderful escape I ever witnessed. The hill down which he rolled was almost perpendicular and broken by large, irregular, and broken rocks.

19th Sept., 1805

Set out early. Proceeded on up the Hungry Creek, passing through a small glade at 6 miles, at which place we found a horse. I directed him killed and hung up for the party after taking a breakfast off for ourselves, which we thought fine.

20th September, 1805

I set out early and proceeded on through a country as rugged as usual. Passed over a low mountain into the forks of a large creek which I kept down 2 miles, and ascended a high steep mountain leaving the creek to our left hand. Passed the head of several drains on a dividing ridge, and at 12 miles descended the mountain to a level pine country. Proceeded on through a beautiful country for three miles to a small plain in which I found many Indian lodges.

At the distance of 1 mile from the lodges, I met 3 Indian boys. When they saw me, they ran and hid themselves in the grass.[7] I dismounted, gave my gun and horse to one of the men, searched in the grass, and found 2 of the boys. Gave them small pieces of ribbon, and sent them forward to the village. Soon after, a man came out to meet me with great caution, and conducted me [us] to a large spacious lodge, which he told me, by signs, was the lodge of his great chief, who had set out 3 days previous with all the warriors of the nation to war, on a southwest direction, and would return in 15 or 18 days. The few men that were left in the village, and great numbers of women, gathered around me with much

---

[7] As they dropped down on the other side of the Rockies, the explorers came into the country of the Nez Percés. Though Lewis and Clark believed the tribe had been friendly from the beginning, the Indians had, at first, considered having a massacre—on general principles. Tribal tradition says they were dissuaded by a squaw named Stray Away, whose life had once been saved by friendly white trappers. The tradition is probably correct, as other Nez Percé legends of the expedition, when they can be checked by existing documents, are surprisingly accurate.

apparent signs of fear, and appear pleased.[8] They (those people) gave us a small piece of buffalo meat, some dried salmon berries, and roots in different states—some round and much like an onion, which they call *pas-she-co*.[9] Of this they make bread and soup. They also gave us the bread made of this root, all of which we ate heartily. I gave them a few small articles as presents and proceeded on with a chief to his village—2 miles in the same plain.

21st Sept., 1805

[Clark]

A fine morning. Sent out all the hunters in different directions to hunt deer. I myself delayed with the chief to prevent suspicion, and to collect, by signs, as much information as possible about the river and country in advance. The chief drew me a kind of chart of the river, and informed me that a greater chief than himself was fishing at the river half a day's march from his village; that he was called The Twisted Hair; and that the river forked a little below his camp. At a long distance below, and below two large forks—one from the left and the other from the right—the river passed through the mountains, at which place was a great fall of the water passing through the rocks. At those falls, white people lived from whom they procured the white beads, and brass, &c., which the women wore.

A chief of another band visited me today and smoked a pipe. I gave my handkerchief and a silver cord with a little tobacco to those chiefs. The hunters all return without anything. I purchased as much provisions as I could with what few things I chanced to have in my pockets, such as salmon, bread, roots, and berries, and sent one man—R. Fields—with an Indian to meet Captain Lewis, and at 4 o'clock P.M. set out to the river.

Met a man at dark on his way from the river to the village, whom I hired and gave the neck handkerchief of one of the men, to pilot me to the camp of The Twisted Hair. We did

[8] Within the last three decades it was still possible to enter an Ojibway village in the deeper Canadian woods and be received with this odd mixture of fear and pleasure, though the fear was by that time confined to children—obviously pleased and curious, but keeping a good, safe distance.

[9] Pas-she-co was camas, or quamash, bulbous root of one or more species of the genus *Camassia,* in the lily family. The name given by Clark appears to be related to the modern Shoshone word, *pah-see-go.*

not arrive at the camp of The Twisted Hair, but opposite, until half past 11 o'clock P.M. Found at this camp five squaws and 3 children. My guide called to the chief, who was encamped with 2 others on a small island in the river. He soon joined me. I found him a cheerful man with apparent sincerity. I gave him a medal, &c., and smoked until one o'clock A.M., and went to sleep.

September 22nd, 1805

[Lewis]

We had proceeded about two and a half miles when we met Reuben Fields, one of our hunters, whom Captain Clark had dispatched to meet us with some dried fish and roots that he had procured from a band of Indians, whose lodges were about eight miles in advance. I ordered the party to halt for the purpose of taking some refreshment. I divided the fish, roots, and berries, and was happy to find a sufficiency to satisfy completely all our appetites. Fields also killed a crow.

After refreshing ourselves, we proceeded to the village— due west 7½ miles—where we arrived at 5 o'clock in the afternoon. Our route was through lands heavily timbered, the larger wood entirely pine. The country, except the last 3 miles, was broken and descending. The pleasure I now felt in having triumphed over the Rocky Mountains, and descending once more to a level and fertile country, where there was every rational hope of finding a comfortable subsistence for myself and party, can be more readily conceived than expressed. Nor was the flattering prospect of the final success of the expedition less pleasing.

On our approach to the village, which consisted of eighteen lodges, most of the women fled to the neighboring woods on horseback with their children—a circumstance I did not expect, as Captain Clark had previously been with them and informed them of our pacific intentions toward them, and also the time at which we should most probably arrive. The men seemed but little concerned, and several of them came to meet us at a short distance from their lodges, unarmed.

22nd Sept., 1805

[Clark]

Set out with the chief and his son on a young horse for the village, at which place I expected to meet Captain Lewis. This young horse in fright threw himself and me 3 times, on the side of a steep hill, and hurt my hip much. Caught a colt which we found on the road, and I rode it for several miles until we saw the chief's horses. He caught one, and we arrived at his village at sunset, and himself and myself walked up to the second village, where I found Captain Lewis and the party encamped, much fatigued and hungry, much rejoiced to find something to eat, of which they appeared to partake plentifully. I cautioned them of the consequences of eating too much, &c.

The plains appeared covered with spectators viewing the white men and the articles which we had. Our party weakened and much reduced in flesh as well as strength. The horse I left hung up they received at a time they were in great want; and the supply I sent by R. Fields proved timely, and gave great encouragement to the party with Captain Lewis. He lost 3 horses, one of which belonged to our guide. Those Indians stole out of R.F.'s shot pouch his knife, wipers, compass, and steel, which we could not procure from them. We attempted to have some talk with those people, but could not, for the want of an interpreter through which we could speak. We were compelled to converse altogether by signs. I got The Twisted Hair to draw the river from his camp down, which he did with great cheerfulness on a white elk skin.

Chapter *XVI*

DOWNSTREAM TOWARD
THE COAST

September 23—November 1, 1805

23rd September, 1805

[Clark]

We assembled the principal men as well as the chiefs and by signs informed them where we came from, where bound, our wish to inculcate peace and good understanding between all the red people, &c., which appeared to satisfy them much. We then gave two other medals to other chiefs of bands, a flag to The Twisted Hair. Left a flag and handkerchief to the grand chief, gave a shirt to The Twisted Hair, and a knife and handkerchief with a small piece of tobacco to each. Finding that those people gave no provisions today, we determined to purchase with our small articles of merchandise; accordingly, we purchased all we could, such as roots dried, in bread, and in their raw state, berries of red haws and fish, and in the evening set out and proceeded on to the 2nd village, 2 miles distant, where we also purchased a few articles, all amounting to as much as our weak horses could carry to the river. Captain Lewis and 2 men very sick this evening.[1] My hip very painful. The men trade a few old tin canisters for dressed elk skin to make themselves shirts.

24th September, 1805

Dispatched J. Colter back to hunt the horses lost in the

[1] Most of the party recovered from the terrible struggle across the mountains in about a week, but some showed the effect of the strain and exertion much longer. Sergeant Gass remarks that Clark administered "Dr. Rush's pills" (presumably some remedy the Philadelphia physician recommended that the expedition carry) to the men "to see what effect that would have."

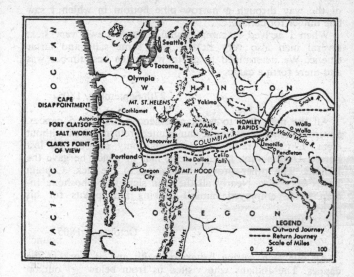

mountains and bring up some shot left behind, and at 10 o'clock we all set out for the river and proceeded on by the same route I had previously traveled, and at sunset we arrived at the island on which I found The Twisted Hair, and formed a camp on a large island a little below. Captain Lewis scarcely able to ride on a gentle horse which was furnished by the chief. Several men so unwell that they were compelled to lie on the side of the road for some time. Others obliged to be put on horses. I gave Rush's pills to the sick this evening.

25th of September, 1805

A very hot day. Most of the party complaining, and 2 of our hunters left here on the 22nd very sick; they had killed only two bucks in my absence. I set out early with the chief and 2 young men to hunt some trees calculated to build canoes, as we had previously determined to proceed on by water. I was furnished with a horse, and we proceeded on down the river. Crossed a creek at 1 mile and passed down on the north side of the river to a fork. We halted about an hour. One of the young men took his gig and killed 6 fine salmon; two of them were roasted and we ate. I crossed the south fork and proceeded up on the south side, the most of the way through a narrow pine bottom in which I saw fine timber for canoes.

When I arrived at camp, found Captain Lewis very sick, several men also very sick. I gave some salts and tartar emetic. We determined to go to where the best timber was and there form a camp.

27th September, 1805

All the men able to work commenced building 5 canoes. Several taken sick at work. Our hunters returned sick without meat. J. Colter returned. He found only one of the lost horses. On his way, killed a deer, half of which he gave the Indians. The other proved nourishing to the sick. Captain Lewis very sick. Nearly all the men sick. Our Shoshone Indian guide employed himself making flint points for his arrows.

October 3, 1805

All our men getting better in health and at work at the canoes. The Indians who visited us from below set out on their return early. Several others come from different directions.

October 7, 1805

I feel myself very unwell. All the canoes in the water. We load and set out, after fixing all our poles, &c. The afternoon cloudy. Proceed on, passing many bad rapids. One canoe, that in which I went in front, sprung a leak in passing the third rapid.

October 8th, 1805

A cloudy morning. Loaded our canoes, which were unloaded last night, and set out at 9 o'clock. Passed a creek on the starboard side at 16 miles, just below which one canoe, in which Sergeant Gass was steering, was near turning over. She sprung a leak or split open on one side, and bottom filled with water and sunk on the rapid. The men, several of whom could not swim, hung on to the canoe. I had one of the other canoes unloaded and, with the assistance of our small canoe and one Indian canoe, took out everything and towed the empty canoe on shore. One man, Thompson, a little hurt. Everything wet, particularly the greater part of our small stock of merchandise. Had everything opened, and two sentinels put over them to keep off the Indians, who are inclined to thievery, having stolen several small articles. Those people appeared disposed to give us every assistance in their power during our distress.

October 9th, 1805

In examining our canoe, found that by putting knees and strong pieces primed to her sides and bottom, &c., she could be made fit for service by the time the goods dried. Set 4 men to work at her: Sergeants Pryor and Gass, Joe Fields and Gibson; others to collect resin. At 1 o'clock she was finished, stronger than ever. The wet articles, not sufficiently dried to pack up, obliged us to delay another night. During that time, one man was trading for fish for our voyage. At dark, we were informed that our old guide and his son had left us, and had been seen running up the river several miles above. We could not account for the cause of his leaving us at this time, without receiving his pay for the services he had rendered us or letting us know anything of his intention.

We requested the chief to send a horseman after our old guide, to come back and receive his pay, &c., which he advised us not to do, as his nation would take his things from him before he passed their camps.

October 10, 1805

Loaded and set out at 7 o'clock. Passed a creek on the larboard with wide cotton willow bottoms, having passed an island and a rapid.

We arrived at the head of a very bad riffle, at which place we landed. After viewing this riffle, two canoes were taken over very well. The third stuck on a rock which took us an hour to get her off, which was effected without her receiving a greater injury than a small split in her side, which was repaired in a short time. We purchased fish and dogs of those people, dined, and proceeded on. Here we met with an Indian from the falls, at which place he says he saw white people, and expressed an inclination to accompany us. Arrived at a large southerly fork. This South Fork or Lewis's River has two forks, which fall into it on the south.[2]

---

[2] The names are confusing, partly because they are not those used today, partly because Clark does not always agree with modern map-makers on which is main stream and which tributary. At this point, he was at the junction of the Clearwater (Kooskooskee) with the Snake, not far from Lewiston, Idaho.

October 11th, 1805

We set out early and proceeded on. Passed a rapid at two miles. At 6 miles we came to at some Indian lodges and took breakfast. We purchased all the fish we could, and seven dogs, of those people for stores of provisions down the river. At this place I saw a curious sweat house underground, with a small hole at top to pass in or throw in the hot stones, which those inside threw on as much water as to create the temperature of heat they wished. At 9 mile, passed a rapid. At 15 miles, halted at an Indian lodge to purchase provisions, of which we procured some roots, five dogs, and a few fish dried. After taking some dinner of dog, &c., we proceeded on. Came to and encamped at 2 Indian lodges at a great place of fishing. Here we met an Indian of a nation near the mouth of this river. We purchased three dogs and a few fish of those Indians. We passed today nine rapids, all of them great fishing places. At different places on the river, saw Indian houses and slabs and split timber raised from the ground, being the different parts of the houses of the natives.

October 14th, 1805

A very cold morning. At 2½ miles passed a remarkable rock, very large and resembling the hull of a ship. Passed rapids at 6 and 9 miles. At 12 miles we came to at the head of a rapid which the Indians told me was very bad. We viewed the rapid, found it bad in descending. Three stern canoes stuck fast for some time on the head of the rapid, and one struck a rock in the worst part. Fortunately, all landed safe below the rapid, which was nearly 3 miles in length. Here we dined, and for the first time for three weeks past, I had a good dinner of blue-winged teal.

After dinner we set out and had not proceeded on two miles before our stern canoe, in passing through a short rapid opposite the head of an island, ran on a smooth rock and turned broadside. The men got out on the rock, all except one of our Indian chiefs, who swam on shore. The canoe filled and sank. A number of articles floated out, such as the men's bedding, clothes, and skins, the lodge,[3] &c., &c., the greater part of which were caught by 2 of the canoes, while a third was unloading and stemming the swift current to the relief of the men on the rock, who could with

---

[3] The "lodge" was the tent used by the two officers.

much difficulty hold the canoe. However, in about an hour we got the men and canoe to shore, with the loss of some bedding, tomahawks, shot pouches, skins, clothes, &c., &c., all wet. We had every article exposed to the sun to dry on the island.

Our loss in provisions is very considerable. All our roots were in the canoe that sank, and cannot be dried sufficient to save. Our loose powder was also in the canoe and is all wet. This I think may be saved. In this island we found some split timber, the parts of a house which the Indians had very securely covered with stone. We also observed a place where the Indians had buried their fish. We have made it a point at all times not to take anything belonging to the Indians, even their wood. But at this time we are compelled to violate that rule and take a part of the split timber we find here buried for firewood, as no other is to be found in any direction.

October 16th, 1805

A cool morning. Determined to run the rapids. Put our Indian guide in front, our small canoe next, and the other four following each other. The canoes all passed over safe except the rear canoe, which ran fast on a rock at the lower part of the rapids. With the early assistance of the other canoes and the Indians, who were extremely alert, everything was taken out, and the canoe got off without any injury further than the articles with which it was loaded getting all wet. At 14 miles passed a bad rapid, at which place we unloaded and made a portage of ¾ of a mile, having passed 4 smaller rapids, three islands, and the parts of a house above. I saw Indians and horses on the south side below. Five Indians came up the river in great haste. We smoked with them and gave them a piece of tobacco to smoke with their people, and sent them back. After getting safely over the rapid and having taken dinner, set out and proceeded on seven miles to the junction of this river and the Columbia, which joins from the northwest.[4]

We halted above the point on the river Kimooenim to smoke with the Indians who had collected there in great numbers to view us.[5] Here we met our 2 chiefs who left us

[4] They are now at the junction of the Snake and Columbia Rivers.

[5] The arrival of the white men was a great sensation among Nez Percé villages, far and wide. In our century, perhaps as late as 1908, an old woman still treasured the cap she had worn

two days ago and proceeded on to this place to inform those bands of our approach and friendly intentions toward all nations, &c. We also met the 2 men who had passed us several days ago on horseback; one of them, we observed, was a man of great influence with those Indians—harangued them. After smoking with the Indians who had collected to view us, we formed a camp at the point near which place I saw a few pieces of driftwood.

After we had our camp fixed and fires made, a chief came up from this camp, which was about ¼ of a mile up the Columbia River, at the head of about 200 men singing and beating on their drums and keeping time to the music. They formed a half-circle around us and sang for some time. We gave them all smoke, and spoke to their chief as well as we could by signs, informing them of our friendly disposition to all nations, and our joy in seeing those of our children around us. Gave the principal chief a large medal, shirt, and handkerchief; a second chief a medal of small size, and to the chief who came down from the upper villages a small medal and handkerchief.

October 18th, Friday, 1805

The Great Chief and one of the Chimnâpum nation drew me a sketch of the Columbia and the tribes of his nation living on the banks, and its waters, and the Tâpetett River which falls in 18 miles above on the westerly side.

We thought it necessary to lay in a store of provisions for our voyage, and the fish being out of season, we purchased forty dogs, for which we gave articles of little value, such as bells, thimbles, knitting pins, brass wire, and a few beads, with all of which they appeared well satisfied and pleased.

Everything being arranged, we took in our two chiefs, and set out on the great Columbia River, having left our guide and the two young men. Two of them inclined not to proceed on any further, and the third could be of no service to us as he did not know the river below.

Passed 4 islands. At the upper point of the 3rd is a rapid. On this island are two lodges of Indians, drying fish. On the fourth island are nine large lodges of Indians, drying fish on scaffolds. At this place we were called to to land. As it

---

the day her mother took her to see these strange creatures, The squaw Washkin, perhaps the same woman, remembered being strapped to a cradle and taken three miles to see the white men. The Kimooenim is the Snake River.

was near night and no appearance of wood, we proceeded on about 2 miles lower to some willows, at which place we observed a drift log. Formed a camp on the larboard side.

Soon after we landed, our old chiefs informed us that the large camp above "was the camp of the 1st chief of all the tribes in this quarter, and that he had called to us to land and stay all night with him, that he had plenty of wood for us." This would have been agreeable to us, if it had been understood, particularly as we were compelled to use dried willows for fuel for the purpose of cooking. We requested the old chiefs to walk up on the side we had landed and call to the chief to come down and stay with us all night, which they did. Late at night, the chief came down accompanied by 20 men, and formed a camp a short distance above. The chief brought with him a large basket of mashed berries, which he left at our lodge as a present.

October 19th, 1805

The Great Chief Yelleppit, two other chiefs, and a chief of a band below presented themselves to us very early this morning. We smoked with them, informed them, as we had all others above, as well as we could by signs, of our friendly intentions toward our red children, particularly those who opened their ears to our counsels. We gave a medal, a handkerchief, and a string of wampum to Yelleppit and a string of wampum to each of the others. Yelleppit is a bold, handsome Indian, with a dignified countenance, about 35 years of age.

Great numbers of Indians came down in canoes to view us before we set out, which was not until 9 o'clock A.M. We arrived at the head of a very bad rapid. As the channel appeared to be close under the opposite shore and it would be necessary to lighten our canoe, I determined to walk down on the larboard side, with the two chiefs, the interpreter, and his woman, and directed the small canoe to proceed down on the larboard side to the foot of the rapid, which was about 2 miles in length.

I sent on the Indian chief &c. down, and I ascended a high cliff, about 200 feet above the water, from the top of which is a level plain, extending up the river and off for a great extent. From this place I discovered a high mountain of immense height, covered with snow. This must be one of the mountains laid down by Vancouver, as seen from the mouth of the Columbia River. From the course which it bears, which is west, I take it to be Mt. St. Helens,[6] distant about 120 miles, a range of mountains in the direction crossing a conical mountain southwest, topped with snow.

I observed a great number of lodges on the opposite side at some distance below, and several Indians on the opposite bank passing up to where Captain Lewis was with the canoes. Others I saw on a knob nearly opposite to me, at which place they delayed but a short time before they returned to their lodges as fast as they could run. I was fearful that those people might not be informed of us. I determined to take the little canoe which was with me, and proceed with the three men in it, to the lodges. On my approach, not one person was to be seen except three men off in the plains, and they sheered off as I approached near the shore.

I landed in front of five lodges which were at no great distance from each other. Saw no person. The entrances or doors of the lodges were shut, with the same materials of which they were built—a mat. I approached one, with a pipe in my hand, entered a lodge which was the nearest to me. Found 32 persons—men, women, and a few children—sitting promiscuously in the lodge, in the greatest agitation; some crying and wringing their hands, others hanging their heads. I gave my hand to them all, and made signs of my friendly disposition, and offered the men my pipe to smoke, and distributed a few small articles which I had in my pockets. This measure pacified those distressed people very much. I then sent one man into each lodge, and entered a second myself, the inhabitants of which I found more frightened than those of the first lodge. I distributed sundry small articles among them, and smoked with the men.

I then entered the third, fourth, and fifth lodges, which I found somewhat pacified, the three men, Drouilliard, Joe and R. Fields, having used every means in their power to convince them of our friendly disposition to them. I then

---

[6] Captain George Vancouver, of the Royal Navy, failed to find the Columbia during his exploration of the coast but met the American ship *Columbia,* commanded by Captain Robert Gray, who had himself just discovered it. Learning of the river from Gray, Vancouver sent Lieutenant William Broughton, in H.M.S. *Chatham,* 119 miles upstream, using a rough chart that Gray had given him. The peak Clark saw was actually Mt. Adams, not Mt. St. Helens.

Clark omits from this entry a note he had made in his first draft for it: "P. Cruzat played on the violin, which pleased and astonished those wretches." After being carried hundreds of miles through all kinds of weather, the violin must have been in pretty bad condition.

sat myself on a rock and made signs to the men to come and smoke with me. Not one came out until the canoes arrived with the two chiefs, one of whom spoke aloud and as was their custom to all we had passed. The Indians came out and sat by me, and smoked. They said we came from the clouds, &c., &c., and were not men, &c., &c.

This time Captain Lewis came down with the canoes in which the Indians were. As soon as they saw the squaw wife of the interpreter, they pointed to her and informed those who continued yet in the same position I first found them. They immediately all came out and appeared to assume new life. The sight of this Indian woman, wife to one of our interpreters, confirmed those people of our friendly intentions, as no woman ever accompanies a war party of Indians in this quarter. Captain Lewis joined us, and we smoked with those people in the greatest friendship, during which time one of our old chiefs informed them who we were, from whence we came, and where we were going; giving them a friendly account of us. Passed a small rapid and 15 lodges below the five, and encamped below an island close under the larboard side, nearly opposite to 24 lodges on an island near the middle of the river, and the main starboard shore. Soon after we landed, which was at a few willow trees, about 100 Indians came from the different lodges, and a number of them brought wood, which they gave us. We smoked with all of them, and two of our party—Peter Cruzat and Gibson—played on the violin, which delighted them greatly.

October 21st, 1805

One of our party, J. Collins, presented us with some very good beer made of the *pa-shi-co-quar-mash* [7] bread, which bread is the remains of what was laid in as a part of our stores of provisions, at the first Flatheads, [8] or Chopunnish nation at the head of the Kooskooskee river, which, by being frequently wet, molded and soured.

October 23rd, 1805

I, with the greater part of the men, crossed in the canoes to

[7] This was root beer, the *pa-shi-co-quar-mash* being an unidentified edible root.

[8] Clark is a little mixed up, which is not remarkable, as the names of these tribes are confusing. In modern terminology, the Flatheads are Salish; but they did not flatten their heads as some other tribes did! The Chopunnish are the Nez Percés.

opposite side above the falls and hauled them across the portage of 457 yards, which is on the larboard side and certainly the best side to pass the canoes. I then descended through a narrow channel, about 150 yards wide, forming a kind of half-circle in its course of a mile, to a pitch of 8 feet, in which the channel is divided by 2 large rocks.

At this place we were obliged to let the canoes down by strong ropes of elkskin which we had for the purpose. One canoe, in passing this place, got loose by the cords breaking, and was caught by the Indians below. I accomplished this necessary business and landed safe with all the canoes at our camp below the falls by 3 o'clock P.M. Nearly covered with fleas, which were so thick among the straw and fish skins at the upper part of the portage, at which place the natives had been camped not long since, that every man of the party was obliged to strip naked during the time of taking over the canoes, that they might have an opportunity of brushing the fleas off their legs and bodies.

Great numbers of sea otter in the river below the falls. I shot one in the narrow channel today, which I could not get. Great numbers of Indians visit us both from above and below.

We purchased 8 small fat dogs for the party to eat. The natives not being fond of selling their good fish, compels us to make use of dog meat for food, the flesh of which the most of the party have become fond of, from the habit of using it for some time past.

October 24th, 1805

Our two old chiefs expressed a desire to return to their band from this place, saying that they could be of no further service to us, as their nation extended no further down the river than those falls; they could no longer understand the language of those below the falls, till then not much difference in the vocabularies; and as the nation below had expressed hostile intentions against us, would certainly kill them, particularly as they had been at war with each other. We requested them to stay with us two nights longer, and we would see the nation below and make a peace between them. They replied that they were anxious to return and see "our horses." We insisted on their staying with us two nights longer, to which they agreed. Our views were to detain those chiefs with us until we should pass the next falls, which we were told were very bad, and at no great distance below; that they might inform us of any designs of the natives; and, if possible, to bring about a peace between them and the tribes below.

At 9 o'clock A.M. I set out with the party and proceeded on down a rapid stream about 400 yards wide. At 2½ miles, the river widened into a large basin to the starboard side, on which there are five lodges of Indians. Here a tremendous black rock presented itself, high and steep, appearing to choke up the river. Nor could I see where the water passed further than the current was drawn with great velocity to the larboard side of this rock, at which place I heard a great roaring.

I landed at the lodges, and the natives went with me to the top of the rock, which makes from the starboard side; from the top of which I could see the difficulties we had to pass for several miles below. At this place, the water of this great river is compressed into a channel between two rocks, not exceeding forty-five yards wide, and continues for ¼ of a mile, when it again widens to 200 yards, and continues this width for about 2 miles, when it is again intercepted by rocks. This obstruction in the river accounts for the water in high floods rising to such a height at the last falls. The whole of the current of this great river must at all stages pass through this narrow channel of 45 yards wide. As the portage of our canoes over this high rock would be impossible with our strength, and the only danger in passing through those narrows was the whorls and swells arising from the compression of the water; and which I thought—as also our principal waterman, Peter Cruzat—by good steering we could pass down safe. Accordingly, I determined to pass through this place notwithstanding the horrid appearance of this agitated gut, swelling, boiling, and whorling in every direction, which, from the top of the rock, did not appear as bad as when I was in it. However, we passed safe—to the astonishment of all the Indians of the last lodges, who viewed us from the top of the rock.

Passed one lodge below this rock, and halted on the starboard side to view a very bad place: the current divided by 2 islands of rocks, the lower of them large and in the middle of the river. This place being very bad, I sent by land all the men who could not swim and such articles as were most valuable to us—such as papers, guns, and ammunition—and proceeded down with the canoes, two at a time, to a village of 20 wood houses in a deep bend to the starboard side, below which was a rugged black rock about 20 feet higher than the common high floods of the river, with several dry channels which appeared to choke the river up, quite across. This I took to be the second falls, or the place the natives above call timm.

The natives of this village received me very kindly; one of whom invited me into his house, which I found to be large and commodious, and the first wooden houses in which Indians have lived, since we left those in the vicinity of the Illinois. I dispatched a sufficient number of the good swimmers back for the 2 canoes above the last rapid, and with 2 men walked three miles down to examine the river. I returned through a rocky open country infested with polecats, to the village, where I met with Captain Lewis, the two old chiefs who accompanied us, and the party and canoes, who had all arrived safe.

October 25th, 1805

Captain Lewis and myself walked down to see the place the Indians pointed out as the worst place in passing through the gut, which we found difficult of passing without great danger. But, as the portage was impractical with our large canoes, we concluded to make a portage of our most valuable articles and run the canoes through. Accordingly, on our return, divided the party: some to take over the canoes, and others to take our stores across a portage of a mile, to a place on the channel below this bad whorl and suck; with some others I had fixed on the channel with ropes to throw out to any who should unfortunately meet with difficulty in passing through. Great numbers of Indians viewing us from the high rocks under which we had to pass. The three first canoes passed through very well; the fourth nearly filled with water; the last passed through by taking in a little water. Thus, safely below what I conceived to be the worst part of this channel, felt myself extremely gratified and pleased.

We loaded the canoes and set out, and had not proceeded more than 2 miles before the unfortunate canoe which filled crossing the bad place above, ran against a rock and was in great danger of being lost. This channel is through a hard, rough black rock, from 50 to 100 yards wide, swelling and boiling in a most tremendous manner. Several places on which the Indians inform me they take the salmon as fast as they wish. We passed through a deep basin to the starboard side of 1 mile, below which the river narrows and is divided by a rock. The current we found quite gentle.

Here we met with our two old chiefs, who had been to a village below to smoke a friendly pipe, and at this place they met the chief and party from the village above, on his return from hunting, all of whom were then crossing over their horses. We landed to smoke a pipe with this chief, whom we found to be a bold, pleasing-looking man of about 50 years of age, dressed in a war jacket, a cap, leggings, and moccasins. He gave us some meat, of which he had but little, and informed us he, in his route, met with a war party of Snake Indians from the great river of the S.E., which falls in a few miles above, and had a fight. We gave this chief a medal, &c. Had a parting smoke with our two faithful friends, the chiefs who accompanied us from the head of the river.

Chapter *XVII*

...AND GAZED AT THE PACIFIC!

November 2—December 10, 1805

November 2nd, 1805

[Clark]

Examined the rapid below us more particularly. The danger appearing too great to hazard our canoes loaded, dispatched all the men who could not swim with loads to the end of the portage below. I also walked to the end of the portage with the carriers, where I delayed until every article was brought over, and the canoes arrived safe.

November 3rd, 1805

A mountain which we suppose to be Mt. Hood is S. 85° E., about 47 miles distant from the mouth of Quicksand River. This mountain is covered with snow and in the range of mountains which we have passed through and is of a conical form, but rugged. After taking dinner at the mouth of this river, we proceeded on.

November 4th, 1805

Several canoes of Indians from the village above came down, dressed for the purpose, as I supposed, of paying us a friendly visit. They had scarlet and blue blankets, sailor jackets, overalls, shirts and hats, independent of their usual dress. The most of them had either war axes, spears, or bows sprung with quivers of arrows, muskets or pistols, and tin flasks to hold their powder. Those fellows we found assuming and disagreeable. However, we smoked with them and treated them with every attention and friendship.

During the time we were at dinner, those fellows stole

my pipe tomahawk [1] which they were smoking with. I immediately searched every man and the canoes, but could find nothing of my tomahawk. While searching for the tomahawk, one of those scoundrels stole a capote [greatcoat] of one of our interpreters, which was found stuffed under the root of a tree near the place they sat. We became much displeased with those fellows, which they discovered, and moved off on their return home to their village, except two canoes which had passed on down. We proceeded on.

November 6th, 1805

We overtook two canoes of Indians, going down to trade. One of the Indians spoke a few words of English, and said that the principal man who traded with them was Mr. Haley, and that he had a woman in his canoe who Mr. Haley was fond of, &c. He showed us a bow of iron and several other things, which, he said, Mr. Haley gave him. We came to, to dine on the long narrow island. Found the woods so thick with undergrowth that the hunters could not get any distance into the island.

November 7th, 1805

Encamped under a high hill on the starboard side, opposite to a rock situated half a mile from the shore, about 50 feet high and 20 feet in diameter. We with difficulty found a place clear of the tide and sufficiently large to lie on, and the only place we could get was on round stones on which we laid our mats. Rain continued moderately all day, and two Indians accompanied us from the last village. They were detected in stealing a knife and returned. Our small canoe, which got separated in a fog this morning, joined us this evening from a large island situated nearest the larboard side, below the high hills on that side, the river being too wide to see either the form, shape, or size of the islands on the larboard side.

Great joy in camp. We are in view of the ocean, this great Pacific Ocean which we have been so long anxious to see, and the roaring or noise made by the waves breaking on the rocky shores (as I suppose) may be heard distinctly.[2]

[1] The pipe tomahawk had a pipe bowl opposite its cutting edge and a hollow handle, so that it served as a weapon, a camp axe, and a tobacco pipe.

[2] If Thwaites identifies this point correctly, it was quite impossible to see the ocean. The explorers could see the estuary, which is fifteen miles wide and was easily mistaken for the Pacific.

November 8th, 1805

We took the advantage of a returning tide and proceeded on to the second point on the starboard. Here we found the swells or waves so high that we thought it imprudent to proceed. We landed, unloaded, and drew up our canoes. Some rain all day at intervals. We are all wet and disagreeable, as we have been for several days past, and our present situation a very disagreeable one inasmuch as we have not level land sufficient for an encampment, and for our baggage to lie clear of the tide. The high hills jutting in so close and steep that we cannot retreat back, and the water of the river too salt to be used. Added to this, the waves are increasing to such a height that we cannot move from this place. In this situation, we are compelled to form our camp between the height of the ebb and flood tides, and raise our baggage on logs. We are not certain as yet if the white people who trade with those people, or from whom they procure their goods, are stationary at the mouth, or visit this quarter at stated times for the purpose of traffic, &c. I believe the latter to be the most probable conjecture. The seas rolled and tossed the canoes in such a manner this evening that several of our party were seasick.

November 9th, 1805

The tide of last night obliged us to unload all the canoes, one of which sank, before she was unloaded, by the high waves or swells which accompanied the returning tide. The others we unloaded, and 3 others were filled with water soon after by the swells or high seas which broke against the shore immediately where we lay. Rained hard all the fore part of the day. The tide, which rose until 2 o'clock P.M. today, brought with it such immense swells or waves— added to a hard wind from the south which loosened the drift trees, which are very thick on the shore, and tossed them about in such a manner—as to endanger our canoes very much. Every exertion and the strictest attention by the party was scarcely sufficient to defend our canoes from being crushed to pieces between those immensely large trees, many of them 200 feet long and 4 feet through.

November 10th, 1805

Rained very hard the greater part of last night and continues this morning. The wind has lulled and the waves are not high. We loaded our canoes and proceeded on. Passed several small and deep niches on the starboard side. We proceeded on about 10 miles; saw great numbers of sea gulls. The wind rose from the N.W., and the waves became so high that we were compelled to return about 2 miles to a place we could unload our canoes, which we did in a small niche at the mouth of a small run, on a pile of drift logs, where we continued until low water. When the river appeared calm, we loaded and set out, but were obliged to return, finding the waves too high for our canoes to ride. We again unloaded the canoes and stowed the loading on a rock above the tidewater, and formed a camp on the drift logs which appeared to be the only situation we could find to lee—the hills being either a perpendicular cliff or steep ascent, rising to about 500 feet. Our canoes we secured as well as we could. We are all wet, the rain having continued all day— our bedding and many other articles. Employ ourselves drying our blankets. Nothing to eat but dried fish, pounded, which we brought from the Falls. We made 10 miles today.

November 12th, 1805

Our situation is dangerous. We took the advantage of a low tide and moved our camp around a point to a small wet bottom, at the mouth of a brook, which we had not observed when we came to this cove, from its being very thick and obscured by drift trees and thick bushes. It would be distressing to see our situation—all wet and cold, our bedding also wet (and the robes of the party which compose half the bedding are rotten, and we are not in a situation to supply their places), in a wet bottom scarcely large enough to contain us, our baggage half a mile from us, and canoes at the mercy of the waves, although secured as well as possible—sunk, with immense parcels of stone to weight them down to prevent their dashing to pieces against the rocks. One got loose last night and was left on a rock a short distance below, without receiving more damage than a split in her bottom. Fortunately for us, our men are healthy.

November 14th, 1805

Captain Lewis concluded to proceed on by land and find, if possible, the white people the Indians say are below, and examine if a bay is situated near the mouth of this river, as laid down by Vancouver, in which we expect, if there are white traders, to find them. At 3 o'clock, he set out with four men, Drouilliard, Joseph and Reuben Fields, and R.

Frazer, in one of our large canoes, and 5 men to set them around the point on the sand beach. This canoe returned nearly filled with water, at dark, which it received by the waves dashing into it on its return, having landed Captain Lewis and his party safe on the sand beach. The rain continues all day. All wet.

November 15th, Friday, 1805

Shannon informed me that he met Captain Lewis at an Indian hut about 10 miles below, who had sent him back to meet me. He also told me the Indians were thievish, as the night before they had stolen both his and Willard's rifles from under their heads [they threatened them with a large party from above, which Captain Lewis's arrival confirmed]; that they set out on their return and had not proceeded far up the beach before they met Captain Lewis, whose arrival was at a timely moment and alarmed the Indians, so that they instantly produced the guns.

I told those Indians who accompanied Shannon that they should not come near us, and if anyone of their nation stole anything from us, I would have him shot, which they understood very well.

November 17, 1805

Captain Lewis returned, having traversed Haley Bay to Cape Disappointment, and the seacoast to the north for some distance. Several Chinook Indians followed Captain Lewis, and a canoe came up with roots, mats, &c., to sell.

Cape Disappointment at the entrance of the
Columbia River into the Great
South Sea, or Pacific Ocean

November the 19th, 1805

I arose early this morning from under a wet blanket caused by a shower of rain which fell in the latter part of the last night, and sent two men on ahead with directions to proceed on near the seacoast and kill something for breakfast and that I should follow myself in about half an hour. After drying our blankets a little, I set out with a view to proceed near the coast, the direction of which induced me to conclude that at the distance of 8 or 10 miles, the bay was no great distance across. I overtook the hunters at about 3 miles. They had killed a small deer, on which we breakfasted. It commenced raining and continued moderately until 11 o'clock A.M.

After taking a sumptuous breakfast of venison, which was roasted on sticks exposed to the fire, I proceeded on through rugged country of high hills and steep hollows on a course from the cape, N. 20° W., 5 miles on a direct line to the commencement of a sandy coast which extended N. 10° W. from the top of the hill above the sand shore to a point of high land, distant near 20 miles. This point I have taken the liberty of calling after my particular friend, Lewis.

November the 20th, 1805

Found many of the Chinooks with Captain Lewis, of whom there were 2 chiefs, Comcommoly and Chillarlawil, to whom we gave medals, and to one a flag. One of the Indians had on a robe made of two sea-otter skins. The fur of them was more beautiful than any fur I had ever seen. Both Captain Lewis and myself endeavored to purchase the robe with different articles. At length, we procured it for a belt of blue beads which the squaw wife of our interpreter Charbonneau wore around her waist.

November 21st, 1805

An old woman and wife to a chief of the Chinooks came and made a camp near ours. She brought with her 6 young squaws—her daughters and nieces—I believe for the purpose of gratifying the passions of the men of our party and receiving for those indulgences such small presents as she (the old woman) thought proper to accept of.

Those people appear to view sensuality as a necessary evil, and do not appear to abhor it as a crime in the unmarried state. The young females are fond of the attention of our men and appear to meet the sincere approbation of their friends and connections for thus obtaining their favors. The women of the Chinook nation have handsome faces, low and badly made with large legs and thighs, which are generally swelled from a stoppage of the circulation in the feet (which are small) by many strands of beads or curious strings which are drawn tight around the leg above the ankle. Their legs are also picked [tattooed] with different figures. I saw on the left arm of a squaw the following letters: *J. Bowman.* All those are considered by the natives of this quarter as handsome decorations.

November 22nd [3rd], 1805

Captain Lewis branded a tree with his name, date, &c. I marked my name, the day and year, on an alder tree. The party all cut the first letters of their names on different trees in the bottom. Our hunters killed 3 bucks, 4 brant, and 3 ducks today.

In the evening, seven Indians of the Clatsop nation came over in a canoe. They brought with them two sea-otter skins, for which they asked blue beads &c., and such high prices that we were unable to purchase them without reducing our small stock of merchandise on which we depended for subsistence on our return up this river. Merely to try the Indian who had one of those skins, I offered him my watch, handkerchief, a bunch of red beads, and a dollar of the American coin, all of which he refused and demanded *ti-â-co-mo-shack,* which is "chief beads," and the common blue beads, but few of which we have at this time.

November 29th, 1805

[Lewis]

The wind being high, the party were unable to proceed with the pirogues. I determined, therefore, to proceed down the river on its east side in search of an eligible place for our winter's residence, and accordingly set out early this morning in the small canoe, accompanied by 5 men.

December 3rd, 1805

[Clark]

I marked my name and the day of the month and year on a large pine tree on this peninsula:

Capt. William Clark December 3d 1805. By Land.
U. States in 1804-1805

The squaw broke the two shank bones of the elk after the marrow was taken out; boiled them, and extracted a pint of grease or tallow from them. Sergeant Pryor and Gibson returned after night and informed me they had been lost the greater part of the time they were out, and had killed six elk which they left lying, having taken out their entrails.

December 7th, 1805

We set out at 8 o'clock down to the place Captain Lewis

pitched on for winter quarters when he was down. We
stopped and dined in the commencement of a bay, after
which we proceeded on around the bay to S.E. and ascended
a creek 8 miles to a high point and camped. At this place
of encampment we propose to build and pass the winter.
The situation is in the center of, as we conceive, a hunting
country.

December 8th, 1805

We having fixed on this situation as the one best calculated for our winter quarters, I determined to go as direct
a course as I could to the seacoast, which we could hear
roar and appeared to be at no great distance from us. My
principal object is to look out a place to make salt, blaze
the road or route that the men out hunting might find the
direction to the fort if they should get lost in cloudy
weather; and see the probability of game in that direction,
for the support of the men we shall send to make salt.

9th December, 1805

I set out in a westerly direction, crossed 3 slashes, and arrived at a creek. Met 3 Indians loaded with fresh salmon.
Those Indians made signs that they had a town on the seacoast at no great distance, and invited me to go to their
town. They had a canoe hid in the creek; we crossed in this
little canoe. After crossing, 2 of the Indians took the canoe
on their shoulders and carried it across to the other creek,
about ¼ of a mile. We crossed the 2nd creek and proceeded
on to the mouth of the creek, which makes a great bend.
Above the mouth of this creek, or to the south, are 3 houses
and about 12 families of the Clatsop nation. We crossed
to those houses.

Those people treated me with extraordinary friendship.
One man attached himself to me as soon as I entered the hut,
spread down new mats for me to sit on, gave me fish, berries,
roots, etc. All the men of the other houses came and smoked
with me. In the evening an old woman presented in a bowl
made of a light-colored horn, a kind of syrup made of dried
berries which the natives call *shele-well*. They gave me a
kind of soup made of bread of the shele-well berries mixed
with roots, which they presented in neat trenchers made of
wood.

When I was disposed to go to sleep, the man who had been
most attentive, named Cuscalah, produced 2 new mats and
spread them near the fire, and directed his wife to go to his

bed, which was the signal for all to retire. I had not been long on my mats before I was attacked most violently by the fleas, and they kept up a close siege during the night.

10th December, 1805

One of the Indians pointed to a flock of brant sitting in the creek a short distance below and requested me to shoot one. I walked down with my small rifle and killed two at about 40 yards' distance. On my return to the houses, two small ducks sat at about 30 steps from me. The Indians pointed at the ducks. They were near together. I shot at the ducks and accidentally shot the head of one off. This duck and brant were carried to the house, and every man came around, examined the duck, looked at the gun, the size of the ball, which was 100 to the pound, and said in their own language, *Clouch musket*, (English word, "musket") *wake, com-ma-tax, musket, Kloshe musket, wake kumtuks musket*, which is, "A good musket, do not understand this kind of musket," &c. I entered the same house I slept in; they immediately set before me their best roots, fish, and syrup. I attempted to purchase a small sea-otter skin for red beads which I had in my pockets. They would not trade for those beads, not prizing any other color than blue or white. I purchased a little of the berry bread and a few of their roots for which I gave small fishhooks, which they appeared fond of.

Chapter *XVIII*

FORT CLATSOP
December 12, 1805—March 17, 1806

12th December, 1805

All hands that are well employed in cutting logs and raising our winter cabins. Detached two men to split boards. Some rain at intervals all last night and today. The fleas were so troublesome last night that I made but a broken night's rest. We find great difficulty in getting those troublesome insects out of our robes and blankets. In the evening, two canoes of Clatsops visited us. They brought with them wappato,[1] a black sweet root they call shanataque, and a small sea-otter skin, all of which we purchased for a few fishing hooks and a small sack of Indian tobacco which was given us by the Snake Indians.

Those Indians appear well disposed. We gave a medal to the Principal Chief, named Connyau or Commowol [*Coboway*], and treated those with him with as much attention as we could. I can readily discover that they are close dealers, and stickle for a very little; never close a bargain except they think they have the advantage. Value blue beads highly, white they also prize, but no other color do they value in the least.

24th December 1805

Cuscalah, the Indian who had treated me so politely when I was at the Clatsops' village, came up in a canoe with his young brother and two squaws. He laid before Captain Lewis and myself each a mat and a parcel of roots. Some time in the evening, two files were demanded for the presents

---

[1] Wappato was the edible root of *Sagittaria latifolia,* or arrowhead; shanataque is the root of a thistle, *Cnicus edulis.*

of mats and roots. As we had no files to part with, we each returned the present which we had received, which displeased Cuscalah a little. He then offered a woman to each of us, which we also declined accepting of, which displeased the whole party very much. The female part appeared to be highly disgusted at our refusing to accept of their favors.

Christmas, 25th December, 1805

At daylight this morning, we were awakened by the discharge of the firearms of all our party and a salute, shouts, and a song which the whole party joined in under our windows, after which they retired to their rooms. Were cheerful all the morning. After breakfast we divided our tobacco, which amounted to 12 carrots, one half of which we gave to the men of the party who used tobacco, and to those who do not use it we made a present of a handkerchief. The Indians left us in the evening. All the party snugly fixed in their huts. I received a present of Captain Lewis of a fleece hosiery shirt, drawers and socks, a pair of moccasins of Whitehouse, a small Indian basket of Goodrich, two dozen white weasels' tails of the Indian woman, and some black root of the Indians before their departure. Drouilliard informs me that he saw a snake pass across the path today. The day proved showery, wet, and disagreeable.

We would have spent this day, the nativity of Christ, in feasting, had we had anything either to raise our spirits or even gratify our appetites. Our dinner consisted of poor elk, so much spoiled that we ate it through mere necessity, some spoiled pounded fish, and a few roots.

The 28th of December, 1805

Directed Drouilliard, Shannon, Labiche, Reuben Fields, and Collins to hunt; Joseph Fields, Bratton, Gibson to proceed to the ocean, at some convenient place form a camp, and commence making salt with 5 of the largest kettles, and Willard and Wiser to assist them in carrying the kettles to the seacoast. All the other men to be employed about putting up pickets and making the gates of the fort. My man York very unwell from a violent cold, and strain by carrying meat from the woods and lifting the heavy logs on the works, &c.

30th December, 1805

Our fortification is completed this evening, and at sunset we let the natives know that our custom will be in future to shut the gates at sunset, at which time all Indians must go out of the fort and not return into it until next morning after sunrise, at which time the gates will be opened.

31st December, 1805

With the party of Clatsops who visited us last was a man of much lighter color than the natives generally. He was freckled, with long, dusky red hair, about 25 years of age, and must certainly be half white at least. This man appeared to understand more of the English language than the others of his party, but did not speak a word of English. He possessed all the habits of the Indians.

Fort Clatsop, 1806
January 1st

[Lewis]

This morning I was awakened at an early hour by the discharge of a volley of small arms, which was fired by our party in front of our quarters to usher in the New Year. This was the only mark of respect which we had it in our power to pay this celebrated day. Our repast of this day, though better than that of Christmas, consisted principally in the anticipation of the 1st day of January, 1807, when, in the bosom of our friends, we hope to participate in the mirth and hilarity of the day; and when, with the zest given by the recollection of the present, we shall completely, both mentally and corporally, enjoy the repast which the hand of civilization has prepared for us. At present we were content with eating our boiled elk and wappato, and solacing our thirst with our only beverage, *pure water*. Two of our hunters who set out this morning returned in the evening having killed two buck elk. They presented Captain Clark and myself each a marrowbone and tongue, on which we supped.

We were uneasy with respect to two of our men, Willard and Wiser, who were dispatched on the 28th ult. with the salt makers, and were directed to return immediately. Their not having returned induces us to believe it probable that they have missed their way.

January 3rd, 1806

Our party, from necessity having been obliged to subsist some length of time on dogs, have now become extremely fond of their flesh. It is worthy of remark that while we lived principally on the flesh of this animal, we were much more healthy, strong, and more fleshy than we had been since we left the buffalo country. For my own part, I have become so perfectly reconciled to the dog that I think it an agreeable food and would prefer it vastly to lean venison or elk.

5th of January, 1806

[Clark]

At 5 P.M., Willard and Wiser returned. They had not been lost as we expected. They informed us that it was not until the fifth day after leaving the fort that they could find a convenient place for making salt; that they had at length established themselves on the seacoast about 15 miles S.W. from this, near the houses of some Clatsop and Tillamook families; that the Indians were very friendly and had given them a considerable quantity of the blubber of the whale which perished on the coast some distance S.E. of them. It was white and not unlike the fat of pork, though the texture was more spongy and somewhat coarser. We had part of it cooked and found it very palatable and tender. It resembles the beaver in flavor.

Those men also informed us that the salt makers with their assistance had erected a comfortable camp, had killed an elk and several deer and secured a good stock of meat. They commenced the making of salt and found that they could make from 3 quarts to a gallon a day. They brought with them a specimen of the salt, of about a gallon. We found it excellent, white, and fine, but not so strong as the rock salt, or that made in Kentucky or the western parts of the U. States. This salt was a great treat to most of the party, having not had any since the 20th ult. As to myself, I care but little whether I have any with my meat or not, provided the meat is fat, having from habit become entirely careless about my diet; and I have learned to think that if the cord be sufficiently strong which binds the soul and body together, it does not so much matter about the materials which compose it.

I determined to set out early tomorrow with two canoes and 12 men in quest of the whale, or at all events to purchase from the Indians a parcel of the blubber. For this purpose I made up a small assortment of merchandise and directed the men to hold themselves in readiness.

6th of January, 1806

The last evening Charbonneau and his Indian woman were very impatient to be permitted to go with me and were therefore indulged. She observed that she had traveled a long way with us to see the great waters and, now that monstrous fish was also to be seen, she thought it very hard that she could not be permitted to see either. (She had never yet been to the ocean.)

7th of January, 1806

I found our salt makers, and with them Sergeant Gass. George Shannon was out in the woods assisting Joe Fields and Gibson to kill some meat. The salt makers had made a neat, close camp, convenient to wood, salt water, and the fresh water of the Clatsop river, which at this place was within 100 paces of the ocean.[2] They were also situated near four houses of Clatsops and Tillamooks, who, they informed me, had been very kind and attentive to them.

I hired a young Indian to pilot me to the whale, for which service I gave him a file in hand and promised several other small articles on my return. Left Sergeant Gass and one man of my party, Warner, to make salt, and permitted Bratton to accompany me.

8th January, 1806

Proceeded to the place the whale had perished. Found only the skeleton of this monster on the sand, between 2 of the villages of the Tillamook nation. The whale was already pillaged of every valuable part by the Tillamook Indians in the vicinity, of whose villages it lay on the strand, where the waves and tide had driven up and left it. This skeleton measured 105 feet. I returned to the village of 5 cabins on the creek, which I shall call *Ecola* or Whale Creek. Found the natives busily engaged boiling the blubber, which they performed in a large, square wooden trough, by means of hot stones. The oil, when extracted, was secured in bladders and the guts of the whale. The blubber, from which the oil was only partially extracted by this process, was laid by in their cabins, in large flitches for use. Those flitches they usually expose to the fire on a wooden spit, until it is pretty well warmed through, and then eat it either alone or with roots of the rush, *shanataque*,[3] or dipped in the oil.

[2] The salt-making party built large fireplaces on which to boil down the sea water. These still exist, though now only heaps of stone.

[3] Though Clark spells this *shaw na tâk-we* and here identifies it as a rush, there seems little doubt it was the thistle *Cnicus edulis*, usually called *shanataque*.

The Tillamooks, although they possessed large quantities of this blubber and oil, were so penurious that they disposed of it with great reluctance, and in small quantities only; insomuch that my utmost exertions, aided by the party, with the small stock of merchandise I had taken with me, were not able to procure more blubber than about 300 pounds and a few gallons of oil. Small as this stock is, I prize it highly; and thank Providence for directing the whale to us; and think Him much more kind to us than He was to Jonah, having sent this monster to be swallowed *by* us, instead of swallowing *of* us, as Jonah's did.

January 9, 1806

[Lewis]

The persons who usually visit the entrance of this river for the purpose of traffic or hunting, I believe are either English or Americans. The Indians inform us that they speak the same language with ourselves, and give us proofs of their veracity by repeating many words of English, as *musket, powder, shot, knife, file, damned rascal, son of a bitch,* &c. Whether these traders are from Nootka Sound, from some other late establishment on this coast, or immediately from the U. States or Great Britain, I am at a loss to determine, nor can the Indians inform us.

The Indians whom I have asked in what direction the traders go when they depart from hence or arrive here, always point to the S.W.,[4] from which it is presumable that Nootka cannot be their destination; and as, from Indian information, a majority of these traders annually visit them about the beginning of April and remain with them six or seven months, they cannot come immediately from Great Britain or the U. States, the distance being too great for them to go and return in the balance of the year. From this circumstance I am sometimes induced to believe that there is some other establishment on the coast of America, southwest of this place, of which little is but yet known to the world, or it may be perhaps on some little island in the Pacific Ocean, between the continents of Asia and America, to the southwest of us.

This traffic on the part of the whites consists in vending

[4] The Indians were quite right. The traders were heading for China, to sell their furs. As this trade developed, merchants made three profits, first on the goods they exchanged with the Pacific Coast Indians for furs, then on the furs they exchanged with Orientals, then on the Oriental wares—silks, china, wallpaper, etc.—that they sold for cash on their return home.

guns (principally old British or American muskets), powder, balls and shot, copper and brass kettles, brass teakettles and coffeepots, blankets from two to three points,[5] scarlet and blue cloth (coarse), plates and strips of sheet copper and brass, large brass wire, knives, beads, and tobacco, with fishing hooks, buttons, and some other small articles. Also a considerable quantity of sailors' clothes, as hats, coats, trousers, and shirts. For these they receive in return from the natives dressed and undressed elk skins, skins of the seaotter, common otter, beaver, common fox, spuck,[6] and tiger cat; also dried and pounded salmon in baskets, and a kind of biscuit which the natives make of roots, called by them shappellel.[7]

9th of January, 1806

[Clark]

A fine morning. Wind from the N.E. Last night about 10 o'clock, while smoking with the natives, I was alarmed by a loud shrill voice from the cabins on the opposite side. The Indians all ran immediately across to the village. My guide, who continued with me, made signs that someone's throat was cut. By inquiry, I found that one man, McNeal, was absent. I immediately sent off Sergeant N. Pryor and four men in quest of McNeal, whom they met coming across the creek in great haste, and informed me that the people were alarmed on the opposite side at something, but what he could not tell; a man had very friendlily invited him to go and eat in his lodge; that the Indian had locked arms with him and went to a lodge in which a woman gave him some

[5] The word "point," as here used, is a measure of the size of blankets, which the Hudson's Bay Company has used for two or three centuries. The "points" are short lines woven into one margin of the blanket. Originally they indicated the cost to an Indian, in beaver skins, of the blanket. Thus a three-and-a-half-point blanket cost three big beaverskins and one small one. A four-point blanket cost four beaverskins. The points are still woven into the blankets, but today they indicate dimensions and weight. Clark evidently refers to one of the blanket-coats still used. Lewis and Clark were not the last explorers to use Hudson's Bay blankets. Admiral Byrd and at least one Mt. Everest expedition also used them.

[6] "Spuck" was a native word for the young of the sea-otter.

[7] A bread made of roots baked in the sun. There is some doubt exactly what root was used. Sergeant Gass thought the food "strong and palatable."

blubber, that the man invited him to another lodge to get something better, and the woman—knowing his design—held him [McNeal] by the blanket which he had around him. He, not knowing her object, freed himself and was going off, when this woman—a Chinook, an old friend of McNeal's— and another, ran out and hallooed, and his pretended friend disappeared.

I immediately ordered every man to hold himself in a state of readiness, and sent Sergeant Pryor and four men to know the cause of the alarm, which was found to be a premeditated plan of the pretended friend of McNeal to assassinate him for his blanket and what few articles he had about him, which was found out by a Chinook woman, who alarmed the men of the village who were with me, in time to prevent the horrid act. This man was of another band, at some distance, and ran off as soon as he was discovered.

We have now to look back and shudder at the dreadful road on which we have to return, of 45 miles S.E. of Point Adams and 35 miles from Fort Clatsop. I had the blubber and oil divided among the party, and set out about sunrise, and returned by the same route we had gone out. Met several parties of men and women of the Chinook and Clatsop nations on their way to trade with the Tillamooks for blubber and oil.

On the steep descent of the mountain, I overtook five men and six women with immense loads of the oil and blubber of the whale. Those Indians had passed by some route by which we missed them as we went out yesterday. One of the women, in the act of getting down a steep part of the mountain, her load by some means had slipped off her back, and she was holding the load by a strap which was fastened to the mat bag in which it was in, in one hand and holding a bush by the other. As I was in front of my party, I endeavored to relieve this woman by taking her load until she could get to a better place a little below, and to my astonishment found the load as much as I could lift, and must exceed 100 pounds. The husband of this woman, who was below, soon came to her relief.

Those people proceeded on with us to the salt works, at which place we arrived late in the evening. Found them without meat, and three of the party—J. Fields, Gibson, and Shannon—out hunting. As I was excessively fatigued, and my party appeared very much so, I determined to stay until the morning and rest ourselves a little. The Clatsops proceeded on with their loads. The Clatsops, Chinooks, Tillamooks, &c., are very loquacious and inquisitive. They possess good memories and have repeated to us the names, capacities of the vessels, &c., of many traders and others who have visited the mouth of this river.

They are generally low in stature, proportionally small, rather lighter-complexioned, and much more illy formed than the Indians of the Missouri and those of our frontiers. They are generally cheerful, but never gay. With us, their conversation generally turns upon the subject of trade, smoking, eating, or their women. About the latter they speak without reserve in their presence—of their every part, and of the most familiar connection. They do not hold the virtue of their women in high estimation, and will even prostitute their wives and daughters for a fishing hook or a strand of beads.

16th January, 1806

This evening we finished curing the meat. No occurrence worthy of relation took place today. We have a plenty of elk beef for the present, and a little salt. Our houses dry and comfortable. Having made up our minds to stay until the first of April, everyone appears contented with his situation and his fare.

February 14th, 1806

I completed a map [8] of the country through which we have been passing from the Mississippi, at the mouth of the Missouri, to this place. On the map, the Missouri, Jefferson's River, the S.E. branch of the Columbia or Lewis's River, Kooskooskee, and Columbia from the entrance of the S.E. fork to the Pacific Ocean, as well as a part of Clark's River and our track across the Rocky Mountains, are laid down by celestial observations and survey. The rivers are also connected at their sources with other rivers, agreeably to the information of the natives and the most probable conjecture, arising from their capacities and the relative positions of their respective entrances, which last have, with but few exceptions, been established by celestial observations.

February 20th, 1806

[Lewis]

This forenoon we were visited by Tâhcum, a principal chief of the Chinooks, and 25 men of his nation. We had never seen this chief before. He is a good-looking man about

[8] There is a large collection of Clark's original maps, not all of which were made on the expedition, in the Coe Collection of Western Americana, Yale University Library.

50 years of age, rather larger in stature than most of his nation. As he came on a friendly visit, we gave himself and party something to eat and plied them plentifully with smoke. We gave this chief a small medal, with which he seemed much gratified.

In the evening at sunset we desired them to depart, as is our custom, and closed our gates. We never suffer parties of such number to remain within the fort all night; for, notwithstanding their apparent friendly disposition, their great avarice and hope of plunder might induce them to be treacherous. At all events, we determined always to be on our guard as much as the nature of our situation will permit us, and never place ourselves at the mercy of any savages. [9] We well know that the treachery of the aborigines of America and the too great confidence of our countrymen in their sincerity and friendship has caused the destruction of many hundreds of us.

March 15th, 1806

[Clark]

We were visited this afternoon, in a canoe 4 feet 2 inches wide, by Delashelwilt, a Chinook chief, his wife, and six women of his nation, which the Old Bawd, his wife, had brought for market. This was the same party which had communicated the venereal to several of our party in November last, and of which they have fully recovered. I therefore gave the men a particular charge with respect to them, which they promised me to observe.

March 17th, 1806

[Lewis]

Old Delashelwilt and his women still remain. They have formed a camp near the fort and seem determined to lay close seige to us, but I believe, notwithstanding every effort of their winning graces, the men have preserved their constancy to the vow of celibacy which they made on this occasion to Captain Clark and myself. We have had our pirogues

[9] Both leaders had served in Indian country. Clark had actually fought Indians in small campaigns. He had also learned a great deal from his brother, General George Rogers Clark, who had plenty of experience with both the courage and the treachery of American Indians and who also took a strong anthropological interest in them—genuinely scientific, by the standards of the period. The apparently extreme security measures of Lewis and Clark made it possible for them to make the entire journey with only one small Indian fight, in which no one in the party was even wounded.

prepared for our departure, and shall set out as soon as the weather will permit.

Drouilliard returned late this evening from the Cathlah-mahs with our canoe, which Sergeant Pryor had left some days since, and also a canoe which he had purchased from those people. For this canoe he gave my uniform laced coat and nearly half a carrot of tobacco. It seems that nothing except this coat would induce them to dispose of a canoe, which, in their mode of traffic, is an article of the greatest value except a wife, with whom it is nearly equal, and is generally given in exchange to the father for his daughter. I think that the United States are indebted to me another uniform coat for that of which he has disposed of on this occasion. It was but little worn.

Chapter *XIX*

THE RETURN JOURNEY BEGINS

March 18—April 24, 1806

March 18th, 1806

[Lewis]

This morning we gave Delashelwilt a certificate of his good deportment, &c., and also a list of our names, after which we dispatched him to his village with his female band. These lists of our names we have given to several of the natives, and also pasted up a copy in our room. The object of these lists we stated in the preamble of the same, as follows:

"The object of this list is that, through the medium of some civilized person who may see the same, it may be known to the informed world that the party consisting of the persons whose names are hereunto annexed, and who were sent out by the government of the U. States in May 1804 to explore the interior of the continent of North America, did penetrate the same by way of the Missouri and Columbia rivers, to the discharge of the latter into the Pacific Ocean, where they arrived on the 14th of November, 1805, and from whence they departed the [blank in MS.] day of March, 1806, on their return to the United States by the same route they had come out." [1]

[1] The brig *Lydia*, of Boston, had been in the Columbia estuary in November, 1805, and her commander had been told that Lewis and Clark were somewhere near. The captain did not find them, though a few signal guns would certainly have attracted the explorers' attention. *Lydia* stood off and on the Pacific Coast till August, 1806, by which time Lewis and Clark were nearly home. Soon after they left Oregon, one copy of their message fell into the hands of the brig's captain, who carried it to Canton, where an American copied it and sent a copy to Boston. The *Lydia* herself reached Boston in 1807, nearly a year after Lewis and Clark had returned.

On the back of some of these lists we added a sketch of the connection of the upper branches of the Missouri with those of the Columbia, particularly of its main S.E. branch, on which we also delineated the track we had come out and that we meant to pursue on our return where the same happened to vary. There seemed so many chances against our government ever obtaining a regular report through the medium of the savages and the traders of this coast, that we declined making any. Our party are also too small to think of leaving any of them to return to the U. States by sea, particularly as we shall be necessarily divided into three or four parties on our return in order to accomplish the objects we have in view; and at any rate, we shall reach the United States, in all human probability, much earlier than a man could who must in the event of his being left here depend for his passage to the United States on the traders of the coast who may not return immediately to the U. States, or if they should, might probably spend the next summer in trading with the natives before they would set out on their return.

March 20th, 1806

Although we have not fared sumptuously this winter and spring at Fort Clatsop, we have lived quite as comfortably as we had any reason to expect we should; and have accomplished every object which induced our remaining at this place, except that of meeting with the traders who visit the entrance of this river. Our salt will be very sufficient to last us to the Missouri, where we have a stock in store. It would have been very fortunate for us had some of those traders arrived previous to our departure from hence, as we should then have had it in our power to obtain an addition to our stock of merchandise, which would have made our homeward-bound journey much more comfortable.

23rd March, 1806

[Clark]

The rain ceased and it became fair about Meridian, at which time we loaded our canoes and at 1:00 P.M. left Fort Clatsop on our homeward-bound journey. At this place we had wintered and remained from the 7th of December, 1805, to this day, and have lived as well as we had any right to expect, and we can say that we were never one day without three meals of some kind a day, either poor elk meat or roots, notwithstanding the repeated fall of rain which has fallen almost constantly since we passed the long narrows on the [blank in MS.] of November last. Indeed, we have had only [blank in MS.] days fair weather since that time.

Soon after we had set out from Fort Clatsop, we were met by Delashelwilt and 8 men of the Chinook and Delashelwilt's wife, the Old Bawd, and his six girls. They had a canoe, a sea otter skin, dried fish, and hats for sale. We purchased a sea otter skin, and proceeded on.

March 30th, 1806

[Lewis]

We had a view of Mount St. Helens and Mount Hood. The first is the most noble-looking object of its kind in nature. Its figure is a regular cone. Both these mountains are perfectly covered with snow—at least the parts of them which are visible. The highlands in this valley are rolling, though by no means too steep for cultivation. They are generally fertile, of a dark rich loam and tolerably free of stone.

April 2nd, 1806

The men who went in quest of the elk and deer which were killed yesterday returned at 8 A.M. We now informed the party of our intention of laying in a store of meat at this place and immediately dispatched two parties, consisting of nine men, to the opposite side of the river.

About this time, several canoes of the natives arrived at our camp, among others two from below with eight men of the Shahala nation. Those men informed us that they reside on the opposite side of the Columbia near some pine trees which they pointed to, in the bottom south of the Dimond Island. They singled out two young men who, they informed us, lived at the falls of a large river which discharges itself into the Columbia on its south side, some miles below us.

We readily prevailed on them to give us a sketch of this river, which they drew on a mat with a coal. It appeared that this river, which they call Multnomah, discharged itself behind the island we call the Image Canoe Island, and as we had left this island to the south in descending and ascending the river we had never seen it. They informed us that it was a large river, and runs a considerable distance to the south between the mountains.

I determined to take a small party and return to this river and examine its size, and collect as much information of the natives on it or near its entrance into the Columbia of its extent; the country which it waters; and the natives who inhabit its banks, &c. I took with me six men: Thompson, J. Potts, Peter Cruzat, P. Wiser, T. P. Howard, Joseph Whitehouse, and my man York in a large canoe, with an Indian whom I hired for a sun-glass to accompany me as a pilot.

At 11:30 A.M., I set out and had not proceeded far ere I saw four large canoes, at some distance above, descending and bending their course toward our camp, which at this time is very weak, Captain Lewis having only 10 men with him. I hesitated for a moment whether it would not be advisable for me to return and delay until a part of our hunters should return to add more strength to our camp, but on a second reflection and reverting to the precautions always taken by my friend Captain Lewis on those occasions, banished all apprehensions, and I proceeded on down.

At 3 P.M. I landed at a large double house of the Ne-er-che-ki-oo tribe of the Shahala nation. I entered one of the rooms of this house and offered several articles to the natives in exchange for wappato. They were sulky, and they positively refused to sell any.

I had a small piece of port fire match [2] in my pocket, off of which I cut a piece one inch in length and put it into the fire, and took out my pocket compass and sat myself down on a mat on one side of the fire, and also showed a magnet, which was in the top of my inkstand. The port fire caught and burned vehemently, which changed the color of the fire. With the magnet I turned the needle of the compass about very briskly, which astonished and alarmed these natives, and they laid several parcels of wappato at my feet, and begged of me to take out the bad fire. To this I consented. At this moment, the match being exhausted was of course extinguished, and I put up the magnet, &c. This measure alarmed them so much that the women and children took shelter in their beds, and behind the men. All this time, a very old blind man was speaking with great vehemence, apparently imploring his god.

I lit my pipe and gave them a smoke, and gave the women the full value of the roots which they had put at my feet. They appeared somewhat pacified, and I left them and proceeded on. At the distance of thirteen miles below the last village and at the place I had supposed was the lower point of

---

[2] Port fire match was a paper case, filled with a slow-burning composition, used by the artillery of that day. What Clark was doing with it is not clear. It may have been useful in kindling sulky campfires.

Image Canoe Island, I entered this river which the natives had informed us of, called Multnomah River, so called by the natives from a nation who reside on Wappetoe Island a little below the entrance of this river. Multnomah discharges itself in the Columbia on the S.E., and may be justly said to be ¼ the size of that noble river.

April 7, 1806

I prevailed on an old Indian to mark the Multnomah River down on the sand, which he did, and it perfectly corresponded with the sketch given me by sundry others, with the addition of a circular mountain which passes this river at the falls and connects with the mountains of the seacoast. He also laid down the Clackamas, passing a high conical mountain near its mouth on the lower side and heading in Mount Jefferson, which he laid down by raising the sand as a very high mountain and covered with eternal snow. The high mountain which this Indian laid down near the entrance of Clackamas River we have not seen, as the hills in its direction from this valley are high and obscure the sight of it from us. Mt. Jefferson we can plainly see from the entrance of Multnomah, from which place it bears S.E. This is a noble mountain and I think equally as high or something higher than Mt. St. Helens, but its distance being much greater than that of the latter, so great a portion of it does not appear above the range of mountains which lie between both those stupendous mountains and the mouth of Multnomah. Like Mt. St. Helens, its figure is a regular cone and is covered with eternal snow.

April 11th, 1806

[Lewis]

As the tents and skins which covered both our men and baggage were wet with the rain which fell last evening, and as it continued still raining this morning, we concluded to take our canoes first to the head of the rapids, hoping that by evening the rain would cease and afford us a fair afternoon to take our baggage over the portage. This portage is two thousand eight hundred yards along a narrow, rough, and slippery road. The duty of getting the canoes above the rapid was by mutual consent confided to my friend Captain Clark, who took with him for that purpose all the party except Bratton, who is yet so weak he is unable to work, three others who were lamed by various accidents, and one other to cook for the party.

A few men were absolutely necessary, at any rate, to guard our baggage from the Wahclellahs,[3] who crowded about our camp in considerable numbers. These are the greatest thieves and scoundrels we have met with. By the evening, Captain Clark took four of our canoes above the rapids, though with much difficulty and labor. The canoes were much damaged by being driven against the rocks in spite of every precaution which could be taken to prevent it. The men complained of being so much fatigued in the evening that we postponed taking up our fifth canoe until tomorrow.

These rapids are much worse than they were in the fall when we passed them. At that time there were only three difficult points within seven miles. At present the whole distance is extremely difficult of ascent, and it would be impracticable to descend except by letting down the empty vessels by a cord, and even then the risk would be greater than in taking them up by the same means. The water appears to be considerably upwards of 20 feet higher than when we descended the river. The distance by way of the river between the points of the portage is 3 miles.

Many of the natives crowded about the bank of the river where the men were engaged in taking up the canoes. One of them had the insolence to cast stones down the bank at two of the men who happened to be a little detached from the party at the time. On the return of the party in the evening from the head of the rapids, they met with many of the natives on the road, who seemed but illy disposed. Two of these fellows met with John Shields, who had delayed some time in purchasing a dog and was a considerable distance behind the party on their return with Captain Clark. They attempted to take the dog from him and pushed him out of the road. He had nothing to defend himself with, except a large knife which he drew with an intention of putting one or both of them to death before they could get themselves in readiness to use their arrows; but, discovering his design, they declined the combat and instantly fled through the woods.

Three of this same tribe of villains, the Wahclellahs, stole my dog this evening, and took him toward their village. I was shortly afterward informed of this transaction by an Indian who spoke the Clatsop language, some of which we had learned from them during the winter, and sent three men in pursuit of the thieves with orders that, if they made

[3] The Wahclellahs were a division of the Shahala tribe, Indians living along the Multnomah River, in Oregon.

the least resistance or difficulty in surrendering the dog, to fire on them. They overtook these fellows, or rather came within sight of them at the distance of about 2 miles. The Indians, discovering the party in pursuit of them, left the dog and fled. They also stole an ax from us, but scarcely had it in their possession before Thompson detected them and wrested it from them.

We ordered the sentinel to keep them out of camp, and informed them by signs that if they made any further attempts to steal our property, or insulted our men, we should put them to instant death. A chief of the Wahclellahs tribe informed us that there were two very bad men among the Wahclellahs who had been the principal actors in these scenes of outrage of which we complained, and that it was not the wish of the nation by any means to displease us. We told him that we hoped it might be the case, but we should certainly be as good as our word if they persisted in their insolence. I am convinced that no other consideration but our number at this moment protects us. The chief appeared mortified at the conduct of his people, and seemed friendly disposed toward us. As he appeared to be a man of consideration, and we had reason to believe much respected by the neighboring tribes, we thought it well to bestow a medal of small size upon him.

April 12th, 1806

[Clark]

We employed all hands in attempting to take up the last canoe. In attempting to pass by a rock against which the current ran with immense force, the bow unfortunately took the current at too great a distance from the rock, she turned broadside to the stream, and the exertions of every man were not sufficient to hold her. The men were compelled to let go the rope, and both the canoe and rope went with the stream. The loss of this canoe will, I fear, compel us to purchase another at an extravagant price.

April 13th, 1806

The loss of one of our large canoes rendered it necessary to divide the loading and men of that canoe between the remaining four, which was done, and we loaded and set out at 8 o'clock A.M. Passed the village immediately above the rapids, where only one house remains entire, the other 8 having been taken down and moved to the opposite side of the Columbia, as already mentioned. The additional men and baggage in each canoe render them crowded and unsafe. Captain Lewis, with two of the smallest canoes of Sergeant Pryor and Gibson, crossed above the rapids to the village on the S.E. side with a view to purchase a canoe of the natives if possible. He took with him some cloth and a few elk skins and deer skins.

At ½ past 2 P.M. set out and proceeded on to the bottom, 6 miles, and halted at the next bottom. Formed a camp and sent out all the hunters. I also walked out myself on the hills, but saw nothing. On my return, found Captain Lewis at camp with two canoes which he had purchased at a village for two robes and four elk skins. He also purchased four paddles and three dogs from the natives, with deer skins. The dogs now constitute a considerable part of our subsistence, and with most of the party has become a favorable food. Certain I am that it is a healthy, strong diet.

April 16th, 1806

About 8 o'clock this morning I passed the river with the two interpreters and nine men, in order to trade with the natives for their horses, for which purpose I took with me a good part of our stock of merchandise. Captain Lewis sent out the hunters and set several men at work making pack saddles. I formed a camp on the north side.

17th of April, 1806

I rose early after a bad night's rest, and took my merchandise to a rock which afforded an eligible situation for my purpose and divided the articles of merchandise into parcels of such articles as I thought best calculated to please the Indians. And in each parcel I put as many articles as we could afford to give, and thus exposed them to view, informing the Indians that each parcel was intended for a horse.

They tantalized me the greater part of the day, saying that they had sent out for their horses and would trade as soon as they came. Several parcels of merchandise were laid by for which they told me they would bring horses. I made a bargain with the chief for two horses. About an hour after, he canceled the bargain, and we again bargained for three horses, which were brought forward. Only one of the three could be possibly used; the other two had such intolerable backs as to render them entirely unfit for service. I refused to take two of them, which displeased him, and he refused to part with the third.

I then packed up the articles and was about setting out for the village above, when a man came and sold me two horses, and another man sold me one horse, and several others informed me that they would trade with me if I would continue until their horses could be driven up. This induced me to continue at this village another day. Many of the natives from different villages on the Columbia above offered to trade, but asked such things as we had not, and double as much of the articles which I had as we could afford to give. This was a very unfavorable circumstance, as my dependence for procuring a sufficiency of horses rested on the success above, where I had reasons to believe there was a greater abundance of those animals, and was in hopes of getting them on better terms. I purchased three dogs for the party with me to eat, and some shappellel for myself.

Before procuring the three horses, I dispatched Cruzat, Willard, and McNeal and Peter Wiser to Captain Lewis with a note informing him of my ill success in procuring horses, and advised him to proceed on to this place as soon as possible. That I would, in the meantime, proceed on to the Eneeshur nation, above the Great Falls, and try to purchase some horses of that people.

Soon after I had dispatched this party, the chief of the Eneeshurs and 15 or 20 of his people visited me, and appeared to be anxious to see the articles I offered for the horses. Several of them agreed to let me have horses if I would add sundry articles to those I offered, which I agreed to do, and they laid those bundles by and informed me they would deliver me the horses in the morning. I proposed going with them to their town. The chief informed me that their horses were all in the plains with their women gathering roots. They would send out and bring the horses to this place tomorrow.

This intelligence was flattering, though I doubted the sincerity of those people, who had several times disappointed me in a similar way. However, I determined to continue until tomorrow. In the meantime, industriously employed ourselves with the great multitude of Indians of different nations about us, trying to purchase horses. Charbonneau purchased a very fine mare for which he gave ermine, elk's teeth, a belt, and some other articles of no great value. No other purchase was made in the course of this day.

In the evening, I received a note from Captain Lewis by Shannon, informing me that he should set out early on tomorrow morning.

18th April, 1806

Collected the four horses purchased yesterday, and sent Frazer and Charbonneau with them to the basin, where I expected they would meet Captain Lewis, and commence the portage of the baggage on those horses. About 10 A.M. the Indians came down from the Eneeshur villages and I expected would take the articles which they had laid by yesterday. But to my astonishment, no one would make the exchange today. Two other parcels of goods were laid by, and the horses promised at 2 P.M. I paid but little attention to this bargain. However, suffered the bundles to lie.

I dressed the sores of the principal chief, gave some small things to his children, and promised the chief some medicine for to cure his sores. His wife, whom I found to be a sulky bitch, was somewhat afflicted with pains in her back. This I thought a good opportunity to get her on my side, giving her something for her back. I rubbed a little camphor on her temples and back and applied warm flannel to her back, which, she thought had nearly restored her to her former feelings. This I thought a favorable time to trade with the chief, who had more horses than all the nation besides. I accordingly made him an offer, which he accepted, and sold me two horses. Sergeant Ordway and three men arrived from Captain Lewis. They brought with them several elk skins, two of my coats, and four robes of the party, to add to the stores I had with me for the purchase of horses.

Sergeant Ordway informed me that Captain Lewis had arrived with all the canoes into the basin two miles below, and wished some dogs to eat. I had three dogs purchased and sent down. At 5 P.M. Captain Lewis came up. He informed me that he had passed the river to the basin with much difficulty and danger, having made one portage.

April 19th, 1806

[Lewis]

There was great joy with the natives last night, in consequence of the arrival of the salmon. One of those fish was caught. This was the harbinger of good news to them. They informed us that these fish would arrive in great quantities in the course of about five days. This fish was dressed and, being divided into small pieces, was given to each child in the village. This custom is founded on a superstitious opinion that it will hasten the arrival of the salmon. With much difficulty we obtained four other horses from the Indians today. We were obliged to dispense with two of our kettles in order to acquire those. We now have only one small kettle to a mess of eight men.

In the evening Captain Clark set out with four men to the Eneeshur village at the Grand Falls in order to make a further attempt to procure horses. These people are very faithless in their contracts. They frequently receive the merchandise in exchange for their horses and, after some hours, insist on some additional article being given them or revoke the exchange. They have pilfered several small articles from us this evening.

I directed the horses to be hobbled [4] and suffered to graze at a little distance from our camp under the immediate eye of the men who had them in charge. One of the men, Willard, was negligent in his attention to his horse and suffered it to ramble off. It was not to be found when I ordered the others to be brought up and confined to the pickets. This, in addition to the other difficulties under which I labored, was truly provoking. I reprimanded him more severely for this piece of negligence than had been usual with me. I had the remaining horses well secured by pickets.

April 21st, 1806

Notwithstanding all the precautions I had taken with respect to the horses, one of them had broken his cord of five strands of elk skin and had gone off spanceled. I sent several men in search of the horse with orders to return at 10 A.M., with or without the horse, being determined to remain no longer with these villains. They stole another tomahawk from us this morning. I searched many of them but could not find it. I ordered all the spare poles, paddles, and the balance of our canoe put on the fire, as the morning was cold, and also that not a particle should be left for the benefit of the Indians.

I detected a fellow in stealing an iron socket of a canoe pole, and gave him several severe blows, and made the men kick him out of camp. I now informed the Indians that I would shoot the first of them that attempted to steal an

---

[4] To "hobble," or "spancel" a horse is to tie the hind legs or one fore and one hind leg with a short length of rope. The animal can then move about to graze but cannot wander far and is easily caught when wanted. Bells were sometimes attached, but this was dangerous, because Indian war parties liked to steal the horse, ring the bell till the owner came, and scalp him.

article from us; that we were not afraid to fight them; that I had it in my power at that moment to kill them all and set fire to their houses; but it was not my wish to treat them with severity provided they would let my property alone. That I would take their horses if I could find out the persons who had stolen the tomahawks, but that I had rather lose the property altogether than take the horse of an innocent person. The chiefs who were present hung their heads and said nothing.

At 9 A.M. Windsor returned with the lost horse. The others who were in search of the horse soon after returned also. The Indian who promised to accompany me as far as the Chopunnish [Nez Percé] country produced me two horses, one of which he politely gave me the liberty of packing. We took breakfast and departed, a few minutes after 10 o'clock, having nine horses loaded, and one which Bratton rode, not being able as yet to march. The two canoes I had dispatched early this morning.

At 1 P.M., I arrived at the Eneshur village, where I found Captain Clark and party. After dinner, we proceeded on about four miles to a village of 9 mat lodges of the Eneeshur, a little below the entrance of Clark's river [Des Chutes] and encamped.

Our guide continued with us. He appears to be an honest, sincere fellow. He tells us that the Indians a little above will treat us with much more hospitality than those we are now with. We purchased another horse this evening, but his back is in such a horrid state that we can put but little on him.

April 22nd, 1806

At 7 A.M. we set out, having previously sent on our small canoe with Colter and Potts. We had not arrived at the top of a hill over which the road leads, opposite the village, before Charbonneau's horse threw his load and, taking fright at the saddle and robe which still adhered, ran at full speed down the hill. Near the village he disengaged himself from the saddle and robe. An Indian hid the robe in his lodge.

I sent our guide and one man who was with me in the rear, to assist Charbonneau in retaking his horse, which having done, they returned to the village on the track of the horse, in search of the lost articles. They found the saddle but could see nothing of the robe. The Indians denied having seen it. They then continued on the track of the horse to the place from whence he had set out with the same success.

Being now confident that the Indians had taken it, I sent the Indian woman on, to request Captain Clark to halt the party and send back some of the men to my assistance, being determined either to make the Indians deliver the robe or burn their houses. They have vexed me in such a manner by such repeated acts of villainy that I am quite disposed to treat them with every severity. Their defenseless state pleads forgiveness so far as respects their lives. With this resolution, I returned to their village, which I had just reached when Labiche met me with the robe, which, he informed me, he found in an Indian lodge hidden behind their baggage. I now returned and joined Captain Clark who was waiting my arrival with the party.

We now made the following regulations as to our future order of march, viz., that Captain Clark and myself should divide the men who were disencumbered by horses and march alternately each day, the one in front and the other in rear. Having divided the party agreeably to this arrangement, we proceeded on through an open plain country about 8 miles to a village of 6 houses of the Eneeshur nation. Here we observed our two canoes passing up on the opposite side. The wind being too high for them to pass the river, they continued on.

24th April, 1806

[Clark]

We sold our canoes for a few strands of beads. The natives had tantalized us with an exchange of horses for our canoes in the first instance, but when they found that we had made our arrangements to travel by land they would give us nothing for them. We sent Drouilliard to cut them up. He struck one and split her. They discovered that we were determined to destroy the canoes and offered us several strands of beads, which were accepted. Most of the party complain of their feet and legs this evening being very sore. It is no doubt caused by walking over the rough stone and deep sand after being accustomed to a soft soil. My legs and feet give me much pain. I bathed them in cold water from which I experienced considerable relief.

Chapter XX

WALLAWALLAS AND NEZ PERCÉS

April 27—June 6, 1806

April 27, 1806

[Lewis]

The principal chief of the Wallawallas joined us with six men of his nation. This chief, by name Yellept, had visited us on the morning of the 19th of October [1805] at our encampment a little below this place. We gave him at that time a small medal and promised him a larger one on our return. He appeared much gratified at seeing us return, invited us to remain at his village three or four days, and assured us that we should be furnished with a plenty of such food as they had themselves, and some horses to assist us on our journey. After our scanty repast we continued our march, accompanied by Yellept and his party, to the village.

Yellept harangued his village in our favor, entreated them to furnish us with fuel and provision, and set the example himself by bringing us an armful of wood and a platter of three roasted mullets. The others soon followed his example with respect to fuel, and we soon found ourselves in possession of an ample stock.

April 28th, 1806

This morning early, Yellept brought a very elegant white horse to our camp and presented him to Captain Clark, signifying his wish to get a kettle, but, on being informed that we had already disposed of every kettle we could possibly spare, he said he was content with whatever he thought proper to give him. Captain Clark gave him his sword, for which he had expressed a great desire, a hundred balls and powder, and some small articles, with which he appeared perfectly satisfied.

It was necessary before we entered on our route through the plains, where we were to meet with no lodges or resident Indians, that we should lay in a stock of provision and not depend altogether on the gun.

We directed Frazer, to whom we have entrusted the duty of making those purchases, to lay in as many fat dogs as he could procure. He soon obtained ten.

Being anxious to depart, we requested the chief to furnish us with canoes to pass the river, but he insisted on our remaining with him this day at least, that he would be much pleased if we would consent to remain two or three, but he would not let us have canoes to leave him today. That he had sent for the Chymnappos,[1] his neighbors, to come down and join his people this evening and dance for us.

We urged the necessity of our going on immediately in order that we might the sooner return to them with the articles which they wished, but this had no effect. He said that the time he asked could not make any considerable difference. I at length urged that there was no wind blowing and that the river was consequently in good order to pass our horses; and, if he would furnish us with canoes for that purpose, we would remain all night at our present encampment. To this proposition he assented, and soon produced us a couple of canoes by means of which we passed our horses[2] over the river safely, and hobbled them as usual.

We found a Shoshone woman, prisoner among these people, by means of whom and Sacagawea we found the means of conversing with the Wallawallas. We conversed with them for several hours and fully satisfied all their inquiries with respect to ourselves and the objects of our pursuit. They were much pleased.

They brought several diseased persons to us for whom they requested some medical aid. One had his knee contracted by the rheumatism, another with a broken arm, &c.,

---

[1] The Chymnappo (also called Chymnappum) Indians were the Yakima tribe, part of the large Shahaptian group of tribes, which included the Salish and Nez Percés. They did not cede their Washington lands to the United States and move to a reservation until 1855.

[2] It was, of course impossible to put horses in canoes. The horses were led into the water and then guided across by men in the canoes, holding the halters.

to all of which we administered, much to the gratification of those poor wretches.

We gave them some eye-water, which I believe will render them more essential service than any other article in the medical way which we had it in our power to bestow on them. Captain Clark splinted the arm of the man which was broke. Sore eyes seem to be a universal complaint among these people. I have no doubt but the fine sand of these plains and river—fishing on the waters, too—contribute much to this disorder. Ulcers and eruptions of the skin on various parts of the body are also common diseases among them.

A little before sunset, the Chymnappos arrived. They were about 100 men and a few women. They joined the Walla-wallas, who were about the same number, and formed a half-circle around our camp, where they waited very patiently to see our party dance. The fiddle was played and the men amused themselves with dancing about an hour. We then requested the Indians to dance, which they very cheer-fully complied with. They continued their dance until ten at night.

April 30th, 1806

[Lewis]

At 10 A.M., we had collected all our horses except the white horse which Yellept had given Captain Clark. The whole of the men soon after returned without being able to find this horse. I lent my horse to Yellept to search for Captain Clark's. About half an hour after he set out, our Chopunnish man brought up Captain Clark's horse. We now determined to leave one man to bring on my horse when Yellept returned, and to proceed on with the party. Accordingly, took leave of these friendly, honest people.

May 1st, 1806

Some time after we had encamped, three young men arrived from the Wallawalla village bringing with them a steel trap belonging to one of our party which had been negligently left behind. This is an act of integrity rarely witnessed among Indians. During our stay with them, they several times found the knives of the men which had been carelessly lost by them and returned them. I think we can justly affirm to the honor of these people that they are the most hospitable, honest, and sincere people that we have met with in our voyage.

May 3rd, 1806

We met with Wearkkoomt, whom we have usually distinguished by the name of the Bighorn Chief, from the circumstance of his always wearing a horn of that animal suspended by a cord to the left arm. He is the first chief of a large band of the Chopunnish nation. He had 10 of his young men with him. This man went down Lewis's River by land as we descended it by water last fall, quite to the Columbia, and I believe was very instrumental in procuring us a hospitable and friendly reception among the natives. He had now come a considerable distance to meet us.

May 4th, 1806

The hills of the creek which we descended this morning are high and in most parts rocky and abrupt. One of our pack horses slipped from one of those heights and fell into the creek with its load, consisting principally of ammunition, but fortunately neither the horse nor load suffered any material injury. The ammunition being secured in canisters, the water did not affect it. After dinner, we continued our route up the west side of the river 3 miles opposite to 2 lodges, the one containing 3 and the other 2 families of the Chopunnish nation. Here we met with Tetoharsky, the youngest of the two chiefs who accompanied us last fall to the Great Falls of the Columbia. We also met with our pilot who descended the river with us as far as the Columbia.

Wearkkoomt, whose people resided on the west side of Lewis's River above, left us when we determined to pass the river, and went on to his lodge.

May 5th, 1806

Collected our horses and set out at 7 A.M. At 4½ miles we arrived at the entrance of the Kooskooskee, up the N. Eastern side of which we continued our march 12 miles to a large lodge of 10 families, having passed two other large mat lodges.

At the second lodge, we passed an Indian man who gave Captain Clark a very elegant gray mare, for which he requested a phial of eye-water, which was accordingly given him. While we were encamped last fall at the entrance of the Chopunnish river, Captain Clark gave an Indian man some volatile liniment to rub his knee and thigh for a pain of which he complained. The fellow soon after recovered, and has never ceased to extol the virtues of our medicines, and the skill of my friend Captain Clark as a physician. This occurrence, added to the benefit which many of them experienced from the eye-water we gave them about the same time, has given them an exalted opinion of our medicine.

My friend Captain Clark is their favorite physician and has already received many applications. In our present situation, I think it pardonable to continue this deception, for they will not give us any provision without compensation in merchandise, and our stock is now reduced to a mere handful. We take care to give them no article which can possibly injure them.

While at dinner, an Indian fellow very impertinently threw a poor, half-starved puppy nearly into my plate by way of derision for our eating dogs, and laughed very heartily at his own impertinence. I was so provoked at his insolence that I caught the puppy and threw it with great violence at him and struck him in the breast and face, seized my tomahawk, and showed him by signs, if he repeated his insolence I would tomahawk him.

We had several applications to assist their sick, which we refused unless they would let us have some dogs or horses to eat. A chief, whose wife had an abscess formed on the small of her back, promised a horse in the morning, provided we would administer to her. Accordingly, Captain Clark opened the abscess, introduced a tent, and dressed it with basilicon.[3] Captain Clark soon had more than fifty applications. I prepared some doses of flower of sulphur and cream of tartar, which were given with directions to be taken on each morning.

A little girl and sundry other patients were offered for cure, but we postponed our operations until morning. They produced us several dogs, but they were so poor that they were unfit for use.

This is the residence of one of the four principal chiefs of the nation, whom they call Neeshneparkkeook, or The Cut Nose, from the circumstance of his nose being cut by the Snake [Shoshone] Indians with a lance, in battle. To this man we gave a medal of the small size, with the like-

---

[3] A "tent" is a roll of lint inserted in a wound. The word "basilicon" means "royal" and was applied to an ointment of wax, pitch, resin, and olive oil, which was supposed to have "sovereign" healing powers.

ness of the President. He may be a great chief, but his countenance has but little intelligence, and his influence among his people seems but inconsiderable. A number of Indians besides the inhabitants of these lodges gathered about us this evening and encamped in the timbered bottom on the creek near us.

We met with a Snake Indian man at this place, through whom we spoke at some length to the natives this evening with respect to the objects which had induced us to visit their country. This address was induced at this moment by the suggestions of an old man who observed to the natives that he thought we were bad men and had come, most probably, in order to kill them. This impression, if really entertained, I believe we effaced. They appeared well satisfied with what we said to them, and, being hungry and tired, we retired to rest at 11 o'clock.

May 6th, 1806

This morning the husband of the sick woman was as good as his word. He produced us a young horse in tolerable order, which we immediately killed and butchered. The inhabitants seemed more accommodating this morning; they sold us some bread. We received a second horse for medicine and prescription for a little girl with the rheumatism. Captain Clark dressed the woman again this morning, who declared that she had rested better last night than she had since she had been sick.

Sore eyes are a universal complaint with all the natives we have seen on the west side of the Rocky Mountains. Captain Clark was busily engaged for several hours this morning in administering eye-water to a crowd of applicants. We once more obtained a plentiful meal, much to the comfort of all the party.

May 7th, 1806

This morning we collected our horses and set out early, accompanied by the brother of The Twisted Hair as a guide. Wearkkoomt and his party left us. We proceeded up the river 4 miles to a lodge of 6 families just below the entrance of a small creek. Here our guide recommended our passing the river. He informed us that the road was better on the south side, and that game was more abundant also on that side near the entrance of the Chopunnish River. We determined to pursue the route recommended by the guide, and accordingly unloaded our horses and prepared to pass the river, which we effected by means of one canoe in the course of four hours.

A man of this lodge produced us two canisters of powder, which he informed us he had found by means of his dog where they had been buried in a bottom near the river some miles above. They were the same which we had buried as we descended the river last fall. As he kept them safe and had honesty enough to return them to us, we gave him a fire steel by way of compensation.

The Shoshone man of whom I have before made mention overtook us this evening with Neeshneparkkeook, and remained with us this evening. We supped this evening, as we had dined, on horse beef. We saw several deer this evening, and a great number of the tracks of these animals. We determined to remain here until noon tomorrow in order to obtain some venison, and accordingly gave orders to the hunters to turn out early in the morning.

May 8th, 1806

Most of the hunters turned out by light this morning; a few others remained without our permission or knowledge until late in the morning. We chided them severely for their indolence and inattention to the order of last evening. About 8 o'clock Shields returned with a small deer, on which we breakfasted. By 11 A.M. all our hunters returned. Drouilliard and Cruzat brought each a deer. Collins wounded another, which my dog caught at a little distance from the camp. Our stock of provision now consisted of 4 deer and the remnant of the horse which we killed at Colter's Creek.

At half after 3 P.M., we departed for the lodge of The Twisted Hair, accompanied by the chief and sundry other Indians. The relation of The Twisted Hair left us. The road led us up a steep and high hill to a high and level plain mostly untimbered, through which we passed parallel with the river about 4 miles when we met The Twisted Hair and a party of six men. To this chief we had confided the care of our horses and a part of our saddles when we descended the river last fall.

The Twisted Hair received us very coolly, an occurrence as unexpected as it was unaccountable to us. He shortly began to speak with a loud voice and in an angry manner. When he had ceased to speak, he was answered by the Cutnose Chief, or Neeshneparkkeook. We readily discovered that a violent quarrel had taken place between these chiefs, but at that instant knew not the cause. We afterwards learned that it was on the subject of our horses. This controversy between the chiefs detained us about 20 minutes.

In order to put an end to this dispute, as well as to relieve our horses from the embarrassment of their loads, we informed the chiefs that we should continue our march to the first water and encamp. Accordingly, we moved on and the Indians all followed. About two miles on the road, we arrived at a little branch which ran to the right. Here we encamped for the evening, having traveled 6 miles today. The two chiefs with their little bands formed separate camps a short distance from ours. They all appeared to be in an ill humor. To obtain our horses and saddles as quickly as possible is our wish, and we are somewhat apprehensive that this difference which has taken place between these chiefs may militate against our operations in this respect. We were therefore desirous to bring about a good understanding between them as soon as possible.

The Shoshone boy refused to speak. He alleged it was a quarrel between two chiefs, and that he had no business with it. It was in vain that we urged that his interpreting what we said on this subject was not taking the responsibility of the interference on himself. He remained obstinately silent.

About an hour after we had encamped, Drouilliard returned from hunting. We sent him to The Twisted Hair to make some inquiries relative to our horses and saddles, and to ask him to come and smoke with us. The Twisted Hair accepted the invitation and came to our fire.

The Twisted Hair informed us that, according to the promise he had made us when he separated from us at the falls of the Columbia, he collected our horses on his return and took charge of them. That about this time The Cut Nose, or Neeshneparkkeook, and Tunnachemootoolt, or The Broken Arm, returned from a war excursion against the Shoshones on the south branch of Lewis's River which had caused their absence when we were in this neighborhood. That these men had become dissatisfied with him in consequence of our having confided the horses to his care, and that they were eternally quarreling with him insomuch that he thought it best, as he was an old man, to relinquish any further attention to the horses; that they had consequently become scattered; that most of the horses were near this place, a part were in the Forks between the Chopunnish and Kooskooskee rivers, and three or four others were at the lodge of The Broken Arm, about half a day's march higher up the river.

He informed us with respect to our saddles that on the rise of the water this spring, the earth had fallen from the door of the cache and exposed the saddles. He, being informed of their situation, had taken them up and placed them in another cache, where they were at this time. He said it was probable that a part of them had fallen into the water, but of this he was not certain. The Twisted Hair said if we would spend the day, tomorrow, at his lodge, which was a few miles only from hence and on the road leading to The Broken Arm's lodge, he would collect such of our horses as were near this place, and our saddles; that he would also send some young men over the Kooskooskee to collect those in the forks and bring them to the lodge of The Broken Arm, to meet us. He advised us to go to the lodge of The Broken Arm, as he said he was a chief of great eminence among them, and promised to accompany us thither if we wished him.

May 9th, 1806

Late in the evening, The Twisted Hair and Willard returned. They brought about half of our saddles, and some powder and lead which had been buried at that place. My saddle was among the number of those which were lost. About the same time, the young men arrived with 21 of our horses. The greater part of our horses were in fine order. Five of them appeared to have been so much injured by the Indians riding them last fall, that they had not yet recovered and were in low order.

May 10th, 1806

At four in the afternoon, we descended the hills to Commearp Creek [*Lawyer's Canyon Creek*] and arrived at the village of Tunnachemootoolt, the chief at whose lodge we had left the flag last fall. This flag was now displayed on a staff placed at no great distance from the lodge. Underneath the flag, the chief met my friend Captain Clark, who was in front, and conducted him about 80 yards to a place on the bank of the creek where he requested we should encamp. I came up in a few minutes and we collected the chiefs and men of consideration, smoked with them, and stated our situation with respect to provision. The chief spoke to his people, and they produced us about two bushels of the quamash [4] roots, dried, four cakes of the bread of cows, and a dried salmon trout. We thanked them for this store of provision but informed them that, our men not being accustomed to live on roots alone, we feared it would make them sick, to obviate which we proposed exchanging a horse in rather low order for a young horse in tolerable order with a view to kill. The hospitality of the chief revolted at the idea of an exchange. He told us that his young men had a great abundance of young horses, and if we wished to eat them we should be furnished with as many as we wanted. Accordingly, they soon produced us two fat young horses, one of which we killed. The other we informed them we would postpone killing until we had consumed the one already killed.

A principal chief by name Hohâstillpilp, arrived with a party of fifty men mounted on elegant horses. He had come on a visit to us from his village, which is situated about six miles distant near the river. We invited this man into our circle and smoked with him. His retinue continued on horseback at a little distance. After we had eaten a few roots, we spoke to them as we had promised, and gave Tunnachemooltoolt and Hohâstillpilp each a medal; the former one of the small size with the likeness of Mr. Jefferson, and the latter one of the sowing medals struck in the presidency of Washington. We explained to them the design and the importance of medals in the estimation of the whites as well as the red men who had been taught their value. The chief had a large conic lodge of leather erected for our reception, and a parcel of wood collected and laid at the door; after which he invited Captain Clark and myself to make that lodge our home while we remained with him.

May 11, 1806

At 8 A.M. a chief of great note among these people arrived from his village or lodge on the south side of Lewis's River. This is a stout fellow of good countenance, about 40 years of age, and has lost the left eye. His name is Yoomparkkartim. To this man we gave a medal of the small kind.

---

[4] The quamash, or camas, is the bulb of a species related to our domestic lilies, growing in California or Montana. The roots, dug in early summer, could be eaten either raw or cooked. "Cows" is another Indian root, which the Indians pounded and formed into large, flat cakes, which they dried in the sun. These cakes were either eaten as bread or boiled into a thick paste or soup.

Those with the likeness of Mr. Jefferson have all been disposed of except one of the largest size, which we reserve for some great chief on the Yellow Rock River.

We now pretty fully informed ourselves that Tunnachemootoolt, Neeshneparkkeook, Yoomparkkartim, and Hohâstillpilp were the principal chiefs of the Chopunnish nation and rank in the order here mentioned. As all those chiefs were present in our lodge, we thought it a favorable time to repeat what had been said yesterday and to enter more minutely into the views of our government with respect to the inhabitants of this western part of the continent; their intention of establishing trading houses for their relief; their wish to restore peace and harmony among the natives; the strength, power, and wealth of our nation, &c. To this end we drew a map of the country, with a coal on a mat in their way, and, by the assistance of the Snake boy and our interpreters, were enabled to make ourselves understood by them, although it had to pass through the French, Minnetaree, Shoshone, and Chopunnish languages. The interpretation being tedious, it occupied nearly half the day before we had communicated to them what we wished. They appeared highly pleased. After this council was over we amused ourselves with showing them the power of magnetism, the spyglass, compass, watch, air gun, and sundry other articles equally novel and incomprehensible to them.

12th May, 1806

[Clark]

After breakfast I began to administer eye-water and in a few minutes had near 40 applicants with sore eyes, and many others with other complaints—most common rheumatic disorders and weaknesses in the back and loins, particularly the women. The Indians had a grand council this morning, after which we were presented each with a horse by two young men at the instance of the nation. We caused the chiefs to be seated and gave them each a flag, a pint of powder, and 50 balls; to the two young men who had presented the horses we also gave powder and ball. The Broken Arm, or Tunnachemootoolt, pulled off his leather shirt, and gave me. In return, I gave him a shirt.

We retired into the lodge, and the natives spoke to the following purpose: i.e., they had listened to our advice and that the whole nation were determined to follow it; that they had only one heart and one tongue on this subject. Explained the cause of the war with the Shoshones. They wished to be at peace with all nations, &c. Some of their men would accompany us to the Missouri, &c., &c., as a great number of men, women, and children were waiting and requesting medical assistance, many of them with the most simple complaints which could be easily relieved, independent of many with disorders entirely out of the power of medicine —all requesting something!

We agreed that I should administer, and Captain Lewis hear and answer the Indians. I was closely employed until 2 P.M., administering eye-water to about 40 grown persons, some simple cooling medicines to the disabled chief, to several women with rheumatic affections, and a man who had a swelled hip, &c., &c. In the evening, three of our horses were brought—all in fine order.

22nd May, 1806

Charbonneau's son, a small child, is dangerously ill. His jaw and throat much swelled. We apply a poultice of onions, after giving him some cream of tartar, &c. This day proved to be fine and fair, which afforded us an opportunity of drying our baggage, which had got a little wet.

23rd May, 1806

The child is something better this morning than it was last night. We applied a fresh poultice of the wild onion, which we repeated twice in the course of the day. The swelling does not appear to increase any since yesterday. The 4 Indians who visited us today informed us that they came from their village on Lewis's River, two days' ride from this place, for the purpose of seeing us and getting a little eye-water. I washed their eyes with some eye-water, and they all left us at 2 P.M. and returned to the villages on the opposite side of this river.

24th May, 1806

The child was very restless last night. Its jaw and back of its neck is much more swollen than it was yesterday. I gave it a dose of cream of tartar and a fresh poultice of onions. Ordered Shields, Gibson, Drouilliard, Cruzat, Collins, and Joe and Reuben Fields to turn out hunting and if possible cross Collins Creek and hunt toward the quamash fields. W. Bratton is yet very low. He eats heartily, but he is so weak in the small of his back that he can't walk. We have made use of every remedy to restore him without its having the desired effect.

One of our party, John Shields, observed that he had seen men in similar situations restored by violent sweats, and Bratton requested that he might be sweated in the way Shields proposed, which we agreed to.

Shields dug a round hole 4 feet deep and 3 feet in diameter, in which he made a large fire so as to heat the hole, after which the fire was taken out, a seat placed in the hole. The patient was then set on the seat with a board under his feet and a can of water handed him to throw on the bottom and the sides of the hole, so as to create as great a heat as he could bear, and the hole covered with blankets supported by hoops. After about twenty minutes, the patient was taken out and put in cold water a few minutes and returned to the hole, in which he was kept about an hour, then taken out and covered with several blankets, which were taken off by degrees until he became cool. This remedy took place yesterday and Bratton is walking about today, and is much better than he has been.

At 11 A.M. a canoe came down with the Indian man who had applied for medical assistance while we lay at The Broken Arm's village. This man I had given a few doses of flowers of sulphur and cream of tartar and directed that he should take the cold bath every morning. He conceded himself a little better than he was at that time. He had lost the use of all his limbs, and his fingers are contracted. We are at a loss to determine what to do for this unfortunate man. I gave him a few drops of laudanum and some portable soup as medicine.

26th May, 1806

The child something better this morning, though the swelling yet continues. We still apply the onion poultice. I directed what should be done for the disabled man, gave him a few doses of cream of tartar and flowers of sulphur, and some portable soup and directed that he should be taken home and sweated, &c.

27th May, 1806

Charbonneau's child is much better today, though the swelling on the side of his neck, I believe, will terminate in an ugly imposthume,[5] a little below the ear. The Indians were so anxious that the sick chief (who has lost the use of his limbs) should be sweated under our inspection, they requested me to make a second attempt today. Accordingly, the hole was enlarged, and his father—a very good-looking old man—performed all the drudgery, &c. We could not make him sweat as copiously as we wished, being compelled to keep him erect in the hole by means of cords. After the operation, he complained of considerable pain. I gave him thirty drops of laudanum, which soon composed him, and he rested very well.

May 28th, 1806

The Chopunnish held a council in the morning of the 12th, among themselves, in respect to the subject on which we had spoken to them the day before. The result, as we learned, was favorable. They placed confidence in the information they had received, and resolved to pursue our advice. After this council was over, the principal chief, or The Broken Arm, took the flour of the roots of cows and thickened the soup in the kettles and baskets of all his people. This being ended, he made a harangue, the purpose of which was making known the deliberations of their councils and impressing the necessity of unanimity among them, and a strict attention to the resolution which had been agreed on in council. He concluded by inviting all such men as had resolved to abide by the decree of the council to come and eat, and requested such as would not be so bound to show themselves by not partaking of the feast. I was told by one of our men who was present in the house that there was not a dissenting voice on this great national question, but all swallowed their objections if any they had, very cheerfully—with their mush.

During the time of this loud animated harangue of the chief, the women cried, wrung their hands, tore their hair, and appeared to be in the utmost distress. After this ceremony was over, the chiefs and considerable men came in a body to where we were seated at a little distance from our tent, and two young men at the instance of the nation presented Captain Lewis and myself each a fine horse; and informed us that they had listened with attention to what we had said and were resolved to pursue our counsels, &c. That as we had not seen the Blackfoot Indians and the Minnetarees of Fort de Prairie, they did not think it safe to venture over

---

[5] Imposthume" is an old word for an abscess of any kind.

to the plains of the Missouri, where they would fondly go provided those nations would not kill them. That when we had established a trading house on the Missouri as we had promised, they would come over and trade for arms, ammunition, &c., and live about us. That it would give them much pleasure to be at peace with those nations although they had shed much of their blood. They said that they were poor but their hearts were good.

May 30th, 1806

Lepage and Charbonneau set out early this morning to the Indian village in order to trade with them for roots. Sergeant Gass was sent this morning to obtain some goat's hair to stuff the pads of our saddles. He ascended the river on this side and, being unable to pass the river to the village he wished to visit, returned in the evening unsuccessful. Shannon and Collins were permitted to pass the river in order to trade with the natives and lay in a store of roots and bread for themselves, with their proportion of the merchandise, as others had done. On landing on the opposite shore, the canoe was driven broadside, with the full force of a very strong current, against some standing trees and instantly filled with water and sank. Potts, who was with them, is an indifferent swimmer. It was with difficulty he made the land. They lost three blankets and a blanket capote and their pittance of merchandise.

In our bare state of clothing this was a serious loss. I sent Sergeant Pryor and a party over in the Indian canoe in order to raise and secure ours but the depth of the water and the strength of the current baffled every effort. I fear that we have also lost our canoe. All our invalids are on the recovery. We gave the sick chief a severe sweat today, shortly after which he could move one of his legs and thighs and work his toes pretty well. The other leg he can move a little. His fingers and arms seem to be almost entirely restored. He seems highly delighted with his recovery. I begin to entertain strong hope of his recovering by these sweats.

June 1st, 1806

[Lewis]

Yesterday evening Charbonneau and Lepage returned, having made a broken voyage. They ascended the river on this side nearly opposite to a village eight miles above us. Here their led horse, which had on him their merchandise, fell into the river from the side of a steep cliff and swam over. They saw an Indian on the opposite side whom they prevailed on to drive their horse back again to them. In swimming the river the horse lost a dressed elk skin of Lepage's and several small articles, and their paint (vermilion) was destroyed by the water. Here they remained and dried their articles.

The evening of the 30th ult., the Indians at the village, learning their errand and not having a canoe, made an attempt yesterday morning to pass the river to them on a raft, with a parcel of roots and bread in order to trade with them. The Indian raft struck a rock, upset, and lost their cargo. The river having fallen heir to both merchandise and roots, our traders returned with empty bags.

June 2nd, 1806

McNeal and York were sent on a trading voyage over the river this morning. Having exhausted all our merchandise, we are obliged to have recourse to every subterfuge in order to prepare in the most ample manner in our power to meet that wretched portion of our journey, the Rocky Mountains, where hunger and cold in their most rigorous forms assail the wearied traveler. Not any of us has yet forgotten our suffering in those mountains in September last, and I think it probable we never shall.

Our traders McNeal and York were furnished with the buttons which Captain Clark and myself cut off our coats, some eye-water and basilicon which we made for that purpose, and some phials and small tin boxes which I had brought out with phosphorus. In the evening they returned with about three bushels of roots and some bread.

Drouilliard arrived this morning with Neeshneparkkeook and Hohâstillpilp, who had accompanied him to the lodges of the persons who had our tomahawks. He obtained both the tomahawks, principally by the influence of the former of these chiefs. The one which had been stolen we prized most, as it was the private property of the late Sergeant Floyd, and Captain Clark was desirous of returning it to his friends. The man who had this tomahawk had purchased it from the Indian that had stolen it, and was himself, at the moment of their arrival, just expiring. His relations were unwilling to give up the tomahawk as they intended to bury it with the deceased owner, but were at length induced to do so for the consideration of a handkerchief, two strands of beads, which Captain Clark sent by Drouilliard, gave them, and two horses given by the chiefs to be killed, agreeably to their custom, at the grave of the deceased.

June 4th, 1806

About noon the 3 chiefs left us and returned to their villages. While they were with us, we repeated the promises we had formerly made them and invited them to the Missouri with us. They declined going until the latter end of the summer, and said it was their intention to spend the ensuing winter on the east side of the Rocky Mountains. They gave us no positive answer to a request which we made, that two or three of their young men should accompany me to the Falls of the Missouri, and there wait my return from the upper part of Maria's River, where it was probable I should meet with some of the bands of the Minnetarees from Fort de Prairie; that, in such case, I should endeavor to bring about a good understanding between those Indians and themselves, which when effected they would be informed of it through the young men thus sent with me, and that on the contrary, should I not be fortunate enough to meet with these people nor to prevail on them to be at peace, they would equally be informed through those young men, and they might still remain on their guard with respect to them until the whites had it in their power to give them more effectual relief. The Broken Arm invited us to his village and said he wished to speak to us before we set out, and that he had some roots to give us for our journey over the mountains.

June 6th, 1806

This morning Frazer returned, having been in quest of some roots and bread, which he had left at the lodge of The Twisted Hair, when on his way to the fishery on Lewis's River. The Twisted Hair came with him, but I was unable to converse with him for the want of an interpreter, Drouilliard being absent with Captain Clark. This chief left me in the evening and returned to his village. Captain Clark visited The Broken Arm today agreeably to his promise. He took with him Drouilliard and several others. They were received in a friendly manner. The Broken Arm informed Captain Clark that the nation would not pass the mountain until the latter end of the summer, and that with respect to the young men who we had requested should accompany us to the Falls of the Missouri, they were not yet selected for that purpose, nor could they be so until there was a meeting of the nation in council.

Chapter *XXI*

THE BITTERROOT RANGE

June 8—June 29, 1806

June 8th, 1806

[Lewis]

The sick chief is fast on the recovery; he can bear his
weight on his legs and has acquired a considerable portion
of strength. The child is nearly well. Bratton has so far recovered that we cannot well consider him an invalid any
longer. He has had a tedious illness, which he bore with much
fortitude and firmness.

June 9th, 1806

We ate the last of our meat yesterday evening and have
lived on roots today. Our party seem much elated with the
idea of moving on toward their friends and country. They all
seem alert in their movements today. They have everything
in readiness for a move, and notwithstanding the want of
provision have been amusing themselves very merrily today
in running foot races, pitching quoits, prisoner's base, etc.
The river has been falling for several days and is now
lower by near six feet than it has been. This we view as a
strong evidence that the great body of snow has left the
mountains.

June 10th, 1806

At 11 A.M., we set out with the party, each man being well
mounted and a light load on a second horse; besides which,
we have several supernumerary horses, in case of accident or

the want of provision. We therefore feel ourselves perfectly equipped for the mountains.

June 15th, 1806

We had some little difficulty in collecting our horses this morning; they had straggled off to a greater distance than usual. It rained very hard in the morning, and after collecting our horses we waited an hour for it to abate; but, as it had every appearance of a settled rain, we set out at 10 A.M. We passed a little prairie at the distance of 8½ miles to which we had previously sent R. Fields and Willard. We found two deer which they had killed and hung up. At the distance of 2½ miles further we arrived at Collins's Creek, where we found our hunters. They had killed another deer and had seen two large bear together—the one black, and the other white. We halted at the creek, dined, and grazed our horses.

June 16th, 1806

The difficulty we met with from the fallen timber detained us until 11 o'clock before we reached this place. Here is a handsome little glade, in which we found some grass for our horses. We therefore halted to let them graze and took dinner, knowing that there was no other convenient situation for that purpose short of the glades on Hungry Creek, where we intended to encamp as the last probable place at which we shall find a sufficient quantity of grass for many days. This morning Windsor busted [sic] his rifle near the muzzle.

Before we reached this little branch on which we dined, we saw in the hollows and N. hillsides large quantities of snow yet undissolved. In some places it was from two to three feet deep. The snow has increased in quantity so much that the greater part of our route this evening was over the snow, which has become sufficiently firm to bear our horses; otherwise it would have been impossible for us to proceed, as it lay in immense masses, in some places 8 or ten feet deep. We found much difficulty in pursuing the road, as it was so frequently covered with snow.

The air was cold. My hands and feet were benumbed. We knew that it would require five days to reach the fish weirs at the entrance of Colt Creek, provided we were so fortunate as to be enabled to follow the proper ridges of the mountains to lead us to that place. Of this, Drouilliard, our principal dependence as a woodman and guide, was entirely doubtful.

Short of that point we could not hope for any food for our horses, not even underwood itself, as the whole was covered many feet deep in snow. If we proceeded and should get bewildered in these mountains, the certainty was that we should lose all our horses and consequently our baggage, instruments, perhaps our papers, and thus eminently risk the loss of the discoveries which we had already made if we should be so fortunate as to escape with life. The snow bore our horses very well and the traveling was therefore infinitely better than the obstruction of rocks and fallen timber which we met with in our passage over, last fall, when the snow lay on this part of the ridge in detached spots only.

Under these circumstances we conceived it madness in this stage of the expedition to proceed without a guide who could certainly conduct us to the fish weirs on the Kooskooskee (Traveler's Creek Rest), as our horses could not possibly sustain a journey of more than five days without food. We therefore came to the resolution to return with our horses while they were yet strong and in good order and endeavor to keep them so, until we could procure an Indian to conduct us over the snowy mountains; and again to proceed as soon as we could procure such a guide, knowing from the appearance of the snow that, if we remained until it had dissolved sufficiently for us to follow the road, we should not be enabled to return to the United States within this season.

Having come to this resolution, we ordered the party to make a deposit for all the baggage which we had not immediate use for and also all the roots and bread of cows which they had, except an allowance for a few days to enable them to return to some place at which we could subsist by hunting until we procured a guide. We left our instruments, papers, &c., believing them safer here than to risk them on horseback over the roads and creeks which we had passed.

Our baggage being laid on scaffolds and well covered, we began our retrograde march at 1 P.M., having remained about 3 hours on this snowy mountain. We returned by the route we had come to Hungry Creek, which we ascended about 2 miles, and encamped. We had here more grass for our horses than the preceding evening, yet it was but scant. The party were a good deal dejected, though not as much so as I had apprehended they would have been. This is the first time since we have been on this long tour that we have ever been compelled to retreat or make a retrograde march. It rained on us most of this evening.

June 18th, 1806

This morning we had considerable difficulty in collecting our horses, they having straggled off to a considerable distance in search of food on the sides of the mountains among the thick timber. At 9 o'clock we collected them all except one of Drouilliard's and one of Shields's. We set out, leaving Shields and Lepage to collect the two lost horses and follow us. We dispatched Drouilliard and Shannon to the Chopunnish Indians in the plains beyond the Kooskooskee in order to hasten the arrival of the Indians who had promised to accompany us, or to procure a guide at all events and rejoin us as soon as possible. We sent by them a rifle, which we offered as a reward to any of them who would engage to conduct us to Traveler's Rest. We also directed them, if they found difficulty in inducing any of them to accompany us, to offer the reward of two other guns to be given them immediately, and ten horses at the Falls of Missouri.

We had not proceeded far this morning before Potts cut his leg very badly with one of the large knives. He cut one of the large veins on the inner side of the leg. I found much difficulty in stopping the blood, which I could not effect until I applied a tight bandage with a little cushion of wood and tow, on the vein below the wound.

Colter's horse fell with him in passing Hungry Creek and himself and horse were driven down the creek a considerable distance rolling over each other among the rocks. Fortunately he escaped without injury or the loss of his gun.

By 1 P.M., we returned to the glade on the branch of Hungry Creek, where we had dined on the 16th inst. Here we again halted and dined. As there was much appearance of deer about this place, we left R. and J. Fields with directions to hunt this evening and tomorrow morning at this place, and to join us in the evening at the meadows of Collins's Creek, where we intend remaining tomorrow in order to rest our horses and hunt. After dinner we proceeded on to Collins's Creek and encamped in a pleasant situation at the upper part of the meadows about 2 miles above our encampment of the 15th inst. We sent out several hunters, but they returned without having killed anything.

They saw a number of salmon [trout] in the creek and shot at them several times, without success. We directed Colter and Gibson to fix each of them a gig in the morning and endeavor to take some of the salmon. The hunters saw much fresh appearance of bear but very little of deer. We hope by means of the fish, together with what deer and bear we can kill, to be enabled to subsist until our guide arrives, without the necessity of returning to the quamash flats. There is a great abundance of good food here to sustain our horses.

June 19th, 1806

At 2 P.M. J. and R. Fields arrived with two deer. John Shields and Lepage came with them; they had not succeeded in finding their horses. Late in the evening Frazer reported that my riding horse, that of Captain Clark, and his mule had gone on toward the quamash flats, and that he had pursued their tracks on the road about 2½ miles. We determined to send out all the hunters in the morning, in order to make a fair experiment of the practicability of our being able to subsist at this place; and if not we shall move, the day after, to the quamash flats. The mosquitoes have been excessively troublesome to us since our arrival at this place, particularly in the evening. Cruzat brought me several large morels which I roasted and ate without salt, pepper, or grease.[1] In this way, I had for the first time the true taste of the morel, which is truly an insipid, tasteless food. Our stock of salt is now exhausted except two quarts, which I have reserved for my tour up Maria's River, and that I left the other day on the mountain.

June 20th, 1806

[Clark]

The hunters turned out early in different directions. Our giggers also turned out with two gigs, a bayonet fixed on a pole, a scooping net, and a snare made of horsehair. Near the ford of the creek, in a deep hole, we killed six salmon trout and two others were killed in the creek above in the

[1] Fortunately for the explorers, North American mushrooms of the genus *Morcella* (morels) are not poisonous. No one, at that time, knew much about American fungi, since the early settlers, like the Indians, rarely if ever ate wild American mushrooms—some of which are very good eating indeed. Only with the arrival of Italian and Slavic immigration did real mycophagy begin in this country, and even today there are not very many Americans of the older racial stocks who can be persuaded to try them. Veteran woodsmen though they were, Lewis and Clark had to be forced by hunger to taste mushrooms, and even then didn't like them! It was pure luck that they had stumbled on an edible, nontoxic species.

evening. Reuben Fields killed a reddish brown bear, which was very meager. The talons of this bear were remarkably short, broad at their base and sharply pointed. This was the species the Chopunnish call *yah-kar*. As it was in very low order, the flesh was indifferent. Labiche and Cruzat returned late in the evening with one deer which the former had killed. The hunters assured us that their greatest exertions would not enable them to support us here more than one or two days longer, from the great scarcity of game and the difficult access of the country, the underbrush being very thick and great quantities of fallen timber.

As we shall necessarily be compelled to remain more than two days for the return of Drouilliard and Shannon, we determined to return in the morning as far as the quamash flats and endeavor to lay in another stock of meat for the mountains, our former stock now being nearly exhausted as well as what we have killed on our route. By returning to the quamash flats we shall sooner be informed whether or not we can procure a guide to conduct us through the mountains.

June 21st, 1806

We collected our horses early and set out on our return to the flats. We all felt some mortification in being thus compelled to retrace our steps through this tedious and difficult part of our route, obstructed with brush and innumerable logs and fallen timber, which renders the traveling distressing and even dangerous to our horses. One of Thompson's horses is either choked this morning or has the distemper badly. I fear he is to be of no further service to us. An excellent horse of Cruzat's snagged himself so badly in the groin in jumping over a parcel of fallen timber that he will eventually be of no further service to us.

At the pass of Collins's Creek, we met two Indians who were on their way over the mountains. They had brought with them the three horses and the mule which had left us and returned to the quamash ground. Those Indians returned with us about ½ a mile down the creek, where we halted to dine and graze our horses.

As well as we could understand the Indians, they informed us they had seen George Drouilliard and Shannon, and that they would not return until the expiration of two days. At 7:00 in the evening we found ourselves once more at our old encampment, where we shall anxiously await the return of Drouilliard and Shannon.

June 23rd, 1806

Apprehensive from Drouilliard's and Shannon's delay that they had met with some difficulty in procuring a guide and also that the two Indians, who had promised to wait two nights for us, would set out today, we thought it most advisable to dispatch Wiser and Frazer to them this morning, with a view if possible to detain them a day or two longer; and directed that, in the event of their not being able to detain the Indians, Sergeant Gass, Joe and R. Fields, and Wiser should accompany the Indians, by whatever route they might take, to Traveler's Rest and blaze the trees well as they proceeded, and wait at that place until our arrival with the party. The hunters, as usual, were dispatched early this morning.

At 4 P.M. Shannon, Drouilliard, and Whitehouse returned. Shannon and Drouilliard brought with them three Indians who had consented to accompany us to the Falls of the Missouri, for the compensation of two guns. One of those men is the brother of The Cut Nose; and the other two are the same who presented Captain Lewis and myself with a horse on a former occasion, at the lodge of The Broken Arm; and the two who promised to pursue us in nine nights after we left the river, or on the 19th inst. Those are all young men of good character and much respected by their nation.

June 25th, 1806

Last evening the Indians entertained us with setting the fir trees on fire. They have a great number of dry limbs near their bodies, which, when set on fire, create a very sudden and immense blaze, from top to bottom of those tall trees. They are a beautiful object in this situation at night. This exhibition reminded me of a display of fireworks. The natives told us that their object in setting those trees on fire was to bring fair weather for our journey.

We collected our horses and set out at an early hour this morning. One of our guides complained of being unwell, a symptom which I did not much like, as such complaints with an Indian are generally the prelude to his abandoning any enterprise with which he is not well pleased. We left 4 of those Indians at our encampment. They promised to pursue us in a few hours. At 11 A.M. we arrived at the branch of Hungry Creek, where we found Joe and R. Fields. They had not killed anything. Here we halted and dined, and our guides overtook us.

At this place the squaw collected a parcel of roots of which the Shoshones eat. It is a small knob root a good deal in flavor and consistency like the Jerusalem artichoke.[2]

After dinner we continued our route to Hungry Creek and encamped about 1½ miles below our encampment of the 16th inst. The Indians all continue with us and, I believe, are disposed to be faithful to their engagements.

June 26th, 1806

We collected our horses and set out early and proceeded on down Hungry Creek a few miles and ascended to the summit of the mountain where we deposited our baggage on the 17th inst. Found everything safe as we had left them. The snow, which was 10 feet 10 inches deep on the top of the mountain, had sunk to 7 feet, though perfectly hard and firm. We made some fire, cooked dinner, and dined, while our horses stood on snow 7 feet deep at least. After dinner we packed up and proceeded on.

The Indians hastened us off and informed us that it was a considerable distance to the place they wished to reach this evening, where there was grass for our horses. Accordingly we set out with our guides, who led us over and along the steep sides of tremendous mountains entirely covered with snow except about the roots of the trees, where the snow was partially melted and exposed a small spot of earth. We ascended and descended several steep, lofty heights, but, keeping on the dividing ridge of the Chopunnish and Kooskooskee rivers, we passed no stream of water.

Late in the evening, much to the satisfaction of ourselves and the comfort of the horses, we arrived at the desired spot, and encamped on the steep side of a mountain convenient to a good spring. Soon after we had encamped, we were overtaken by a Chopunnish man who had pursued us with a view to accompany Captain Lewis to the Falls of Missouri.

---

[2] The "Jerusalem artichoke," is, of course, not an artichoke at all but a sunflower growing from potatolike tubers. The Italian word for sunflower, "girasole," became "Jerusalem" in early American speech; and the roots do have a flavor more or less like that of a real artichoke. It is rare in modern American gardens, though it was, at one time, a rather popular vegetable.

June 27th, 1806

We collected our horses early and set out. The road still continued on the heights of the dividing ridge on which we had traveled yesterday, for 9 miles or to our encampment of the 16th September last. About 1 mile short of the encampment, we halted by the request of the guides a few minutes on an elevated point and smoked a pipe. On this eminence the natives have raised a conic mound of stones, 6 or 8 feet high, and erected a pine pole of 15 feet long. From hence they informed us that when passing over with their families some of the men were usually sent on foot by the fishery at the entrance of Colt Creek in order to take fish and again meet the party at the quamash glade on the head of Kooskooskee River. From this place we had an extensive view of these stupendous mountains principally covered with snow like that on which we stood. We were entirely surrounded by those mountains, from which, to one unacquainted with them, it would have seemed impossible ever to have escaped. In short, without the assistance of our guides, I doubt much whether we who had once passed them could find our way to Traveler's Rest, in their present situation, for the marked trees, on which we had placed considerable reliance, are much fewer and more difficult to find than we had apprehended. Those Indians are most admirable pilots. We find the road wherever the snow has disappeared, though it be only for a few paces.

After having smoked the pipe and contemplating this scene sufficient to have dampened the spirits of any except such hardy travelers as we have become, we continued our march and at the distance of 3 miles descended a steep mountain, and passed two small branches of the Chopunnish River just above their fork, and again ascended the ridge on which we passed. At the distance of 7 miles, arrived at our encampment of 16th September last.

Our meat being exhausted, we issued a pint of bear's oil to a mess with which their boiled roots made an agreeable dish. Joe Potts's leg, which had been much swollen and inflamed for several days, is much better this evening and gives him but little pain. We applied the pounded root and leaves of wild ginger, from which he found great relief.

June 29th, 1806

After dinner we continued our march 7 miles further to

the warm springs, where we arrived early in the evening and sent out several hunters, who, as well as R. Fields and Drouilliard, returned unsuccessful. Late in the evening, Joe Fields and Colter joined us with the lost horses and brought with them a deer, which J.F. had killed. This furnished us with a supper.

The principal spring is about the temperature of the warmest baths used at the Hot Springs in Virginia. In this bath, which had been prepared by the Indians by stopping the river with stone and mud, I bathed and remained in 10 minutes. It was with difficulty I could remain this long, and it caused a profuse sweat. Two other bold springs adjacent to this are much warmer, their heat being so great as to make the hand of a person smart extremely when immersed. We think the temperature of those springs about the same as that of the hottest of the Hot Springs of Virginia.

Both the men and the Indians amused themselves with the use of the bath this evening. I observe the Indians, after remaining in the hot bath as long as they could bear it, run and plunge themselves into the creek, the water of which is now as cold as ice can make it. After remaining here a few minutes, they return again to the warm bath, repeating this transition several times, but always ending with the warm bath. Saw the tracks of two barefooted Indians.

Chapter **XXII**

THE EXPEDITION DIVIDED: LEWIS AND THE INDIANS

July 1—August 12, 1806

July 1st, 1806

[Lewis]

From this place I determined to go with a small party by the most direct route to the Falls of the Missouri, there to leave Thompson, McNeal, and Goodrich to prepare carriages and gear for the purpose of transporting the canoes and baggage over the portage; and myself and six volunteers to ascend Maria's River with a view to explore the country and ascertain whether any branch of that river lies as far north as latitude 50, and again return and join the party who are to descend the Missouri, at the entrance of Maria's River. I now called for the volunteers to accompany me on this route. Many turned out, from whom I selected Drouilliard, the two Fieldses, Warner, Frazer, and Sergeant Gass.

The other part of the men are to proceed with Captain Clark to the head of Jefferson's River, where we deposited sundry articles and left our canoes. From thence, Sergeant Ordway and a party of 9 men are to descend the river with the canoes. Captain Clark, with the remaining ten, including Charbonneau and York, will proceed to the Yellowstone River at its nearest approach to the Three Forks of the Missouri. Here he will build a canoe and descend the Yellowstone River with Charbonneau, the Indian woman, his servant York, and five others to the Missouri, where, should he arrive first, he will await my arrival. Sergeant Pryor with two other men is to proceed with the horses by land to the Mandans, and thence to the British posts on the Assiniboine with a letter to Mr. Haney,[1] whom we wish to engage to pre-

[1] Hugh Haney was a friendly Canadian trader, whom the expedition had met in 1804. Only Mandans went back to Washington with the expedition. It was quite impossible to take any Sioux.

vail on the Sioux chiefs to join us on the Missouri and accompany them with us to the seat of the general government.

July 2nd, 1806

[Clark]

Had all of our arms put in the most prime order. Two of the rifles have unfortunately burst near the muzzle. Shields cut them off, and they shoot tolerably well. One which is very short we exchanged with the Indian to whom we had given a longer gun to induce them to pilot us across the mountains. We caused every man to fill his horn with powder and have a sufficiency of balls, &c. The last day in passing down Traveler's Rest Creek, Captain Lewis fell down the side of a steep mountain near 40 feet but fortunately received no damage. His horse was near falling on him but fortunately recovered, and they both escaped unhurt.

July 3rd, 1806

[Lewis]

All arrangements being now completed for carrying into effect the several schemes we had planned for execution on our return, we saddled our horses and set out. I took leave of my worthy friend and companion, Captain Clark, and the party that accompanied him. I could not avoid feeling much concern on this occasion, although I hoped this separation was only momentary.

I proceeded down Clark's River seven miles with my party of nine men and five Indians. Here the Indians recommended our passing the river, which was rapid and 150 yards wide.

As we had no other means of passing the river, we busied ourselves collecting dry timber for the purpose of constructing rafts. Timber being scarce, we found considerable difficulty in procuring as much as made three small rafts. We arrived at 11 A.M., and had our rafts completed by 3 P.M., when we dined and began to take over our baggage, which we effected in the course of three hours, the rafts being obliged to return several times. The Indians swam over their horses, and drew over their baggage in little basins of deerskin, which they constructed in a very few minutes for that purpose. We drove our horses in after them, and they followed to the opposite shore.

I remained myself with two men who could scarcely swim until the last. By this time the raft, by passing so frequently,

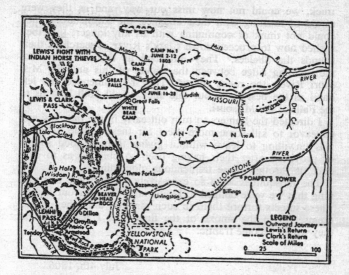

had fallen a considerable distance down the river to a rapid and difficult part of it, crowded with several small islands and willow bars which were now overflowed. With these men, I set out on the raft and was soon hurried down with the current a mile and a half before we made shore. On our approach to the shore the raft sank, and I was drawn off the raft by a bush and swam on shore.[2] The two men remained on the raft and fortunately effected a landing at some little distance below. I wet the chronometer by this accident, which I had placed in my fob, as I conceived, for greater security.

I now joined the party and we proceeded with the Indians about 3 miles to a small creek and encamped at sunset. I sent out the hunters, who soon returned with three very fine deer, of which I gave the Indians half. These people now informed me that the road which they showed me at no great distance from our camp would lead us up the east branch of Clark's River and to a river they called Cokahlarishkit, or the River of the Road to Buffalo, and thence to Medicine River and the Falls of the Missouri, where we wished to go. They alleged that as the road was a well-beaten

---

[2] When the raft "sank," it didn't stay under water. It had been pushed under by the current and, relieved of Lewis's weight, bobbed up again with enough buoyancy to hold two men instead of three.

track, we could not now miss our way, and as they were afraid of meeting with their enemies, the Minnetarees, they could not think of continuing with us any longer; that they wished now to proceed down Clark's River in search of their friends the Shalees.[3] They informed us that not far from the dividing ridge between the waters of this and the Missouri River, the roads forked. They recommended the left hand as the best route but said they would both lead us to the Falls of the Missouri.

I directed the hunters to turn out early in the morning and endeavor to kill some more meat for these people, whom I was unwilling to leave without giving them a good supply of provision after their having been so obliging as to conduct us through those tremendous mountains.

The mosquitoes were so excessively troublesome this evening that we were obliged to kindle large fires for our horses. These insects torture them in such manner, until they placed themselves in the smoke of the fires, that I really thought they would become frantic.

July 4th, 1806

I gave a shirt, a handkerchief, and a small quantity of ammunition to the Indians. At half after eleven the hunters returned from the chase, unsuccessful. I now ordered the houses saddled, smoked a pipe with these friendly people, and at noon bid them adieu. They had cut the meat which I gave them last evening, thin, and exposed it in the sun to dry, informing me that they should leave it in this neighborhood until they returned, as a store for their homeward journey.

These affectionate people, our guides, betrayed every emotion of unfeigned regret at separating from us. They said that they were confident that the Pahkees (the appellation they give the Minnetarees) would cut us off.

July 11th, 1806

It is now the season at which the buffalo begin to copulate, and the bulls keep a tremendous roaring. We could hear them for many miles, and there are such numbers of them

---

[3] The Shalees were a branch of the Tushepaws, living along Clark's River. These Indians really did flatten the heads of their children by pressure in infancy.

that there is one continual roar. Our horses had not been acquainted with the buffalo. They appeared much alarmed at their appearance and bellowing. When I arrived in sight of the White Bear islands, the Missouri bottoms on both sides of the river were crowded with buffalo. I sincerely believe that there were not less than 10 thousand buffalo within a circle of 2 miles around that place. I met with the hunters at a little grove of timber opposite to the island where they had killed a cow and were awaiting our arrival. They had met with no elk.

I directed the hunters to kill some buffalo as well for the benefit of their skins to enable us to pass the river [4] as for their meat for the men I meant to leave at this place. We unloaded our horses and encamped opposite to the islands; had the cow skinned and some willow sticks collected to make canoes of the hides. By 12 o'clock they killed eleven buffalo, most of them in fine order. The bulls are now generally much fatter than the cows and are fine beef. I sent out all hands with the horses to assist in butchering and bringing in the meat. By 3 in the evening we had brought in a large quantity of fine beef and as many hides as we wanted for canoes, shelters, and gear. I then set all hands to prepare two canoes. The one we made after the Mandan fashion, with a single skin in the form of a basin, and the other we constructed of two skins, on a plan of our own.

July 12, 1806

Two of the men whom I had dispatched this morning in quest of the horses returned with seven of them only. The remaining ten of our best horses were absent and not to be found. I fear that they are stolen. I dispatched two men on horseback in search of them. The wind blew so violently that I did not think it prudent to attempt passing the river. At noon Warner returned, having found three others of the horses near Fort Mountain. Sergeant Gass did not return until 3 P.M., not having found the horses. He had been about 8 miles up Medicine River. I now dispatched Joseph Fields and Drouilliard in quest of them. The former returned at dark, unsuccessful, and the latter continued absent all night.

---

[4] The buffalo skins would help them cross the river, because they could be used to make "bull boats," or buffalo-hide canoes. The horses, brought from the other side of the Rockies or the eastern uplands, had never seen buffalo.

13th July

Removed above to my old station opposite the upper point of the White Bear island. Formed our camp and set Thompson, etc., at work to complete the gear for the horses. Had the cache opened, found my bear skins entirely destroyed by the water, the river having risen so high that the water had penetrated. All my specimens of plants also lost. The chart of the Missouri fortunately escaped. Opened my trunks and boxes and exposed the articles to dry. Found my papers damp and several articles damp. The stopper had come out of a phial of laudanum and the contents had run into the drawer and destroyed a great part of my medicine in such manner that it was past recovery.

14th July

Had the carriage wheels dug up. Found them in good order. The iron frame of the boat had not suffered materially. Had the meat cut thinner and exposed to dry in the sun, and some roots of cows, of which I have yet a small stock, pounded into meal for my journey. I find the fat buffalo meat a great improvement on the mush of these roots.

The wolves are in great numbers howling around us and lolling about in the plains in view, at the distance of two or three hundred yards. I counted 27 about the carcass of a buffalo which lies in the water at the upper point of the large island. These are generally of the large kind.

July 15th, 1806

Dispatched McNeal early this morning to the lower part of the portage in order to learn whether the cache and white pirogue remained untouched or in what state they were. The men employed in drying the meat, dressing deer skins, and preparing for the reception of the canoes. At 1 P.M., Drouilliard returned without the horses and reported that, after a diligent search of 2 days, he had discovered where the horses had passed Dearborn's River, at which place there were 15 lodges that had been abandoned about the time our horses were taken. He pursued the tracks of a number of horses from these lodges to the road which we had traveled over the mountains, which they struck about 3 miles south of our encampment of the 7th inst., and had pursued this road west-wardly.

I have no doubt but they are a party of the Tushepaws, who have been on a buffalo hunt. Drouilliard informed that their camp was in a small bottom on the river of about 5 acres enclosed by the steep and rocky and lofty cliffs of the river, and that so closely had they kept themselves and horses within this little spot that there was not a track to be seen of them within a quarter of a mile of that place. Every spire of grass was eaten up by their horses near their camp, which had the appearance of their having remained here some time. His horse being much fatigued with the ride he had given him and finding that the Indians had at least two days the start of him, he thought it best to return.

His safe return has relieved me from great anxiety. I had already settled it in my mind that a white bear had killed him, and should have set out tomorrow in search of him, and if I could not find him to continue my route to Maria's River. I knew that if he met with a bear, in the plains even, he would attack him; and that, if any accident should happen to separate him from his horse in that situation, the chances in favor of his being killed would be as 9 to 10. I felt so perfectly satisfied that he had returned in safety that I thought but little of the horses, although they were seven of the best I had.

This loss, great as it is, is not entirely irreparable or at least does not defeat my design of exploring Maria's River. I have yet 10 horses remaining, two of the best and two of the worst of which I leave, to assist the party in taking the canoes and baggage over the portage, and take the remaining six with me. These are but indifferent horses, most of them, but I hope they may answer our purposes. I shall leave three of my intended party—Gass, Frazer, and Warner, and take the two Fieldses and Drouilliard. By having two spare horses, we can relieve those we ride.

Having made this arrangement, I gave orders for an early departure in the morning. Indeed, I should have set out instantly, but McNeal rode one of the horses which I intend to take and has not yet returned. A little before dark, Mc-Neal returned with his musket broken off at the breach, and informed me that on his arrival at Willow Run (on the portage) he had approached a white bear within ten feet without discovering him, the bear being in the thick brush.

The horse took the alarm and, turning short, threw him immediately under the bear. This animal raised himself on his hind feet for battle, and gave him time to recover from his fall, which he did in an instant, and with his clubbed musket he struck the bear over the head and cut him with the guard of the gun and broke off the breach. The bear, stunned with the stroke, fell to the ground and began to scratch his head with his feet. This gave McNeal time to climb a willow tree [5] which was near at hand and thus fortunately made his escape. The bear waited at the foot of the tree until late in the evening before he left him.

July 17th, 1806

We killed a buffalo cow as we passed through the plains, and took the hump and tongue, which furnish ample rations for four men one day. At 5 P.M., we arrived at Rose (Tansy) River, where I purposed remaining all night, as I could not reach Maria's River this evening, and unless I did there would be but little probability of our finding any wood, and very probably no water either. On our arrival at the river we saw where a wounded and bleeding buffalo had just passed and concluded it was probable that the Indians had been running them and were near at hand. The Minnetarees of Fort de Prairie and the Blackfoot Indians rove through this quarter of the country, and as they are a vicious, lawless, and rather abandoned set of wretches, I wish to avoid an interview with them if possible.

July 26th, 1806

The country through which this portion of Maria's River passes to the fork which I ascended appears much more broken than that above and between this and the mountains. I had scarcely ascended the hills before I discovered, to my left, at the distance of a mile, an assemblage of about 30 horses. I halted and used my spyglass, by the help of which I discovered several Indians on the top of an eminence just above them, who appeared to be looking down toward the river—I presumed, at Drouilliard. About half the horses were saddled.

This was a very unpleasant sight. However, I resolved to make the best of our situation and to approach them in a friendly manner. I directed J. Fields to display the flag which I had brought for that purpose, and advanced slowly toward

---

[5] Though bears of some species climb trees, grizzlies do not, though they sometimes *walk* up a trunk growing at a suitable slope.

them. About this time they discovered us and appeared to run about in a very confused manner as if much alarmed. Their attention had been previously so fixed on Drouilliard that they did not discover us until we had begun to advance upon them. Some of them descended the hill on which they were, and drove their horses within shot of its summit and again returned to the height as if to wait our arrival or to defend themselves.

I calculated on their number being nearly or quite equal to that of their horses, that our running would invite pursuit, as it would convince them that we were their enemies, and our horses were so indifferent that we could not hope to make our escape by flight. Added to this, Drouilliard was separated from us, and I feared that his not being apprised of the Indians in the event of our attempting to escape, he would most probably fall a sacrifice.

Under these considerations, I still advanced toward them. When we had arrived within a quarter of a mile of them, one of them mounted his horse and rode full speed toward us, which when I discovered, I halted and alighted from my horse. He came within a hundred paces, halted, looked at us, and turned his horse about, and returned as briskly to his party as he had advanced.

While he halted near us, I held out my hand and beckoned him to approach, but he paid no attention to my overtures. On his return to his party, they all descended the hill and mounted their horses, and advanced toward us, leaving their horses behind them.[6] We also advanced to meet them. I counted eight of them but still supposed that there were others concealed, as there were several other horses saddled.

I told the two men with me that I apprehended that these were the Minnetarees of Fort de Prairie, and from their known character I expected that we were to have some difficulty with them; that if they thought themselves sufficiently strong, I was convinced that they would attempt to rob us, in which case, be their numbers what they would, I should resist to the last extremity, preferring death to being deprived of my papers, instruments, and gun; and desired that they would form the same resolution, and be alert and on their guard.

When we arrived within a hundred yards of each other, the

---

[6] This is a choice example of the explorers' wilder prose, which has been somewhat edited in this edition. The Indians left their *spare* horses behind. They were still mounted when they approached the white men and only then dismounted.

Indians, except one, halted. I directed the two men with me to do the same and advanced singly to meet the Indian, with whom I shook hands and passed on to those in his rear, as he did also to the two men in my rear. We now all assembled and alighted from our horses. The Indians soon asked to smoke with us, but I told them that the man whom they had seen pass down the river had my pipe and we could not smoke until he joined us. I requested, as they had seen which way he went, that they would one of them go with one of my men in search of him. This they readily consented to, and a young man set out with R. Fields in search of Drouilliard.

I now asked them by signs if they were the Minnetarees of the North which they answered in the affirmative. I asked if there was any chief among them, and they pointed out three. I did not believe them. However, I thought it best to please them and give to one a medal, to a second a flag, and to the third a handkerchief, with which they appeared well satisfied. They appeared much agitated with our first interview, from which they had scarcely yet recovered. In fact, I believe they were more alarmed at this accidental interview than we were.

From no more of them appearing, I now concluded they were only eight in number, and became much better satisfied with our situation, as I was convinced that we could manage that number should they attempt any hostile measures. As it was growing late in the evening, I proposed that we should remove to the nearest part of the river and encamp together. I told them that I was glad to see them and had a great deal to say to them.

We mounted our horses and rode toward the river, which was at but a short distance. On our way we were joined by Drouilliard, Fields, and the Indian. We descended a very steep bluff about 250 feet high to the river, where there was a small bottom of nearly ½ a mile in length. In this bottom, there stand three solitary trees, near one of which the Indians formed a large semicircular camp of dressed buffalo skins and invited us to partake of their shelter, which Drouilliard and myself accepted, and the Fieldses lay near the fire in front of the shelter. With the assistance of Drouilliard, I had much conversation with these people in the course of the evening. I learned from them that they were a part of a large band which lay encamped at present near the foot of the Rocky Mountains, on the main branch of Maria's river, 1½ days' march from our present encampment; that there was a white man with their band; that there was another large band of their nation hunting buffalo near the broken mountains and were on their way to the mouth of Maria's River, where they would probably be in the course of a few days.

I told these people that I had come a great way from the East, up the large river which runs toward the rising sun, that I had been to the great waters where the sun sets and had seen a great many nations, all of whom I had invited to come and trade with me, on the rivers on this side of the mountains; that I had found most of them at war with their neighbors and had succeeded in restoring peace among them. That I was now on my way home and had left my party at the Falls of the Missouri with orders to descend that river to the entrance of Maria's River and there wait my arrival, and that I had come in search of them in order to prevail on them to be at peace with their neighbors, particularly those on the west side of the mountains, and to engage them to come and trade with me when the establishment is made at the entrance of this river; to all of which they readily gave their assent, and declared it to be their wish to be at peace with the Tushepaws who they said had killed a number of their relations lately, and pointed to several of those present who had cut their hair, as an evidence of the truth of what they had asserted.

I found them extremely fond of smoking and plied them with the pipe until late at night. I told them that if they intended to do as I wished them, they would send some of their young men to their band with an invitation to their chiefs and warriors to bring the white man with them and come down and counsel with me at the entrance of Maria's River, and that the balance of them would accompany me to that place, where I was anxious now to meet my men, as I had been absent from them some time and knew that they would be uneasy until they saw me. That if they would go with me, I would give them ten horses and some tobacco. To this proposition they made no reply.

I took the first watch tonight and sat up until half after eleven. The Indians by this time were all asleep. I roused up R. Fields and lay down myself. I directed Fields to watch the movements of the Indians, and if any of them left the camp, to awake us all, as I apprehended they would attempt to steal our horses.

This being done, I fell into a profound sleep and did not wake until the noise of the men and Indians awoke me a little after light, in the morning.

July 27th, 1806

This morning at daylight the Indians got up and crowded

around the fire. J. Fields, who was on post, had carelessly laid his gun down behind him, near where his brother was sleeping. One of the Indians—the fellow to whom I had given the medal last evening—slipped behind him and took his gun and that of his brother, unperceived by him. At the same instant two others advanced and seized the guns of Drouilliard and myself.

J. Fields, seeing this, turned about to look for his gun and saw the fellow just running off with her [7] and his brother's. He called to his brother, who instantly jumped up and pursued the Indian with him, whom they overtook at the distance of 50 or 60 paces from the camp, seized their guns and wrested them from him; and R. Fields, as he seized his gun, stabbed the Indian to the heart with his knife. The fellow ran about fifteen steps and fell dead. Of this I did not know until afterward. Having recovered their guns, they ran back instantly to the camp.

Drouilliard, who was awake, saw the Indian take hold of his gun and instantly jumped up and seized her and wrested her from him, but the Indian still retained his pouch. His jumping up and crying, "Damn you, let go my gun!" awakened me.

I jumped up and asked what was the matter, which I quickly learned when I saw Drouilliard in a scuffle with the Indian for his gun. I reached to seize my gun, but found her gone. I then drew a pistol from my holster and, turning myself about, saw the Indian making off with my gun. I ran at him with my pistol and bid him lay down my gun, which he was in the act of doing when the Fieldses returned and drew up their guns to shoot him, which I forbade as he did not appear to be about to make any resistance or commit any offensive act.

He dropped the gun and walked slowly off. I picked her up instantly. Drouilliard, having about this time recovered his gun and pouch, asked me if he might not kill the fellow, which I also forbade as the Indian did not appear to wish to kill us. As soon as they found us all in possession of our arms, they ran and endeavored to drive off all the horses.

I now hallooed to the men and told them to fire on them if they attempted to drive off our horses. They accordingly pursued the main party who were driving the horses up the

---

[7] Reference to a rifle as "she" and "her" was not unusual. Their arms were almost persons to Virginia and Kentucky frontiersmen, and often had names. Daniel Boone treasured a rifle he called "Ticklicker." One of his contemporaries named his rifle "Beelzebub."

river, and I pursued the man who had taken my gun, who, with another, was driving off a part of the horses which were to the left of the camp. I pursued them so closely that they could not take twelve of their own horses, but continued to drive one of mine with some others. At the distance of three hundred paces, they entered one of those steep niches in the bluff with the horses before them. Being nearly out of breath, I could pursue no further. I called to them, as I had done several times before, that I would shoot them if they did not give me my horse and raised my gun.

One of them jumped behind a rock and spoke to the other, who turned around and stopped at the distance of thirty steps from me, and I shot him through the belly. He fell to his knees and on his right elbow, from which position he partly raised himself and fired at me and, turning himself about, crawled in behind a rock, which was a few feet from him. He overshot me. Being bareheaded, I felt the wind of his bullet very distinctly.

Not having my shot pouch I could not reload my piece, and as there were two of them behind good shelters from me, I did not think it prudent to rush on them with my pistol, which had I discharged. I had not the means of reloading until I reached camp. I therefore returned leisurely toward camp. On my way, I met with Drouillard who, having heard the report of the guns, had returned in search of me and left the Fieldses to pursue the Indians. I desired him to hasten to the camp with me and assist in catching as many of the Indian horses as were necessary, and to call to the Fieldses, if he could make them hear, to come back—that we still had a sufficient number of horses. This he did, but they were too far to hear him. We reached the camp and began to catch the horses and saddle them and put on the packs.

The reason I had not my pouch with me was that I had not time to return about fifty yards to camp, after getting my gun, before I was obliged to pursue the Indians or suffer them to collect and drive off all the horses. We had caught and saddled the horses and begun to arrange the packs when the Fieldses returned with four of our horses. We left one of our horses and took four of the best of those of the Indians.

While the men were preparing the horses, I put four shields and two bows and quivers of arrows, which had been left on the fire, with sundry other articles. They left all their baggage at our mercy. They had but two guns, and one of them they left. The others were armed with bows and arrows

and eyedaggs.[8] The gun we took with us. I also retook the
flag, but left the medal about the neck of the dead man that
they might be informed who we were.

We took some of their buffalo meat and set out, ascending
the bluffs by the same route we had descended last evening,
leaving the balance of nine of their horses, which we did not
want. The Fieldses told me that three of the Indians whom
they pursued swam the river—one of them on my horse;
and that two others ascended the hill and escaped from
them with a part of their horses; two I had pursued into the
niche—one lay dead near the camp; and the eighth we could
not account for but suppose that he ran off early in the con-
test.[9]

Having ascended the hill, we took our course through a
beautiful level plain a little to the S. of east. My design was
to hasten to the entrance of Maria's River as quick as possible,
in the hope of meeting with the canoes and party at that
place, having no doubt but that the Indians would pursue
us with a large party. No time was therefore to be lost, and
we pushed our horses as hard as they would bear.

By dark, we had traveled about 17 miles further. We now
halted to rest ourselves and horses about two hours. We
killed a buffalo cow and took a small quantity of the meat.
After refreshing ourselves, we again set out by moonlight and
traveled leisurely. Heavy thunderclouds lowered around us
on every quarter but that from which the moon gave us
light. We continued to pass immense herds of buffalo all
night, as we had done in the latter part of the day. We
traveled until 2 o'clock in the morning, having come, by my
estimate, after dark about 20 miles. We now turned out our
horses and laid ourselves down to rest in the plain, very
much fatigued, as may be readily conceived. My Indian horse
carried me very well—in short, much better than my own

---

[8] No one, including a number of museums and anthropologists,
seems to know what an "eyedagg" was—probably a war club.

[9] Toward the end of the nineteenth century, the Indian side
of the story was revealed by a Blackfoot warrior, Wolf Calf, who
had been a mere boy when he accompanied the band Lewis met.
George Bird Grinnell, who heard his story, gathered that the
Indians "flew north about as fast as Lewis flew south and east."
In 1807, the Canadian explorer, David Thompson, found the
Blackfeet still watching the Missouri to avenge the "murder" by
Lewis, whose name he mentions. But the St. Louis trader, Manuel
Lisa, found that some of the Blackfeet justified Lewis. The long-
continued hostility of the Blackfeet is often, but rather dubiously,
attributed to this incident.

would have done—and leaves me with but little reason to complain of the robbery.

July 28th, 1806

The morning proved fair. I slept sound, but fortunately awoke as day appeared. I awakened the men and directed the horses to be saddled. I was so sore from my ride yesterday that I could scarcely stand. And the men complained of being in a similar situation; however, I encouraged them by telling them that our own lives as well as those of our friends and fellow travelers depended on our exertions at this moment. They were alert, soon prepared the horses, and we again resumed our march.

It was my determination that if we were attacked in the plains on our way to the point, that the bridles of the horses should be tied together and we would stand and defend them, or sell our lives as dear as we could.

We had proceeded about 12 miles on an east course when we found ourselves near the Missouri. We heard a report which we took to be that of a gun but were not certain. Still continuing down the N.E. bank of the Missouri about 8 miles further, being then within about five miles of the grog spring,[10] we heard the report of several rifles very distinctly on the river to our right. We quickly repaired to this joyful sound and on arriving at the bank of the river had the unspeakable satisfaction to see our canoes coming down. We hurried down from the bluff on which we were and joined them; stripped our horses and gave them a final discharge, embarking without loss of time with our baggage.

I now learned that they had brought all things safe, having sustained no loss, nor met with any accident of importance. Wiser had cut his leg badly with a knife and was unable, in consequence, to work. We descended the river opposite to our principal cache, which we proceeded to open after reconnoitering the adjacent country. We found that the cache had caved in and most of the articles buried therein were injured. I sustained the loss of two very large bear skins, which I much regret. Most of the fur and baggage belonging to the men were injured. The gunpowder, corn, flour, pork, and salt had sustained but little injury. The parched meal was spoiled, or nearly so. Having no time to air these things, which

[10] Sergeant Gass mentions a spring in this area where, on the outward journey, a detached party of the expedition had "refreshed ourselves with a good drink of grog."

they much wanted, we dropped down to the point to take in the several articles which had been buried at that place in several small caches. These we found in good order, and recovered every article except three traps belonging to Drouilliard, which could not be found. Here, as good fortune would have it, Sergeant Gass and Willard, who brought the horses from the Falls, joined us at 1 P.M. I had ordered them to bring down the horses to this place in order to assist them in collecting meat, which I directed them to kill and dry here for our voyage, presuming that they would have arrived with the pirogue and canoes at this place several days before my return.

Having now nothing to detain us, we passed over immediately to the island in the entrance of Maria's River to launch the red pirogue, but found her so much decayed that it was impossible with the means we had to repair her, and therefore merely took the nails and other iron works about her which might be of service to us and left her. We now re-embarked on board the white pirogue and five small canoes.

August 3rd, 1806

I arose early this morning and had the pirogue and canoes loaded and set out at half after 6 A.M. We soon passed the canoe of Colter and Collins, who were on shore hunting. The men hailed them but received no answer. We proceeded, and shortly after overtook J. and R. Fields, who had killed 25 deer since they left us yesterday. Deer are very abundant in the timbered bottoms of the river and extremely gentle. We did not halt today to cook and dine as usual, having directed that in future the party should cook as much meat in the evening after encamping as would be sufficient to serve them the next day. By this means we forward our journey at least 12 or 15 miles per day.

August 4th, 1806

Ordway and Willard delayed so much in hunting today that they did not overtake us until about midnight. They killed one bear and two deer. In passing a bend just below the gulf, it being dark, they were drawn by the current in among a parcel of sawyers, under one of which the canoe was driven and threw Willard, who was steering, overboard. He caught the sawyer and held by it. Ordway, with the canoe, drifted down about half a mile among the sawyers under a falling bank. The canoe struck frequently but did not over-set. He at length gained the shore, and returned by land to learn the fate of Willard, who, he found, was yet on the saw-yer. It was impossible for him to take the canoe to his relief.

Willard at length tied a couple of sticks together which had lodged against the sawyers on which he was, and set himself adrift among the sawyers, which he fortunately es-caped, and was taken up about a mile below by Ordway with the canoe.

August 7th, 1806

At 4 P.M. we arrived at the entrance of the Yellowstone River. I landed at the point and found that Captain Clark had been encamped at this place and from appearances had left it about 7 or 8 days. I found a paper on a pole at the point, which merely contained my name in the hand-writing of Captain Clark. We also found the remnant of a note which had been attached to a piece of elkhorn in the camp. From this fragment I learned that game was scarce at the point and mosquitoes troublesome, which were the rea-sons given for his going on. I also learned that he intended halting a few miles below, where he intended waiting for my arrival.

I now wrote a note directed to Colter and Collins pro-vided they were behind, ordering them to come on without loss of time. This note I wrapped in leather and attached to the same pole which Captain Clark had planted at the point. This being done, I instantly re-embarked and descended the river in the hope of reaching Captain Clark's camp be-fore night.

About 7 miles below the point on the S.W. shore I saw some meat that had been lately fleeced and hung on a pole. I directed Sergeant Ordway to go on shore and examine the place. On his return, he reported that he saw the tracks of two men which appeared so recent that he believed they had been there today. The fire he found at the place was blazing and appeared to have been mended up afresh or within the course of an hour past. He found at this place a part of a Chinook hat, which my men recognized as the hat of Gibson. From these circumstances we concluded that Cap-tain Clark's camp could not be distant and pursued our route until dark with the hope of reaching his camp. In this, however, we were disappointed; and night coming on com-pelled us to encamp on the northeast shore in the next bottom above our encampment of the 23rd and 24th of April, 1805.

August 8th, 1806

Believing, from the recent appearances about the fire which we passed last evening, that Captain Clark could be at no great distance below, I set out early. The wind hard from the northeast, but by the force of the oars and current we reached the center of the beaver bends (about 8 miles by water and 3 by land) above the entrance of the White Earth River.

Not finding Captain Clark, I knew not what calculation to make with respect to his halting, and therefore determined to proceed as though he was not before me and leave the rest to the chapter of accidents. At this place I found a good beach for the purpose of drawing out the pirogue and one of the canoes, which wanted corking and repairing.

The men with me have not had leisure since we left the west side of the Rocky Mountains to dress any skins or make themselves clothes, and most of them therefore are extremely bare. I therefore determined to halt at this place until the pirogue and canoe could be repaired and the men dress skins and make themselves the necessary clothing. We encamped on the N.E. side of the river.

August 10th, 1806

I hastened the repairs which were necessary to the pirogue and canoe, which were completed by 2 P.M. Those not engaged about this business employed themselves as yesterday. At 4 in the evening, it clouded up and began to rain, which putting a stop to the operation of skin dressing, we had nothing further to detain us. I therefore directed the vessels to be loaded, and at 5 P.M. we got under way. We descended this evening as low nearly as the entrance of White Earth River and encamped on the southwest side.

August 11th, 1806

We set out very early this morning, it being my wish to arrive at the Burnt Hills by noon in order to take the latitude of that place, as it is the most northern point of the Missouri. I informed the party of my design and requested that they would exert themselves to reach the place in time, as it would save us the delay of nearly one day. Being as anxious to get forward as I was, they plied their oars faithfully, and we proceeded rapidly.

Half after 11 A.M., we saw a large herd of elk on the northeast shore, and I directed the men in the small canoes to halt and kill some of them, and continued on in the pirogue to the Burnt Hills. When I arrived here, it was about 20 minutes after noon, and of course, the observation of the sun's meridian altitude was lost.

Just opposite to the Burnt Hills, there happened to be a herd of elk on a thick willow bar, and finding that my observation was lost for the present, I determined to land and kill some of them. Accordingly, we put to, and I went out with Cruzat only. We fired on the elk. I killed one and he wounded another. We reloaded our guns and took different routes through the thick willows in pursuit of the elk.

I was in the act of firing on the elk a second time when a ball struck my left thigh about an inch below my hip joint. Missing the bone, it passed through the left thigh and cut the thickness of the bullet across the hinder part of the right thigh. The stroke was very severe. I instantly supposed that Cruzat had shot me in mistake for an elk, as I was dressed in brown leather and he cannot see very well. Under this impression I called out to him, "Damn you, you have shot me," and looked toward the place from whence the ball had come. Seeing nothing, I called Cruzat several times as loud as I could, but received no answer.

I was now persuaded that it was an Indian that had shot me, as the report of the gun did not appear to be more than 40 paces from me and Cruzat appeared to be out of hearing of me. In this situation, not knowing how many Indians there might be concealed in the bushes, I thought it best to make good my retreat to the pirogue, calling out as I ran for the first hundred paces as loud as I could to Cruzat to retreat, that there were Indians, hoping to alarm him in time to make his escape also. I still retained the charge in my gun which I was about to discharge at the moment the ball struck me.

When I arrived in sight of the pirogue, I called the men to their arms, to which they flew in an instant. I told them that I was wounded but I hoped not mortally—by an Indian, I believed—and directed them to follow me, that I would return and give them battle and relieve Cruzat if possible, who I feared had fallen into their hands. The men followed me as they were bid and I returned about a hundred paces, when my wounds became so painful and my thigh so stiff that I could scarcely get on. In short, I was compelled to halt, and ordered the men to proceed and, if they found themselves overpowered by numbers, to retreat in order, keeping up a fire. I now got back to the pirogue as well as I could, and prepared myself with a pistol, my rifle, and air gun, being determined—as a retreat was impracticable—to sell my life as dearly as possible.

In this state of anxiety and suspense I remained about 20 minutes, when the party returned with Cruzat and reported that there were no Indians nor the appearance of any. Cruzat seemed much alarmed, and declared if he had shot me it was not his intention, that he had shot an elk in the willows after he left or separated from me. I asked him whether he did not hear me when I called to him so frequently, which he absolutely denied. I do not believe that the fellow did it intentionally but after finding that he had shot me, was anxious to conceal his knowledge of having done so.

The ball had lodged in my breeches, which I knew to be the ball of the short rifles such as that he had; and there being no person out with me but him and no Indians that we could discover, I have no doubt in my own mind of his having shot me. With the assistance of Sergeant Gass, I took off my clothes and dressed my wounds myself as well as I could, introducing tents of patent lint into the ball holes. The wounds bled considerably, but I was happy to find that it had touched neither bone nor artery.

I sent the men to dress the two elk which Cruzat and myself had killed, which they did in a few minutes and brought the meat to the river. My wounds being so situated that I could not, without infinite pain, make an observation, I determined to relinquish it and proceeded on. At 4 P.M. we passed an encampment which had been evacauted this morning by Captain Clark. Here I found a note from Captain Clark informing me that he had left a letter for me at the entrance of the Yellowstone River, but that Sergeant Pryor, who had passed that place since he left it, had taken the letter; that Sergeant Pryor, having been robbed of all his horses, had descended the Yellowstone River in skin canoes and had overtaken him at this encampment.

August 12th, 1806

Being anxious to overtake Captain Clark, who from the appearance of his camps could be at no great distance before me, we set out early and proceeded with all possible expedition. At 8 A.M. the bowsman informed me that there was a canoe and a camp, he believed of white men, on the N.E. shore. I directed the pirogue and canoes to come to at this place, and found it to be the camp of two hunters from the Illinois, by name Joseph Dickson and Forest Hancock.

These men informed me that Captain Clark had passed them about noon the day before. They also informed me that they had left the Illinois in the summer of 1804, since which time they had been ascending the Missouri, hunting and trapping beaver; that they had been robbed by the Indians, and the former wounded last winter by the Tetons of the Burnt Woods; that they had hitherto been unsuccessful in their voyage, having as yet caught but little beaver, but were still determined to proceed.

I gave them a short description of the Missouri, a list of distances to the most conspicuous streams and remarkable places on the river above, and pointed out to them the places where the beaver most abounded. I also gave them a file and a couple of pounds of powder with some lead. These were articles which they assured me they were in great want of. I remained with these men an hour and a half, when I took leave of them and proceeded.

While I halted with these men, Colter and Collins—who separated from us on the 3rd inst.—rejoined us. They were well, no accident having happened. They informed me that after proceeding the first day and not overtaking us, they had concluded that we were behind and had delayed several days in waiting for us, and had thus been unable to join us until the present moment.

My wounds felt very stiff and sore this morning but gave me no considerable pain. There was much less inflammation than I had reason to apprehend there would be. I had, last evening, applied a poultice of Peruvian barks.

At 1 P.M. I overtook Captain Clark and party and had the pleasure of finding them all well. As writing in my present situation is extremely painful to me, I shall desist until I recover, and leave my friend Captain Clark the continuation of our journal.

Chapter *XXIII*

THE EXPEDITION DIVIDED: CLARK IN THE YELLOWSTONE

July 3—August 12, 1806

July 3rd, 1806

[Clark]

We collected our horses, and after breakfast I took my leave of Captain Lewis and the Indians, and at 8 A.M. set out with [blank in MS.] men, interpreter Charbonneau and his wife and child (as an interpreter and interpretress for the Crow Indians, and the latter for the Shoshone) with fifty horses.

July 5th, 1806

I rose at daylight this morning. Dispatched Labiche after a buck, which he killed late last evening; and I went with the three men whom I had sent in search of a ford across the west fork of Clark's River, and examined each ford. Neither of them I thought would answer to pass the fork without wetting all the loads. Near one of those places pointed out by Colter I found a practicable ford and returned to camp. Ordered everything packed up, and after breakfast we set out. I saw fresh sign of two horses, and a fire burning on the side of the road. I presume that those Indians are spies from the Shoshones.

7th July, 1806

This morning our horses were very much scattered. I sent out men in every direction in search of them. They brought all except 9 by 6 o'clock, and informed me that they could not find those 9. I then ordered 6 men to take horses and go different directions and at a greater distance. Those men all returned by 10 A.M., and informed me that they had made circles in every direction to 6 or 8 miles around camp and could not see any signs of them. That they had reasons to believe that the Indians had stolen them in the course of the night, and founded their reasons on the quality of the horses, all being the most valuable horses we had, and several of them so attached to horses of inferior quality which we have, they could not be separated from each other when driving with their loads on in the course of the day.

I thought it probable that they might be stolen by some skulking Shoshones; but, as it was yet possible that they might have taken our back route or rambled to a greater distance, I determined to leave a small party to hunt for them today and proceed on with the main party and all the baggage to the canoes, raise them out of the water, and expose them to the sun to dry by the time this party should overtake me.

I left Sergeant Ordway, Shannon, Gibson, Collins, and Labiche, with directions to hunt this day for the horses without [*i.e., unless*] they should discover that the Indians had taken them into the mountains, and pursue our trail, &c.

8th July, 1806

After dinner we proceeded on down the fork which is here but small, 9 miles, to our encampment of 17th August, at which place we sank our canoes, and buried some articles as before mentioned. The most of the party with me, being chewers of tobacco, became so impatient to be chewing it that they scarcely gave themselves time to take their saddles off their horses before they were off to the deposit.

I found every article safe, except a little damp. I gave to each man who used tobacco about two feet off a part of a roll, took one third of the balance myself, and put up 2/3 in a box to send down with the most of the articles which had been left at this place, by the canoes to Captain Lewis. As it was late, nothing could be done with the canoes this evening. I examined them and found them all safe except one of the largest, which had a large hole in one side and split in bow.

9th July, 1806

Set several men to work digging for the tobacco Captain Lewis informed me he had had buried in the place the lodge stood when we lay here last summer. They searched diligently without finding anything. At 10 A.M. Sergeant Ordway and party arrived with the horses we had lost. He reported that he found those horses near the head of the creek on which we encamped, making off as fast as they could, and much scattered.

10th July, 1806

I had all the canoes put into the water and every article, which was intended to be sent down, put on board, and the horses collected and packed with what few articles I intend taking with me to the Yellowstone; and after breakfast we all set out at the same time and proceeded on down Jefferson's River on the east side through Service Valley and Rattlesnake Mountain and into that beautiful and extensive valley, open and fertile, which we call the Beaverhead Valley, which is the Indian name.

At meridian, I halted to let the horses graze, having come 15 miles. I ordered the canoes to land. Sergeant Ordway informed me that the party with him had come on very well and he thought the canoes could go as fast as the horses, &c. As the river now becomes wider and not shoal, I determined to put all the baggage, &c., which I intend taking with me to the Yellowstone, in the canoes and proceed on down with them myself to the Three Forks, or Madison's and Gallatin's rivers, leaving the horses to be taken down by Sergeant Pryor; and six of the men of the party to accompany me to the Yellowstone; and directed Sergeant Pryor to proceed on moderately and, if possible, encamp with us every night.

12th July, 1806

Sergeant Pryor did not join me last night. He has proceeded on down. The beaver were flapping their tails in the river about us all the last night. This morning I was detained until 7 A.M. making paddles and drawing the nails of the canoe to be left at this place, and the one we had before left here. After completing the paddles, &c., and taking some breakfast, I set out.

13th July, 1806

Set out early this morning and proceeded on very well to the entrance of Madison's River at our old encampment of the 27th July last, at 12 o'clock, where I found Sergeant Pryor and party with the horses. They had arrived at this place one hour before us. His party had killed 6 deer and a white bear. I had all the horses driven across Madison and Gallatin rivers and halted to dine, and let the horses feed immediately below the entrance of Gallatin. Had all the baggage of the land party taken out of the canoes, and after dinner the 6 canoes and the party of 10 men under the direction of Sergeant Ordway set out. Previous to their departure I gave instructions how they were to proceed, &c. I also wrote to Captain Lewis by Sergeant Ordway. My party now consists of the following party, viz., Sergeant N. Pryor, Joe Shields, G. Shannon, William Bratton, Labiche, Windsor, H. Hall, Gibson, Interpreter Charbonneau, his wife and child, and my man York—with 49 horses and a colt. The horses' feet are very sore, and several of them can scarcely proceed on. The Indian woman, who has been of great service to me as a pilot through this country, recommends a gap in the mountain more south, which I shall cross.[1]

14th July, 1806

Sent Shields ahead to kill a deer for our breakfast, and at an early hour set out with the party. Crossed Gallatin River, which makes a considerable bend to the N.E. and proceeded on nearly S. 78° E. through an open level plain. At 6 miles I struck the river and crossed a part of it and attempted to proceed on through the river bottoms, which were several miles wide at this place. I crossed several channels of the river running through the bottom in different directions. I proceeded on about two miles, crossing those different channels, all of which were dammed with beaver in such a manner as to render the passage impracticable, and after being swamped, as I may say, in this bottom of beaver, I was

---

[1] This is one of the few occasions when Sacagawea really did serve as a guide, this being country not too far from her native mountains for her to know.

compelled to turn short about to the right, and after some difficulty made my way good to an open, low, but firm plain which was an island, and extended nearly the course I wished to proceed.

Here the squaw informed me that there was a large road passing through the upper part of this low plain from Madison River through the gap, which I was steering my course to. I proceeded up this plain 4 miles, and crossed the main channel of the river, having passed through a skirt of cotton timber to an open low plain on the N.E. side of the river, and nooned it. The river is much divided, and on all the small streams innumerable quantities of beaver dams, though the river is yet navigable for canoes. I overtook Shields soon after I set out. He had killed a large fat buck. I saw elk, deer, and antelopes, and a great deal of old signs of buffalo. Their roads are in every direction.

The Indian woman informs me that a few years ago buffalo were very plenty in those plains and valleys, quite as high as the head of Jefferson's River, but few of them ever come into those valleys of late years, owing to the Shoshones, who are fearful of passing into the plains west of the mountains, and subsist on what game they can catch in the mountains, principally, and the fish which they take in the east fork of Lewis's River. Small parties of Shoshones do pass over to the plains for a few days at a time and kill buffalo for their skins and dried meat, and return immediately into the mountains.

15th July, 1806

In the evening [*i.e., afternoon*], after the usual delay of three hours to give the horses time to feed and rest, and allowing ourselves time also to cook and eat dinner, I proceeded on down the river on an old buffalo road. The horses' feet are very sore; many of them can scarcely proceed on over the stone and gravel. In every other respect they are sound and in good spirits. I saw two black bear on the side of the mountains this morning. Several gangs of elk, from 100 to 200 in a gang, on the river. Great numbers of antelopes.

16th July, 1806

Saw a large gang of about 200 elk and nearly as many antelope; also two white or gray bears in the plains. One of them I chased on horseback about 2 miles to the rugged part of the plain, where I was compelled to give up the chase, two of the horses were so lame owing to their feet being worn quite smooth and to the quick. The hind feet were much the worse. I had moccasins made of green buffalo skin and put on their feet, which seems to relieve them very much in passing over the stony plains.

18th July, 1806

At 11 A.M., I observed a smoke rise to the S.S.E. in the plains toward the termination of the Rocky Mountains in that direction (which are covered with snow). This smoke must be raised by the Crow Indians in that direction, as a signal for us or other bands. I think it most probable that they have discovered our trail and, taking us to be Shoshones, &c., in search of them, the Crow Indians—now at peace with them—to trade, as is their custom, have made this smoke to show where they are; or, otherwise, taking us to be their enemy, made this signal for other bands to be on their guard.

19th July, 1806

Charbonneau informed me that he saw an Indian on the high lands on the opposite side of the river, at the time I was absent in the woods. I saw a smoke in the same direction with that which I had seen on the 7th inst. It appeared to be in the mountains.

20th July, 1806

I directed Sergeant Pryor and Shields, each of them good judges of timber, to proceed on down the river six or 8 miles and examine the bottoms, if any larger trees than those near which we are encamped can be found, and return before twelve o'clock. They set out at daylight. I also sent Labiche, Charbonneau, and Hall to bring the skin and some of the flesh of the elk Labiche had killed last evening. They returned with one skin, the wolves having eaten the most of the other four elk.

I also sent two men in search of wood suitable for ax handles. They found some chokecherry, which is the best wood which can be procured in this country. Saw a bear on an island opposite, and several elk.

Sergeant Pryor and Shields returned at half past 11 A.M., and informed me that they had proceeded down the timbered bottoms of the river for about 12 miles without finding a tree better than those near my camp. I determined to have two canoes made out of the largest of those trees and lash them together, which will cause them to be sturdy and fully sufficient to take my small party and self with what little baggage we have down this river. Had handles put in the three axes and after sharpening them with a file felled the two trees which I intended for the two canoes. Those trees appeared tolerably sound and will make canoes of 28 feet in length and about 16 or 18 inches deep and from 16 to 24 inches wide. The men with the three axes set in and worked until dark.

21st July, 1806

This morning I was informed that half of our horses were absent. Sent out Shannon, Bratton, and Charbonneau to hunt them. Charbonneau went up the river, Shannon down; and Bratton in the bottom near the camp. Charbonneau and Bratton returned at 10 A.M., and informed me that they saw no signs of the horses.

Shannon proceeded on down the river about 14 miles and did not return until late in the evening. He was equally unsuccessful. Shannon informed me that he saw a remarkably large lodge about 12 miles below, covered with bushes, and the top decorated with skins, &c., and had the appearance of having been built about 2 years.

I sent out two men on horseback to kill a fat cow, which they did, and returned in 3 hours. The men work very diligently on the canoes; one of them nearly finished—ready to put in the water.

This evening late a very black cloud from the S.E. accompanied with thunder and lightning with hard winds, which shifted about and was warm and disagreeable. I am apprehensive that the Indians have stolen our horses, and probably those who had made the smoke a few days past toward the S.W. I determined to have the balance of the horses guarded, and for that purpose sent out 3 men. On their approach near, the horses were so alarmed that they ran away and entered the woods, and the men returned.

22nd of July, 1806

I sent Sergeant Pryor and Charbonneau in search of the horses with directions to proceed up the river as far as the first narrows and examine particularly for their tracks. They returned at 3 P.M. and informed me that they had proceeded up the distance I directed them to go and could see neither horses nor tracks. The plains immediately out from camp are so dry and hard that the track of a horse cannot be seen without close examination.

I therefore directed Sergeant Pryor, Shannon, Charbonneau, and Bratton to encircle the camp at some distance around and find the tracks of the horses and pursue them. They searched for tracks all the evening without finding which course the horses had taken, the plains being so remarkably hard and dry as to render it impossible to see a track of a horse passing through the hard parts of them.

I begin to suspect that they are taken by the Indians, and taken over the hard plains to prevent our following them. My suspicion is grounded on the improbability of the horses' leaving the grass and rushes of the river bottoms, of which they are very fond, and taking immediately out into the open dry plains, where the grass is but short and dry. If they had continued in the bottoms, either up or down, their tracks could be followed very well. I directed Labiche, who understands tracking very well, to set out early in the morning and find what route the horses had taken, if possible.

23rd July, 1806

Last night the wolves or dogs came into our camp and ate the most of our dried meat, which was on a scaffold. Labiche went out early, agreeable to my directions of last evening. Sergeant Pryor and Windsor also went out. Sergeant Pryor found an Indian moccasin and a small piece of a robe, the moccasin worn out on the bottom and yet wet and has every appearance of having been worn but a few hours before. Those Indian signs are conclusive with me that they have taken the 24 horses which we lost on the night of the 20th instant, and that those who were about last night were in search of the balance of our horses, which they could not find as they had fortunately got into a small prairie surrounded with thick timber in the bottom.

Labiche returned, having taken a great circle, and informed me that he saw the tracks of the horses making off into the open plains and were, by the tracks, going very fast. The Indians who took the horses bent their course rather down the river. The men finished both canoes by 12 o'clock today, and I sent them to make oars and get poles, after which I sent Shields and Labiche to kill a fat buffalo out of a gang which has been within a few miles of us all day.

I gave Sergeant Pryor his instructions and a letter to Mr. Haney and directed that he, G. Shannon, and Windsor take the remaining horses to the Mandans, where he is to inquire for Mr. Haney. If at the establishments on the Assiniboine River, to take 12 or 14 horses and proceed on to that place, and deliver Mr. Haney the letter, which is with a view to engage Mr. Haney to prevail on some of the best-informed and most influential chiefs of the different bands of Sioux to accompany us to the seat of our government, with a view to let them see our population and resources, &c., which I believe is the surest guarantee of savage fidelity to any nation —that of a government possessing the power of punishing promptly every aggression.

Sergeant Pryor is directed to leave the balance of the horses with the grand chief of the Mandans until our arrival at his village, also to keep a journal of his route— courses, distances, water courses, soil productions, and animals to be particularly noted. Shields and Labiche killed three buffalo, two of them very fat. I had as much of the meat saved as we could conveniently carry. In the evening had the two canoes put into the water and lashed together, oars and everything fixed ready to set out early in the morning, at which time I have directed Sergeant Pryor to set out with the horses and proceed on to the entrance of the Bighorn River (which we suppose to be at no great distance), at which place the canoes will meet him and set him across the Yellowstone, below the entrance of that river.

24th July, 1806

Had all our baggage put on board of the two small canoes which, when lashed together, are very sturdy and, I am convinced, will carry the party I intend taking down with me. At 8 A.M., we set out and proceeded on very well to a riffle. At this riffle the small canoes took a good deal of water, which obliged us to land to dry out articles and bail the canoes. I also had a buffalo skin tacked on, so as to prevent the water's flacking in between the two canoes.

After dinner, I proceeded on past the entrance of a small creek and some wood on the starboard side, where I met with Sergeant Pryor, Shannon, and Windsor with the horses. They had but just arrived at that place.

Sergeant Pryor informed me that it would be impossible for the two men with him to drive on the horses after him without tiring all the good ones in pursuit of the more indifferent, to keep them on the course; that in passing every gang of buffalo, several of which he had met with, the loose horses, as soon as they saw the buffalo, would immediately pursue them and run around them. All those that had speed sufficient would head the buffalo, and those of less speed would pursue on as fast as they could.

He at length found that the only practical method would be for one of them to proceed on and whenever they saw a gang of buffalo to scare them off before the horses got up.

This disposition in the horses is no doubt owing to their being frequently exercised in chasing different animals by their former owners, the Indians, as it is their custom to chase every species of wild animal with horses, for which purpose they train all their horses. I had the horses driven across the river, and set Sergeant Pryor and his party across. H. Hall, who cannot swim, expressed a willingness to proceed on with Sergeant Pryor by land, and as another man was necessary to assist in driving the horses, but observed he was naked, I gave him one of my two remaining shirts, a pair of leather leggings, and three pairs of moccasins, which equipped him completely, and sent him on with the party by land to the Mandans.

25th July, 1806

The wind continued high until 2 P.M. I proceeded on after the rain, lay a little, and at 4 P.M., arrived at a remarkable rock situated in an extensive bottom on the starboard side of the river and 250 paces from it. This rock I ascended and from its top had a most extensive view in every direction. This rock, which I shall call Pompey's Tower,[2] is 200 feet high and 400 paces in circumference, and only accessible on one side, which is from the N.E., the other parts of it being a perpendicular cliff of lightish-

[2] Pompey's Tower, now usually called Pompey's Pillar, had nothing to do with the old Roman. "Pomp" was a Shoshone word for "first born." Clark habitually called Sacagawea's child that and later used it as a nickname for one of his own boys. Clark's signature is still cut into the rock, a close facsimile of his written signature. A U.S. Army expedition, passing that way in 1875, included a stonecutter, who somewhat deepened the cutting, but apparently did not disturb the outline. It is now protected from vandals by an iron grating. As a Virginian, Clark had, of course, often heard "Pomp" and "Pompey" used as a name for slaves.

colored gritty rock. On the top there is a tolerable soil about 5 or 6 feet thick covered with short grass. The Indians have made two piles of stone on the top of this tower. The natives have engraved on the face of this rock the figures of animals, &c., near which I marked my name and the day of the month and year. From the top of this tower I could discover two low mountains and the Rocky Mountains covered with snow.

1st of August, 1806

At 2 P.M. I was obliged to land to let the buffalo cross over. Notwithstanding an island half a mile in width over which this gang of buffalo had to pass, and the channel of the river on each side nearly ¼ of a mile in width, this gang of buffalo was entirely across and as thick as they could swim. The channel on the side of the island they went into the river, was crowded with those animals for half an hour (I was obliged to lay to for one hour); the other side of the island for more than ¾ of an hour. I took four of the men and killed four fat cows for their fat and what portion of their flesh the small canoes could carry, that which we had killed a few days ago being nearly spoiled from the wet weather. Encamped on an island close to the larboard shore. Two gangs of buffalo crossed a little below us, as numerous as the first.

August 2nd, 1806

About 8 A.M. this morning, a bear of the large vicious species, being on a sand bar, raised himself up on his hind feet and looked at us as we passed down near the middle of the river. He plunged into the water and swam toward us, either from a disposition to attack or from the scent of the meat which was in the canoes. We shot him with three balls, and he returned to shore badly wounded. In the evening I saw a very large bear take the water above us. I ordered the boat to land on the opposite side with a view to attack him when he came within shot of the shore. When the bear was in a few paces of the shore, I shot it in the head. The men hauled it on shore, and it proved to be an old she, which was so old that her tusks had worn smooth, and much the largest female bear I ever saw.

4th August, 1806

Mosquitoes excessively troublesome—so much so that the

men complained that they could not work at their skins for those troublesome insects. And I find it entirely impossible to hunt in the bottoms, those insects being so numerous and tormenting as to render it impossible for a man to continue in the timbered lands, and our best retreat from those insects is on the sand bars in the river, and even those situations are only clear of them when the wind should happen to blow, which it did today for a few hours in the middle of the day. The evenings, nights, and mornings they are almost unendurable, particularly by the party with me, who have no biers, to keep them off at night, and nothing to screen them but their blankets, which are worn and have many holes.

The torments of those mosquitoes and the want of a sufficiency of buffalo meat to dry—those animals not to be found in this neighborhood—induce me to determine to proceed on to a more eligible spot on the Missouri below, at which place the mosquitoes will be less troublesome and buffalo more plenty. Wrote a note to Captain Lewis, informing him of my intentions, and tied it to a pole which I had stuck up in the point. At 5 P.M., set out and proceeded on down to the second point, which appeared to be an eligible situation for my purpose. [Killed a porcupine.] On this point the mosquitoes were so abundant that we were tormented much worse than at the point. The child of Charbonneau has been so much bitten by the mosquitoes that his face is much puffed up and swollen.

5th August, 1806

The mosquitoes were so troublesome to the men last night that they slept but very little. Indeed, they were excessively troublesome to me. My mosquito bier has a number of small holes worn, through which they pass in. I set out at an early hour intending to proceed to some other situation. I had not proceeded on far before I saw a ram of the bighorn animal near the top of a larboard bluff. I ascended the hill with a view to kill the ram. The mosquitoes were so numerous that I could not keep them off my gun long enough to take sight, and by that means missed.

6th August, 1806

This morning a very large bear of the white species discovered us floating in the water and taking us, as I presume, to be buffalo, immediately plunged into the river and pursued us. I directed the men to be still. This animal came

within about 40 yards of us and tacked about. We all fired
into him without killing him, and the wind so high that we
could not pursue him, by which means he made his escape
to the shore, badly wounded. I have observed buffalo floating
down, which I suppose must have been drowned in crossing
above. More or less of those animals drown or mire in passing this river. I observed several floating buffalo on the river
Yellowstone immediately below where large gangs had crossed.

8th of August, 1806

At 8 A.M., Sergeant N. Pryor, Shannon, Hall, and Windsor
came down the river in two canoes made of buffalo skins.
Sergeant Pryor informed me that the second night after he
parted with me on the Yellowstone, he arrived about 4 P.M.
on the banks of a large creek, which contained no running
water. He halted to let the horses graze, during which time
a heavy shower of rain raised the creek so high that several
horses which had straggled across the channel of this creek
were obliged to swim back. Here he determined to continue
all night, it being in good food for the horses. In the morning he could see no horses.

In looking about their camp, they discovered several tracks
within 100 paces of their camp, which they pursued. Found
where they [Indians] had caught and driven off all the
horses. They pursued on five miles. The Indians there divided
into two parties. They continued in pursuit of the largest
party five miles further. Finding that there was not the smallest chance of overtaking them, they returned to their camp
and packed up their baggage on their backs, and steered a
N.E. course to the river Yellowstone, which they struck at
Pompey's Tower.

There they killed a buffalo bull and made a canoe in the
form and shape of the Mandans and Arikaras—the form of
a basin.

On the night of the 26th ulto., the night after the horses
had been stolen, a wolf bit Sergeant Pryor through his hand
when asleep, and this animal was so vicious as to make an
attempt to seize Windsor, when Shannon fortunately shot
him. Sergeant Pryor's hand has nearly recovered. The country through which Sergeant Pryor passed after he parted
with me is a broken open country. He passed one small
river, which I have called Pryor's River, which rises in
a mountain to the south of Pompey's Tower. The note I left
on a pole at the mouth of the Yellowstone Sergeant Pryor,
concluding that Captain Lewis had passed, took and brought

with him. Captain Lewis, I expect, will be certain of my passing by the sign which I have made, and the encampment immediately in the point.

Sergeant Pryor, being anxious to overtake me, set out some time before day this morning, and forgot his saddlebags, which contain his papers, &c. I sent Bratton back with him in search of them. After dark, Sergeant Pryor returned with his saddlebags, &c. They were much further up than he expected.

11th August, 1806

At meridian I set out and had not proceeded more than 2 miles before I observed a canoe near the shore. I directed the canoes to land. Here I found two men from the Illinois, Joseph Dixon and Hancock.[3] Those men are on a trapping expedition up the Yellowstone. They inform me that they left the Illinois in the summer of 1804. The last winter they spent with the Tetons, in company with Mr. Coartong, who brought up goods to trade. The Tetons robbed him of the greater part of the goods and wounded this Dixon in the leg with a hard wad. The Tetons gave Mr. Coartong some few robes for the articles they took from him.

Those men further informed me that they met the boat and party we sent down from Fort Mandan, near the Kansas River, on board of which was a chief of the Arikaras; that he met the Yankton chiefs with Mr. Dorion, McClellan, and several other traders on their way down.

12th August, 1806

At meridian, Captain Lewis hove in sight with the party which went by way of the Missouri, as well as that which accompanied him from Traveler's Rest on Clark's River. I was alarmed, on the landing of the canoes, to be informed that Captain Lewis was wounded by an accident. I found him lying in the pirogue. He informed me that his

[3] Joseph Dickson, or Dixon, and Forest Hancock were hunters and fur traders, the former from the Illinois country, the latter from Daniel Boone's settlement on the lower Missouri. Charles McKenzie was one of the Canadians the explorers had met at the Mandan village in 1804. Robert McClellan was another fur trader, whom the explorers were soon to meet. Mr. Coartong remains a mystery. Joseph Dickson does not appear to have been related to Robert Dickson, whom the explorers meet soon after.

wound was slight and would be well in 20 or 30 days. This information relieved me very much. I examined the wound and found it a very bad flesh wound. The ball had passed through the fleshy part of his left thigh, below the hipbone, and cut the cheek of the right buttock for three inches in length, and the depth of the ball. Captain Lewis informed me the accident happened the day before, by one of the men, Peter Cruzat, mistaking him in the thick bushes to be an elk.

14th August, 1806

Set out at sunrise and proceeded on. When we were opposite the Minnetarees' grand village, we saw a number of the natives viewing us. Soon after we came to at a crowd of the natives on the bank opposite the village of the Shoe Indians, or Mahas, at which place I saw the principal chief of the little village of the Minnetarees and the principal chief of the Mahas. I proceeded on to the Black Cats' [Mandan] village, where I intended to encamp, but the sand blew in such a manner that we determined not to continue on that site. I walked up to the Black Cats' village.

I had, as soon as I landed, dispatched Charbonneau to the Minnetarees, inviting the chiefs to visit us, and Drouilliard down to the lower village of the Mandans to ask Mr. Jussome to come and interpret for us.

After assembling the chiefs and smoking one pipe, I informed them that I still spoke the same words which we had spoken to them when we first arrived in their country. We then invited them to visit their Great Father, the President of the U. States, and to hear his own counsels and receive his gifts from his own hands, as also to see the population of a government which can, at their pleasure, protect and secure you from all your enemies and chastise all those who will shut their ears to his counsels. They were all afraid of the Sioux. They would not go down.

16th August, 1806

We sent for Mr. Jussome and told him to use his influence to prevail on one of the chiefs to accompany us. He informed us soon after that the Big White [Sheheke] would go if we would take his wife and son and Jussome's wife and two children, which we were obliged to agree to do.

17th of August, 1806

We were visited by all the principal chiefs of the Minnetarees, to take their leave of us. At 2 o'clock we left our encampment. We also took our leave of Toussaint Charbonneau, his Snake Indian wife, and their child. We dropped down to the Big White's Mandan village, half a mile below on the south side. I walked to the lodge of the chief, whom I found surrounded by his friends. He sent his baggage with his wife and son, with the interpreter Jussome and his wife and two children to the canoes provided for them. He informed me that he was ready, and we were accompanied to the canoes by all the village.[4] We saluted them with a gun and set out.

---

[4] Sheheke, "the Big White," made the journey to Washington, was received by President Jefferson and was eventually sent back to St. Louis. After many difficulties, he was eventually returned to his home late in 1807.

Chapter *XXIV*

LAST LAP
August 29—September 24, 1806

29th August, 1806

[Clark]

I ascended to the high country, and from an eminence I had a view of the plains for a great distance. From this eminence I had a view of a greater number of buffalo than I had ever seen before at one time. I must have seen near 20,000 of those animals feeding on this plain. I have observed that in the country between the nations which are at war with each other, the greatest numbers of wild animals are to be found.

30th of August, 1806

I saw several men on horseback which with the help of a spyglass I found to be Indians on the high hill to the N.E. We landed on the S.W. side, and I sent out two men to a village of barking squirrels to kill some of those animals.

Immediately after landing, about 20 Indians were discovered on an eminence a little above us on the opposite side. One of those men I took to be a Frenchman from his having a blanket capote and a handkerchief around his head. Immediately after, 80 or 90 Indian men—all armed with fusees and bows and arrows—came out of a wood on the opposite bank, about a quarter of a mile below us. They fired off their guns as a salute. We returned the salute with two rounds.

We were at a loss to determine of what nation those Indians were. From their hostile appearance, we were apprehensive they were Tetons, but from the country through which they roved we were willing to believe them either the Yanktons, Poncas, or Mahas, either of which nations are well disposed toward the white people. I determined to find out who they were without running any risk of the party and Indians, and therefore took three Frenchmen who could speak the Maha, Pawnee, and some Sioux, and in a small canoe I went over to a sand bar which extended sufficiently near the opposite shore to converse. Immediately after I set out, three young men set out from the opposite side and swam next me on the sand bar. I directed the men to speak to them in the Pawnee and Maha languages first, neither of which they could understand. I then directed the man who could speak a few words of Sioux to inquire what nation or tribe they belong to. They informed me that they were Tetons and their chief was the Black Buffalo. This chief I knew very well to be the one we had seen with his band at Teton river, which band had attempted to detain us in the fall of 1804 as we ascended this river, and with whom we were near coming to blows.

I told those Indians that they had been deaf to our counsels, and ill-treated us as we ascended this river two years past; that they had abused all the whites who had visited them since. I believed them to be bad people and should not suffer them to cross to the side on which the party lay, and directed them to return with their band to their camp; that if any of them came near our camp we should kill them certainly. I left them on the bar and returned to the party and examined the arms, &c. Those Indians, seeing some corn in the canoe, requested some of it, which I refused, being determined to have nothing to do with those people.

Several others swam across, one of which understood Pawnee; and as our Pawnee interpreter was a very good one, we had it in our power to inform what we wished. I told this man to inform his nation that we had not forgotten their treatment to us as we passed up this river, &c., that they had treated all the white people who had visited them very badly—robbed them of their goods, and had wounded one man whom I had seen. We viewed them as bad people and no more traders would be suffered to come to them, and whenever the white people wished to visit the nations above, they would come sufficiently strong to whip any villainous party who dared to oppose them, and words to the same purpose.

I also told them that I was informed that a part of all their bands were going to war against the Mandans, &c., and that they would be well whipped, as the Mandans and Minnetarees, &c., had a plenty of guns, powder and ball, and we had given them a cannon to defend themselves. And directed them to return from the sand bar and inform their chiefs what we had said to them, and to keep away from the river or we should kill every one of them, &c., &c. Those fellows requested to be allowed to come across and make comrades, which we positively refused, and I directed them to return immediately, which they did; and after they had informed the chiefs, &c., as I suppose, what we had said to them, they all set out on their return to their camps back of a high hill. Seven of them halted on the top of the hill and blackguarded us, told us to come across and they would kill us all, &c., of which we took no notice. We all this time were extremely anxious for the arrival of the two Fieldses and Shannon, whom we had left behind, and were somewhat concerned as to their safety. To our great joy, those men hove in sight at 6 P.M.

1st of September, 1806

About two miles below the Quicurre, 9 Indians ran down the bank and beckoned us to land. They appeared to be a war party, and I took them to be Tetons and paid no kind of attention to them further than an inquiry to what tribe they belonged. They did not give me any answer. I presume they did not understand the man who spoke to them, as he spoke but little of their language. As one canoe was yet behind, we landed in an open, commanding situation, out of sight of the Indians, determined to delay until they came up.

About 15 minutes after we had landed, several guns were fired by the Indians, which we expected was at the three men behind. I called out 15 men and ran up with a full determination to cover them if possible, let the number of Indians be what they might. Captain Lewis hobbled up on the bank and formed the remainder of the party in a situation well calculated to defend themselves and the canoes, &c. When I had proceeded to the point about 250 yards, I discovered the canoe about 1 mile above, and the Indians where we had left them.

I then walked on the sand beach and the Indians came down to meet me. I gave them my hand and inquired of them what they were shooting at. They informed me that they were shooting off their guns at an old keg which we had thrown out of one of the canoes and was floating down. Those Indians informed me they were Yanktons. One of the men with me knew one of the Indians to be the brother of young Dorion's wife.

Finding those Indians to be Yanktons, I invited them down to the boats to smoke. When we arrived at the canoes, they all eagerly saluted the Mandan chief, and we all sat and smoked several pipes. I told them that we took them to be a party of Tetons, and the firing, I expected, was at the three men in the rear canoe, and I had gone up with a full intention to kill them all if they had been Tetons and fired on the canoe as we first expected; but, finding them Yanktons and good men, we were glad to see them and take them by the hand as faithful children who had opened their ears to our counsels.

One of them spoke and said that their nation had opened their ears and done as we had directed them ever since we gave the medal to their great chief, and should continue to do as we had told them. We inquired if any of their chiefs had gone down with Mr. Dorion. They answered that their great chief and many of their brave men had gone down, that the white people had built a house near the Maha village where they traded. We tied a piece of ribbon to each man's hair and gave them some corn, of which they appeared much pleased.

The Mandan chief gave a pair of elegant leggings to the principal man of the Indian party, which is an Indian fashion (to make presents). The canoe and three men having joined us, we took our leave of this party telling them to return to their band and listen to our counsels which we had before given to them. Their band of 80 lodges were on Plum Creek, a few miles to the north. Those nine men had five fusees and 4 bows and quivers of arrows.

3rd September, 1806

At half past 4 P.M. we spied two boats and several men. Our party plied their oars, and we soon landed on the side of the boats. The men of these boats saluted us with their small arms. I landed and was met by a Mr. James Aird [1] from

[1] James Aird was a Scotch fur trader, based in the Wisconsin-Michigan country for many years, who made frequent trips along the Missouri. He was equally respected by whites and Indians. Both he and Robert Dickson, of Dickson & Co., Prairie du Chien, were arrayed against Clark's forces in the War of 1812.

"Cady" Chouteau was Pierre Chouteau, Junior—in other words the "cadet" of Pierre Chouteau, Senior, of the great St. Louis trading family. Wilkinson is the notorious James Wilkinson,

Mackinaw by way of Prairie du Chien and St. Louis. This gentleman is of the house of Dickson and Co., of Prairie du Chien, who has a license to trade for one year with the Sioux. He has two bateaux loaded with merchandise for that purpose. This gentleman received both Captain Lewis and myself with every mark of friendship. He was himself at the time with a chill of the ague on him which he has had for several days.

Our first inquiry was after the President of our country, and then our friends, and the state of politics of our country, &c., and the state of Indian affairs, to all of which inquiries Mr. Aird gave us as satisfactory information as he had it in his power to have collected in the Illinois, which was not a great deal. Soon after we landed, a violent storm of thunder, lightning, and rain from the N.W., which was violent, with hard claps of thunder and sharp lightning which continued until 10 P.M., after which the wind blew hard. I sat up late and partook of the tent of Mr. Aird, which was dry. Mr. Aird unfortunately had his boat sunk on the 25th of July last, by a violent storm of wind and hail, by which accident he lost the most of his useful articles, as he informed us.

This gentleman informed us of many changes and misfortunes which had taken place in the Illinois, amongst others the loss of Mr. Cady Chouteau's house and furniture by fire. For this misfortune of our friend Chouteau, I feel myself very much concerned, &c. He also informed us that General Wilkinson was the governor of the Louisiana and at St. Louis. Three hundred of the American troops had been cantoned [2] on the Missouri a few miles above its mouth. Some disturbance with the Spaniards in the Natchitoches country is the cause of their being called down to that country.

The Spaniards had taken one of the U. States' frigates in the Mediterranean. Two British ships of the line had fired on an American ship in the port of New York and killed the captain's brother. Two Indians had been hanged in St. Louis for murder, and several others in jail. And that Mr. Burr and General Hamilton fought a duel, the latter was killed, &c., &c. I am happy to find that my worthy friend Captain Lewis is so well as to walk about with ease to himself,

a spy in Spanish pay while also a U. S. Army officer. In 1805-1806 he was governor of Louisiana. Clark had known him while both were serving under Wayne in 1794.

[2] "Cantoned" is a military term, now obsolete, meaning "placed in cantonment," i.e., "quartered, stationed, camped."

&c., and we made 60 miles today. The river much crowded with sand bars, which are very differently situated from what they were when we went up.

4th September, 1806

The mosquitoes became troublesome early this morning. I rose at the usual hour, found all the party as wet as rain could make them. As we were in want of some tobacco, I proposed to Mr. Aird to furnish us with 4 carrots, for which we would pay the amount to any merchant of St. Louis. He very readily agreed to furnish us with tobacco, and gave to each man as much as it is necessary for them to use between this and St. Louis, an instance of generosity for which every man of the party appears to acknowledge. Mr. Aird also insisted on our accepting a barrel of flour.

We gave to this gentleman what corn we could spare, amounting to about 6 bushels. This corn was well calculated for his purpose, as he was about to make his establishment and would have it in his power to hull the corn, &c. The flour was very acceptable to us. We have yet a little flour, part of what we carried up from the Illinois as high as Maria's River and buried it there until our return, &c.

At 8 A.M., we took our leave and set out, and proceeded on very well. At 11 A.M., passed the entrance of the Big Sioux River, which is low, and at meridian we came to at Floyd's Bluff below the entrance of Floyd's River, and ascended the hill with Captain Lewis and several men. Found the grave had been opened by the natives and left half covered. We had this grave completely filled up, and returned to the canoes.

6th September, 1806

We met a trading boat of Mr. Auguste Chouteau, of St. Louis, bound to the River Jacques to trade with the Yanktons. This boat was in the care of a Mr. Henry Delaunay.[3] He had exposed all his loading to dry, and sent out five of his hands to hunt. They soon arrived with an elk. We purchased a gallon of whiskey of this man—promised to pay Chouteau, who would not receive any pay—and gave to each man of the

[3] Nothing is known of Henry Delaunay, except that he was a fur trader, working for Chouteau. However, he was probably one of the St. Louis family of that name.

party a dram, which is the first spirituous liquor which had
been tasted by any of them since the 4th of July, 1805.
Several of the party exchanged leather for linen shirts, and
beaver for coarse hats.

Those men could inform us nothing more than that all the
troops had moved from the Illinois and that General Wilkinson was preparing to leave St. Louis. We advised this trader
to treat the Tetons with as much contempt as possible and
stated to him where he would be benefited by such treatment, &c., &c. and at 1 P.M. set out. Those men gave us
two shots from a swivel they had on the bow of their boat,
which we returned in our turn.

Proceeded on about 3 miles and came up with two of the
hunters. They had not killed anything. At 5 miles we overtook the canoe of the other hunters, with Shannon in it,
floating down—the two Fieldses being in the woods behind.

10th September, 1806

We met a Mr. Alexander La Fass and three Frenchmen
from St. Louis in a small pirogue, on his way to the River
Platte to trade with the Pawnee Loup, or Wolf Indians. This
man was extremely friendly to us; he offered us anything he
had. We accepted of a bottle of whiskey only, which we gave
to our party. Mr. La Fass informed us that General Wilkinson
and all the troops had descended the Mississippi, and Mr.
Pike and young Mr. Wilkinson [4] had set out on an expedition up the Arkansas River, or in that direction.

After a delay of half an hour, we proceeded on about 3
miles and met a large pirogue and 7 men from St. Louis
bound to the Mahas for the purpose of trade. This pirogue
was in charge of a Mr. LaCroix. We made some few inquiries
of this man and again proceeded on through a very bad part
of the river, crowded with snags and sawyers, and encamped
on a sand bar.

12th of September, 1806

We set out at sunrise, the usual hour, and proceeded on
very well. About 7 miles we met 2 pirogues from St. Louis.

[4] Mr. Pike was Zebulon Pike, the explorer. "Young Mr.
Wilkinson" was James D. Wilkinson, the general's son. Lewis
later identified Joseph LaCroix as a British merchant. La Fass is
obscure.

One contained the property of Mr. Chouteau bound to the Pawnees, or River Platte; the other going up trapping as high as the Mahas. Here we met one of the Frenchmen who had accompanied us as high as the Mandans. He informed us that Mr. McClellan [5] was a few miles below. The wind blew ahead. Soon after we passed those pirogues, we saw a man on shore who informed us that he was one of Mr. McClellan's party, and that he was a short distance below. We took this man on board and proceeded on and met Mr. McClellan at the St. Michael's Prairie. We came to here.

We found Mr. Jo. Gravelines, the Arikara interpreter whom we had sent down with an Arikara chief in the spring of 1805; and old Mr. Dorion, the Sioux interpreter. We examined the instructions of those interpreters and found that Gravelines was ordered to the Arikaras with a speech from the President of the U. States to that nation, and some presents which had been given the Arikara chief who had visited the U. States, and unfortunately died at the city of Washington. He was instructed to teach the Arikaras agriculture and make every inquiry after Captain Lewis, myself, and the party.

Mr. Dorion was instructed to accompany Gravelines and, through his influence, pass him with his presents &c., by the Teton bands of the Sioux, and to prevail on some of the principal chiefs of those bands, not exceeding six, to visit the seat of the government next spring. He was also instructed to make every inquiry after us. We made some small additions to his instructions by extending the number of chiefs to 10 or 12—or 3 from each band, including the Yanktons, &c. Mr. McClellan received us very politely, and gave us all the news and occurrences which had taken place in the Illinois within his knowledge. The evening proving to be wet and cloudy, we concluded to continue all night. We dispatched the two canoes ahead to hunt with 5 hunters in them.

13th September, 1806

Rose early. Mr. McClellan (an old acquaintance in the army) gave each man a dram, and a little after sunrise we set out, the wind hard ahead from the S.E. At 8 A.M., we landed at the camp of the five hunters whom we had sent

---

[5] McClellan was Robert McClellan, whom Clark must have known as a scout on Wayne's expedition. McClellan was to spend the next few years of his brief life in the fur trade.

ahead. They had killed nothing. The wind being too high for us to proceed in safety through the immensity of snags which were immediately below, we concluded to lay by and sent on the small canoes a short distance to hunt and kill some meat.

17th September, 1806

At 11 A.M., we met a Captain McClallan,[6] late a Captain of Artillery of the U. States Army, ascending in a large boat. This gentleman, an acquaintance of my friend Captain Lewis, was somewhat astonished to see us return and appeared rejoiced to meet us. We found him a man of information and from him we received a partial account of the political state of our country. We were making inquiries and exchanging answers, &c., until near midnight.

This gentleman informed us that we had been long since given up by the people of the U.S. generally, and almost forgotten. The President of the U. States had yet hopes of us. We received some civilities of Captain McClallan. He gave us some biscuit, chocolate, sugar, and whiskey, for which our party were in want, and for which we made a return of a barrel of corn and much obliged to him.

20th September, 1806

The party, being extremely anxious to get down, ply their oars very well. We saw some cows on the bank, which was a joyful sight to the party and caused a shout to be raised for joy. At [blank in MS.] P.M., we came in sight of the little French village called Charrette. The men raised a shout and sprang upon their oars, and we soon landed opposite to the village.

Our party requested to be permitted to fire off their guns, which was allowed, and they discharged three rounds with a hearty cheer, which was returned from five trading boats which lay opposite the village. We landed and were very politely received by two young Scotsmen from Canada—one in the employ of Mr. Aird, a Mr. [blank in MS.], and the other, Mr. Reed. Two other boats, the property of Mr. Lacomb and Mr. [blank in MS.]. All of those boats were bound to the Osage and Otos.

---

[6] Lewis's friend, Captain John McClallan, the artilleryman, must not be confused with Robert McClellan.

Those two young Scotch gentlemen furnished us with beef, flour, and some pork for our men, and gave us a very agreeable supper. As it was like to rain, we accepted of a bed in one of their tents. We purchased of a citizen two gallons of whiskey for our party, for which we were obliged to give eight dollars in cash, an imposition on the part of the citizen.

Every person, both French and Americans, seemed to express great pleasure at our return, and acknowledged themselves much astonished in seeing us return. They informed us that we were supposed to have been lost long since, and were entirely given out by every person, &c.

21st September, 1806

Rose early this morning. Collected our men. Several of them had accepted of the invitation of the citizens and visited their families. At half after 7 A.M. we set out. Passed 12 canoes of Kickapoos ascending on a hunting expedition. Saw several persons, also stock of different kinds on the bank, which revived the party very much. At 3 P.M. we met two large boats ascending. At 4 P.M. we arrived in sight of St. Charles. The party, rejoiced at the sight of this hospitable village, plied their oars with great dexterity, and we soon arrived opposite the town.

This day being Sunday, we observed a number of gentlemen and ladies walking on the bank. We saluted the village by three rounds from our blunderbusses and the small arms of the party, and landed near the lower part of the town. We were met by great numbers of the inhabitants. We found them excessively polite. The inhabitants of this village appear much delighted at our return, and seem to vie with each other in their politeness to us all. We came only 48 miles today. The banks of the river thinly settled, &c. Some settlements since we went up.

22nd of September, 1806

This morning being very wet and the rain still continuing hard, and our party being all sheltered in the houses of those hospitable people, we did not think proper to proceed on until after the rain was over, and continued at the house of Mr. Proulx. I took this opportunity of writing to my friends in Kentucky, &c. At 10 A.M. it ceased raining, and we collected our party and set out, and proceeded on down to the cantonment at Coldwater Creek, about 3 miles up the Missouri on its southern banks. At this place we found Colonel Thomas Hunt and a Lieutenant Peters, and one company of artillery. We were kindly received by the gentlemen of this place. Mrs. Wilkinson, the lady of the Governor and General, we were sorry to find in delicate health.

We were honored with a salute of [blank in MS.] guns and a hearty welcome. At this place there is a public store kept in which I am informed the U.S. has $60,000 worth of Indian goods.

23rd September, 1806

We rose early. Took the chief to the public store and furnished him with some clothes, &c. Took an early breakfast with Colonel Hunt and set out. Descended to the Mississippi and down that river to St. Louis, at which place we arrived about 12 o'clock. We suffered the party to fire off their pieces as a salute to the town. We were met by all the village and received a hearty welcome from its inhabitants.

Here I found my old acquaintance, Major W. Christy, who had settled in this town in a public line as a tavernkeeper. He furnished us with storerooms for our baggage, and we accepted of the invitation of Mr. Peter Chouteau and took a room in his house. We paid a friendly visit to Mr. August Chouteau and some of our old friends this evening. As the post had departed from St. Louis, Captain Lewis wrote a note to Mr. Hays in Cahokia to detain the post in that place till 12 tomorrow, which is rather later than his usual time of leaving it.

24th of September, 1806

I slept but little last night. However, we rose early and commenced writing our letters.[7] Captain Lewis wrote one to the President, and I wrote Governor Harrison and my friends in Kentucky.

---

[7] The postal rider who carried the mail from Cahokia, a little way down the Mississippi from St. Louis, received special orders to hold the U. S. mails, the letter to the President being of so much importance.